THE SECRET GARDEN

THE SECRET GARDEN

FRANCES HODGSON BURNETT

Retold by
Louise Betts

Illustrated by
Karen Pritchett

Troll Associates

Library of Congress Cataloging in Publication Data

Betts, Louise.
  The secret garden.

  Summary: Ten-year-old Mary comes to live in a
lonely house on the Yorkshire moors and discovers an
invalid cousin and the mysteries of a locked garden.
  [1. Orphans—Fiction. 2. Gardens—Fiction.
3. Physically handicapped—Fiction. 4. Yorkshire—
Fiction] I. Pritchett, Karen, 1952-   , ill.
II. Burnett, Frances Hodgson, 1849-1924. Secret
Garden. III. Title.
PZ7.B934Se   1988   [Fic]   87-15490
ISBN 0-8167-1203-4 (lib. bdg.)
ISBN 0-8167-1204-2 (pbk.)

Nearly everyone agreed Mary Lennox was a most disagreeable child. She wore a sour expression on her face. And her face, like her hair and body, was thin. She appeared frail and ill. And much of the time, she was.

Mary lived in a big house in India. Although she was an only child, she hardly ever saw her parents. Her father was always too busy to play with Mary. Her mother, who was admired for her great beauty, cared only for parties and fun—not for her little daughter.

Mary's mother had not wanted a daughter at all. So when Mary was born, her mother hired a nanny to take care of her. The nanny's job was to keep Mary as quiet as possible and out of sight. Mary was a sickly, complaining baby.

In time, she grew up to become a sickly, complaining young girl, who was completely used to having her own way. Her nanny and the servants gave in to Mary so that she would not cry and disturb her mother. It was obvious to all that Mary was a selfish, spoiled little girl.

Mary's life stayed the same until she was ten years old. Then, without warning, a terrible disease swept through India. Many people died. Even servants at Mary's house began to die from the disease.

One very hot morning, Mary awoke with a strange feeling. She could hear people outside moaning and wailing and running around. Mary was afraid and called to her nanny. No one came. As the sounds outside grew louder, Mary grew more frightened. She hid in the nursery all day. She had to eat biscuits and fruit left from the day before. Most of the time, Mary cried. Soon she had cried herself to sleep.

When Mary awoke the following morning, everything was silent. She felt alone, but she also felt angry that everyone had forgotten about her. Suddenly, the door opened and two soldiers came in. They were surprised to find Mary there.

"Why did nobody come?" Mary demanded, stamping her foot.

"Poor little kid!" said one of the men. "There's nobody *left* to come."

That was how Mary learned that her parents had died from the terrible disease. Most of the servants had also died, while the rest had run away. With no one left in India to look after her, Mary was put on a ship and sent to live with her uncle. His name was Archibald Craven, and he lived at Misselthwaite Manor in Yorkshire, England.

When Mary arrived in London, she was met by her uncle's housekeeper, Mrs. Medlock. She was a stout woman with very red cheeks and sharp black eyes. The housekeeper thought Mary was a spoiled child. Mary thought Mrs. Medlock was the most unpleasant person she had ever met. Mary often thought people were unpleasant, but of course she didn't know she was unpleasant herself.

On the train north to Yorkshire, Mrs. Medlock told Mary about Misselthwaite Manor. She said the house was big and gloomy. It had hundreds of rooms that were almost all closed up and locked. Around the house was a big park, and beyond that was the moor.

"What's the moor like?" asked Mary.

"It's just miles and miles of dreary, bare land. Nothing grows on it but wildflowers and shrubs, and nothing lives there but wild ponies and sheep," said Mrs. Medlock.

The two were quiet for a while. Then, in the carriage ride to Misselthwaite Manor, Mrs. Medlock said, "Don't expect to see your uncle. He never troubles himself about anyone. He's got a crooked back and was always a bitter person until he got married. His wife was sweet and pretty, and he adored her. But when she died, it made him stranger than ever. He's away from home most of the time, so you must look after yourself."

When they arrived, Misselthwaite Manor was dark, except for one dim light. A butler opened a huge oak door and told Mrs. Medlock, "You're to take her to her room. Mr. Craven is going to London in the morning and won't see her now."

Mary was led upstairs and down many long hallways to a room with a fire in it. Supper was on the table.

"Here," said Mrs. Medlock. "You'll live in this room and the next. Just see that you stay here. I don't want you poking about the rest of the house."

On this first night at Misselthwaite Manor, Mary had never felt quite so sad in all her life.

The next morning, Mary was awakened by a young housemaid. She was raking the ashes from the bedroom fireplace. Her name was Martha. She smiled and chatted as she worked. Mary thought it was odd that a servant would speak so freely to her. In India, Mary had slapped her nanny's face once in anger. Somehow, Mary knew she could not treat Martha that way.

As the girl talked on in her good-natured way, Mary gradually began to listen. Martha was describing her eleven brothers and sisters who lived in a little cottage on the moor. "It's hard for my mother to feed them all. But the fresh air on the moor makes them strong and healthy. My brother Dickon, who's twelve, is always out on the moor. He's a kind lad and animals like him. Why, he's even tamed a wild pony!"

Mary was impressed with anyone who could tame a wild pony. She thought about that while picking at her breakfast. Martha thought Mary was wasteful not to eat it all, but Mary never did have much of an appetite. After Martha finished cleaning, she showed Mary the way outside.

"Go out and look at the gardens," Martha suggested.

"There's not much there now, but they'll be beautiful in summer." She thought a moment, then added, "One of the gardens has been locked up. No one's been in it for ten years."

"Why?" asked Mary.

"Mr. Craven had it shut after his wife died so suddenly," said Martha. "It was her garden, but now he hates it. He locked the door, dug a hole, and buried the key."

Mary idly strolled through the grounds of Misselthwaite Manor. They were huge, divided by high brick walls surrounding gardens that looked bare and wintry. Green doors led from one garden to the next. Suddenly, an old man with a large spade over his shoulder walked into the vegetable garden where Mary was standing. He seemed startled to see Mary and stared at her with his grouchy, old face. Mary looked coldly back at him.

"Can I look at the other gardens?" Mary asked.

"If you like. But there's nothing to see," said the man.

Mary shrugged and walked from garden to garden through the green doors. She hoped to find a door that wouldn't open, for that would be the mysterious garden.

Finally, she came to an orchard that was also surrounded by a wall—but there was no door anywhere. Behind the wall Mary could see the tops of trees and a robin perched on one of the highest branches. The bird was singing a song, and its cheerful whistle gave Mary a pleasant feeling. She listened until the robin flew away.

Mary found the old man digging in the vegetable garden. "There was no door into one of the gardens," she said.

"Which garden?" the man asked gruffly.

"The one on the other side of that wall. I could see the treetops where a robin was singing."

To Mary's surprise, a smile spread over the old man's face. She had never realized how much nicer a person looked smiling. Then the gardener whistled, and the robin came flying over the wall. It landed near the man's foot.

"Here he is!" said the old man, as he watched the red-breasted bird hop about, pecking at the earth. "He always comes when I call him. Poor critter. You see, he got sick and was too weak to fly south with his family for the winter. So they had to leave him here. He's lonely. I'm lonely myself, except when he's with me."

"I'm lonely too," said Mary. "I've never had any friends."

"We're probably a good bit alike then, you and me," said the old man. "We're as sour as we seem." He then introduced himself as Ben Weatherstaff, the gardener of Misselthwaite Manor.

Mary told him who she was. She was still hurt from what he said about her. Mary had never heard the truth about herself. Now that she did, she did not like it. Her thoughts were interrupted by the robin's singing from an apple tree.

"He wants to be friends with you," said Ben.

Mary moved toward the bird and asked gently, "Will you be my friend?"

Her soft, kind voice surprised Ben. "Why, you said that like a real child."

Just then the robin flew away, over the wall beyond the orchard. "There must be a door to that garden," said Mary.

"None that anyone can find," said Ben. "And don't be nosy." He walked off without saying goodbye.

13

Mary spent most of her days outdoors. The fresh air and walking brought a healthy glow to her skin. At night, she liked to sit by the fireplace and talk with Martha.

"Why does Mr. Craven hate the garden?" Mary asked Martha one evening.

Martha answered in a quiet voice. "It was Mrs. Craven's garden, you see. She made it when they first got married. They were the only ones allowed in it. But one day, while Mrs. Craven was sitting on a tree branch, it snapped. She fell and was hurt so badly that the next day she died. Mr. Craven never recovered from the shock of her death. So he had the garden locked up. And no one's been in it since."

Outside, the wind howled. Mary thought she heard something else too. "Do you hear anyone crying?"

Martha looked surprised. "N-no," she said quickly. "It's the wind . . . or the cook. She's had a toothache all day."

Mary did not believe Martha. She felt Martha was hiding something from her. But what?

The following morning, it rained heavily. Both girls were huddled again by the fire, talking.

"On a day like this at home," said Martha, "we stay inside too. All of us but Dickon, that is. He goes out rain or shine. And he's always making new animal friends. Some he even brings home with him, like the fox cub and young crow he found." Martha spoke a little while longer about Dickon and the rest of her family, then left to do her chores.

With the rain still beating down outside, Mary decided to spend the morning exploring inside. Most of the doors to the manor's rooms were locked. But one was open. She entered a room full of curious furniture and ornaments. There were embroidered hangings on the wall. Inside a cabinet were little carved ivory elephants. Mary took them out and played with them on the carpet. She hardly noticed the tiny gray mice on the couch nearby.

On the way back to her room, Mary lost her way. Finally, she found her floor, but she was still some distance from her room when she heard a cry. It was a short, fretful, childish whine. She leaned against the wall to hear better.

"What are you doing here?" said an angry Mrs. Medlock, startling Mary. The housekeeper took Mary by the arm and pulled her away.

"I heard someone crying!" said Mary

"You heard nothing of the sort!" snapped Mrs. Medlock. She then dragged Mary down the hall and pushed her through the door of her room. "You stay where you're told," the woman hissed.

Mary sat on the rug. She was angry herself now. "There *was* someone crying!" she said. "And someday I'm going to find out who it was!"

Two days later, the storm ended. The sky was clear, and everything seemed fresh and lovely. It was Martha's day off, and the young maid was getting ready to cross the moor and visit her family.

"You'd like my mother," said Martha.

"I'd like her and Dickon too," Mary said, "even though I've never met them."

"Everyone likes Dickon. I wonder what he'd think of you."

"He wouldn't like me," said Mary sadly. "Nobody does."

"Do you like yourself?" Martha asked.

"Not really," replied Mary. "I never thought of that before."

As Martha headed home in high spirits, Mary felt lonelier than ever. She went outside and ran around the flower garden ten times. This made her feel much better. Wandering into the kitchen vegetable garden, she found Ben Weatherstaff.

"Springtime's coming," Ben said. "You can smell it in the soil."

Mary sniffed. The soil smelled nice and fresh and damp. "What kind of things will grow?" she asked.

"Oh, crocuses and snowdrops and daffodils."

Just then the robin fluttered down and landed close to Mary's feet. "Are any plants poking through in the robin's garden?" she asked.

Ben said gruffly, "I don't know anything about that garden and neither should you." Then he turned and walked away.

Mary shrugged and headed slowly down the path to the ivy-covered wall that had no door. Hearing a chirp and a twitter, she turned and saw that the robin had followed her.

Mary smiled. The robin was playing with her, pretending to peck for food. Mary made some robin sounds and crept slowly toward it. The robin let Mary get close. It liked her. This made Mary extremely happy.

She watched while the robin pecked and scratched at a hole in the ground. Mary thought she could see something rusty, like a brass ring, in the dirt. When the robin flew away, Mary rushed to the hole and pulled the rusty object out. It was an old key. "Hurray!" she shouted. "Maybe it's the key to the garden!"

With the key in her hand, Mary walked up and down the wall looking for a door. She looked hard but could not find one. Disappointed, she slipped the key into her pocket and decided to carry it with her whenever she went out. That way, she'd be ready if she ever did find the door.

The next day, Martha returned to Misselthwaite Manor in the best of spirits. "Everyone liked hearing about you," she said. "They wanted to hear all about India and the ship you came in."

"Did Dickon and your mother like to hear you talk about me?" asked Mary.

"Why, Dickon's eyes nearly popped out of his head, they got so round," replied Martha, smiling. "But Mother worried that you were alone too much. Look, " she said, pulling something from her apron, "I've brought you a present from my mother."

It was a jump rope, with a striped red-and-blue handle at each end. Mary had never seen one before, so Martha showed her how to skip with it. Mary was delighted and grateful. She knew Martha's mother did not have much money to buy such gifts.

The jump rope was a wonderful thing. Mary skipped rope down to the fountain garden, then up one walk and down another. At last she skipped into the kitchen garden and saw Ben Weatherstaff and the robin.

"Upon my word!" exclaimed Ben. "Jumping rope like a sweet child. Maybe you're not made of sour buttermilk, after all. What pink cheeks it's given you!"

Mary liked hearing this, and Ben encouraged her to keep on skipping. Soon, she went to her own special path to see if she could skip down it the whole way. Halfway down, Mary stopped to catch her breath. She saw the robin swaying on a long branch of ivy. The bird greeted her with a chirp. As Mary skipped toward it, she could feel the brass key strike against her pocket.

"You found the key for me yesterday," she said to the robin. "I wish you could show me the door today, but I don't think you know how!"

Just then, something happened that Mary would always say was magic. A gust of wind parted the trailing sprays of ivy hanging from the wall. It was then that Mary saw a round object—a doorknob! Mary's heart began to pound, and her hands shook as she pulled back the ivy and took out the brass key she always carried in her pocket.

She put the key into the lock and turned it. It took two hands to do it, but she finally turned the knob. Making sure no one was coming, she held back the swinging curtains of ivy and pushed back the door. It opened slowly. Then she slipped through the door and shut it behind her.

There she was, standing *inside* the secret garden. It was the sweetest, strangest-looking place anyone could imagine. The high walls were thickly matted with the leafless stems of climbing roses. The ground was covered with wintry brown grass and out of it grew clumps of bushes, possibly rosebushes, Mary thought. There were trees in the garden too. Climbing roses had run all over them, though Mary did not know if the roses were dead or alive. A hazy mantle of gray and brown branches spread over everything—walls, and trees, and even the brown grass. It all looked so mysterious.

"How still it is!" Mary whispered to the robin perched in one of the trees. "But no wonder. I'm the first person here in ten years."

She moved softly away from the door. Mary was glad that her steps made no sound, preserving the quiet. I hope the garden isn't completely dead, Mary thought, seeing no sign of leaves or buds anywhere. With her jump rope, Mary began to skip around the garden. Suddenly, she stopped and

23

knelt down. In an alcove, she saw what once must have been a flowerbed, and she saw some little flower sprouts pushing up through the soil.

Remembering what Ben Weatherstaff had said, Mary thought the sprouts might be crocuses or snowdrops or daffodils. Slowly, she walked around the garden and looked for more sprouts. Finding many more, Mary became excited again.

"It isn't a dead garden!" she cried out softly to herself. "Even if the roses are dead, other things are alive!"

Mary did not know anything about gardening. But she noticed that some of the flower sprouts might not have enough room to grow because of the thick grass around them. Mary knelt down and, with a sharp piece of wood, dug and weeded until she cleared some space around them.

After she finished with the first flowerbeds, Mary went to the others, clearing the way for more sprouts and smiling the whole time without knowing it. The hours passed quickly before Mary realized she was late for her mid-day meal. "I'll come back this afternoon," she said, speaking to the trees and the rosebushes as if they heard her. Then she ran lightly across the grass, pushed open the old door and slipped through it under the ivy.

That noon, Mary ate a large dinner. Martha watched with

pleasure, wondering what brought on Mary's sudden appetite. Mary wanted to share her new secret with Martha. But Mary was afraid if Mr. Craven found out, he would get a new key and lock up the garden for good—something that Mary could not bear!

Instead, Mary said, "If Ben Weatherstaff would give me some seeds and lend me a small spade, I could make a little garden for myself."

"That's a lovely idea!" said Martha. "Dickon knows which flowers are the prettiest and how to make them grow. We could send him a letter and ask him to bring some garden tools and seeds." For the rest of the afternoon, Martha told Mary what to write in their letter to Dickon. Mary wrote it all down and then mailed the letter.

The sun shone down for nearly a week on the secret garden, the name Mary had given it. She liked the name and the beautiful walls that surrounded it. Best of all, she liked feeling she was in her own private world that no one else knew about.

Mary loved to garden, and the plants seemed to know how much she cared about them. With the grass cleared away, the sun could warm the flowers and the rain would be able to reach them at once. The plants began to feel very much alive.

Mary also liked talking with Ben Weatherstaff because he seemed to know everything about gardening. Ben himself seemed to enjoy talking with Mary, for she had stopped speaking to him as if he were a servant.

"The fresh air is doing you good," he said one day. "You're a bit healthier and not so pale. The first time I saw you, you looked like a young plucked crow."

"I know I'm heavier," said Mary. "My stockings don't wrinkle anymore."

Though Ben still got angry when she asked him about the walled-in garden, Mary liked him anyway.

25

One afternoon, Mary skipped down a path that led to a wooded park. At the park gate, she heard a low, peculiar whistling sound. Walking through the gate, she saw a boy sitting under a tree. He was playing a wooden pipe. The boy had a turned-up nose and the bluest eyes Mary had ever seen. A brown squirrel watched him from the tree, a cock pheasant peeked out from the bushes, and two rabbits sat up and sniffed. It actually seemed as if they were drawing near to listen to the boy's music.

When he saw Mary, the boy stopped his music and rose slowly. He didn't want to frighten the animals. "I'm Dickon," he said, "and I know you're Mary." He had a wide, curving mouth, and his smile brightened his entire face. Mary knew nothing about boys and felt rather shy, but Dickon did not seem to notice. He had received Martha's letter and had come with the garden tools and flower seeds they had requested. Excited, Mary asked to see the seeds.

"I've got a lot of mignonette and poppy seeds," Dickon said. "Mignonette's the sweetest-smelling thing that grows. It'll grow wherever you plant it, just like poppies." Dickon spoke quickly and easily. Mary liked him right off, and she soon forgot her shyness. "I'll plant the seeds for you myself," Dickon continued. "Where's your garden?"

Mary was not sure what to say. At last, clutching his sleeve, she asked, "Can you keep a secret?"

"Of course," he said. "If I couldn't keep secrets about such things as foxes' cubs and birds' nests, there'd be nothing safe on the moor."

Mary thought about this, but sharing her precious secret made her nervous.

"I've stolen a garden," she said. "But I'm the only one in the world who wants it to be alive."

Mary saw the puzzled look on Dickon's face. "Come, I'll show you," she said. Mary led Dickon to the wall, lifted the hanging ivy, and slowly pushed the door open. They entered together, and Mary waved her hand around proudly. "It's this," she said. "Have you heard of the secret garden?"

Dickon nodded, as he looked at the lovely tangle of trees and bushes. "What an odd, pretty place!" he said.

Dickon knew how to tell the dead branches from the live ones, and soon he was busy at work. He cut away the dead ones with his knife. Then he spotted Mary's own clearings around the flower sprouts. "Why, I thought you didn't know anything about gardening!" he exclaimed. "A gardener couldn't have taught you better."

Mary showed him more clearings, which Dickon said were full of crocuses, snowdrops, narcissuses, and daffodils. A chirp came from one of the trees. "Who's that robin calling?" he asked.

"Ben Weatherstaff," said Mary. "But it knows me too."

Dickon moved closer to the tree and made a sound almost like the robin's twitter. When the robin answered, Dickon said, "Yes, the bird's a friend of yours."

Mary thought Dickon was just as nice as she'd imagined he would be. And he could talk to birds and animals too! "You're the fourth person I like," she confessed to Dickon. The other three were Martha, Martha's mother, and Ben Weatherstaff. And there was also the robin, of course.

Later that same day, Mary rushed through her noon meal to get back to Dickon and the garden. Martha stopped her, however. "Mrs. Medlock says Mr. Craven wants to see you," she said. "He's going away for a long time to travel in foreign places, and he wants to meet you first."

Martha helped Mary into her best dress and brushed her hair. By the time Mary followed Mrs. Medlock down the long hallways to Mr. Craven's study, she was very nervous. Although she had been at Misselthwaite Manor for several weeks, Mary had never met her mysterious uncle. All she knew about him was that he had a crooked back and had acted strangely ever since his wife died. He must be some kind of monster! she thought, knocking on the study door.

"Come in!" Mr. Craven said. Mary entered and moved slowly toward him.

He's not too frightening, she thought to herself. He's just a man with high, crooked shoulders, and black hair streaked with white. If he didn't look so miserable, he might even be handsome. Still, Mary felt a little scared.

"Come here," Mr. Craven said. Mary stepped closer.

"What do you do here at Misselthwaite?" he asked.

"I play outdoors," gasped Mary. "I skip and run—and I look at the flower sprouts sticking up out of the earth."

"Don't look so scared," he said. "A child like you could not do any harm. What do you want—toys, books, dolls?"

Mary shook her head. "Could I have a bit of earth to plant seeds in?"

Mr. Craven studied Mary and answered slowly, "You remind me of someone else who loved the earth and things that grow. Take as much as you want that's not being used and make it come alive."

Mary was relieved. Now she could call the secret garden her own! She politely curtsied and left the study.

That night, Mary awoke to the rain beating against her window and the wind blowing around the corners and chimneys of the old house. She lay awake for some time, listening to the wind. It sounded to her like someone crying out on the moor.

Suddenly, something made her sit up and listen. "That isn't the wind," she whispered. "It's that crying I heard before!" Determined to find out what it was, Mary took the candle by her bedside and crept down the corridor. Soon she saw a glimmer of light beneath a door. The crying she heard was coming from that room.

Mary pushed the door open slowly, not knowing what to expect. Before her, on a carved, four-poster bed, was a boy crying fretfully. He had a sharp, delicate face and gray eyes. His thick hair tumbled over his forehead and made his face seem even smaller.

Seeing Mary's candlelight, he turned and stared. "Are you a ghost?" he asked in a frightened whisper.

Mary half-wondered if *he* might be a ghost, but she whispered back, "No, I'm Mary Lennox. Mr. Craven is my uncle."

"Oh. I'm his son, Colin," said the boy, no longer whispering or afraid.

"No one ever told me he had a son!" Mary exclaimed.

"They wouldn't dare. I don't like people to talk about me."

"Why?" asked Mary, feeling more curious every moment.

"Because I am always ill like this. If I live, I may have a crooked back, like my father's. But I won't live."

"What a strange house this is!" Mary said. "Everything is so secret. Have you been locked up?"

31

"No," said Colin. "I stay in this room because it would tire me to move out."

"Does your father come to see you?" asked Mary.

"Sometimes, but mostly when I'm asleep. My mother died when I was born, and I've heard people say it makes him miserable to look at me. He thinks I don't know, but I've heard people talking. He almost hates me."

"Do you ever go outside?" Mary asked.

"No," he said. "I hate people looking at me."

"In that case, shall I go away?"

"No," said Colin. "I want you to stay and talk with me."

Mary was glad. She wanted to know more about this mysterious boy. And Colin wanted to know all about her—when she had come to Misselthwaite, where her room was, and where she had lived before. Mary learned from Colin that he always got everything he wanted and never had to do anything he did not want to do. Mary realized she had been that way herself.

"I won't live long anyway," said Colin. He spoke as if the idea of dying had ceased to matter to him. "How old are you?" he asked suddenly.

"Ten. And so are you," said Mary, immediately wishing she had not said that.

"How do you know how old I am?" Colin demanded.

Mary clutched her hands nervously and said, "Because you were born when the garden was locked, ten years ago."

Now Colin wanted to know more about the garden, so Mary told him how it had come to be locked. She did not tell him she had found the key or that she had gone inside. It was too early to trust him with that.

Colin loved hearing about the garden. "I'll make the servants take me there and I'll let you go too," he said.

"Oh, no!" Mary cried.

"But you said you wanted to see it."

"I do," she said, "but we must keep it a secret for now!" Mary was terrified Colin would tell about the garden. If that happened, Dickon might not come back, the robin might fly away, and everything would be spoiled!

"If we keep the garden a secret and get into it someday," Mary said, "we could plant daffodils and lilies and snowdrops and watch them grow bigger every day. No one would know about it but us! Don't you think that would be wonderful?"

"I've never had a secret," Colin said, smiling. "But I'd like that."

The next day, Mary told Martha that she had met Colin. This upset the maid terribly. Martha was afraid she would be blamed for telling Mary. But Mary said that Colin was glad he had met her and wanted to see her every day. Mary then asked Martha if Colin really had a crooked back.

"Nobody knows for sure," said Martha. "Mr. Craven went crazy when he was born because Mrs. Craven had just died. He wouldn't set eyes on the baby. Mr. Craven said that it would have a crooked back like his and that it would be better off dead."

"But Colin doesn't look like he has a crooked back," said Mary.

"Not yet, but he began all wrong. The doctors said his back is weak, so they've always kept him lying down. They don't let him walk."

Mary thought a moment. "It's done me a lot of good to be outside," she said. "Do you think it would help Colin?"

"Oh, I don't know," replied Martha. "He was taken outside once and had such a fit of bad temper. He cried and cried, and made himself ill all night. Afterward, he said he never wanted to go outside again."

"He's a very spoiled boy," said Mary. "If he ever gets angry with me, I won't go see him again."

That afternoon, Colin ordered Martha to bring Mary to him. Poor Martha was shaking in her shoes when she brought Mary to the room. "I'm afraid Mrs. Medlock will think I told Mary about you," she said to Colin.

The boy frowned. "If I order you to bring Mary to me, that's your duty," he said. "Medlock has to do what I please, just as you do. Now, you may go."

After Martha left, Mary said to Colin, "You remind me of a little Indian prince, the way you order everyone around! You're so different from Dickon!"

"Who's Dickon?" Colin asked.

"He's Martha's brother," she said, "and he's not like anyone else in the world. He can charm foxes and squirrels and birds on the moor. When he plays his pipe, they come and listen."

"I couldn't go to the moor," Colin said. "I'm going to die." It was almost as if Colin were boasting about it.

"See here," said Mary crossly, "let's not talk about dying. Let's talk about living. Let's start by talking about Dickon." And that's what they did. They enjoyed themselves so much that they forgot about the time. For a while, Colin even forgot about his back.

It rained for a week. So there had been no chance to see the secret garden or Dickon. But Mary enjoyed herself by spending many hours each day with Colin in his room. They often looked at beautiful books and pictures, and they took turns reading to each other. They laughed about silly things, and Colin liked to talk about the secret garden and what might be in it.

In their talks, Mary tried to find out if Colin could really be trusted not to tell about the garden. If he could, she had to think of a way to get him there without anyone finding out.

Finally, the rain stopped one morning and the sun returned. Sunshine poured through the blinds. Mary jumped out of bed and ran to open the window. The sky was blue again, and fresh, cool air blew in. No one else was awake yet, but Mary could not wait to see her garden.

Once inside the secret walls, Mary was surprised to see Dickon already there. "I couldn't stay in bed!" he exclaimed. "When the sun jumped up, I ran all the way here."

The rain and warmth had pushed the crocuses up into whole clumps of purple and orange and gold. Leaf buds were bursting on the rose branches that had once seemed dead. Mary and Dickon found so many more wonders that they kept forgetting to keep their voices low. Best of all, Mary thought, was seeing Ben Weatherstaff's robin building a nest in the garden.

"He'll get nervous if we watch too closely," warned Dickon.

To take their minds off the robin, Mary told Dickon about Colin. "He always thinks about how a lump's going to form on his back," she said.

Dickon shook his head. "If we could get him out here, he wouldn't be watching for lumps to grow on his back. He'd be watching for buds to grow on the rosebushes."

"I've been thinking that too," said Mary. "If he could keep a secret, maybe you could push his wheelchair out here without anyone seeing us."

"I'm sure the garden in springtime would be better than doctor's stuff for Colin," said Dickon.

Mary spent the whole delightful day in the garden with Dickon. But that evening, Martha stood at her door with a worried face. "I wish you'd gone to see Colin today," she said. "He was nearly having a fit!"

Colin was still in a rage when Mary went to see him. "I won't let that boy come here if you go and play with him instead of me," he said.

This made Mary angry. "Then I'll never come into this room again!"

"I'll make you," said Colin. "They'll drag you in."

"That they may, " said Mary fiercely. "But I'll just sit here and clench my teeth and never tell you one thing."

"You are so selfish!" cried Colin.

"You're more selfish than I am," said Mary. "You're the most selfish boy I ever saw."

"That's not true!" Colin shouted. "Besides, I'm going to die!"

"I don't believe it," said Mary firmly. "You just say that to make people feel sorry for you." With that, Colin picked up his pillow and threw it at her. Furious, Mary walked to the door, then turned. "I was going to tell you about Dickon and his fox and crow," Mary said, her face pinched tight. "But now I won't." She marched out the door and closed it behind her.

Back in her room, Mary found Martha waiting for her with a box that Mr. Craven had sent. Though Mary had felt cross after her fight with Colin, her anger melted when she saw the beautiful books that her uncle had sent. Two were about gardening. She had never expected him to remember her and wanted to thank him immediately.

As she wrote a letter to Mr. Craven, she thought of Colin. Normally, she would be sharing these new treasures with him. She remembered how Colin thought about his back most when he'd been cross or tired, which he certainly had been today. "I'll go see him tomorrow," Mary decided.

In the middle of the night, Mary was awakened by such dreadful sounds that she jumped out of bed in an instant. "It's Colin!" she said to herself. He was sobbing and screaming at the top of his lungs. "Somebody must stop him!" she said angrily. "He'll upset everyone in the house!"

Her temper mounted as she flew down the corridor and into Colin's room. "Stop it!" she shouted. "You'll scream yourself to death!"

Colin looked dreadful, all pale and swollen, and he was gasping and choking. But Mary did not seem to care.

"If you scream," she said, "I'll scream, too. And I can scream louder!"

"I can't stop! I felt the lump on my back and now I shall die!" Colin wept.

"There's nothing the matter with your stupid back," said Mary. "Sobbing and screaming make lumps. Turn over and let me look at it." Mary looked carefully at Colin's thin back. "There's no lump," she announced. "And if you ever say there's a lump there again, I'll laugh!"

"Do you think...I could...live to grow up?" he said.

"You probably could if you'd stop having these fits of anger and spend some time outside every day," said Mary.

Colin was relieved. He was weak with crying, but his temper tantrum had passed. He put his hand out toward Mary.

"I'll...I'll go outdoors with you, Mary," he said. Mary sat by his bed and described how the coming of spring had changed the garden. Her voice was soft, and Colin slowly relaxed until he was fast asleep. Then Mary quietly returned to her own room and slept.

Up with the morning sun, Mary dressed quickly and went out to the secret garden. Dickon was already there. He was surrounded by the two squirrels he called Nut and Shell and by the crow he named Soot. When she told him what happened the night before, he said, "Yup! We've got to get him out here quick!"

Just then Nut scampered up onto Dickon's shoulder, causing his cap to fall on Nut's head. The two burst out laughing. "I'll tell Colin what your clever pet did today!" Mary said.

"That'll make him laugh," agreed Dickon. "And there's nothing as good as laughing for sick folks."

When Mary visited Colin that morning, he exclaimed, "You smell like flowers—and fresh things!"

"It comes from sitting on the grass and watching a squirrel called Nut knock Dickon's cap off his head and onto its own!" Mary said, laughing.

Colin began to laugh as she told him what happened. Pretty soon, the two of them could not stop themselves from laughing. When they could speak again, Colin told Mary he did not mean what he said about sending Dickon away.

"I'm glad you said that," said Mary, ready to burst with the news of the garden. "He's coming to see you tomorrow with his animal friends." Colin was delighted.

"But that's not all," Mary said. "There's a door to the garden. I found it and went inside weeks ago. But I couldn't tell you until I was sure I could trust you."

Colin was cheerful and wide awake when Mary came in the next morning. At breakfast, he said to Mrs. Medlock in his most prince-like manner, "A boy and a fox, a crow, two squirrels, and a newborn lamb are coming to see me today. I want them brought up as soon as they arrive."

Mrs. Medlock gasped. "Yes, sir," she said.

Mary and Colin had just finished eating when Mary said, "Listen! Did you hear a caw? That must be Soot!"

Dickon's boots went *clump, clump, clump* as he walked down the hall. He entered the room smiling broadly with the newborn lamb in his arms and the fox trotting by his side. Soot sat on one shoulder, Nut trailed behind, and Shell's head poked out of Dickon's coat pocket.

Colin stared in wonder, but Dickon did not mind. He put the newborn lamb in Colin's lap and gave him a bottle to feed it. Dickon, Colin and Mary talked about animals and about the garden, which Dickon and Mary said had a new patch of flowers.

A week of cold, windy weather passed before Mary and Dickon were able to take Colin out. During this time, the three children discussed over and over just how they were going to get Colin to the garden without Mrs. Medlock or the servants seeing them.

When the day finally came, the strongest footman in the house carried Colin into a wheelchair waiting outside. The footman was then promptly excused. Dickon pushed the wheelchair slowly and steadily, while Mary walked beside it. Colin leaned back and looked at the bright sky. Not another human creature was to be found on the paths they took. Even so, as they approached the ivy-covered wall, they began to speak in excited whispers.

"Here's the handle and here's the door," Mary said. "Push him in quickly, Dickon!" And Dickon did it with one strong push.

Inside, Colin looked around at all the leaves and splashes of color and the trees with birds twittering in them. A pink glow of color crept into his face.

"I shall get well!" Colin cried out. "I shall live forever and ever and ever!"

From his chair, placed beneath the plum tree's snow-white blossoms, Colin watched as Mary and Dickon worked around the garden. Sometimes they all got to talking and giggling so loudly that they had to put their hands over their mouths. Colin had been told about the law of whispers and low voices, and he liked the secrecy of it.

"I don't want this afternoon to end," Colin said. "But I'll come back tomorrow and all the days after that."

"You certainly will," said Dickon, "and we'll have you walking about here like other people before long."

"Walk!" exclaimed Colin, turning bright red. "Do you think I will?"

Just then Colin looked up at the wall. "Who's that man?" he asked in a loud whisper. Mary and Dickon looked up, scrambling to their feet.

Ben Weatherstaff glared at them from the top of a ladder behind the wall. He shook his fist at Mary and shouted, "You nosy girl, always poking about where you aren't wanted!"

"But the robin showed me the way," Mary protested.

"Do you know who I am?" Colin demanded.

Ben Weatherstaff stared and answered at last in a shaky voice, "Yes, yes, I do—with your mother's eyes staring at me out of your face. You're the boy with the crooked back."

"I do not have a crooked back!" Colin shouted.

Ben did not know what to say. "Y—you mean you don't even have crooked legs?"

Now the strength that usually threw Colin into a fit of anger rushed through him in a new way. In a moment, he was filled with a power he had never known. He began to throw off his blankets, and Dickon rushed to help him. Suddenly, Colin's thin legs pushed out from the wheelchair and his feet touched the grass.

"Come on, you can do it!" whispered Mary.

And in a moment Colin was standing upright.

Ben Weatherstaff forgot his anger, then tears ran down his cheeks. "Why, the lies people tell!" he exclaimed. "You'll be a man yet. And a healthy one at that!"

Colin stood straighter and straighter as he spoke. "I want to talk to you," he said to Ben, gesturing for him to come down to the garden. "Now that you've seen us, you'll have to be in on the secret. What work do you do in the gardens, Ben?" he asked.

"Anything I'm told to do," replied the gardener. "I'm kept on by favor. You see, your mother liked me."

"Was this her garden?" asked Colin, surprised.

"Yes, and she was very fond of it."

Colin told Ben that he could help in the garden as long as he kept it a secret. Ben surprised all of them when he said, "After your mother died, I came here once a year until I got too old to climb over the wall. I did a bit of pruning, for your mother once said to me, 'Ben, if I ever go away, you must take care of my roses'."

Colin, Mary, and Dickon saw that they could trust Ben. After a while, Ben said to Colin, "How'd you like to plant a rose I have in a pot?"

Colin was thrilled. "Just think! Not only have I stood up for the first time today, but now I'm also going to dig!"

Dickon and Mary helped Colin dig the hole for the rose. His face flushed as he set the rose in the mold. Ben then filled the hole with earth and packed it down firmly.

As the strange, lovely afternoon ended, Dickon helped Colin to his feet. Colin stood up and, looking into the setting sun, laughed as he had never laughed before.

That evening, Colin said to Mary, "I'm not going to be a poor sick thing anymore. I stood on my feet this afternoon." Colin and Mary believed there was good magic—or *something*—in the garden that made the flowers bloom and made them strong and healthy. And in the happy months that followed, it did seem the garden worked magic.

Colin spent every day in the garden, even gray days. He would lie on the grass watching the insects, plants, and birds with equal fascination. If the magic in the garden made things grow, he thought it had also gotten him to stand.

One day, Colin said to Mary, Dickon, and Ben: "When I was going to try to stand that first time, I remember Mary whispering to me, 'You can do it!' And I did. Now I am going to walk around the whole garden!"

Colin rose slowly, with Mary and Dickon on either side. Ben Weatherstaff walked behind and the lamb, fox cub, Soot, and a white rabbit trailed after them. The procession moved slowly, stopping every few yards to rest, until Colin had walked all the way around the garden.

"I did it!" he cried. "This is to be the biggest secret of all. No one will know anything about it until I can walk and run like any boy." Most of all, Colin wanted to surprise his father when he returned home from his trip abroad.

During the time Colin was discovering the joys of the secret garden, his father was walking through a quiet forest in Austria. Archibald Craven had traveled throughout Europe, seeing some of the most beautiful places in the world. But their beauty did not seem to touch him.

In the silence of the Austrian forest, Mr. Craven decided to rest for a while. He lay down on a carpet of moss next to a stream. Soon he fell into a deep, deep sleep. When he awoke, he shook his head in wonder.

"What a strange, wonderful dream I had!" he exclaimed. "There was Colin, clear as day, crying out, 'I am going to live forever and ever and ever!'"

Mr. Craven was puzzled by the dream, but did not think much more about it. Still, as he continued traveling, Mr. Craven slowly felt stronger and happier. He slept well at night. And when he looked in the mirror, his back no longer seemed so crooked.

Gradually, he began to think of Misselthwaite Manor. One night, he dreamed he was in his wife's garden. The dream seemed so real that he thought he smelled the roses. A few days later, Mr. Craven decided to go home.

As the train whirled him through mountain passes and grassy plains, Mr. Craven thought about his son. He had not meant to be a bad father, but he had never really felt like a father at all. Now that he felt so much better, Mr. Craven looked at his life in a new way.

Perhaps I have been wrong all these years, he thought. Suddenly, he wanted very much to see the son he had neglected for so long.

When he arrived back home at last, Mr. Craven asked, "Where is Colin?"

"In the garden, sir," replied Mrs. Medlock.

Mr. Craven went immediately to the ivy-covered door. Then he stopped and listened. There were sounds inside the garden—sounds of running, scuffling feet, exclamations, and happy cries. As he listened, the sounds grew louder and louder. Curious, he yanked the door wide open.

At that moment a boy burst through the door and dashed headlong into him. Caught by surprise, Mr. Craven held out his arms just in time to save the boy from falling.

This was not the meeting Colin had planned. "Father!" he said, standing as tall as he could. "It's me, Colin."

Mr. Craven could scarcely believe his eyes.

"No one knows I can walk," his son continued breathlessly. "We kept it a secret so you would be the first to know. I'm well, and I just beat Mary in a footrace. I'm going to be an athlete!"

He said it all like a healthy boy—his face flushed, his words tumbling over each other in eagerness. Mr. Craven shook with joy as he embraced his son. For the rest of the day, Mary, Dickon, and Colin took turns telling him about the garden and its magic.

As the sun set that day, Martha and Mrs. Medlock looked out toward the garden. They could hardly believe their eyes. Walking along one side of Mr. Craven were Mary and Dickon and a parade of little animals. On the other side, Mr. Craven had his arm around his son's shoulders. He was beaming. And Colin, feeling stronger than ever, proudly walked beside him. It was the first of what would be many walks together.

BUSINESS AND
GENERAL
REFERENCE
BOOK SERIES
FROM IDG

Annuals For Du...

W9-AXW-998

An Annual by Any Other Name . . .

Many annuals go by several different common names. If you're having trouble finding information about a particular plant, you might try looking for it under another name.

Looking for This:	Try This Name:	Looking for This:	Try This Name:
alcea rosea	hollyhock	gaillardia	blanket flower
annual coreopsis	calliopsis	godetia	clarkia
bachelor's button	cornflower	golden fleece	Dahlberg daisy
black-eyed Susan	gloriosa daisy	Madagascar periwinkle	vinca rosea
black-eyed Susan vine	thunbergia	moss rose	portulaca
blue marguerite	felicia	mum	chrysanthemum
burning bush	kochia	nigella	love-in-a-mist
butterfly flower	schizanthus	ornamental cabbage	kale
China aster	aster	painted tongue	salpiglossis
cleome	spider flower	pot marigold	calendula
cockscomb	celosia	rudbeckia	gloriosa daisy
cupflower	nierembergia	sweet scabious	pincushion flower
dianthus	sweet William	tithonia	Mexican sunflower
firecracker plant	cigar plant	toadflax	linaria
floss flower	ageratum	tree mallow	lavatera
flowering tobacco	nicotiana	wax begonia	bedding begonia

Caring for Your Annuals

Follow these tips as you go about your gardening routine:

- ✔ Water as needed to keep soil moist but not soggy (Chapter 11).
- ✔ Pull weeds when they are small to prevent competition (Chapter 15).
- ✔ Fertilize annual flowers every 4 to 6 weeks (Chapter 12).
- ✔ Watch for and control pests and diseases (Chapter 14).
- ✔ Mulch with organic matter to preserve moisture and smother weeds (Chapter 15).
- ✔ Remove faded flowers regularly to prolong bloom (Chapter 13).

IDG
BOOKS
WORLDWIDE

...For Dummies: Bestselling Book Series for Beginners

Annuals For Dummies®

Quick Reference Card

Buying the Best Seedlings

Chapter 10 is chock-full of great information about choosing the best seedlings for your needs. Keep the following quick tips in mind before you set out to your local nursery.

- ✔ Plan your garden on paper first so that you have a good estimate of how many transplants you need to buy.

- ✔ Choose annuals suited to the amount of sun or shade at your site.

- ✔ Pick transplants that are compact, healthy, and just starting to flower.

- ✔ Avoid buying plants that are root-bound or have outgrown their pots.

- ✔ Select colors and flower forms that you like and that look good together.

- ✔ Buy flowers that are the right height and size for the scale of your garden.

Planting Annual Flowers

Follow these basic steps. Refer to Chapters 9 and 10 for specific instructions on planting seeds and seedlings.

1. Prepare your bed for planting by removing all vegetation, digging up the dirt, working in your soil amendments, and leveling off the bed. (See Chapter 8 for details.)

2. If necessary, water the bed so that it's thoroughly damp but not soggy.

3. Dig planting holes a little bigger than the transplant going into them.

4. Carefully remove transplants from their containers, keeping the soil and root mass intact. Divide seedlings grown in flats with a knife if their roots have grown together.

5. Separate and loosen tangled plant roots so that they will grow out.

6. Place the plant in its hole and firm the soil around transplant roots with your hands. The surface should be level with the ground.

7. Gently water the bed again and keep the soil moist until your new plants get established.

Metric to U.S. Style, and Back Again

The following table gives approximate equivalents between metric and U.S. measurements.

Metric to U.S. weights and measures	
1 centimeter	.4 inch
1 meter	39 inches (just over 3 feet)
1 kilometer	.6 mile
1 liter	1.1 quarts
1 kilogram	2.2 pounds

U.S. to metric weights and measures	
1 inch	2.5 centimeters
1 foot	30.5 centimeters
1 yard	.9 meter
1 mile	1.6 kilometers
1 quart	.9 liter
1 pint	.6 liter
1 fluid ounce	29.6 milliliters
1 pound	.4 kilogram
1 ounce	31 grams

...For Dummies: Bestselling Book Series for Beginners

Praise for Annuals For Dummies

"*Annuals For Dummies* is a masterful blend of tips, tricks, and techniques that even an experienced gardener can use to create a successful and spectacular flower garden. It's like having a garden designer at your fingertips."
— Doug Jimerson, Editor-in-Chief, *Garden Escape,*
www.garden.com

"The subject of annuals was just waiting for the straightforward, quiet-humor delivery of Californian Bill Marken. (The *Californian* tag is part of Bill's mastery: In growing annuals year around, mild-climate gardeners accumulate twice the lifetime experience available to cold-winter people.) In small takes, the book gives you the full range of instructions for growing and displaying these charming one-act plants."
— Joseph F. Williamson, Former Garden Editor and
Managing Editor of *Sunset Magazine*

Praise for the NGA

". . . you'll find you're in the company of the real geniuses — the folks who can help you dig through the mounds of gardening information available and get growing soon."
— Amy Green, *The Journal-Constitution,*
Atlanta, Georgia

"We have used GrowLab and other NGA publications in many aspects of our programming for years. The curriculum and other resources NGA has produced are innovative, high quality and enormously popular with users. . . . Based on our experience to date, we have great regard for NGA as a national leader in supporting science education reform and an inquiry-based approach."
— Sandy Tanck, Manager, Youth Education

"The GrowLab curriculum and other resources NGA has produced are innovative, high-quality, and enormously popular with users here in the Twin Cities. The Growing Ideas newsletter is the best newsletter we receive on any topic in science."
— Arboretum Education Manager

Praise for Gardening . . ., Perennials . . ., and Roses For Dummies

"[*Gardening For Dummies*] is an outstanding reference for beginners and first-time homeowners . . . clearly explains how to retrieve garden information online."
— Carol Stocker, *Boston Globe,*
Boston, Massachusetts

"[*Gardening For Dummies* is] a thorough, readable beginners' guide. . . . Readers will enjoy the straightforward, yet light-hearted tone."
— Cheryl Dorschner, *Burlington Free Press,*
Burlington, Vermont

". . . easy-to-read and fun to thumb through . . . a wealth of information on all aspects of gardening. . . . A good choice for beginning gardeners, *Gardening For Dummies* would also be a good gift for longtime growers."
— Beth Dolan, *The Tampa Tribune,* Tampa, Florida

"The beauty of *Gardening For Dummies* . . . is its clear, jargon-free text. This should be a great relief for you if you're truly interested in learning about the subject, but afraid to spend big bucks on a serious gardening book that will only amaze and confuse you."
— *Country Decorator* magazine

"Humorous, down-to-earth information anyone can understand. *[Perennials For Dummies]* covers every detail of creating a flower garden from beginning to end. I'm impressed — a book filled with valuable lessons covering each phase of building a garden, keeping one from making timely mistakes. It could help any beginner have a successful, flourishing flower garden."
— Judy Wigand, owner of Judy's Perennials,
San Marcos, CA

"Whether you live in the sun-bleached subtropics or the misty snow belt, [with *Perennials For Dummies*] you will be able to determine just what perennials grow best for you, how to combine them for the optimal effect through the season, and perhaps most importantly, you will have some real design concepts instilled in you. . . . I know no other book that presents these ideas more intelligently."
— Panayoti Kelaidis, Plant Evaluation Coordinator,
Denver Botanic Gardens

"As an all-organic gardener, I've always dreamed of having a rose expert/ enthusiast come to my gardens for tea and spend the afternoon sharing and teaching me all about roses. *Roses For Dummies* is written as a friend, answering all my puzzling questions and providing easy solutions that are budget friendly."
— Jan Weverka, Editor of *The Rose Garden,*
a monthly organic newsletter

ANNUALS FOR DUMMIES®

by Bill Marken and The Editors of The National Gardening Association

IDG Books Worldwide, Inc.
An International Data Group Company

Foster City, CA ♦ Chicago, IL ♦ Indianapolis, IN ♦ Southlake, TX

Annuals For Dummies®

Published by
IDG Books Worldwide, Inc.
An International Data Group Company
919 E. Hillsdale Blvd.
Suite 400
Foster City, CA 94404
www.idgbooks.com (IDG Books Worldwide Web site)
www.dummies.com (Dummies Press Web site)

Library of Congress Catalog Card No.: 97-81233

ISBN: 0-7645-5056-X

Printed in the United States of America

10 9 8 7 6 5 4 3 2

1E/RR/QT/ZY/IN

Distributed in the United States by IDG Books Worldwide, Inc.

Distributed by Macmillan Canada for Canada; by Transworld Publishers Limited in the United Kingdom; by IDG Norge Books for Norway; by IDG Sweden Books for Sweden; by Woodslane Pty. Ltd. for Australia; by Woodslane Enterprises Ltd. for New Zealand; by Longman Singapore Publishers Ltd. for Singapore, Malaysia, Thailand, and Indonesia; by Simron Pty. Ltd. for South Africa; by Toppan Company Ltd. for Japan; by Distribuidora Cuspide for Argentina; by Livraria Cultura for Brazil; by Ediciencia S.A. for Ecuador; by Addison-Wesley Publishing Company for Korea; by Ediciones ZETA S.C.R. Ltda. for Peru; by WS Computer Publishing Corporation, Inc., for the Philippines; by Unalis Corporation for Taiwan; by Contemporanea de Ediciones for Venezuela; by Computer Book & Magazine Store for Puerto Rico; by Express Computer Distributors for the Caribbean and West Indies. Authorized Sales Agent: Anthony Rudkin Associates for the Middle East and North Africa.

For general information on IDG Books Worldwide's books in the U.S., please call our Consumer Customer Service department at 800-762-2974. For reseller information, including discounts and premium sales, please call our Reseller Customer Service department at 800-434-3422.

For information on where to purchase IDG Books Worldwide's books outside the U.S., please contact our International Sales department at 650-655-3200 or fax 650-655-3295.

For information on foreign language translations, please contact our Foreign & Subsidiary Rights department at 650-655-3021 or fax 650-655-3281.

For sales inquiries and special prices for bulk quantities, please contact our Sales department at 650-655-3200 or write to the address above.

For information on using IDG Books Worldwide's books in the classroom or for ordering examination copies, please contact our Educational Sales department at 800-434-2086 or fax 817-251-8174.

For press review copies, author interviews, or other publicity information, please contact our Public Relations department at 650-655-3000 or fax 650-655-3299.

For authorization to photocopy items for corporate, personal, or educational use, please contact Copyright Clearance Center, 222 Rosewood Drive, Danvers, MA 01923, or fax 978-750-4470.

is a trademark under exclusive license to IDG Books Worldwide, Inc., from International Data Group, Inc.

About the Authors

Bill Marken is an editor and writer who lives in the San Francisco Bay Area. He served as editor-in-chief of *Sunset, the Magazine of Western Living,* from 1981 to 1996. Early in his career at *Sunset,* he worked as a writer for the magazine's garden section, pitched in on several editions of the best-selling *Western Garden Book,* and generally nurtured his interests in subjects related to gardening, landscaping, travel, and other aspects of the good life in the West. Having developed an early interest in gardening by working at nurseries while going to school, Bill may have been the only English major at the University of California at Berkeley who knew what U.C. soil mix was.

Bill's interest in the natural world includes a strong dose of environmentalism. He has served three terms as president of the League to Save Lake Tahoe, the major watchdog of the threatened lake. A vacation garden at 6,200-feet elevation gives him insight into cold-winter climates with 100-day growing seasons; he knows what it feels like to see Father's Day snow wipe out containers that were just planted.

Bill is currently serving as an editorial consultant to Hearst Magazines Enterprises, developing a new magazine based on the television show *Rebecca's Garden.* He is also California editor for *Garden Escape,* an Internet publisher and catalog. He is a past winner of the American Horticultural Society's Horticultural Communication award.

The National Gardening Association is the largest member-based, nonprofit organization of home gardeners in the U.S. Founded in 1972 (as "Gardens for All") to spearhead the community garden movement, today's National Gardening Association is best known for its bimonthly magazine, **National Gardening** ($18 per year). Reporting on all aspects of home gardening, each issue is read by some half-million gardeners worldwide. NGA supplements these publishing activities by online efforts, such as on the World Wide Web (www.garden.org), and on America Online (type Keyword, "HouseNet").

Other NGA activities include

- ✔ **Growing Science Inquiry and GrowLab** (funded in part by the National Science Foundation): Provides kindergarten through grade 8 with science-based curricula.
- ✔ **The *National Gardening Survey*** (conducted by the Gallup Company since 1972): The most detailed research about gardeners and gardening in North America.
- ✔ **Youth Garden Grants:** Grants of gardening tools and seeds, worth more than $500 each, which the NGA makes yearly to schools, youth groups, and community organizations.

Mission statement: "The mission of the National Gardening Association is to sustain the essential values of life and community, renewing the fundamental links between people, plants, and the earth. Through gardening, we promote environmental responsibility, advance multi-disciplinary learning and scientific literacy, and create partnerships that restore and enhance communities."

For more information about the National Gardening Association, write to 180 Flynn Ave., Burlington, Vermont, U.S.A. 05401.

ABOUT IDG BOOKS WORLDWIDE

Welcome to the world of IDG Books Worldwide.

IDG Books Worldwide, Inc., is a subsidiary of International Data Group, the world's largest publisher of computer-related information and the leading global provider of information services on information technology. IDG was founded more than 25 years ago and now employs more than 8,500 people worldwide. IDG publishes more than 275 computer publications in over 75 countries (see listing below). More than 60 million people read one or more IDG publications each month.

Launched in 1990, IDG Books Worldwide is today the #1 publisher of best-selling computer books in the United States. We are proud to have received eight awards from the Computer Press Association in recognition of editorial excellence and three from *Computer Currents'* First Annual Readers' Choice Awards. Our best-selling *...For Dummies*® series has more than 30 million copies in print with translations in 30 languages. IDG Books Worldwide, through a joint venture with IDG's Hi-Tech Beijing, became the first U.S. publisher to publish a computer book in the People's Republic of China. In record time, IDG Books Worldwide has become the first choice for millions of readers around the world who want to learn how to better manage their businesses.

Our mission is simple: Every one of our books is designed to bring extra value and skill-building instructions to the reader. Our books are written by experts who understand and care about our readers. The knowledge base of our editorial staff comes from years of experience in publishing, education, and journalism — experience we use to produce books for the '90s. In short, we care about books, so we attract the best people. We devote special attention to details such as audience, interior design, use of icons, and illustrations. And because we use an efficient process of authoring, editing, and desktop publishing our books electronically, we can spend more time ensuring superior content and spend less time on the technicalities of making books.

You can count on our commitment to deliver high-quality books at competitive prices on topics you want to read about. At IDG Books Worldwide, we continue in the IDG tradition of delivering quality for more than 25 years. You'll find no better book on a subject than one from IDG Books Worldwide.

John Kilcullen
CEO
IDG Books Worldwide, Inc.

Steven Berkowitz
President and Publisher
IDG Books Worldwide, Inc.

Eighth Annual
Computer Press
Awards ≥1992

Ninth Annual
Computer Press
Awards ≥1993

Tenth Annual
Computer Press
Awards ≥1994

Eleventh Annual
Computer Press
Awards ≥1995

IDG Books Worldwide, Inc., is a subsidiary of International Data Group, the world's largest publisher of computer-related information and the leading global provider of information services on information technology. International Data Group publishes over 275 computer publications in over 75 countries. Sixty million people read one or more International Data Group publications each month. International Data Group's publications include: **ARGENTINA:** Buyer's Guide, Computerworld Argentina, PC World Argentina; **AUSTRALIA:** Australian Macworld, Australian PC World, Australian Reseller News, Computerworld, IT Casebook, Network World, Publish, Webmaster; **AUSTRIA:** Computerwelt Österreich, Networks Austria, PC Tip Austria; **BANGLADESH:** PC World Bangladesh; **BELARUS:** PC World Belarus; **BELGIUM:** Data News; **BRAZIL:** Anuário de Informática, Computerworld, Connections, Macworld, PC Player, PC World, Publish, Reseller News, Supergamepower; **BULGARIA:** Computerworld Bulgaria, Network World Bulgaria, PC & MacWorld Bulgaria; **CANADA:** CIO Canada, Client/Server World, ComputerWorld Canada, InfoWorld Canada, NetworkWorld Canada, WebWorld; **CHILE:** Computerworld Chile, PC World Chile; **COLOMBIA:** Computerworld Colombia, PC World Colombia; **COSTA RICA:** PC World Centro America; **THE CZECH AND SLOVAK REPUBLICS:** Computerworld Czechoslovakia, Macworld Czech Republic, PC World Czechoslovakia; **DENMARK:** Communications World Danmark, Computerworld Danmark, Macworld Danmark, PC World Danmark, Techworld Denmark; **DOMINICAN REPUBLIC:** PC World Republica Dominicana; **ECUADOR:** PC World Ecuador; **EGYPT:** Computerworld Middle East, PC World Middle East; **EL SALVADOR:** PC World Centro America; **FINLAND:** MikroPC, Tietoverkko, Tietoviikko; **FRANCE:** Distributique, Hebdo, Info PC, Le Monde Informatique, Macworld, Reseaux & Telecoms, WebMaster France; **GERMANY:** Computer Partner, Computerwoche, Computerwoche Extra, Computerwoche FOCUS, Global Online, Macwelt, PC Welt; **GREECE:** Amiga Computing, GamePro Greece, Multimedia World; **GUATEMALA:** PC World Centro America; **HONDURAS:** PC World Centro America; **HONG KONG:** Computerworld Hong Kong, PC World Hong Kong, Publish in Asia; **HUNGARY:** ABCD CD-ROM, Computerworld Szamitastechnika, Internetto online Magazine, PC World Hungary, PC-X Magazin Hungary; **ICELAND:** Tolvuheimur PC World Island; **INDIA:** Information Communications World, Information Systems Computerworld, PC World India, Publish in Asia; **INDONESIA:** InfoKomputer PC World, Komputek Computerworld, Publish in Asia; **IRELAND:** ComputerScope, PC Live!; **ISRAEL:** Macworld Israel, People & Computers/Computerworld; **ITALY:** Computerworld Italia, Macworld Italia, Networking Italia, PC World Italia; **JAPAN:** DTP World, Macworld Japan, Nikkei Personal Computing, OS/2 World Japan, SunWorld Japan, Windows NT World, Windows World Japan; **KENYA:** PC World East African; **KOREA:** Hi-Tech Information, Macworld Korea, PC World Korea; **MACEDONIA:** PC World Macedonia; **MALAYSIA:** Computerworld Malaysia, PC World Malaysia, Publish in Asia; **MALTA:** PC World Malta; **MEXICO:** Computerworld Mexico, PC World Mexico; **MYANMAR:** PC World Myanmar; **NETHERLANDS:** Computer! Totaal, LAN Internetworking Magazine, LAN World Buyers Guide, Macworld Netherlands, Net, WebWereld; **NEW ZEALAND:** Absolute Beginners Guide and Plain & Simple Series, Computer Buyer, Computer Industry Directory, Computerworld New Zealand, MTB, Network World, PC World New Zealand; **NICARAGUA:** PC World Centro America; **NORWAY:** Computerworld Norge, CW Rapport, Datamagasinet, Financial Rapport, Kursguide Norge, Macworld Norge, Multimediaworld Norge, PC World Ekspress Norge, PC World Nettverk, PC World Norge, PC World ProduktGuide Norge; **PAKISTAN:** Computerworld Pakistan; **PANAMA:** PC World Panama; **PEOPLE'S REPUBLIC OF CHINA:** China Computer Users, China Computerworld, China InfoWorld, China Telecom World Weekly, Computer & Communication, Electronic Design China, Electronics Today, Electronics Weekly, Game Software, PC World China, Popular Computer Week, Software Weekly, Software World, Telecom World; **PERU:** Computerworld Peru, PC World Profesional Peru, PC World SoHo Peru; **PHILIPPINES:** Click!, Computerworld Philippines, PC World Philippines, Publish in Asia; **POLAND:** Computerworld Poland, Computerworld Special Report Poland, Cyber, Macworld Poland, Networld Poland, PC World Komputer; **PORTUGAL:** Cerebro/PC World, Computerworld/Correio Informático, Dealer World Portugal, Mac*In/PC*In Portugal, Multimedia World; **PUERTO RICO:** PC World Puerto Rico; **ROMANIA:** Computerworld Romania, PC World Romania, Telecom Romania; **RUSSIA:** Computerworld Russia, Mir PK, Publish, Seti; **SINGAPORE:** Computerworld Singapore, PC World Singapore, Publish in Asia; **SLOVENIA:** Monitor; **SOUTH AFRICA:** Computing SA, Network World SA, Software World SA; **SPAIN:** Communicaciones World España, Computerworld España, Dealer World España, Macworld España, PC World España; **SRI LANKA:** Infolink PC World; **SWEDEN:** CAP&Design, Computer Sweden, Corporate Computing Sweden, Internetworld Sweden, it.branschen, Macworld Sweden, MaxiData Sweden, MikroDatorn, Nätverk & Kommunikation, PC World Sweden, PGaktiv, Windows World Sweden; **SWITZERLAND:** Computerworld Schweiz, Macworld Schweiz, PCtip; **TAIWAN:** Computerworld Taiwan, Macworld Taiwan, NEW ViSiON/Publish, PC World Taiwan, Windows World Taiwan; **THAILAND:** Publish in Asia, Thai Computerworld; **TURKEY:** Computerworld Turkiye, Macworld Turkiye, Network World Turkiye, PC World Turkiye; **UKRAINE:** Computerworld Kiev, Multimedia World Ukraine, PC World Ukraine; **UNITED KINGDOM:** Acorn User UK, Amiga Action UK, Amiga Computing UK, Apple Talk UK, Computing, Macworld, Parents and Computers UK, PC Advisor, PC Home, PSX Pro, The WEB; **UNITED STATES:** Cable in the Classroom, CIO Magazine, Computerworld, DOS World, Federal Computer Week, GamePro Magazine, InfoWorld, I-Way, Macworld, Network World, PC Games, PC World, Publish, Video Event, THE WEB Magazine, and WebMaster; online webzines: JavaWorld, NetscapeWorld, and SunWorld Online; **URUGUAY:** InfoWorld Uruguay; **VENEZUELA:** Computerworld Venezuela, PC World Venezuela; and **VIETNAM:** PC World Vietnam.
3/24/97

Dedication

To the memory of fellow-editor Walter Doty, whose creativity and work habits I've long aspired to and fallen short of, but whose deadline performance I may finally have matched in this book.

Author's Acknowledgments

This book owes a lot to the efforts of a number of contributors. You don't think one person could possibly know all this stuff, do you?

Special thanks go to Lance Walheim, who wrote several chapters and supplied expertise especially on difficult, more technical material such as fertilizer, pests, weeds, and more. He did all this while writing an excellent book of his own, *Lawn Care For Dummies*.

Peggy Henry also made key contributions, with chapters on wildflowers, cutting gardens, and maintenance.

Valerie Easton deserves a lot of credit for her work on the design chapter and the inspired designs themselves.

Big thanks also to Barbara Pleasant, for her contribution to three chapters (planting, seeds, and seedlings).

For help with the regional section (see Chapter 3), I'm indebted to Carrie Chalmers and Nel Newman. Special thanks to Catherine Boyle, who compiled the frost-date chart.

The National Gardening Association thanks Sarah Kennedy, at the Chicago office of IDG Books Worldwide, Inc. for her vision and enthusiasm about both gardening and these books. Also at IDG in Chicago, thanks to Ann Miller, who is always ready to lend her able hand. At the Indianapolis office of IDG, much thanks to Project Editor Shannon Ross, and Copy Editor Tina Sims. Thanks to key participants at NGA: David Els, President; Michael MacCaskey, Editor-in-Chief; Bill Marken, ...*For Dummies* Series Editor; Larry Sommers, Associate Publisher; and Charlie Nardozzi, Senior Horticulturist. Special thanks to Suzanne DeJohn and Kathy Bond-Bori, NGA Staff Horticulturists, for their help.

Publisher's Acknowledgments

We're proud of this book; please register your comments through our IDG Books Worldwide Online Registration Form located at http://my2cents.dummies.com.

Some of the people who helped bring this book to market include the following:

Acquisitions, Development, and Editorial

Project Editor: Shannon Ross

Executive Editor: Sarah Kennedy

Copy Editor: Tina Sims

Technical Editor: Dr. David Beaty

Editorial Manager: Leah P. Cameron

Editorial Assistants: Paul E. Kuzmic, Donna Love

Special Help

Jill Alexander, Acquisitions Assistant;
Nickole Harris, Product Marketing Coordinator;
Maureen Kelly, Editorial Coordinator;
Ann K. Miller, Acquisitions Coordinator;
Linda Stark, Copy Editor;
Allison Solomon, Administrative Assistant

Production

Project Coordinator: Sherry Gomoll

Layout and Graphics: Steve Arany, Lou Boudreau, Linda M. Boyer, J. Tyler Connor, Maridee V. Ennis, Angela F. Hunckler, Todd Klemme, Brent Savage, Janet Seib, Kate Snell, Ian A. Smith

Illustrator: Joanna Koperski and JAK Graphics Ltd.

Photographers: David Cavagnaro, Crandall & Crandall Photography, R. Todd Davis Photography Inc., Derek Fell, Goldsmith Seed Company, Jerry Pavia, Michael S. Thompson

Proofreaders: Kelli Botta, Michelle Croninger, Joel Draper, Rachel Garvey, Nancy Price, Janet M. Withers

Indexer: Sherry Massey

General and Administrative

IDG Books Worldwide, Inc.: John Kilcullen, CEO; Steven Berkowitz, President and Publisher

IDG Books Technology Publishing: Brenda McLaughlin, Senior Vice President and Group Publisher

Dummies Technology Press and Dummies Editorial: Diane Graves Steele, Vice President and Associate Publisher; Mary Bednarek, Director of Acquisitions and Product Development; Kristin A. Cocks, Editorial Director

Dummies Trade Press: Kathleen A. Welton, Vice President and Publisher; Kevin Thornton, Acquisitions Manager

IDG Books Production for Dummies Press: Beth Jenkins Roberts, Production Director; Cindy L. Phipps, Manager of Project Coordination, Production Proofreading, and Indexing; Kathie S. Schutte, Supervisor of Page Layout; Shelley Lea, Supervisor of Graphics and Design; Debbie J. Gates, Production Systems Specialist; Robert Springer, Supervisor of Proofreading; Debbie Stailey, Special Projects Coordinator; Tony Augsburger, Supervisor of Reprints and Bluelines; Leslie Popplewell, Media Archive Coordinator

Dummies Packaging and Book Design: Patti Crane, Packaging Specialist; Kavish + Kavish, Cover Design

◆

The publisher would like to give special thanks to Patrick J. McGovern, without whom this book would not have been possible.

◆

Contents at a Glance

Introduction 1

Part I: Annual Report 7
Chapter 1: Friend to the Beginner, Challenge to the Expert 9
Chapter 2: Growing Annuals in Your Little Corner of the World 21
Chapter 3: Month by Month in Your Garden 31

Part II: Every Annual under the Sun . . .
and the Shade, Too 57
Chapter 4: The Big Ten: Popular, Reliable Annuals 59
Chapter 5: Annuals from A to Z 77

Part III: Designing Annual Beds and Borders 115
Chapter 6: Annuals and the Elements of Design 117
Chapter 7: Planning Beds and Borders 127

Part IV: Starting at Ground Level 143
Chapter 8: Preparing the Soil 145
Chapter 9: Sowing Seeds 159
Chapter 10: Planting Seedlings 171

Part V: The Care and Feeding of Annuals 181
Chapter 11: Quenching Your Flowers' Thirst 183
Chapter 12: Feeding Those Hungry Annuals 195
Chapter 13: Staking, Pruning, Deadheading, and Other Joys of Gardening 207
Chapter 14: Outsmarting Pests and Diseases 219
Chapter 15: Weed Wars and Your Ally, Mulch 237

Part VI: Creating Special Annual Gardens 245
Chapter 16: Growing Annuals in Containers 247
Chapter 17: Growing Annual Wildflower Gardens 263
Chapter 18: Growing Annuals for Cutting 273

Part VII: The Part of Tens 287
Chapter 19: Ten Most Frequently Asked Questions about Annuals 289
Chapter 20: Ten Annuals That Virtually Care for Themselves 293
Chapter 21: Annuals for Special Situations: Ten Sets of Ten 295
Chapter 22: Ten Annuals for Every Color of the Rainbow 301

Appendix: Sources for More Information about Annuals ... 305

Index 313

Book Registration Information .... Back of Book

Table of Contents

Introduction **1**

How to Use This Book.. 1
How This Book Is Organized 2
    Part I: Annual Report... 2
    Part II: Every Annual under the Sun . . . and the Shade, Too 3
    Part III: Designing Annual Beds and Borders 3
    Part IV: Starting at Ground Level................................ 3
    Part V: The Care and Feeding of Annuals 3
    Part VI: Creating Special Annual Gardens 4
    Part VII: The Part of Tens 4
Icons Used in This Book 4
Where to Go Next 5

Part I: Annual Report **7**

Chapter 1: Friend to the Beginner, Challenge to the Expert **9**

What Makes a Plant an Annual? 10
Deciphering Gardenese 11
    It's all in the name.. 12
    Flower shapes and plant sizes 13
Rewarding Projects for Novice Gardeners 15
Challenging Projects for the Expert Gardener 17

Chapter 2: Growing Annuals in Your Little Corner of the World **21**

What You Do (And Don't) Need to Know about Your Climate 21
Warm-Season versus Cool-Season Annuals 24
    The cool cats 25
    Some like it hot 25
Focusing in on Your Garden 27
    Sun or shade 27
    Wind 28
    Soil 28
    Slope 29
    Reflected heat 29

Chapter 3: Month by Month in Your Garden 31

Calendar for the North: Warm Summers, Cold Winters 32
Calendar for the South: Hot Summers, Mild Winters 38
Calendars for the West: Dry Summers, Wet Winters 44
    Growing annuals in most of California 44
    Growing annuals at high altitudes 50
    Growing annuals in lowland deserts 50
    Growing annuals in the Pacific Northwest 53

Part II: Every Annual under the Sun . . . and the Shade, Too 57

Chapter 4: The Big Ten: Popular, Reliable Annuals 59

Dahlias 60
Geraniums *(Pelargonium)* 61
Impatiens 62
Marigolds *(Tagetes)* 65
Pansies and Violas *(Viola wittrochiana)* 67
Petunias 67
Snapdragons *(Antirrhinium majus)* 69
Sunflowers *(Helianthus annuus)* 71
Sweet Peas *(Lathyrus odoratus)* 73
Zinnias *(Zinnia elegans)* 75

Chapter 5: Annuals from A to Z 77

African Daisy to Aster 77
Baby Blue Eyes to Browallia 79
Calendula to Cosmos 81
Dahlberg Daisy to Dusty Miller 90
E Is for English Daisy 91
Felicia to Foxglove 91
Gazania to Gloriosa Daisy 93
Heliotrope, Hollyhock, and Hyacinth Bean 95
Iceland Poppy and Impatiens 96
Kale and Kochia 97
Larkspur to Love-Lies-Bleeding 98
Marigold to Morning Glory 100
Nasturtium to Nierembergia 102
Pansy to Primrose 103
Salpiglossis to Sweet William 106
Thunbergia and Transvaal Daisy 111
Verbena to Viola 112
Wallflower and Wishbone Flower 113
Z Is for Zinnia 114

Part III: Designing Annual Beds and Borders............... 115

Chapter 6: Annuals and the Elements of Design 117

Playing with Color 117
  Spinning your color wheels 118
  Separating the hot from the cold 120
  Don't forget your leafy greens 121
Shape, Height, and Texture 121
Design for Fragrance 122
Four Styles of Annual Gardens 123

Chapter 7: Planning Beds and Borders 127

Getting Bedder All the Time 127
Rightsizing Your Beds and Borders 129
  The big guys 129
  Middle of the pack 130
  Short stuff 130
Choosing the Perfect Spot for Your Beds and Borders 131
Six Designs for Beds and Borders 132
  Sunny patio bed 132
  Shady bed around a large tree 134
  Border for a formal walkway 136
  Border for an informal walkway 137
  Border for a modern-style walkway 138
  Border against a backyard fence 139

Part IV: Starting at Ground Level 143

Chapter 8: Preparing the Soil 145

Taking Stock of What You've Got 145
  Loam is where the heart is 146
  Can you come out and clay? 146
  Sand now for something completely different 147
Building Better Soil 148
  Giving your soil some breathing room 148
  Going organic 149
  Checking your soil's pH 151
Dealing with Delinquent Drainage 152
Making the Bed 152
  Time for a tiller 156
  Bailing out with raised beds 157

Chapter 9: Sowing Seeds 159

Smart Seed Shopping 159
The Needs of Seeds 161
    Starting Seeds Indoors 161
    Sowing seeds directly in the ground 166

Chapter 10: Planting Seedlings 171

Shopping for Seedlings 171
Preventing Transplant Shock by Hardening Off 173
Planning to Plant: Give 'em Some Elbow Room 174
Planting Seedlings, Step by Step 176
    Special care for beautiful beds 179
    Year-round beds 180

Part V: The Care and Feeding of Annuals 181

Chapter 11: Quenching Your Flowers' Thirst 183

Determining a Plant's Water Needs 184
    Considering climate 184
    Watching the weather 184
    Studying your soil 185
    Looking at location 185
    Picking your plants 185
Ways to Water 186
    Hand watering 187
    Sprinklers 188
    Furrow irrigation 189
    Drip irrigation 190
    Soaker-hose irrigation 191
How Much Water to Apply 192

Chapter 12: Feeding Those Hungry Annuals 195

In Need of Nutrients 195
    Nitrogen — once is not enough 196
    Keeping the other nutrients in check 197
Shopping for Fertilizers 197
    Checking the guaranteed analysis 197
    Considering other factors 199
Fertilizing Your Flower Bed 202
Fertilizing Annuals in Containers 205
Using Organic Fertilizers 205

**Chapter 13: Staking, Pruning, Deadheading, and
Other Joys of Gardening** **207**

Tackling the Key Gardening Tasks 208
Using the Right Tool for the Right Job 209
Seven essential tools for growing annuals 209
Nonessential but handy garden supplies 210
Deadheading: Out with the Old 212
Offering Some Support: Basics of Staking............................. 213
Pruning and Pinching: It Hurts You More Than It Hurts the Plant 214
Mulching Miracles 216
Some Final Fun-Filled Activities 217

Chapter 14: Outsmarting Pests and Diseases **219**

An Ounce of Prevention... 220
When Bad Bugs Happen to Nice Gardens 221
Insects that prey on annuals 222
Fighting back 227
Disease — When the Flower Bed Becomes a Sick Bed 231
Prevention and control 232
Five feisty diseases 232

Chapter 15: Weed Wars and Your Ally, Mulch **237**

Outwitting Weeds 237
Before you plant 238
After you plant 239
Battling really tough weeds 239
Thank You Very Mulch... 240
Choosing your mulch 240
Laying it down 242
Knowing when to mulch 242

Part VI: Creating Special Annual Gardens **245**

Chapter 16: Growing Annuals in Containers **247**

Why Grow Annuals in Containers? 247
Having a Pot to Plant In 248
Types of container materials 249
The right size and shape of container 251
Planting Annuals in Containers 252
Soil mix 252
Planting steps 252
Foolproof Annuals for Container Growing 254
Old reliables for sunny spots 254
Annuals for shady containers 255
Combining Annuals in Mixed Plantings 256
Secrets of mixed plantings: Color and form 256
A sampling of mixed plantings for containers.................... 258

Chapter 17: Growing Annual Wildflower Gardens 263

Who's Who Among Wildflowers 264
Getting the Most from Your Wildflowers 265
Picking the Perfect Time to Plant................................... 266
Shopping for Wildflower Seeds or Seedlings 267
Choosing and Preparing Your Site 268
Getting Down to Business 269
    Planting the bed 269
    Alternative planting: Creating a scatter garden 270
Keeping Your Garden Just This Side of Wild 270
When the Show Comes to an End 271

Chapter 18: Growing Annuals for Cutting 273

Seven Reasons to Grow Annuals for Cutting 274
Choosing the Best Annuals for Cutting 274
Mixing Annuals for Cutting into Your Garden 276
A Garden Full of Flowers for Cutting 277
    Designing a cutting garden 278
    Three designs for cutting gardens 278
    Digging in 280
Harvesting and Using Cut Flowers 282
Building a Bouquet 283
Creating Everlasting Beauty with Dried Flowers 284
Ongoing Care 285
Winding Down 285

Part VII: The Part of Tens *287*

Chapter 19: Ten Most Frequently Asked Questions about Annuals 289

Chapter 20: Ten Annuals That Virtually Care for Themselves 293

Chapter 21: Annuals for Special Situations: Ten Sets of Ten 295

Annuals for sunny spots 295
Annuals for shade.. 296
Annuals for hot, dry spots 296
Annuals for containers... 297
Annuals for beds and borders 297
Annuals for edging... 298
Annuals that naturalize (self-seed) 298
Annuals for hanging baskets 299
Annuals that climb or creep... 299
Annuals that are easy to grow from seed outdoors 300

Chapter 22: Ten Annuals for Every Color of the Rainbow **301**

A case of the blues 301
Purple passion 302
Yellow . . . just like this book! 302
A blaze of orange 302
Red hot and spicy 303
Pretty in pink 303
All dressed in white 304
Green with envy 304

Appendix: Sources for More Information
about Annuals **305**

Seeds by mail 305
Tools and supplies by mail 307
Master gardeners in the U.S. and Canada 308
Web sites about annuals 309
Magazines about growing annuals 311

Index *313*

Book Registration Information .... *Back of Book*

Introduction

· ·

Sure, you can live without annual flowers. You can also live without football, rainbow trout, cabernet, and Boston terriers. But why should you?

Annuals are fun to grow for their brilliant colors, for their quick growth, for the life and spirit they add to a garden, for the butterflies and birds they attract, and for the way they can instantly transform something drab into a summer party place.

Growing annuals, of course, is not all fun and games. In this book, along with ideas for using annuals in colorful and creative ways, you can also find plenty of advice on planting and taking care of the little guys. None of the caretaking involved is terribly tough, but following some basic steps can greatly increase your chance for satisfaction.

If I could take the secret to success with annuals and boil it down to three simple steps, I think it would be this: Choose the right plants for your garden's conditions (sun or shade, for example) and for your climate (mild or cold winters, for example), plant them at the right time of year, and provide them with ongoing care. I devote the rest of this book to expanding on these three steps.

How to Use This Book

This book is intended to serve readers in at least two typical situations:

✔ You go to the nursery, are seduced by the beauty of some schizanthus plants, and take them home with you. Now what to do? Pick up your trusty *Annuals For Dummies* book and look up schizanthus. Read about what you can expect from this plant, what conditions it needs, and any special care it may need. If you don't yet have a flower bed in which to plant your lovely new annuals, perhaps you turn to the chapter on preparing the soil (Chapter 8) and planting (Chapter 10) and, with luck, get your seedlings in the ground before they dry out. Later on, after your plants are safely growing and you have time, read up on watering, feeding, pest control, and other things you may need to know to care for the new additions to the family.

✔ The other type of reader is, shall I say, less impulsive. You want to know something about annuals before you start out. You read through the early chapters (2 and 3) that discuss your climate and garden conditions, and you figure out what kinds of annuals best suit your needs. Read the plant descriptions in Chapters 4 and 5, study the color photographs, and choose the plants that most appeal to you. Start making plans for your own garden designs (Chapters 6 and 7) or container plantings (Chapter 16). If you're this kind of gardener, patient and conscientious, congratulations! I'm jealous of you. You will have a beautiful garden.

However you approach this book and whatever your level of experience, you're sure to find tips and information in these pages that will pay off in the garden.

How This Book Is Organized

This book is divided into seven major parts. The first part familiarizes you with your garden, climate, and seasons — all of which are key to what you can grow. The next part introduces a cornucopia of plants and advice on using them in your garden. The third part describes some ways to arrange combinations of flowers in your garden beds and borders for the best design. The fourth part discusses soil preparation and planting, and the fifth part explains how to maintain your annuals. Near the end of the book, I present some more specialized uses for annuals (such as containers and cutting gardens). The final part helps you choose special annuals for different situations and answers any lingering questions you may have.

Part I: Annual Report

I don't want to hold anyone back from getting out there and putting plants in the ground, but you may want to take time to read up on a few of the basics, such as what an annual is. This part includes a list of rewarding projects for first-time gardeners, and a list for more advanced growers of annuals. Chapters 2 and 3 help you figure out how your particular garden, climate, and seasons affect what and how you plant.

Part II: Every Annual under the Sun . . . and the Shade, Too

This part includes descriptions of the annuals that I recommend. Read about over a hundred annuals from A to Z — several hundred if you count all the relatives and varieties covered. Chapter 4 starts you off with ten favorites that are popular for good reasons: They are reliable and rewarding. Chapter 5 lists dozens more you should also consider — less popular, perhaps, but more diverse and just as beautiful. Check out the color section for photographs of nearly every annual listed in this part.

Part III: Designing Annual Beds and Borders

So you want to do more than grow a pot of marigolds? Maybe you want to combine your marigolds with something else, but you're not sure what colors to choose? While you're at it, why not throw in a few more varieties and create a border or bed? The chapters in this part introduce some of the basic principles of design. Chapter 7 presents plans for some typical garden situations. You can follow these plans plant for plant or use them to get started on your own personalized design, one that's suited to your garden's size and conditions.

Part IV: Starting at Ground Level

Preparing a good planting bed is probably the single most important step to growing great annuals. After you have a well-made bed, what do you fill it with, seeds or transplants? Each has its advantage. Chapters 6 and 7 tell you how to start annuals from either method.

Part V: The Care and Feeding of Annuals

Not to scare you off, but this is the kind of stuff that will make or break your success with annuals. Let the chapters in this part lead you by the hand through the major maintenance steps: watering, feeding, staking, and dealing with weeds, pests, and diseases. Don't worry; this stuff sounds worse than it really is.

Part VI: Creating Special Annual Gardens

Annuals are good for more than just sitting around in a flower bed looking pretty. These chapters present ideas for getting more from your annuals. Containers are natural homes for annuals and are a great way to get started. You can also grow gardens especially for cutting flowers to create fresh or dried bouquets. For a less tamed look, throw caution to the wind and grow a wildflower garden.

Part VII: The Part of Tens

Looking for a flower of a particular color? Want to grow fragrant annuals? Or annuals for shade? The chapters in this part have the answers you need, all in tidy bundles of ten.

Icons Used in This Book

Those cute little pictures in the margins of this book aren't just for decoration. They're pointing out some pretty important stuff.

Interested in environmentally friendly suggestions, like composting or conserving water? Look for this icon and do your part to keep the planet green.

Watch out. Something may be lurking about that could damage your annuals. This icon guides you to advice on keeping your plant safe from pests, fertilizer burn, and other disasters of the flower world.

This icon marks an especially challenging project or plant, but one that's worth trying if you're willing to do the extra work.

As long as you're reading about how to grow beautiful flowers, why not pick up a few new words for your gardening vocabulary? Look for this icon when you want to make sense of the strange, new terms you encounter on seed packets, in catalogs, and at the garden center.

Almost everybody has a shady patch of yard where nothing seems to grow. This icon marks information about annuals that grow well in the shade, or other tips about accommodating shady spots.

This book isn't big enough to include everything there is to know about annuals. This icon leads you to resource information such as catalog names, Web sites, phone numbers, and so on. The appendix is another great place to look for this kind of information.

All gardeners have their own bag of tricks. This icon marks nifty tips for growing better plants, saving money or time, or building a better garden.

If you're stuck on an island, you can plant a garden using nothing more than a sharpened stick. (Just ask Gilligan!) But having some basic tools makes your work a lot easier. And when you get serious about growing annuals, you can find some special equipment that will really show your garden who's the boss.

All things considered, gardening is a relatively safe pastime. However, it does have its hazards. This icon warns you of potential harm or injury from such things as poisonous plants, toxic chemicals, dangerous equipment, and so on. Remember, a safe gardener is a happy gardener.

Where to Go Next

If you want to start with buying plants, hit Chapters 4 and 5 and then go to a nursery or garden center. If you want to start dreaming about designs, go out to your yard and then consult Chapters 6 and 7. For a good overview of what's so special about annuals and what they can do for your garden, start with Chapters 1 and 2 — what a concept, start reading on the first page!

Part I
Annual Report

The 5th Wave   By Rich Tennant

"To our new neighbors. May you enjoy your new home, and keep your dog out of our flower beds."

In this part . . .

Have you ever met an annual you didn't love? Most gardeners can't resist the charming nature of annuals, with their bright, assorted colors and their quick response to care. This part of the book gives you even more reasons to love annuals, including the fact that they're versatile and easy to grow. You can also find out what those long, fancy flower names mean, how to choose annuals that are just right for *your* garden, and when to plant your flowers based on where you live. Whether you're a novice or an expert, you're sure to pick up some new ideas for gardening projects. For gardeners who can't live without to-do lists, this part even includes a gardening calendar that tells you what to do each month of the year.

Chapter 1

Friend to the Beginner, Challenge to the Expert

In This Chapter

▶ Ways in which annuals outshine other plants

▶ Bare-bone basics of garden jargon

▶ Seven rewarding projects for first-time gardeners to do with annuals

▶ Challenging ideas for veteran gardeners

*B*rilliantly colorful, yet short-lived. Perhaps this combination of qualities explains why people are so drawn to annuals, the shooting stars of the plant world, streaking across the summer in a burst of color and then burning out.

Even if you don't know what an annual is, you've no doubt seen plenty of them (although you probably just called them "flowers" instead of "annuals"). What many people recognize as the most familiar, friendliest flowers — petunias, marigolds, pansies, and the like — are actually annuals. The orange nasturtiums you see spilling out of window boxes, the yellow-and-white daisies sneaking up through cracks in the sidewalk, the pink hollyhocks standing tall next to grandma's chicken coop — these are the flowers of poetry, music, and fine art, or don't you remember Petunia Pig and Daisy Duck?

Why are annuals especially rewarding plants to grow? For a number of reasons:

✔ **Annuals are fun.** They exhibit the brightest, most endearing colors of the plant world.

✔ **Annuals are versatile.** You can grow them in beds, borders, pots, or baskets, in sun or shade, on top of bulbs, and underneath shrubs or trees. And annuals are the most popular type of flowers for cutting and bringing into the house.

✔ **Annuals don't mess around.** They grow fast and bloom young, even while they're still in little nursery packs. You can see what you're buying instead of having to wait for months until the blooms finally open. And, as a group, annuals give you more color for your money than any other plants.

✔ **Annuals respond to good care and let you know it.** When you provide the proper amount of water and fertilizer, annuals reward you with steady growth and a long bloom season. If you don't give your annuals the care they need, you'll usually know soon enough to replace your plants for that same season. Compare that quick feedback to planting an oak tree for your children to swing in and, years later, discovering that you've been stunting its growth. By that time, your kids have moved out of the house, blaming you for depriving them of the childhood pleasure of a tree swing.

Annuals are easy to grow and easygoing. Yet, they offer enough variety and complexity to challenge an expert gardener . . . and to fill the pages of this book.

What Makes a Plant an Annual?

To be technical for a moment, an *annual* is defined as a plant that undergoes its entire life cycle within one growing season, as illustrated in Figure 1-1. You plant a marigold seed in May, the seedling sprouts quickly, it starts blooming in July, frost kills it in October, seeds scatter and (with luck) sprout the next spring to start the process again. The good news is that nature typically blesses annuals with bright flowers to attract insects that will ensure pollination for seeds to sprout the next season.

Compare an annual with a *perennial.* By definition, a perennial is a plant that can live for several years, sprouting new growth and making new blooms year after year. Plant a typical perennial, such as columbine, from seed in May, and it spends the summer growing foliage, dies completely back to the ground when winter arrives, starts growing again the next spring, blooms that summer, dies back again, and repeats the pattern of blooming and dying back for years. (If you're interested in that kind of plant, too, pick up a copy of *Perennials For Dummies!*)

Also compare an annual to a *biennial,* which takes two years to bloom and complete its life cycle. In general, biennials grow only foliage for the first year and then bloom the second. However, some biennials can bloom in their first year if you plant the seeds early enough or if they happen to be one of the biennials bred for speed.

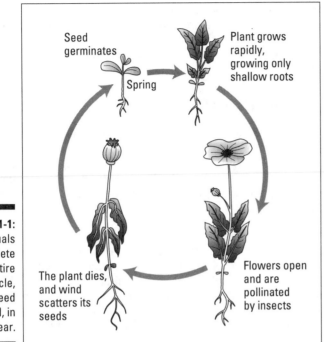

Figure 1-1:
Annuals
complete
their entire
life cycle,
from seed
to seed, in
one year.

As gardening (if not life in general) has no doubt conditioned you to expect, these general rules do come with a couple of qualifications:

- Some plants that appear to be annuals are actually fast-growing bienni-als that can complete their two-year cycle in one year. For simplicity's sake, this book simply refers to such plants as annuals.

- Some perennials act like annuals when you grow them in cold climates. Ivy geraniums *(Pelargonium peltatum),* for example, may not survive the month of June in a climate with late frosts, such as Toronto, but will live longer than you do if planted in a mild climate, such as southern California. For the purposes of this book, I refer to such fair-weather perennials as annuals, as well.

Deciphering Gardenese

Okay, so gardeners don't have an entire language of their own. But when you start growing annuals, you soon encounter new words and jargon at the nursery, in catalogs, on seed packages, and even here, in a book that does its best to demystify garden-speak. Learning a bunch of gardening terminology may not seem important when you're wearing your gardening gloves and are itching to start digging, but knowing these terms makes your planting and growing experiences more pleasant and productive.

It's all in the name

You probably never refer to your family pet as a *Canis familiaris,* even though that's the official scientific term for the domesticated dog. In this tradition of classifying everything under the sun, plant experts created long Latin names for every known annual. Don't worry. In the real world, people rarely use these fancy names in place of a plant's perfectly good (though perhaps less accurate and certainly less impressive sounding) common name.

Every plant has a two-part botanical name, identifying its genus and species. The botanical name always appears underlined or in italics with the genus name (which appears first) capitalized; for example, *Tagetes erecta* is the botanical name for African marigold. The genus name (*Tagetes,* in this case), refers to a group of closely related plants found in nature. The species name (*erecta,* in this case), refers to a specific member of the genus — such as a tall, orange-flowered marigold.

Of course, most plants also have common names. But common names can vary from place to place and from time to time. *Nemophila menziesii* will always be the botanical name for the same plant, no matter where in the world you find it. But when it comes to this plant's common name, some people call it California bluebell, while others know it as baby blue eyes. To add to this confusion, different plants may share the same common name; various kinds of butterfly flowers exist, in addition to butterfly bush and butterfly weed. Sometimes, the common name *is* the botanical name; for example, the botanical name for the petunia is *Petunia hybrida.*

You can see why people who want to be precise use the botanical names, but for most of us, and most of the time, common names work fine. And that's what we're going to use in this book. In case there might be confusion over a common name, check out the botanical name given in parentheses.

Some specialized plants have additional names tacked on to their botanical or common names:

- ✔ **Varieties and cultivars:** Many plants have another name, indicating a group of plants within a species that differ from the species in some particular way, such as flower color. When these subspecies occur naturally, they are called *varieties.* When the groups are manmade, they are referred to as *cultivars.* Variety names appear lowercased and italicized immediately after the species name, as in *Juniperus chinensis sargentii.* Cultivar names are capitalized and set apart in single quotes, as in *Tagetes erecta* 'Snowbird' — a white-flowered variety of marigold. Most of the annuals you see at nurseries or in seed catalogs are cultivars: 'Summer Sun' petunia, 'Freckles' geranium, or 'Pink Castle' celosia, for example.

✔ **Strains and series:** Another important player in the annuals name game is *strain* or *series.* These terms refer to a group of plants that share many similar growth characteristics but also differ among themselves in an important aspect. Many of the most popular annuals sold today are strains. Majestic Giant (note the lack of italics, quote marks, or other fancy punctuation) is a strain of pansies; all members of this strain develop similar big, blotchy flowers, but the blooms come in half a dozen different colors.

Flower shapes and plant sizes

Look what happens when expert plant breeders get their hands on annuals (or other flowering plants, for that matter). In nature, a flower may be yellow and have four petals. But after a few seasons under the guidance of a plant breeder, the same plant may produce a bloom with 16 white petals. Many flowers, but especially annuals, are highly malleable in these ways. Understanding all the whys and hows or plant size and shape isn't particularly important. Just remember that you can't expect a marigold, for example, to always look the same.

GARDEN JARGON

Hybrids: The pinnacle of the breeder's art

Today's flashy and dependable annuals owe a great deal to the hybridization efforts of plant breeders. A *hybrid* is the result of crossing two specific parent plants, such as a petunia with red and white flowers that results from crossing a red petunia with a white one.

An *F1 hybrid* is the result of crossing two carefully controlled parents to create seed that will grow into very predictable offspring. When you plant F1 hybrid seeds, you know exactly what they will grow into (a red and white petunia, for example). However, this second generation of plants won't produce seeds that grow into plants with the same predictability.

The predictable F1 hybrid qualities only last one generation. So this is the bottom line when you come across F1 hybrids: They cost more to develop and are priced higher at the nursery, but they offer benefits such as new flower colors, longer bloom season, bigger plants, or greater resistance to disease.

Hybrids are usually created in greenhouses where pollination can be carefully controlled. *Open pollination,* which occurs when annuals are grown in fields and allowed to be pollinated naturally by insects, yields far less predictable results than with hybridization.

At nurseries, in seed catalogs, and in this book, you'll encounter specific names for certain kinds of flowers. Some examples appear in Figure 1-2 and in the following list:

- ✔ A *single* flower, which is the type most typical in nature, has a single layer of petals.

- ✔ A *double* flower has additional layers of petals, usually the result of breeding that has transformed some of the flower's other parts, such as sepals or stamens, into showy petals.

- ✔ A *bicolor* flower has two prominent colors in its petals. This flower type is similar to, but not the same as, the picotee.

- ✔ A *star* flower is absolutely no surprise: It has a star-shape.

- ✔ The tips of a *picotee* flower have a different color than the rest of the flower petals.

The rest of the annual, as well as its flowers, comes in a wide range of improvements. Most of the breeding efforts have been directed at smaller, more compact plants *(dwarfs),* but you can also find many varieties developed to trail from hanging baskets *(trailers).* Annuals that plant breeders have worked with for a long time (more than a hundred years with marigolds) show the widest range of plant forms. Marigolds have many, many varieties classified as tall, intermediate, and dwarf.

Figure 1-2:
Flowers come in a range of shapes, sizes, and colors, including these favorites.

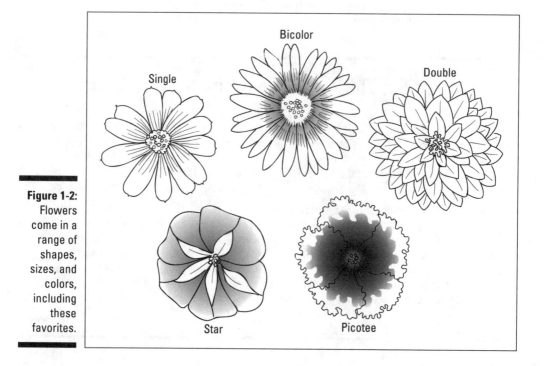

Single

Bicolor

Double

Star

Picotee

There they go, the All-Americas

What do the words *All-America Selections* (AAS) mean when they appear on a nursery label or alongside an annual described in a seed catalog?

In 1932, seed growers developed the All-America Selections program to recognize and promote outstanding new flower and vegetable creations. (Fleuroselect is the European equivalent of All-America Selections.) Each year, plant breeders enter new plant variations in the AAS competition, where they are grown at test gardens across North America. Judges look for improved qualities such as early bloom, disease or pest tolerance, new colors, novel flower forms, and longer bloom periods. The AAS logo on a plant indicates that it's a winner.

Over the years, more than 300 flowers have won AAS honors. Many are great; others have fallen by the wayside. Anytime you see the AAS symbol, you can feel pretty confident that the annual is well worth a try in your garden.

Rewarding Projects for Novice Gardeners

Go to any large garden center in June, and you find impatiens or petunias as far as the eye can see. These are universal flowers, loved by all, especially by beginners. You can't go wrong if you plant them at the right time of year in your climate and in the right conditions. But, as you'll probably find out sometime, put impatiens in too sunny a spot, and you get tinder-dry kindling; plant impatiens too early, and frost will turn them into a pile of slime overnight.

Even if you've never grown anything before, you can create some wonderful effects with annuals just by keeping a few basics in mind. Try any of these projects with annuals; all are fairly easy to do, and all are impressive in the garden:

- **Grow a sunflower taller than your rain gutter.** Children love growing sunflowers. The seeds are big enough to be easily grasped by pudgy, little fingers. Choose one of the monster-sized cultivars, such as 'Giganteus'. Plant the seeds directly in the ground, in a sunny spot, when the weather warms up. Make sure that you water regularly and deeply. You may need to stake the plant; after all, it's growing 10 inches a week. In a few months, your family will be looking up at flower heads more than a foot wide. See Chapter 4 for more information.

- **Create a sophisticated color combination.** If you like gray and purple together as much as I do, this project will make you feel like a master color choreographer. Buy two or three nursery seedlings of dusty miller, a foliage plant with silver-gray leaves, and several seedlings of heliotrope, a plant blessed with deep purple, fragrant flowers and dark, glossy leaves. Pick a sunny spot and plant the heliotrope, which grows taller than dusty miller, in the back. Or combine two or three of each of the plants in a container at least 12 inches in diameter. The soft, gray dusty miller elegantly sets off the regal heliotrope colors.

✔ **Grow flowers for dinner.** Nasturtium flowers are colorful *and* edible — they make a peppery addition to any green salad. The nice big seeds are easy to handle and quick to grow. You can start seeds indoors (see Chapter 9) and then transplant seedlings into containers or garden beds. Or you can start seeds directly in the ground. You can eat the whole nasturtium plant, but the tasty flowers are the best part.

✔ **Plant a flower bed in one step by sowing packs of seeds directly in the ground.** Take advantage of the fact that some annuals are easy to start from seeds. Marigolds and zinnias are noteworthy examples. Mix varieties in your flower bed or devote a bed to a single type. Prepare the planting bed by turning over the soil, raking it smooth, and preparing it as described in Chapter 8. Broadcast seeds evenly, cover lightly with organic matter or soil mix, and keep them moist until seedlings are at least a couple of inches tall. Thin the seedlings so they stand at the spacing recommended on the seed packet.

✔ **Bring in some instant color.** Sometimes, it's smart to pass up the tempting pots of annuals sold in full bloom at many nurseries. Plants this size can be expensive, and younger seedlings in smaller pots or packs can often catch up to and surpass them in just a few weeks. But how can you resist when you want the effect right away? To be smart about such extravagance, select "instant color" plants that have vigorous root systems. (See Chapter 9.) You can buy flower-covered geraniums, petunias, and pansies in 4-inch pots, gallon cans, or even larger containers; these plants perform better than most other annuals available at this size.

When you bring your plants home, show them off by transplanting them into containers or plant them where you can view them close-up. Three 4-inch-pot plants from the nursery fit well into a 12-inch clay pot. If you buy blooming plants in the gallon-can size, move a single plant into a pot just a bit larger (usually 10 inches in diameter).

✔ **Grow bouquets of cut flowers.** A few rows of zinnias, sown directly in the ground in full sun at the back of your garden, can supply a summer's worth of cut flowers for your home. And here's something to feel good about: Zinnias benefit from cutting, which encourages more stems and flowers to develop. Chapter 18 looks at plants that are great for making fresh and dried bouquets.

✔ **Become a container maestro.** Growing annuals in containers can be a fascinating challenge that brings out the artist in you. But it can also be downright simple if you stick with surefire plants. Try this foolproof project for summer annuals: In late spring after frost danger, plant six impatiens seedlings in a 14-inch-diameter terra cotta bowl filled to within $1^1/_2$ inches of the rim with commercial potting mix, keep the bowl in partial shade, water so soil is always moist, and fertilize monthly. Chapter 15 discusses growing annuals in containers in more detail. Or, for even more information about container gardening, hike to your nearest bookstore and pick up a copy of *Container Gardening For Dummies* by Bill Marken and the Editors of the National Gardening Association.

For a colorful spring or early-summer combination, try yellow violas edged with sweet alyssum. Start with a 14-inch terra cotta bowl and commercial potting mix. Buy a six-pack each of violas and alyssum. Plant four of the violas in the center of the pot and surround them with two or three of the alyssum to spill over the sides. Grow in full sun. Use any leftover plants in other pots or transplant them into the ground.

✔ **You can never go wrong with these plants.** If you are not sure what to plant, go to the nursery and buy what looks good from this list of good-looking, foolproof annual flowers: cosmos, impatiens, lobelia, marigolds, nasturtium, petunias, portulaca, sweet alyssum, sweet William, and zinnias.

Challenging Projects for the Expert Gardener

Hundreds and hundreds of annuals are out there, so it's not surprising that among them are plenty of opportunities for anyone who wants to try something new and different. The following projects represent just a few of the more challenging adventures you can have with annuals. Proceed at your own speed.

✔ **Grow beautiful, old-fashioned bouquets.** Can anything match sweet peas for the nostalgic power of their perfume? But sweet peas are notoriously tricky to grow, subject to mildew, affected by hot weather (stems grow too short, flowers don't last), and afflicted by a host of infirmities. Sweet peas make you work for their beautiful fragrance, but it's worth it. Chapter 4 contains the tips and advice you need to please these finicky annuals and create nose-pleasing bouquets.

✔ **Grow a colorful annual border with no flowers.** Not all annuals use blooms to get their color. Coleus, for example, is an annual that's prized for its big, colorful leaves. Such nonflowering annuals are great for shady spots where flowers may not bloom well.

✔ **Create a 365-day border**. If you live in a mild-winter climate (such as much of California, low-elevation Arizona, and parts of the southern U.S.), you can have annuals in bloom every day of the year. The secret is to overlap plantings and be brutal about rotating plants. For example, if you have warm-season annuals still blooming in late summer, replace some of them with cool-season annuals — don't wait until the summer flowers are completely done, or you'll have a bare bed for a while. Remove the rest of the summer annuals when they finish blooming and move in more winter and spring annuals. This juggling act can get complicated. See Chapter 2 for suggestions for your climate.

✔ **Grow a hanging basket as big as your car.** Visitors to Victoria, the capital of British Columbia, Canada, are always amazed at the hanging baskets that decorate the city's lampposts. As one visitor put it, "They're so beautiful, I would have taken a couple home — except they were bigger than my car."

You can make a scaled-down version of these giant beauties by using a 16-inch wire basket, a cubic foot of sphagnum moss, and lightweight soil mix. You need about two dozen warm-season annuals: some that trail (such as ivy geraniums, lobelias, and petunias) and some that stand more upright (such as marigolds and schizanthus). Line the basket with moss and then fill it with soil mix to within $1^1/_2$ inches of the top. Stuff trailing annuals into the sides of the basket and plant a few upright annuals in the center. For more details on planting baskets, see Chapter 16.

✔ **Grow rare tongue-twisters.** Schizanthus and salpiglossis (both covered in Chapter 5) are relatively unknown, but decidedly attractive, annuals. Actually, they're harder to spell than to grow, and they're well worth a try in your summer garden. If you're worried about pronunciation, just point at the nursery label.

✔ **Pamper a prima donna.** Transvaal daisy (*Gerbera*) is a truly beautiful annual with deeply colored, big, flatish, classic-daisy flowers on long, thick stems. It looks hard to grow . . . and it is. This plant requires perfect drainage, perfect weather, and perfect snail control. Are you up to the task? If not, you can do what I do: Buy blooming plants in 4-inch pots at the nursery, transplant extra carefully (the finicky Transvaal daisy is sensitive about transplanting, too) to a larger pot for about a month of glorious bloom on the front porch.

✔ **Take pride in your petunias.** Petunias are easy to grow from transplants, but really difficult to grow from seed. The seeds are about the size of dust, for one thing, and they demand a surprising amount of painstaking care. Why grow petunias from seed? You get a much bigger selection when you buy seeds instead of nursery transplants. And you get a great deal of satisfaction when you start with those dust specks in February and end up with blooming plants in July. Look to Chapter 9 for our step-by-step advice for sowing seeds indoors.

✔ **Coax a miracle from a patio crack.** Think of those unexpected details that make a garden special, like an African daisy poking up between flagstone slabs. Or, as in my garden, blue lobelia spilling from a pot holding a golden barrel cactus. How did I do it? I have no idea. Nature took care of it. Seeds from lobelias growing nearby made their way into the cactus pot, sprouted, found the spot to their liking, and now come back every year from the seeds of those before them.

Expert gardeners sometimes try duplicating nature by planting lobelia or African daisy seedlings between patio cracks, at the base of a brick planter, or in another situation that resembles a natural occurrence. With luck, the plants will adapt and reseed. But here's my big-picture advice that you won't find in fussbudget garden books: Take what nature gives you. Give those little sprouting plants a chance (unless you *know* they're weeds). Seedlings coming up on their own obviously are comfortable in that spot and may do better than anything you intentionally plant there. Tolerate a little disorder and plant improvisation among your annuals.

Chapter 2

Growing Annuals in Your Little Corner of the World

• •

In This Chapter

▶ Enjoying warm-season and cool-season annuals

▶ Knowing when to plant what

▶ Assessing the conditions in your garden

• •

*I*f you plant annuals at the right season and in the right spot in your garden, you can easily have months of glorious blooms. But if you start a marigold too early, place a zinnia in a spot that's too shady, or stick a begonia where it's too dry, you'll get a quick lesson in the importance of understanding your garden's climate patterns and other conditions. (In case you're curious, the results of the unwise plantings suggested in the previous sentence are a blackened, frost-burned marigold; a lanky, bloomless zinnia; and begonia toast.)

Before you head to the nursery to buy your plants, first try to find out a few things about your area's climate and seasons, plus some of your own garden's special conditions. Armed with that knowledge, you can make much wiser selections at planting time and give your annuals a much better chance of flourishing.

What You Do (And Don't) Need to Know about Your Climate

To grow annuals, you don't need to worry about your precise climate zone and temperature extremes as much as you do with permanent plants, such as perennials, trees, and shrubs. If you want to grow roses, for example, you need to know whether the temperature in your area drops to 10°F (−12°C) or −10°F (−23°C). That temperature difference can affect which roses will adapt to your area.

Annuals are more straightforward. You simply have to wait until after the last killing frost to plant. (Use Table 2-1 as a predictor or contact your local weather bureau or cooperative extension service for an idea of the date of the last killing frost in your area.) In fact, no matter where you live, you can probably wait until the first of June to plant impatiens and feel comfortable that you're doing the right thing at the right time for your climate. But if you take this "safe" approach to gardening, you miss a lot of the fun of growing annuals. By experimenting with a variety of annuals, you reap the rewards: flowers that bloom as long as your seasons allow, and flowers that bloom in all the different spots in your garden.

Even though annuals live only for one season, you want to make those few months as pleasant as possible for them. That means planting at the right time in your region.

Table 2-1	Frost Dates and Length of Growing Season		
City	Last Frost in Spring	First Frost in Fall	Length of Growing Season
Birmingham, Alabama	March 19	November 14	240 days
Phoenix, Arizona	January 28	December 16	322 days
Little Rock, Arkansas	March 17	November 10	238 days
Los Angeles (San Fernando), California	*	*	288 days
Santa Ana, California	*	*	338 days
Denver, Colorado	May 3	October 16	166 days
New Haven, Connecticut	April 15	October 27	195 days
Dover, Delaware	April 15	October 26	194 days
Miami, Florida	none	none	365 days
Orlando, Florida	January 31	December 17	320 days
Atlanta, Georgia	March 21	November 18	242 days
Boise, Idaho	May 6	October 12	159 days
Chicago, Illinois	April 8	November 9	215 days
Indianapolis, Indiana	April 17	October 27	193 days
Des Moines, Iowa	April 19	October 22	186 days
Wichita, Kansas	April 5	November 1	210 days
Louisville, Kentucky	April 1	November 7	220 days

City	Last Frost in Spring	First Frost in Fall	Length of Growing Season
New Orleans, Louisiana	February 13	December 12	302 days
Portland, Maine	*	*	136 days
Baltimore, Maryland	March 26	November 19	238 days
Boston, Massachusetts	April 5	November 8	217 days
Detroit, Michigan	April 24	October 22	181 days
Minneapolis-St. Paul, Minnesota	April 30	October 13	166 days
Jackson, Mississippi	March 10	November 13	248 days
St. Louis, Missouri	April 3	November 6	217 days
Billings, Montana	May 15	September 24	132 days
Lincoln, Nebraska	April 20	October 17	180 days
Las Vegas, Nevada	March 13	November 13	245 days
Concord, New Hampshire	May 11	September 30	142 days
Newark, New Jersey	April 3	November 8	219 days
Albuquerque, New Mexico	April 16	October 29	196 days
New York City, New York	April 7	November 12	219 days
Charlotte, North Carolina	March 21	November 15	239 days
Fargo, North Dakota	May 13	September 27	137 days
Cincinnati, Ohio	April 15	October 25	192 days
Oklahoma City, Oklahoma	March 28	November 7	224 days
Portland, Oregon	February 25	December 1	279 days
Pittsburgh, Pennsylvania	April 16	November 3	201 days
Providence, Rhode Island	April 13	October 27	197 days
Charleston, South Carolina	February 19	December 10	294 days
Rapid City, South Dakota	May 7	October 4	150 days
Memphis, Tennessee	March 20	November 12	237 days
Dallas, Texas	March 18	November 12	239 days
Houston, Texas	February 4	December 10	309 days
Salt Lake City, Utah	April 12	November 1	203 days
Burlington, Vermont	May 8	October 3	146 days

(continued)

Table 2-1 *(continued)*

City	Last Frost in Spring	First Frost in Fall	Length of Growing Season
Richmond, Virginia	*	*	206 days
Seattle, Washington	February 23	November 30	280 days
Petersburg, West Virginia	April 30	October 5	158 days
Milwaukee, Wisconsin	April 20	October 25	188 days
Cheyenne, Wyoming	May 20	September 27	130 days

* Data not available

Based on "Climates of the States," by the National Oceanic and Atmospheric Administration

Warm-Season versus Cool-Season Annuals

The first question to ask about any annual that you'd like to add to your garden is not "What's its zodiac sign?" but "Is it a warm-season or a cool-season annual?" Understanding the difference is vital to planting annuals at the right time of year in your area.

Depending on their origin and what's been bred into them, different annuals prefer different conditions. Fortunately, for those who have trouble remembering the growing requirements of every flower, you can focus on only two main categories of annuals: cool season and warm season.

Cool season and *warm season* are, of course, relative terms. Where summers are cool, such as along the foggy California coast or other overcast climates, you can grow cool-season annuals all summer. Where winters are warm and nearly frost-free, such as in low-elevation Arizona, fall through spring is an ideal time to grow cool-season annuals, such as Iceland poppies and stock, and even some warm-season annuals, such as petunias. In fact, winter and early spring make up the main flower-growing season in Arizona — summer there is too hot to grow any annuals except the most heat-tolerant warm-season varieties.

If you live where summer gets hot, which is most of the U.S., plant cool-season annuals as early as possible (even before the last spring frost), and replace them after they fade in hot weather. If you live where summers are hot and winters are *relatively* mild (not dropping too far below freezing), you can plant these cool-season annuals in the fall, leave them over the winter, and they'll bloom in early spring.

The cool cats

Cool-season annuals are those that perform best when temperatures are mild — about 70°F (21°C) — days are short, and soil is cool. In most parts of the U.S. and Canada, these conditions are typical in early spring and early fall. Temperatures may be similarly mild all season in mountain regions or in regions to the far north (or the far south, in the Southern Hemisphere). In some coastal regions, temperatures stay mild year-round.

Cool-season annuals can stand a varying amount of frost, from a little to a lot; some types, in fact, are quite hardy and are actually perennials that live through the winter in many areas. The enemies are hot weather and long days, which cause cool-season annuals to produce fewer blooms and ultimately die. Examples of cool-season favorites are calendulas, pansies, and snapdragons.

You're usually safe planting cool-season annuals a few weeks before the average date of the last spring frost in your area. If you live where weather is cool year-round or during the growing season, plant mostly cool-season annuals. If you live where summer days are hot and winters are mild, such as Phoenix, Palm Springs, or the Gulf Coast, plant cool-season annuals in the fall for a winter garden.

In the typical cold-winter/hot-summer climate, the time to plant cool-season annuals is early spring — from four to eight weeks before the typical last frost or as soon as the ground can be worked (dug and turned over). Their season ends with the arrival of hot weather, when you can replace them with warm-season annuals. Where summers rarely heat up, many cool-season annuals can thrive all summer right alongside warm-season annuals that don't demand hot weather.

Some like it hot

Warm-season annuals are those that thrive in hot summer weather. Most are tender and get damaged or downright destroyed by freezing temperatures. Examples are celosias, marigolds, vinca rosea (also called Madagascar periwinkle), and zinnias. Plant these heat-seekers after soil and air temperatures begin to warm up and expect them to reach their peak in midsummer.

So when is the magic date to plant warm-season annuals? That depends on your climate. (Bet you knew I was going to say that!) Suppose, for example, that you live in the most typical climate, the one that predominates over most of the northern United States, Canada, and northern Europe. This climate typically has cold winters (usually with snow) and warm, often humid summers. In this climate, you can generally grow warm-season annuals from late spring through late summer or early fall. The basic rule for planting: Wait until the danger of frost has passed — by then, the weather is usually also warming enough for growth and blooming.

To determine frost-safe planting dates in your area, refer to Table 2-1. Based on long-term weather records, the chart shows the average dates of the last frost of the spring and the first frost of the fall. To find the planting date for warm-season annuals, take the last date of spring frost in an area near you or in an area with a climate similar to yours and add ten days, to be safe. (Or be ready to protect plants with floating row covers.)

Floating row covers are an essential tool for gardeners who want to squeeze every bit of warmth out of early spring or late fall weather. Several types are available, but all share two traits: They are porous and very lightweight. You can lay floating row covers right over tender growing plants without smothering or crushing them. More importantly, these covers provide just enough insulation to protect plants on those clear, chilly nights when plants are most likely to suffer frost damage.

Use Table 2-1 to calculate another important feature of your climate: the length of the *growing season.* The growing season is simply the typical number of days between spring's last frost and fall's first frost. Generally, the farther north, the shorter the growing season. Growing-season length can be a factor when you're choosing annuals, especially from seed catalogs, which list the number of days to bloom.

Days to bloom is an important number for annuals. It's usually listed right on the seed packet or in the seed catalog, sometimes right after the plant name. Specifically, this figure refers the number of days a plant requires after you plant its seed for the flower to bloom. But this number is an average, not an absolute. The actual number of days a plant takes to bloom in your garden may be more or less, depending on your climate and weather. Your goal is to determine whether a plant's days-to-bloom average fits comfortably within your growing season. If your growing season is 100 days long, and a flower takes, on average, 120 days to bloom, pass it by. If you absolutely must have this flower in your garden, start the seeds indoors a month or more before the last frost. For more information about growing seeds indoors, see Chapter 9.

The date of the last frost is not the only guideline to use when planting annuals. For example, what if you want to grow warm-season annuals in mild-winter climates? If you live in southern California and follow the chart, for example, you might assume that you can plant zinnias in January. Frost isn't a threat then, but January temperatures aren't warm enough to encourage growth. Warm-season annuals need warm temperatures as well as frost-free conditions. Plant when the weather starts to warm up a bit. See more specific dates in Chapter 3 and in the plant descriptions of Chapters 4 and 5. Note that some warm-season annuals need more heat than others.

Do you live in an all-year climate for annuals?

In some places, you can grow annuals all year. Winter temperatures rarely drop much below freezing in these regions, which include California (except for higher elevations), low elevations of the Southwest, and milder sections of the South, such as the Gulf Coast.

In mild-climate regions, you can plant cool-season annuals, such as lobelia and Iceland poppies, in late summer or early fall (after summer cools off). Blooms may appear before Christmas and peak in late winter and early spring. After growth and flowering slow down in spring, replace the cool-season annuals with warm-season annuals.

In mild climates, cool-season annuals can also be planted through the winter and early spring. They miss out on fall's warm weather to push them into growth but surge as soon as temperatures start to warm in late winter and early spring. See Chapter 3 for planting dates in your region.

Truly tropical climates, such as those found in Hawaii and southern Florida, are in a separate category and have their own special guidelines for growing annuals. If you live in a tropical climate, check with local nurseries for advice.

Focusing in on Your Garden

Before you plant, observe the conditions in your garden. Keep the following factors in mind when considering which annuals to plant and where to plant them.

Sun or shade

Plants have natural attributes that enable them to perform better in certain amounts of sunlight. Think about a plant's heredity for a few seconds. Where would a vine native to the jungle grow best in a garden? Probably where it receives some protection from the sun, such as under a high canopy of trees, similar to the shelter that it receives in its native habitat. Give the vine too much sun, and its foliage burns like the skin of an Irish redhead on the beach at Cancun. Or consider a plant with a sunny heredity. Zinnias, originally from Mexico, thrive in full sun. In too much shade, they grow spindly and develop mildew on their leaves.

Most annuals do best in *full sun*. That usually means about seven hours of sunlight during a summer day. Those hours should come during the middle of the day. If a spot in the garden gets its seven hours during the morning or late afternoon when the sun is not as intense, that location probably is not sunny enough for most sun-loving annuals. In those areas, you can plant shade-lovers such as impatiens or begonias.

Try to notice the pattern of sun and shade in your garden. It changes with time and the seasons: as the sun moves higher and lower in the sky, as trees grow taller and develop and lose leaves, and as neighbors build or tear down buildings. The following terms may help you determine what kind of sunlight your garden has:

✔ A northern exposure probably is blocked from the sun all day. This is *full shade*.

✔ The east side of your house, unless it's blocked by trees or buildings, probably gets sun in the morning and shade for the rest of the day. This is a typical *part shade* setting.

✔ A southern exposure gets the most hours of sun — this is *full sun*.

✔ A western exposure may get shade in the morning and full sun in the afternoon — this usually should be considered a sunny location because of the intensity of the light. (Shade plants will probably cook there.)

Pay attention to the sun/shade requirements specified for each plant in Chapters 4 and 5 or as recommended by your local nursery. And watch the flowers that you plant to see how they respond. Signs of too much sun include brown, burned spots on the leaves. Results of too much shade include spindly foliage growth and weak blooming. If you notice those signs, experiment with different plants next time.

Definitions of sun and shade also depend on your climate. For example, near a coast, where it's cool and often overcast, plants generally need more sun than do plants in inland regions. In these cool, cloudy regions, sun-loving plants, such as zinnias, may have trouble growing even in direct sun, and plants that prefer shade, such as begonias, can come out from the shadows to flourish in full sun.

Wind

Will annuals be exposed to wind in your garden? Wind can dry out the soil quickly and rob plants of moisture. Stiff breezes can topple tall plants and break brittle ones. Although you can't do much about the wind, you *can* make sure that you water carefully. Planting shrubs or trees to provide a windbreak also may help. Or you may have to simply find a more protected spot for your annuals.

Soil

You may be stuck with soil that drains poorly or that otherwise makes life tough for annuals. Chapter 8 tells you how to know what kind of soil you have and, if it's lousy, how to improve it.

Slope

Gardening on a hillside presents some special challenges — watering is more difficult, for one thing. Terracing and drip irrigation are ways to ensure that enough moisture gets to plant roots.

Drip irrigation is a very slow and precise way to water plants. This method is great on slopes because the water is applied so slowly that it has time to actually soak in and not run off. Chapter 11 includes more information about drip irrigation, and you can find a list of suppliers of garden tools, including drip irrigation equipment, in the appendix.

Hilly terrain also can affect weather conditions. A sunny, south-facing slope can provide a milder situation for annuals because cold air drains away. You may find a hillside garden to be several degrees warmer and several weeks ahead of the neighbor's garden at the bottom of the hill.

Reflected heat

Pavement, house walls, and other heat-reflective surfaces can warm up a garden. Although these surfaces can be positive factors under certain conditions, reflected heat usually causes plants to burn up. Before you plant, be aware of conditions that are too bright — for example, the pavement around a swimming pool. Unless your plants can take intense heat, you're better off planting them somewhere with a little more shade.

Many annuals thrive on sun and heat. If you've got a hot spot where you want to plant, consider such old favorites as petunias and marigolds, as well as lesser-known annuals such as Mexican sunflower and strawflowers.

Chapter 3

Month by Month in Your Garden

- -

In This Chapter

▶ Calendars for growing annuals in three distinct climate regions

▶ Suggestions for plants that may work well where you live

▶ A time to plant, a time to sow, a time to prune, a time to grow . . .

- -

The calendars in this chapter can help you do all the right things for your annuals at the right time. They show you the best months for planning the garden, preparing the soil, sowing seeds, planting seedlings, cutting and weeding, controlling pests, doing cleanup, and performing other chores. They even list the best times to simply kick back and admire your handiwork.

Because annuals are fairly easy to grow (ranging somewhere between a plastic tulip and a rhododendron in difficulty), these calendars of advice are on the simple side. I divide the United States and much of Canada into big annual-growing regions. You can use this simplified system, rather than the complicated 11-climate USDA zone map, because annuals don't need to survive cold winters year after year the way permanent plants must. You only need to know information such as when to plant what annuals, when insect and disease problems may strike in your area, and how to care for your flowers.

If you live in a country other than the United States or Canada, follow the advice of a climate region in this chapter that comes close to yours — northern Europe, for example, compares most closely with the northern belt of the U.S., and Great Britain's climate is similar to the Pacific Northwest's.

Even though this chapter is relatively simple, climates are, by nature, complex, and weather varies from year to year. Weather is also local, with big swings in cold, heat, rain, snow, and almost everything else occurring over just a few miles. So use the calendars in this chapter as a guideline, but continuing looking to the skies, checking the thermometer, and talking to the friendly folks at your local nursery to make sure that you're on the right track.

Climates not covered in this chapter

Tropical climates, such as you find in the lush southern tip of Florida and in most of Hawaii, don't get a calendar in this chapter because, frankly, they don't need one. The tropics tend to have wet and dry seasons, not so much cold and warm seasons. You can grow annuals year-round in tropical regions as long as you have water. Water, not the temperature, is your limiting factor. If you don't have a storage source, time your planting around the wet seasons so that your plants can get established and last into the dry season.

This chapter also does not cover interior Alaska, which is a climate unto itself.

If you live in any of these regions, you must rely on local advice.

Calendar for the North: Warm Summers, Cold Winters

People tend to think of the northeastern, northern, and midwestern sections of the United States and Canada as separate regions and growing climates. True, these regions encompass a diverse range of climates and gardening conditions. In northern New England, winter temperatures may dip to $-40°F$ ($-40°C$), whereas regions of the lower Midwest, such as southern Kansas and Missouri, may not experience temperatures lower than $-10°F$ ($-23°C$).

For the purposes of this chapter, however, I group all these regions together, along with most of Canada. (British Columbia falls in the Pacific Northwest region, which I cover later in this chapter.) This is possible because the most important concern for growing annuals is not how cold the winter gets, but rather when the first and last frosts of the growing season are likely to occur. The frost dates determine seeding schedules, planting times, duration of garden chores, and the ability to grow fall-blooming annuals. Check the listing of frost dates and season lengths in Chapter 2 to get a more precise idea of when to start annuals and how long the growing season is in your area.

Despite their diversities, all these regions share your basic North American weather: warm summers and cold winters. You won't find annuals growing during the winters in this region; they'd have to hide under a blanket of snow or endure subzero temperatures. The main season for annuals begins with planting time in early or midspring and ends when serious frosts hit in the fall.

January

Settle next to the fire with a stack of new seed catalogs. (See the appendix for a list of sources.) Starting your own annuals from seed can save money, provide a greater selection of varieties and colors, and become a satisfying spring ritual for you.

As you order seeds, think about where you want to plant your annuals and what color combinations you find appealing. Consider planting annuals for drying, fresh-cut bouquets, fragrance, color, and a long bloom period. Think about mixing edible varieties into a vegetable garden, adding tall annuals to a perennial border, or experimenting with annuals in containers.

February

Prepare a space for starting seeds if you haven't already done so. Clear an area in a sunny window or set up fluorescent lights for seedlings to sprout and grow. Buy seed-starting trays or use old trays that you've cleaned with a dilute bleach solution and rinsed well. Consider providing bottom heat, which maintains an even, warm soil temperature and improves germination; many mail-order catalogs offer heating mats specifically for seed starting.

Use a commercial potting mix for starting seeds: a fine germinating mix for tiny seeds, and a coarser, peat-based mix for larger seeds and for growing your seedlings on to maturity. For more about soil mixes and starting seeds, see Chapter 9.

March

March through mid-April is seed-starting time in cold climates.

Plan a seeding schedule — essential in short-season climates where you want to make every day count. Start by figuring when you want to transplant annuals into the ground in the weeks and months ahead, and work backward to calculate the best time to sow the seeds indoors. In most cases, you need to plant four to eight weeks ahead of transplanting time, depending on how long it takes seeds to reach transplanting size. For instance, if you can plant petunias outdoors in your area in mid-May (after frost danger) and petunia seeds take eight weeks to reach transplanting stage after sowing, you should start the seeds indoors around March 15. Consider the following general advice on when to sow seeds indoors:

> ✔ **When to sow tender annuals:** Frost-sensitive types of annuals should go into the garden after the danger of frost has passed. Sow seeds for the following fast-growing annuals indoors four weeks before transplanting: cosmos, hyacinth bean, morning glories, sunflowers, and zinnias. Sow seeds for the following moderate-growing annuals six weeks ahead of transplanting: ageratum, spider flower, marigolds,

salvia, gazania, globe amaranth, strawflower, phlox, moonflower, cup-and-saucer vine, and creeping zinnia. Sow seeds for these slow-growing annuals eight weeks ahead of transplanting: bedding begonia, browallia, coleus, Dahlberg daisy, heliotrope, impatiens, lobelia, nicotiana, petunias, and verbena.

✔ **When to sow hardy annuals:** Sow seeds for fast-growing sweet peas four weeks ahead of transplanting. You can sow seeds for moderate-growing annuals, such as calendula, Chinese forget-me-not, cornflower, love-in-a-mist, stock, and sweet alyssum, six weeks before transplanting. Allow eight weeks before transplanting if you sow seeds for slow-growing annuals, such as snapdragons, poppies, pansies, violas, and larkspur. Because all these hardy annuals can tolerate light frost and cool conditions, you can transplant seedlings 10 to 14 days before the date of the last frost in your region. (Chapter 2 contains a chart of average last frost dates. You can also consult your local weather bureau, cooperative extension office, or local garden center.)

April

You still have time to sow seeds indoors for transplanting next month — especially in colder climates where winters are most severe and the growing season is shortest. If your last-frost date falls around Memorial Day, you should sow seeds for all annuals, except fast-growing, tender plants (cosmos and zinnias, for example), by mid-April.

Watch indoor seedlings for pests and diseases. Plants infested with aphids often exhibit curled leaves and a shiny, sticky substance on their leaves; look under the leaves for clusters of aphids. A soap solution is an effective way to kill aphids, but you must apply it thoroughly and regularly until the population is under control. Try to avoid the conditions that encourage aphids: poor air circulation, overcrowding, and overfertilizing. Damping off is a common disease that affects new seedlings; sprouts rot near soil level and collapse. Prevent this disease by using a sterile soil mix and not overwatering. (See Chapter 14 for more information on pests and diseases.)

If you live in warmer areas with milder winters, you can start sowing seeds of hardy annuals directly into the ground a couple weeks before the last frost date in their region. If it's still cold in April where you live, wait until next month to direct-sow seeds. Hardy annuals that are easy and productive when sown directly include calendula, cornflower, larkspur, and poppies. Make sure that the ground is workable and not too wet. Here's a good test to determine when your ground is ready: Form some garden soil into a ball and drop it from waist-high distance. It should break apart easily when it hits the ground. If it does not crumble apart, the soil is still too wet to plant, and seeds are likely to rot if sown directly into the ground.

If you plant nothing else, sow sweet pea seeds as soon as the ground can be dug. They appreciate the early start — especially if they can bloom before hot weather.

Depending on your region, late April or May is the time to lay out beds and prepare the soil. Adjust the soil pH based on soil tests done in the fall. Amend the soil with a 2- or 3-inch layer of organic matter and a complete fertilizer. (See Chapters 8 and 12 for more details.)

May

Early May is usually the best time to plant hardy annuals (seeds or transplants) in most areas — 10 to 14 days before the last frost is usually safe. Check local garden centers for the following ready-to-plant cool-season annuals: calendula, cornflower, pansies, snapdragons, stock, and violas. Look for stocky, green plants when shopping at garden centers. Avoid plants with dead lower leaves and brown, overcrowded roots, as well as plants that are already flowering.

This month begins the main season for transplanting into the ground tender annuals, such as impatiens, lobelia, and petunias. Wait until frost danger has passed, the soil and air have warmed up, and the nights are no longer cold. Memorial Day is considered optimum timing for planting tender annuals in many places. Tender plants set out too early may not be damaged by frost, but they don't grow during cold weather.

In this region, favorite annuals for containers grown in the sun include creeping zinnia, Dahlberg daisy, geraniums, petunias, scaevola, and verbena. For containers in the shade, try the following: begonias, browallia, impatiens, and lobelia.

If you start seeds indoors, be sure to *harden off* (acclimate) transplants before planting them in the garden. Allow the plants to dry slightly and move them outdoors to a sheltered, shady location for a few days. Gradually move them into full sun and exposure to the elements. Transplant the toughened plants into a prepared bed.

Gardeners in warmer areas of the North can sow seeds of zinnias, morning glories, and cosmos directly in the ground as the weather heats up. In the coldest parts of the North, it makes sense to use transplants, except for sunflowers, which can be direct-seeded easily in most areas.

When seedlings sown directly in the ground reach 2 inches high, thin them according to the spacing recommended for each variety. (See Chapters 4 and 5.)

Beware of rogue frosts. Especially on clear, cold nights, be ready to cover young transplants with a *cloche* (a transparent plastic or glass cover) or lightweight row covers. Also watch for cutworm damage to direct-seeded crops and young transplants; cutworms wrap around the base of seedlings and chew through the stems. A damaged plant appears to be cut by a knife, with the top lying on the ground. Dig around the base of the plant to find the rolled-up grub and destroy it. If the problem is severe, fashion a 2-inch collar of tar paper or cardboard and wrap it around the stem of the plant so that the collar extends into the ground.

June

Continue planting tender annuals according to the guidelines that I describe for May. Old-timers in cold, mountainous areas (such as parts of Vermont) often wait until June 10 to plant the most tender plants, such as impatiens, because cold nights early in the month stress heat-lovers.

Newly planted seeds and transplants are vulnerable. Pay attention to their needs. Water if June is dry. Weeds compete for nutrients and water; hoe or pull the weeds while they are young and easy to remove. Watch for cutworms, slugs, and aphids that can stunt plants.

Mulch to conserve water and slow weed growth. Pull off fading blooms of cool-season annuals to extend their season of color. Pinch back impatiens, petunias, snapdragons, and zinnias to stimulate a branching, bushy habit.

July

July brings hot, dry weather, when plants require extra water and nutrients to keep them at their peak. Container-bound plants, particularly, suffer from heat stress and usually need daily watering if they're located in the sun. Container gardens quickly deplete soil nutrients; feed window boxes and pots with a liquid fertilizer every couple weeks.

Continue feeding annuals to promote steady growth for the remainder of the summer. Stake taller annuals, such as larkspur, cornflower, cosmos, and nicotiana. Deadhead flowers regularly. You can shear some annuals, such as alyssum and lobelia, to encourage them to bloom again in a few weeks.

Japanese beetles make an appearance toward the end of the month. Hand-pick bugs and drop them into a container of soapy water.

In hot climates, cool-season annuals probably have peaked, so pull them out.

August

In northern regions where the growing season is 90 to 110 days long, late July through early August is the garden's peak. It's called "high summer" because so many kinds of plants are blooming all at once. Enjoy the fruits of your work and remember to make notes for next year.

'Indian Spring' gloriosa daisy, Mexican sunflowers *(Tithonia),* sunflowers, and *Verbena bonariensis* add height and color to an August border. If your garden is currently missing any of these flowers, consider adding them next year.

Some late-summer tasks to keep you busy:

- ✔ Continue to deadhead, water, and weed. Containers, especially, still need to be fertilized.

- ✔ Tidy beds and containers by pulling out plants that have been crowded out or have passed their peak.

- ✔ Harvest flowers for drying and enjoy fresh-cut bouquets. You can't go wrong with fresh-cut bouquets of 'Rocket' snapdragons and 'Cut and Come Again' zinnias.

- ✔ Keep picking Japanese beetles. Drop them into a container of soapy water. (See Chapter 14 for more information on these and other garden pests.)

September

Listen to weather reports and be ready with row covers or blankets if an early frost is predicted and you still have tender plants in bloom. You can place bushel baskets over clumps of plants, or you can cover whole beds with sheets.

Use pots of asters, calendulas, and flowering kale to replace frosted or dying annuals.

Collect seed pods, dried flowers, and grasses to make arrangements.

You can pot some annuals — begonias, coleus, impatiens, and geraniums — and bring them indoors. If plants are lanky by summer's end, cut stems back by about a third. Place pots in a sunny window or under grow-lights. Water and fertilize less frequently than you did when the plants were in the ground. Plants seem to need a resting phase after a summer of blooming.

October

Pull out dead plants and add them to your compost pile. If your compost from the summer is almost decomposed, start a new compost pile of garden debris and leaves. Next spring, spread the decomposed pile on your beds and add new debris to the pile started in the fall.

Take soil samples in the fall to know how to amend soil next spring. Use the results of the soil tests to gauge any adjustments that you need to make in soil pH and fertility. Refer to Chapter 8 for more information about amending soil.

November through December

Sharpen, clean, and oil your tools. Keep a record of any extra seed you have. Store the extra seed in an airtight container in a cool location; add packets of silica gel to absorb any moisture in the container. Build your own window boxes or trellises for next year. Build a cold frame for growing and hardening off your transplants.

A *cold frame* is a low box open to the soil but with a "skylight" of glass or plastic on the top. Like a miniature greenhouse, cold frames provide just enough protection from wind and cold to get plants off to a faster start or to acclimate them to outdoors. Several of the companies listed in the appendix sell ready-made cold frames or can tell you how to make your own.

Sort through your notes from the summer and determine what flowers, planting schedules, and gardening practices were successful and decide what areas need improvement. Seek inspiration in books and magazines. Think about what appeals to you when you respond to a photograph of a beautiful garden: Is it the color, the fullness, the simplicity, or the variety?

Calendar for the South: Hot Summers, Mild Winters

The South, as defined in this calendar, ranges from the mountains of North Carolina to just above the tropical tip of south Florida, and from Dallas, Texas, to Savannah, Georgia. Weather may move in from the Midwest, but the region is more often affected by the adjacent oceans and the jet stream's prevailing winds. From north to south, the dates of first and last frosts in this region differ by a month to six weeks — these dates, of course, help you determine when to plant annuals.

This calendar's timing aims for the middle south in the middle of each month. For the lower south, the tasks will fall toward the beginning of the month. For the upper south, wait until month's end. Tropical Florida (Dade County south to the Keys) has its own rules for planting annuals, which are unlike the guidelines for any other gardening region in the continental United States. If you live in tropical Florida, check with local experts for recommended varieties and planting times.

January

Keep pansy blossoms plucked to get more buds and blooms. Remember that winter annuals grow while all else lies dormant, so fertilize garden beds and containers of annuals when you're watering this month.

The best seeds to start indoors now to plant outdoors in six to eight weeks are ageratum, coleus, cosmos, dusty miller, love-lies-bleeding, nicotiana, salvia, and wishbone flower.

Use this simple seed-starting system: Plant seeds in flats of sterile soil mix and put them on top of the refrigerator or clothes dryer next to a sunny window. The bottom heat hastens seed sprouting.

Make the most of a wet, warm day to get rid of winter weeds. Pulling even tiny oak trees is a no-sweat job in this type of weather.

Take advantage of breaking weather to work the soil for spring planting. Turn the soil over with shovel or tiller as described in Chapter 8, add organic matter and a complete fertilizer, and then let it mellow till March.

February

If seedlings recently sown indoors look skinny, they probably need more light. Add a fluorescent lamp or move flats closer to the light source.

Dig through your drawers and check behind the refrigerator for seed packets from last year. If the seeds are moldy, toss them. To check for viability, see if you can make a few seeds sprout in a wet paper towel.

As soon as possible, plant early spring annuals, including petunias and geraniums. If those don't grow over the winter in your area, look for Canterbury bells, delphinium, foxglove, larkspur, and snapdragons to transplant.

Start a garden journal to record what and when you plant, if it bloomed, what bugs bugged you, and which fungus invaded your garden. Knowledge is (flower) power.

Put up a trellis ahead of time to support vigorous vines for summer shade. Use wood, plastic, iron, or bent native wood; anchor legs in 4 inches of concrete.

March

Transplant ageratum, begonia, lobelia, love-lies-bleeding, and nicotiana to slightly shady spots. Plant cosmos, dusty miller, marigolds, and annual verbena in warm, sunny beds or pots. Water transplants well and feed them with fish emulsion or root-stimulator fertilizer, following the directions on the label.

Sow the seeds of the *Ipomoea* family (including cardinal climber, moonflower, and morning glory) and love-in-a-puff *(Cardiospermum haliacacabum)* directly where they'll grow. Plant big-seeded annuals such as globe amaranth, sunflowers, zinnias and in small pots.

If you've had trouble starting seeds in the garden, try this: Top your garden soil with an inch of potting soil or compost. Seeds planted in this way still may dry out before sprouting, however, so lay a board on top to hold in the moisture, just until they sprout.

Make sure that young poppies and larkspur don't dry out; as they put on flower buds, it's okay to water and mulch around the base of the plants. Gently pull the mulch away from pansies and other transplants tucked in last fall.

Make patio pots work overtime: Combine tomato and basil plants with calliopsis, coleus, and marigolds for food plus flowers for the table.

Slugs and snails destroy tender transplants. Limit their numbers by working *diatomaceous earth* (powdery, sharp-edged skeletal remains of tiny sea creatures called *diatoms*) into the top inch of the bed before transplanting.

April

The soil's warming up across the South, so add mulch around spring annuals and don't forget to apply fertilizer and thoroughly water the flowers you transplanted last month.

April is the time to deadhead spring flowers for a second round of flowers; if you allow the seeds to set, the plant's done for the year.

Impatiens are the top transplant this month. You can choose from traditional single flowers or hot, new double blossoms. If your shade is too dense for flowers, nestle pots of impatiens into ground covers.

Coleus is better than ever, with varieties adapted for full sun or part shade. For bushier plants, pinch the third set of leaves that emerges. Those pinched-off stems root easily in water or wet sand.

Now is also the time to plant some of the following up-and-coming annuals: *Angelonia, Bacopas, Evolvulus* 'Blue Daze', *Felicia, Linaria* 'Fantasy', petunia 'Purple Wave', and *Scaevola*.

May

Spider mites and aphids arrive to eat the most tender shoots, but they're slow buggers that dislike water. Water regularly with a sprinkler to discourage both insects.

Plant the following summer annuals from seed directly where you want them to grow: celosia, Mexican sunflower, spider flower, sunflowers, and zinnia.

When night temperatures climb, pansies and violas respond with smaller flowers and skinnier stems. May is the time to make compost of them.

Look for vinca rosea (sold as annual periwinkle in many Southern nurseries) in varieties bred for disease resistance. Even more important, don't plant them until this month at the earliest. Natives of Madagascar, vincas thrive where it's hot and dry.

For pure cottage-garden flair, combine cosmos with zinnias. Unfortunately, both flowers can suffer from leaf spot early and powdery mildew later. To keep leaves looking good, thin plants to stand 4 inches apart and do not mulch.

June

After your transplants are in the ground and your seedlings are up and growing, you need to be watching for signs of trouble. One common warning flag is yellow leaves on young plants. Here's an almost foolproof backyard diagnosis: Yellow lower leaves indicate a need for nitrogen, and yellow leaves at the growing point signal a root problem or that the flower was planted too deep.

New Guinea impatiens are great plants for many locations in your garden, and June is the time to plant them. They tolerate sun or shade, lots of fertilizer or just a little, and life in pots or in beds, but they do not tolerate drought and high temperatures. Water these plants in the containers before setting them out in the garden.

Transplant begonia, bluebell, and wishbone-flower seedlings to shady gardens. Their colors and textures bring welcome contrast to impatiens.

To fertilize beds in dry spells, water them first and then use a fertilizer mixed with more water. Make sure that the water soaks through thick mulches; rake back a bit of mulch if you must or, better yet, use soaker hoses.

July

Plant the second round of heat-loving summer annuals: balsam, celosia, cockscombs, marigolds, and zinnias. Include some of the following "bounce-back" flowers that recover quickly after thunderstorms: dwarf sunflowers, Mexican sunflower, portulaca, scaevola, and vinca rosea.

Off with their heads! Cut back impatiens and all sorts of hanging-basket plants that have become leggy with the heat. Rejuvenated, these plants will bloom again for months.

Choose a spot with late afternoon shade to grow flowers for cutting, to prevent the sun from bleaching out the colors. Include globe amaranth, the best of the South's flowers for drying.

For staying power in the heat, hanging baskets and large containers depend on a rich soil. Measure one part potting soil and an equal amount of bagged compost; then add one-fourth bag of sharp sand (available in most nurseries and hardware stores). Fill baskets and containers with this potting mix and top each pot with a slow-release fertilizer.

Watering practices can make or break the summer garden. Irrigate slowly to soak the bed deeply for best rooting, and finish watering in time for the leaves to dry before darkness falls.

August

Replenish mulch around annual plantings. Adding another inch of pine straw or ground bark now suppresses weeds and moderates the most stressful months of the growing season.

Water container-bound plants daily and soak beds weekly, even if it rains. Use a soaker hose in the garden to ensure that the water stays in the bed. If you aren't sure how much water is reaching your plants, use a rain gauge to measure it.

Plant small chrysanthemum plants during this month.

Whiteflies can be on their tenth generation of the year by now. Long-term control relies on annual garden cleanup and removal of host plants such as privet.

Save the seeds of celosia, cosmos, four o'clock, the morning glory family (including cardinal climber and moonflower), spider flower, and zinnias. Let plants mature as much as possible before gently crushing the flower heads to collect the seeds. Separate the seeds from other materials.

September

Use a complete fertilizer on fall-blooming zinnias, marigolds, balsam *(Impatiens balsama)*, celosia, and other flowers planted in July.

Get to know overwintering annuals, those flowers that perform best when planted in the fall for early spring blooms. Pansies and violas are the most familiar overwintering annuals, along with ornamental cabbage and kale, but depending on how far south you live, other possibilities include candytuft, foxglove, hollyhocks, Johnny-jump-up *(Viola tricolor)*, poppies, snapdragons, and stocks.

The top transplant for this month is the garden chrysanthemum, which you should plant right away. Plants that are already in bloom or covered with flower buds will not grow much larger. For a carpet of flowers, plant chrysanthemums close together. Keep mums moist so that flowers open as they're supposed to. Deadhead first blooms so that side buds can open.

Sow seeds of the following flowers in flats for transplanting next month: calendula, candytuft, pinks, sweet alyssum, and sweet William. Grow outdoors in late-day shade in a mix of half potting soil and half compost. Keep moist; add fertilizer at half-strength every other week.

October

After five consecutive nights with temperatures in the 60s (15 to 20°C), transplant pansies, ornamental cabbage, and flowering kale. After two weeks of those temperatures, transplant the other annuals you started last month after they develop three sets of true leaves.

Sow poppy and larkspur seed with sand for better spacing. Different poppies reseed across the South; single larkspur reseeds almost everywhere.

Take a look at the newer pansy varieties to find flowers with sturdier stems, neater clumps, and more cold-hardiness.

If you feel like taking a chance on a plant in October, try sweet peas. An unseasonably cold and wet winter can do in any of your favorite annuals, but sweet peas prove especially challenging — and they're worth it. Try a tall variety on a trellis under a deciduous tree to provide winter sun and spring shade. (Chapter 4 includes more tips for growing sweet peas.)

November

Don't mulch patches of fall-seeded annuals such as candytuft, larkspur, and poppies. Watch for seedlings and keep the beds weeded. Fertilize once before the end of the year.

Here's a take-a-chance plant idea for November: Fill basket containers with Johnny-jump-up (a member of the *Viola* family) for next month's gift-giving. Add small plants of chives and nasturtiums to fill out the basket. The Johnny-jump-up and nasturium flowers are edible, as well as the chive and the nasturium leaves. It's a feast for the eyes as well as the belly.

As you make out your holiday wish list, consider a bottom-heat mat for starting seeds. This waterproof mat contains a thermostat that plugs into an electrical outlet and heats seed trays to optimum germination temperature. Place these mats under seeded pots, and the warmth transfers to the potting soil and quickens germination and root growth of the young plants.

December

Freezing temperatures are not always the biggest problem annuals face in winter, but wild temperature swings can be deadly to dry plants. Prevent drought damage by watering before plants wilt. For warmer water that's gentler on the plants, set timers for midday, lay your hose out in the sun, or capture rainwater in dark-colored containers before using the water to irrigate.

Sunny days bring out the caterpillars on ornamental cabbage, kale, dill, and parsley. Hand pick the varmints. If you use *Bacillus thuringiensis* (Bt), they'll still be there, but they stop feeding in about 24 hours.

Pile the mulch on transplanted annuals; make excellent, free mulch from leaves chopped up into coin-sized pieces.

Clean up your act! Rake away fallen leaves, spent flowers, and frosted plants, including weeds. Compost this debris, adding kitchen waste and the first cutting of your overseeded rye lawn. Tidying up now can mean fewer weeds, pests, and diseases next season.

Calendars for the West: Dry Summers, Wet Winters

The West exhibits some of the most complex climates in the U.S. In the states west of the Mississippi, annual flowers encounter some of the shortest growing seasons (in the Rocky Mountain region) and the longest (in Southern California). The Pacific Northwest has a long but cool growing season. Arizona's garden-growing season is the opposite of most other climates: Fall, winter, and spring are the seasons to enjoy annuals, because summer is too hot for them.

In this chapter, I divide the West into four subregions for growing annuals: the bulk of California, the high-altitude regions, the low-altitude deserts, and the Pacific Northwest. Each subregion has different seasons, starting times, opportunities, and challenges.

Growing annuals in most of California

The seasonal advice in this section works for the majority of California, with two notable exceptions:

✔ The mountains, where the growing season is much shorter: Refer to "Growing annuals at high altitudes."

✔ The low-elevation desert, where the main growing season for annuals is fall through early spring: See the section "Growing annuals in lowland deserts."

January

Peruse mail-order catalogs or seed racks and select annual seeds for sowing soon (cool-season types) or in several months (warm-season annuals). Check this book's appendix for a list of catalogs to order.

Start seeds of cool-season annuals indoors to set out in four to six weeks; choices include calendulas, Iceland poppies, pansies, snapdragons, and sweet peas.

Brighten your garden with already blooming annuals sold in 4-inch pots and larger sizes at garden centers. Pansies and primroses offer maximum color now — especially if they're planted in containers. Limit your planting to large annuals that are already in bloom. Save smaller-sized plants for warmer weather next month.

February

As the weather starts to warm up, and if the soil is dry enough, set out seedlings of cool-season annuals. You also can fill in empty spots in beds planted last fall. Good choices include calendulas, cinerarias, Iceland poppies, pansies, pinks, primroses, snapdragons, stocks, and violas. These plants can stand up to some frost.

This month or next, start seeds indoors of warm-season annuals, such as cosmos and lobelia. (See the April calendar in this section for more warm-season annuals.) Seeds sown around the middle of the month should be ready for transplanting by late March or early April. Wait until next month to sow seeds if you live in a cooler climate.

Sow seeds of sweet peas directly in the ground. In warm climates, make sure that you choose a heat-resistant type that's able to cope with midspring hot weather that hits at bloom time.

Sow seeds of low-growing annuals to fill in between emerging daffodils, tulips, and other spring bulbs. Good bulb covers include sweet alyssum, baby blue eyes, and wallflowers. The annuals spread and bloom while the bulbs are blooming and then help camouflage the bulb foliage as it dries up.

Fertilize cool-season annuals growing in the ground and in containers. Try to feed regularly — either monthly or twice a month.

Watch for snails and slugs around young plantings, especially if the weather is on the wet and mild side — when the population explodes. Try to eliminate insect hideouts by cleaning up piles of leaves and other garden debris. Hoe or pull out weeds fostered by winter rains before they overtake planting beds.

March

Cool-season annuals (pansies and Iceland poppies, for example) should be at their peak bloom now. Maintain top performance by monthly feeding and pinching off dead blooms. Be especially vigilant in cutting off faded pansy flowers; your goal should be to let no little seedheads form.

Except in the hottest climates, you can still plant cool-season annuals. (See the list of flowers under February in this section.)

In warmer climates, such as southern California and inland valleys, this month begins the planting time for warm-season annuals — make sure that frost danger is past and weather is heating up. (See the April calendar in this section for some suggestions on warm-season annuals.)

Prepare flower beds for major spring planting this month or next month. Improve the soil by incorporating a 2- or 3-inch layer of organic matter and complete fertilizer. (See Chapters 8 and 12.)

Keep watching for snails and slugs. Squish the ones you see, and set out traps for the others. (See Chapter 14.)

April

This is the main planting month for warm-season annuals: Choose from cosmos, pinks, impatiens, lobelia, marigolds, petunias, zinnias, and many others. Wait a month to plant warm-season annuals in cooler coastal climates, where you can still set out most cool-season annuals.

Soon after planting, pinch back warm-season annuals to encourage bushy growth. Impatiens, petunias, and zinnias are among many flowers that respond well to pinching.

Begin a regular fertilizer program several weeks after planting warm-season annuals. Try to feed monthly at full strength or twice monthly at half-strength.

Mulch with a layer of organic matter around young annuals to conserve moisture and curtail weeds. Continue watching for slugs and snails.

May

Plant seedlings of heat-loving annuals, including phlox, portulaca, vinca rosea, and zinnias. You also can plant the warm-season annuals recommended for April. Cosmos, marigolds, and zinnias sprout quickly if sown directly in the ground now.

Sunflowers are easy to grow from seeds sown directly in the ground. If the weather has started to warm up, plant sunflower seeds this month.

If a hot spell strikes, protect newly planted annuals with temporary shading with shade cloth or floating row covers draped over the plants.

In cool coastal climates, you can still plant cool-season annuals (pansies and violas, especially), as well as many warm-season annuals.

Continue grooming and fertilizing. Earwigs emerge as a major threat to annuals. Earwigs love dark, wet places. To create an environment that's unappealing to these pests, don't mulch between plants, cultivate the soil regularly to keep it dry, and in severe cases, spray the plants with an insecticide such as pyrethrum.

June

You still have plenty of time for major planting of warm-season annuals. Choose from the flowers given for April and May in this section. For faster results, select 4-inch pot sizes. It's a fine time to plant shady spots; warm weather encourages rapid growth of bedding begonias, coleus, impatiens, and other shade-lovers.

In all but the mildest climates, cool-season annuals are probably over the hill. Pull them out, clean up planting beds, and refresh them with a layer of organic matter dug in to a depth of 10 or 12 inches. Try to put in replacement warm-season annuals as soon as possible.

Make sure that your watering system (hose, sprinklers, or watering cans) is prepared to carry your annuals through the summer — never let your annuals dry out.

Thin seedlings of annuals sown in the ground at the spacing recommended in Chapters 4 and 5. Pinch back seedlings to encourage bushy growth; zinnias respond with gusto (and lots of side branching) to frequent pinching.

As weather warms, watch for signs of budworm damage (hollowed out buds and tiny black droppings) on petunias and annual geraniums (*Pelargonium*). Control this pest as described in Chapter 14.

July

This can be a surprisingly productive planting month. For quick color, look for warm-season annuals (lobelia, marigolds, petunias, and many more) in 4-inch pots or larger sizes. Transplant these flowers into pots but make sure that you add enough soil mix to encourage continued root growth; pots should have a diameter at least 2 or 3 inches larger than the nursery container.

Or start with smaller seedlings and figure that they'll last well into early fall. Best bets, especially in hotter climates, are the true heat-lovers: celosia, portulaca, salvia, vinca rosea, and zinnias. Plant in the cool of evening and provide temporary shade on hot days.

Watering is the most important chore. If you don't have a sprinkler system for beds of annuals, consider running a soaker hose through your plantings. Mulch to conserve soil moisture.

Continue to watch for budworms, which destroy blooms on geraniums and petunias. Whitish spots on petunia leaves indicate an entirely different problem: smog damage, which you can do nothing about (except, perhaps, write your congressperson).

Keep annuals going at top speed by feeding them regularly, as explained in Chapter 12.

August

Start seeds of cool-season annuals in flats or pots to set out in late summer or early fall. The long list of possibilities includes calendulas, Iceland poppies, and pansies.

Watch for the late-summer destroyers: spider mites and whiteflies. (See Chapter 14 for ways to control these pests.)

Continue to feed and pinch. If lobelia and impatiens look too lanky, cut them back by as much as a third; they'll respond with a burst of late-summer growth.

Figure out a system to water container plants, especially if you go on vacation. Container plants suffer if soil dries out and pulls away from the sides of the pots, allowing water to slip down the sides instead of soaking in. Try a small drip system attached to a faucet; you can easily add a timer.

September

The year's most productive planting season — one of the privileges of gardening in a mild climate — begins in many California gardens this month. Exact timing depends on where you live. In hot areas and much of southern California, wait until late in the month. Near the coast and in most of northern California, aim for midmonth.

Plant cool-season annuals now, and they will bloom by December holidays and continue blooming through spring. Favorite cool-season choices include calendulas, Iceland poppies, pansies, primroses, snapdragons, stocks, and violas. Near the coast, you can plant some flashy annual seedlings such as cineraria, nemesia, and schizanthus, but these flowers will freeze in the parts of California that receive frost.

During hot weather, plant in the evening and provide temporary shade with shade cloth or floating row covers draped over the plants.

Extend plantings of warm-season annuals as long as you can by continuing to water thoroughly, feed, and remove faded flowers. You may want to be ruthless now: Leave summer flowers in too long, and they delay your fall planting. Pull them out when their beauty fades.

Mildew on cosmos and other summer flowers is a sign their season is over. Don't fight it. Pull out the plants.

Start seeds of cool-season annuals in flats or pots for transplanting next month. Calendulas, forget-me-nots, and Iceland poppies are the easiest to grow.

October

Sow wildflowers seeds, such as California poppy and clarkia, as well as seeds of annuals that perform like wildflowers, such as African daisy (*Dimorphotheca*). Plant these seeds before the wet season, and let winter rains take over your watering chores.

If you plant spring-flowering bulbs, follow up with annuals on top. Pansies and violas are classic bulb covers for tulips and daffodils. Or sow seeds such as baby blue eyes, forget-me-nots, sweet alyssum, and wallflowers. Spectacular Shirley poppies can tower over wildflower-type plantings; they're easy to grow from seeds in sunny spots.

This is still a great time to plant all cool-season annuals: See the varieties listed in September in this section.

For wonderfully fragrant sweet peas as early as March, sow seeds between the middle and end of the month. Choose heat-resistant varieties if your area heats up quickly in the spring (inland southern California, for example). Before planting, soak seeds in water overnight or at least for a few hours.

Watch for snails and slugs given new life by cooling weather. If they make an appearance, deal with them as described in Chapter 14.

Start to regularly fertilize fall annuals two or three weeks after planting.

November

Early November is the last chance for planting cool-season annuals with expectation of midwinter flowers. You also can still plant wildflowers and bulb covers as described in October.

Snails and slugs are almost inevitable around newly planted annuals. If you don't believe it, check with a flashlight at night.

Continue regular watering until winter rains keep the soil constantly moist. Check for moisture by digging several inches into the soil.

Watch for a new crop of winter weeds brought up by watering or rainfall. Hoe or pull them while the soil is wet and soft.

December

Make sure that you keep watering if winter rains arrive late.

Plant cool-season annuals if you haven't already. You missed the warm fall weather that pushes annuals into midwinter bloom, but you still can expect a strong spring show from annuals planted now. If rains soak the soil, let it dry out a bit before planting.

Growing annuals at high altitudes

The high-altitude western United States — from California to Colorado, north to Montana, south to mountainous Arizona and New Mexico — offers terrific, albeit abbreviated, growing conditions for annuals. Frosts can hit late in the spring and strike early in the fall, but the cool nights and bright, dry summer weather bring out the best in many annuals. Somehow, they just look brighter in this part of the country.

If you live in a temperate, high-altitude climate (such as the mountains of the western United States and comparable climates around the world, including Switzerland, Chile, Argentina, Korea, or northern China), follow the calendar for the North, earlier in this chapter. Start seeds indoors and set out seedlings as recommended for colder sections in the northern part of the United States. Consult your local extension service, the Department of Agriculture, or the nursery for specific recommendations.

Growing annuals in lowland deserts

The Southwest deserts encompass mild-winter climates of the low-elevation deserts of Arizona and California. (The mountains of Arizona and New Mexico, as well as west Texas, have a more typical cold-winter, summer-only season for growing annuals.) There's nothing else quite like the growing season of low-desert Arizona, primarily around Phoenix and Tucson, and California's Coachella Valley. Summers are hot, to say the least, and winters are sunny and warm in the day but cool at night. Glory time for annuals is late winter and early spring. This calendar starts in September to reflect the true beginning of the planting season — the low desert's "spring."

September

Get planting beds ready for the year's most rewarding planting season in the low-desert Southwest. Lay down 2 or 3 inches of organic matter, such as ground bark. Scatter complete fertilizer according to label directions and work everything into a depth of 10 or 12 inches.

Wait until midmonth or later and set out nursery transplants for winter and spring bloom — maybe even by Christmas. Try these old reliables: calendulas, Iceland poppies, pansies, petunias, snapdragons, stocks, and violas. Provide temporary shade during the hottest weather.

Early in the month, you still have time to start annual flower seeds in flats or pots to transplant into the ground later in the fall. Calendulas and Iceland poppies are easy to start from seed.

Sow African daisy *(Dimorphotheca)* seeds directly in the ground, as you would a wildflower.

If summer annuals are still going strong, keep them watered thoroughly and fertilize monthly or every two weeks.

October

Continue to set out annuals for blooms before the end of the year. (See the list for September in this section.) Water thoroughly after planting and provide temporary shade during extra-hot spells.

Sow seeds of low-spreading annuals to cover bare spots in bulb beds. If your timing is good, everything will bloom all at once. Terrific bulb covers include baby blue eyes, forget-me-nots, and white sweet alyssum. You can also sow wildflower seeds directly in the ground for a big spring show; try California poppy and African daisy.

Start regular feeding a few weeks after planting annuals.

November

There's still time to plant for winter and spring bloom. Top choices for sunny spots are ageratum, calendula, candytuft, clarkia, larkspur, lobelia, petunia, snapdragon, stock, and sweet pea. For shady spots, plant pinks, pansies, primroses, and violas.

This month is the best time of year to sow wildflower seeds, including California poppies and many others. Make sure that the planting area receives full sun all winter.

Cooler weather encourages a new crop of aphids, plus slugs and snails. For information on controlling these insects, see Chapter 14.

December

Where else can you set out annuals over the holidays? You still have time to plant seedlings of calendulas, Iceland poppies, and all the rest.

Watch your soil for signs of dryness, and water as needed.

January

After the holidays, nurseries stock up with blooming annuals in small pots. Shop for color that you can use right away in pots or in gaps in planting beds.

Watch for aphids and take steps to control them.

Winter rains and cool temperatures bring up seasonal weeds, which you can pull or hoe. Or mulch beds with a layer of organic matter to smother weeds and weed seeds.

February

Cool-season annuals — pansies, snapdragons, stocks, and the rest — are peaking this month in the low desert. Maintain top performance by removing dead flowers, watering thoroughly, and feeding regularly.

Indoors, you can start seeds of warm-season annuals (marigold, salvia, and many more) to transplant into the garden in four to six weeks.

Prepare beds for spring planting — as long as plants growing in them have finished their season.

March

In the low desert, transplant warm-season annuals, such as celosia, marigolds, portulaca, and salvia. Pinch back at planting time and snip off flowers to encourage bushier growth.

A few weeks after planting, fertilize young annuals and begin a regular schedule of fertilizing (monthly or twice monthly).

April

Plant heat-loving annuals, such as cosmos, marigolds, and zinnias.

Adjust the frequency of sprinkler systems as the weather heats up. If your annuals aren't on a sprinkler system, consider a soaker hose. (Put it on a timer, if you want.)

May

Spring flowers are winding down. Pull them out and replace them with heat-lovers.

Pinch tips of young annuals for bushier growth, especially marigolds and zinnias.

June

This is your last chance to plant for summer blooms. Make sure that you choose from among the true heat-lovers: globe amaranth, salvia, and the most reliable of all, vinca rosea.

July and August

Water and mulch. Water and mulch. You don't do any planting at this time of year.

Feed summer annuals regularly. Remove faded flowers.

Growing annuals in the Pacific Northwest

Compared with California, the Pacific Northwest, including the milder parts of British Columbia, has a much more straightforward pattern for growing annuals — a long season from spring through fall. West of the Cascade Range, the lingering cool spring tends to favor cool-season annuals, and the relatively cool summers encourage spectacular displays of annuals, such as the legendary Butchart Gardens in Victoria, British Columbia, and magnificent public gardens in Seattle, Washington, and Portland, Oregon. East of the Cascades, where winters are longer and much colder, the annual season is shorter, but the heat and the dry climate are terrific for sun-loving annuals.

January

Study catalogs and order seeds for starting indoors in a few weeks or outdoors in a few months. (The appendix lists a number of catalog sources to feed your mind.)

Prepare an indoor area for starting seeds, as described in Chapter 9.

February

Start seeds of annuals indoors for transplanting in spring. Best bets include ageratum, calendulas, California poppies, cosmos, gloriosa daisies, nicotiana, pansies, Shirley poppies, and snapdragons.

If the ground isn't too wet, you can start seeding the following hardy annuals directly in the ground late this month: calendula, clarkia, cornflower, dwarf pink, English daisy *(Bellis perennis)*, pansy, stock, and sweet alyssum. Optimistic gardeners traditionally sow sweet peas on Washington's Birthday.

Try transplanting hardy annuals, such as pansies and primroses, if nurseries offer them and the soil is dry enough to be dug. Or plant them in containers.

March

Prepare beds for major spring planting as long as the soil isn't too wet. Dig 10 to 12 inches deep and add 2 or 3 inches of organic matter. Blend in thoroughly, along with complete fertilizer.

Sow sweet peas seeds before midmonth; to improve sprouting success, soak seeds in water overnight or at least for a few hours. Also sow seeds of other hardy annuals listed in February in this section.

Continue indoor seeding of annuals listed in February. Begin sowing warm-season annuals, such as marigolds and zinnias, for transplanting when the weather warms up in May.

April

Set out transplants of cool-season annuals, such as calendulas, pansies, and snapdragons.

Begin transplanting warm-season annuals if the weather and soil have warmed up.

Watch for snails and slugs to begin their most damaging season around young annuals.

May

This is the Northwest's prime time for planting annuals. Almost anything will grow if planted now, including transplants of bedding begonias, celosia, cosmos, geraniums *(Pelargonium)*, impatiens, lobelia, marigolds, nicotiana, love-in-a-mist, petunias, salvia, snapdragons, sunflowers, sweet alyssum, and verbena.

Start feeding annuals two or three weeks after planting. (Chapter 12 explains the types and uses of fertilizer.)

Protect young annuals from snails and slugs.

Sow asters, cosmos, marigolds, and zinnias from seed directly in the ground.

June

Planting season continues, but try to finish soon to get the longest season. See the list of choices for May.

Continue to sow seeds of heat-loving annuals, such as marigolds and zinnias.

Soon after planting annuals, pinch them back to encourage bushy growth: Impatiens, petunias, snapdragons, and zinnias are among many flowers that respond well to pinching.

Continue regular feeding and grooming.

Make sure that you're prepared to water annuals through the summer — never let them dry out.

July

Keep annuals going strong by feeding them regularly.

If planting beds need extra watering, run a soaker hose between the plants.

You can still plant annual seeds for later summer bloom. Cosmos is an excellent, reliable late-bloomer.

August

Watch for late-summer invaders, such as spider mites. Treat them according to the instructions in Chapter 14.

If impatiens and lobelia get a bit straggly, cut them back by about a third to encourage a late-summer burst of growth.

September

Extend the summer bloom season by removing dead flowers and watering as needed.

For color until frost strikes, set out dwarf pinks, Johnny-jump-ups, pansies, stocks, and kale.

October

Remove over-the-hill summer annuals. Clean up beds and turn over the soil for fall or spring planting.

Keep hardy annuals, such as pansies, going for another few weeks by continuing to feed, water, and groom them.

Sow wildflowers and other annuals that get off to an early start in spring, including calendula, California poppy, candytuft, larkspur, and linaria. Before planting, clear the area of weeds and rake lightly. Scatter the seeds, cover them with a thin layer of organic matter, and then water thoroughly.

November

You still have time to sow seeds of hardy annuals and wildflowers for blooms next spring: See the list in October in this section.

Clean up all annual planting beds.

Part II
Every Annual under the Sun . . . and the Shade, Too

The 5th Wave   By Rich Tennant

"Well, no, they aren't pretty. But look on the bright side—with your luck growing flowers, they won't live long."

In this part . . .

Petunias, marigolds, geraniums, and impatiens may be vying for first place in the Most Popular Annual competition, but you might decide to cast your vote for a less common annual after reading this part. Chapter 4 contains detailed information about ten of the most popular annuals, including varieties of each of the flowers and when and how to plant them. But if you're looking for out-of-the-ordinary candidates for your garden, peruse Chapter 5. The flower names alone — bells of Ireland, Chinese lantern, love-lies-bleeding, and monkey flower — may arouse your curiosity.

Chapter 4

The Big Ten: Popular, Reliable Annuals

● ●

In This Chapter

▶ Introducing ten darlings of the annuals world

▶ Choosing fail-proof annuals for your garden

▶ Understanding when and how to plant each annual

● ●

*H*ow many different annuals are there? Add up all the basic kinds sold as nursery seedlings, all the new improved varieties and strains, all the rarities marketed by countless seed catalogs, and the total is . . . well, a lot. I may not be able to tell you exactly how many annuals there are altogether, but I can tell you that, in this and the next chapter, you can read about hundreds of kinds (taking into account the many varieties and strains).

This chapter gets you started with what I consider to be the Top Ten, a somewhat arbitrary grouping that, nonetheless, represents some of the most popular and reliable annuals currently available. These plants are where the most plant breeding action has occurred, where you find the most new varieties, and where you encounter the most bewildering array of selections at the nursery or in the seed catalogs.

To be included here, an annual has to do at least a couple of things:

✔ It has to be worth growing without a whole lot of trouble. Remember, though, that it may not perform equally well in all climates and garden situations.

✔ It has to be available through normal channels, either as seedlings at major nurseries and garden centers or as seeds sold by big-time mail-order catalogs or on nursery seed racks.

In the recommendations that follow, plants are listed alphabetically by the most widely used common name. I also include the botanical name for each plant to avoid possible confusion. (Some plants have many common names, and some common names are used to refer to different plants.) Sometimes, you see only one name. Don't feel sorry for the plant and think that it has, sadly, never been given a botanical name. What's happening in these cases is that the common name and botanical name are the same, such as petunia (*Petunia*).

The sections in this chapter don't tell you everything there is to know about each plant, just the important stuff that you need to consider to choose your annuals and grow them successfully. I mention flower size and typical colors, blooming season, size of plants, and how to use the plants in your garden.

You also find advice on when to plant, the best exposure (sun or shade), and the best or most typical way to plant — from nursery transplants or seeds sown directly in the ground. More advanced gardeners take note: You can also start seeds indoors, as described in Chapter 9, and set out your own transplants.

And you find tips on special care needed as well as pests or diseases that are out of the ordinary; refer to Chapter 14 to find out what to do about problems. Remember that you may be able to get additional advice and information specific to your area and conditions from a local nursery or extension service.

Dahlias

Like some people you may know, the loud-colored, dinner-plate-size dahlias insist on being noticed. These big show-offs aren't even true annuals; rather, they are tender perennials grown from tubers. But they have a group of quieter, smaller relatives, reliable and colorful, that are sold as annuals — the dwarf or bedding dahlias. These plants grow about 12 to 15 inches tall, with flowers 2 or 3 inches across. Colors include orange, pink, purple, red, white, and yellow. Virtues of dwarf dahlias are their long bloom season (usually from early summer until frost), an abundance of bloom, and handsome, dark green foliage. And they're easy to grow. Use them in borders, mass plantings, or in containers.

'Figaro' stays less than 12 inches tall; mostly double flowers bloom early in the season. 'Redskin', 12 to 15 inches tall, is an All-America winner with maroon-tinted foliage; mixed-color flowers bloom early.

Dwarf dahlias are sold as nursery transplants. Set them out in full sun or part shade in the spring after frost danger; space plants 12 inches apart. For vigorous growth, dwarf dahlias need lots of water and fertilizer. To encourage bushy growth, pinch stem tips of young plants.

Watch for snails, earwigs, Japanese beetles, and spider mites. Turn to Chapter 14 for advice on dealing with these pests.

Geraniums (Pelargonium)

Some of my most vivid, endearing impressions of annuals involve geraniums: a window box full of bright red geraniums lighting up the stony visage of the only bank in a Swiss village; ground-cover geraniums crawling in and out of the purple bougainvillea on a Laguna Beach hillside as lush and tangled as a Cambodian jungle; the clay pots, unwatered for weeks, outside my dry cleaner's front door, leaves coated with wayward cat hair but bravely hoisting two or three orange flowers.

The annual flower that most people call a geranium is, botanically speaking, a *Pelargonium*. This information is important to know because a very different plant uses *Geranium* as its botanical name. Look for the word *Pelargonium* to be sure that the plant you're buying is the annual described here, and chalk the whole mess up to another case where botanical names create more confusion than they clear up.

Geraniums flourish worldwide and are universal favorites because they're easy to grow and always seem to muster up a bright, crisp look. They're great for beginners — or just about anyone. Geraniums actually have increased in popularity now that so many new varieties are grown from seeds. (Formerly, most geraniums were propagated from cuttings.)

Geraniums are actually perennials and can survive for years in mild climates. In southern California, some people refer to them as "rats of the garden" for their persistence. In cold climates, you can move plants indoors to a sunny spot and keep them through the winter.

Geraniums are usually sold as annuals in pots of various sizes, from 3 inches on up, often in bloom already. Here are the three main types you can find:

- ✔ **Zonal geraniums (*Pelargonium hortorum*):** These are the most familiar, with flower clusters standing tall above deep green, velvety-soft leaves. Colors include white, orange, red, pink, rose, and violet. Some have fancy leaves that are splashed, spotted, and bordered with darker colors. Plants can grow up to 3 feet tall, but usually reach 12 to 18 inches in one season. For a mass planting, space plants 12 inches apart. These are classics for containers of all sizes.

Dozens of varieties are available. Among the strains to check out are Multibloom and Orbit. The Multibloom Strain comes in eight colors, has numerous bloom stems, flowers early, and grows 10 to 12 inches tall. The Orbit Strain grows about the same size, has compact plants, and produces flowers in a dozen and a half colors. You can grow some varieties of this plant from seeds sown indoors in winter, as I discuss in Chapter 9.

✔ **Ivy geraniums (*Pelargonium peltatum*):** These plants seem made for hanging baskets or to cover ground. Branches stretch out like ivy, up to 2 or 3 feet. Foliage is glossy and smooth; flower colors include lavender, pink, red, and white. Look for varieties developed specifically for hanging baskets: Summer Showers, a winner of the European Fleuroselect award, is very pendulous and comes in five colors. Breakaway Hybrid, in red or salmon, has 5- or 6-inch flower heads and bushy spreading growth.

✔ **Scented geraniums (*Pelargonium*):** Crush the foliage to get a sniff of apples, mint, roses, lime, and many other scents that are gentle on the nose. The foliage carries the fragrance. Flowers are small — not the reason you choose to grow scented geraniums. Plants grow 12 to 36 inches tall. Use them in borders, pots, hanging baskets, or in an herb garden. Be sure to grow them where you can appreciate their fragrance at close range. There are countless types — it's fun to choose the ones that smell best to you.

Set out geraniums in the spring. Provide full sun or part shade in hot climates. Try to plant in soil with fast drainage. Geraniums are very responsive to pinching. For bushy growth, pinch out tips of young growth to force side branching. Remove dead flowers.

What are some of the problems that plague geraniums? Budworm is most notorious. It hollows out flowers and can wipe out the bloom season. Look for telltale tiny black droppings in the vicinity of the flowers. Control as described in Chapter 14. Also watch for aphids, spider mites, and whiteflies.

Impatiens

Don't worry if garden snobs look down their noses at impatiens. Every year, I try a few new things by the back fence, but nothing has ever come close to competing with impatiens. Not only do they survive the denizens of the deep shade (snails and who knows what other mysterious creatures lurk there), but they also bloom heavily from early summer to Thanksgiving without a ray of direct sunlight.

Impatiens are easy to grow, bloom better than just about anything else in shady conditions, hardly ever run into problems, stay compact, and have attractive foliage. No wonder they're best-selling annuals in all regions. You can use impatiens for mass plantings under trees, for edging shady borders, or mixed in with ferns or other shade-lovers. They're also great in baskets or containers — try to choose varieties with pendulous stems developed for this purpose.

You can grow impatiens from seeds or cuttings, but nursery transplants are the easiest. Here are the main types:

- The standard impatiens *(Impatiens walleriana)*, sometimes called busy lizzie because of the way that the seed pods pop open, comes in many strains and varieties. The flowers are usually about 1 to 2 inches wide and come in colors including deep classic reds and clean whites, as well as neon shades of lilac and pink — just about every shade except blue and yellow. The plants range from 8 to 24 or 30 inches, depending on the variety.

  The Accent Strain blooms early, with 2-inch flowers in more than a dozen colors plus half a dozen bicolors, and its plants grow 10 inches or so tall. Super Elfin is another popular compact strain with large flowers. Ideal for hanging baskets, the Tempo Series has pendulous stems and early blooms.

  The biggest improvements of recent years have been the double-flowered varieties of impatiens, such as Fiesta and Fancifrills. The blossoms of these plants, shown in Figure 4-1, resemble miniature roses or camellias. 'Victorian Rose' is a 1998 All-America winner, with semi-double dark rose-violet flowers. Try to grow the doubles in containers or in the garden where you can view them up close. What's next for impatiens? The plant breeders are now talking about yellow and blue varieties.

- New Guinea hybrids have larger, less abundant flowers, and some offer additional color with their multicolored leaves. New Guinea impatiens are sturdier and taller than the standard type, and they usually need more sun to bloom well.

- Balsam is another species *(Impatiens balsama)*, with mostly double flowers that are less showy because they tend to become obscured by foliage. Balsam plants grow 24 to 30 inches tall.

Figure 4-1:
One of the most widely planted annuals, shade-loving impatiens come in various flower types, including a roselike double bloom and the larger flowers of the New Guinea hybrids.

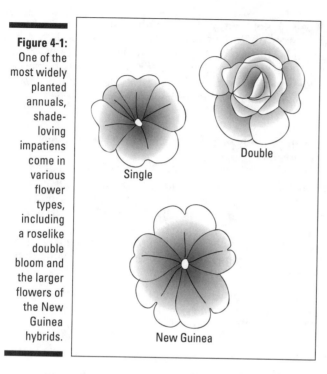

Single

Double

New Guinea

Planting time for impatiens is spring, after frost danger, when the weather has begun to warm up. Plants just sit there if the air and soil are cool. Plant in part shade, or even full shade if that's all you have. In cool coastal climates, impatiens can take a lot of sun, even full sun; they bloom better with more sunlight. (Experiment to see how much sun or shade you can give them and how much they will bloom under different conditions.) Space plants 9 to 12 inches apart, except for dwarf types, which you can plant 6 inches apart. Improve the soil by adding plenty of organic matter and plan to keep it well watered for the whole growing season.

TIP

Don't always count on it, but impatiens have a remarkable ability to bounce back from drying out. Plants that look so withered you'd think they were dead for sure can often bounce back if you provide them with a good soaking.

Don't worry about removing faded flowers. (Where do they go? Another impatiens miracle!) But if plants get leggy late in the season, cut stems back halfway to force new growth. In mild climates, impatiens can grow through the winter and continue blooming, although at a reduced rate. It's up to you whether you want to pull them out as blooms diminish or see what they do the second year.

Marigolds (Tagetes)

Think of marigolds the way football announcers describe offensive line-men — blue-collar, lunch-bucket workers in the garden. They're dependable flower producers over a long season, summer through frost. The flowers can be button-size or whoppers (see Figure 4-2), and they last a long time when cut. Marigolds are fast and easy to grow — so famously unfussy that seed catalogs even advise planting in "ordinary" soil.

So what's the downside? Marigolds have a scent that may be a little too pungent (it's rumored to repel insects). And the colors may be too basic for some people; if a flower can be condemned for being too orange, marigolds deserve at least a 15-yard penalty.

The marigold, like the petunia, has been the subject of decades of plant breeding. As a result, we are blessed with some great plants but a bewildering number of choices. It pays to become a bit familiar with flower forms and plant growth habits.

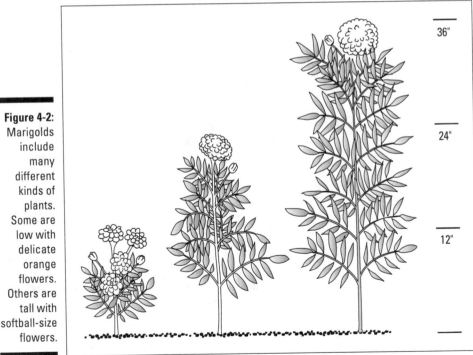

Figure 4-2:
Marigolds include many different kinds of plants. Some are low with delicate orange flowers. Others are tall with softball-size flowers.

✔ **African marigolds** *(Tagetes erecta):* These plants, also called American marigolds, are the towering types — up to 36 inches tall, with huge flowers up to 5 inches across and so thickly double-petaled that they look like round balls. Use them in the background or at the back of borders. Lady Hybrid comes in deep orange, creamy yellow, gold, and other shades. The classic, clear yellow 'First Lady' is an All-America winner, with sturdy plants reaching 20 inches tall. Climax is even taller, up to 36 inches, and has bigger flowers in a range of colors. White marigolds, unknown until recent decades, are now available in several varieties such as 'French Vanilla'. Another white marigold, 'Snowdrift', grows 2 feet tall and is valued for its ability to tolerate afternoon shade.

✔ **French marigolds** *(Tagetes patula):* These plants are much more compact (6 to 12 inches tall) and have single or double, smaller flowers (1 to 2 inches) in great abundance — some varieties have red shades. Also look for striking bicolors, combining yellow and maroon, for instance. Use these for edging borders, mass plantings, and in containers. There are dozens and dozens of kinds: The Aurora Series blooms early, with $2^{1}/_{2}$-inch double flowers on rounded 12-inch plants. 'Naughty Marietta', 10 inches tall, has single flowers that boldly combine golden yellow and maroon.

✔ **Triploid hybrids:** These hybrids are the result of crossing African and French marigolds. They boast numerous 3-inch flowers on compact plants up to a foot tall. One neat thing about these hybrids is that they don't produce seeds, which means that you don't have to bother cutting off dead flowers to sustain the bloom. Look for the outstanding Nugget Supreme Series.

✔ **Signet marigolds** *(Tagetes tenuifolia):* Here is where the word "dainty" enters the marigold lexicon — these dwarf plants are bushy with colorful masses of little flowers only an inch across. Use signets as a border edging or in containers. 'Gem', about 12 inches tall, includes gold, lemon, and orange flowers.

Plant marigolds in the spring after frost danger, when the weather warms up. Nurseries offer dozens of varieties as transplants. Marigolds are as easy as any plant to sow directly in the ground — a perfect opportunity for first-time gardeners in areas with long growing seasons. Choose a sunny spot. Prepare the soil as described in Chapter 8. Broadcast seeds and cover with about $^{1}/_{4}$ inch of soil and keep moist. Seeds usually sprout in a few days if the soil is warm, and plants begin flowering in about 6 to 8 weeks. Thin seedlings so that they stand from 6 inches apart (dwarfs) up to 24 inches apart (biggest, tallest types).

Removing dead flowers greatly prolongs the bloom season and improves the appearance of the plant — it's easier to do, of course, with the big-flowered type than with the prolific bloomers. Marigolds attract no special pests, but watch for slugs and snails when plants are young.

Pansies and Violas (Viola wittrockiana)

The familiar faces of pansies and violas come out to greet us like old friends early each spring. Tolerant of cold, they can stand a light snow cover and are among the first annuals to bloom. In mild climates, they can flower through winter. For generations, pansies and violas have brightened the California racetracks when it's too cold for thoroughbreds and annuals anywhere else.

Technically, pansies are just big violas, having 2- to 4-inch flowers that come in a range of bright colors: blue, purple, rose, yellow, and white, often striped or dramatically blotched. Majestic Giant Strain has 4-inch flowers with big blotches. 'Maxim Marina', an All-America winner, combines light and dark blue and is resistant to heat and cold. Plants grow up to 8 inches tall. Use them in mass plantings, in borders, mixed in with bulbs, in containers, and as an edging.

Violas stay less than 6 or 8 inches tall. Colors are mostly solid, including blue, apricot, red, purple, white, red, and yellow. Johnny-jump-up *(viola tricolor)* looks like a miniature pansy with purple and yellow flowers. It stays low and fits right in nestled among spring bulbs, such as daffodils.

In cold-winter climates, plant pansies and violas in early spring, several weeks before the last frost. In mild-winter climates, plant in the fall or late winter. Check locally to see when to plant pansies in your area. More and more cold-climate gardeners are planting pansies in the fall for a bit of fall color; they are proving to survive through the winter under a light snow and start off strong in the spring.

Set out transplants in full sun or part shade. (Full sun is vital for winter bloom.) Improve the soil by adding plenty of organic matter. Space plants 6 inches apart. Feel free to cut flowers for indoor use — the plants appreciate the effort. Remove all dead flowers. Hot weather tends to end things for pansies and violas; when growth looks shabby, pull them out.

Petunias

What's simpler than a petunia — easily recognizable and pretty easy to grow? Not to make a big deal out of nothing, but what *isn't* so simple is figuring out which kinds of petunia to plant. Allow me to guide you down the baffling rows of the nursery or through the pages of the seed catalog.

The petunia breeding industry spans more than a hundred years. The state-of-the-art petunias you see today are the result of hybridization; they're specially bred for increased vigor and predictability. Modern petunia colors include yellow as well as deep purple, in addition to the traditional pink, red, white, light blue, and bicolors. The blooms can be imaginatively ruffled and frilled, but the typical funnel-shaped, single flower is still the most popular type.

Today's petunias retain one important old-fashioned virtue: a long bloom season, from summer until frost. In the hottest climates of the Southwest and Southeast, summer is too hot; but in some of those climates with mild winters, such as Arizona, petunias can be planted in fall for winter and spring bloom.

Petunias come in single and double blooms and a variety of classes, as shown in Figure 4-3. Pay attention to the two main petunia classes:

- **Grandifloras:** These boast the biggest flowers, usually up to $4^1/_2$ inches wide, in single or ruffled forms. Plants grow up to 24 inches tall and 24 to 36 inches wide — sometimes on the rangy side. Cascade and Supercascade Strains are well-deserved favorites for hanging baskets and containers, where they can spill over the sides. 'Fluffy Ruffles' has frilly, double flowers up to 6 inches wide; plants grow to 18 inches. Look for the 1998 All-America Selection winner, 'Prism Sunshine', with a lovely, large 3-inch-wide bloom.

- **Multifloras:** Compared to grandifloras, the plants are more compact and the flowers are smaller (about 2 inches wide) but more abundant, either single or double. This is the type of petunia you see used by the acre in public gardens — very colorful and very reliable. Look for Ultra Series, 12-inch compact plants, with large, single flowers in more than a dozen colors. Double Delight Series has full double flowers. 'Summer Sun', the original yellow petunia, is still a striking winner.

You may also encounter millifloras, a newer type, with small flowers (about $1^1/_2$ inches wide) and a dwarf habit of growth that's ideal for pots, baskets, and border edging. Fantasy, a 10-inch dwarf in mixed colors, is outstanding.

'Purple Wave', an All-America winner, can rightfully be called a ground-cover petunia, spreading up to 4 feet while growing no more than 6 inches tall. A pink variety is also available. Also look for outstanding new trailing strains, excellent in hanging baskets or as ground covers: Supertunia Strain is fast growing and available in eight colors; Surfinia Strain comes in shades of blue, purple, and pink, as well as white.

Figure 4-3:
With single and double blooms; multiflora, grandiflora, and milliflora classes; and more, petunias are a diverse bunch.

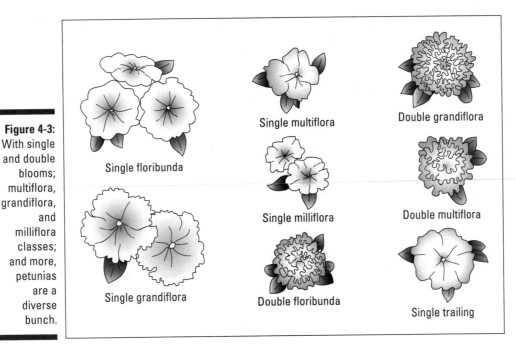

Single floribunda

Single multiflora

Double grandiflora

Single grandiflora

Single milliflora

Double multiflora

Double floribunda

Single trailing

Growing petunias from the tiny seeds is very tricky. It's simplest to start with nursery transplants. Set them out in full sun in spring after frost danger. Space plants 8 to 12 inches apart, depending on variety — new ground-cover types can be spaced farther apart. Soon after planting, begin pinching back tips to encourage bushier growth. Be sure to remove dead flowers. Late in the season, when growth becomes leggy, cut back plants by as much as a half to force a new spurt of growth.

Petunia problems are rare, but watch for tobacco budworms, which devour flowers and leaves. Smog has been a 50-year nemesis to petunias; petunia leaves become splotched during bad-air episodes. You can't do much about smog, but you can be aware of the conditions in your area and choose varieties listed as smog-resistant if pollution is a problem where you live. Also watch for the usual offenders, including aphids, snails, and slugs.

Snapdragons (Antirrhinium majus)

Children find these hinged, dragon-mouth flowers irresistible. Sorry to say, grown-ups usually consider snapdragons difficult to grow. Keys to success: Choose varieties carefully, watch the calendar, and be on guard for rust (a disease discussed in Chapter 14). Rewards are fragrant, striking spikes of blooms in rich colors — purple, red, lavender, and bronze. Snapdragons make great cut flowers and can stand a light frost and still look great.

Snapdragons come in three main height ranges, shown in Figure 4-4. Check the expected mature height of seedlings you buy so you're sure to get the appropriate plant for your garden design.

- **Tall:** Snapdragons in this category grow up to 3 feet tall. Use these flowers for accents in beds and borders, or for cutting. Madam Butterfly Hybrid is 24 to 30 inches tall and has impressive flower spikes in mixed colors. 'Rocket', a few inches taller, is also outstanding.

- **Intermediate:** Height ranges up to 18 inches. These are a good choice for most gardens because they provide spikes plenty long enough for cutting and the plants are compact enough to fit into most borders. Sonnet is a hybrid mix that has many spikes and is more heat-tolerant than most other snapdragons.

- **Dwarfs:** Most stay below 12 inches and are useful for edgings or in containers. The colors are nice, but the stems are too short for cutting. 'Little Darling', an All-America winner, blooms early and is resistant to rust. Royal Carpet is a hybrid mix, also rust-resistant, that grows just 8 to 10 inches tall.

Figure 4-4:
Like marigolds, snapdragons come in a range of heights, from the 6-inch 'Pixie' to the 18-inch 'Liberty Bell' to 3-footers like 'Panorama' and 'Rocket'.

Snapdragons bloom best in cool weather. That means spring to early summer in most places, winter to late spring in mild-winter/hot-summer climates such as the Southwest and part of California. In mild climates, plant in the fall or late winter; plant in early spring elsewhere. Start with nursery transplants; growing snapdragons from seeds takes too long. Plant in full sun, spacing taller types 15 inches apart and dwarfs 9 inches apart.

Never let snapdragons dry out, but don't water them from overhead because doing so can spread *rust* — orangish brown pustules on leaf undersides. (Find out how to avoid or minimize rust damage in Chapter 14.) Pinch the tips of this plant frequently to force bushy growth, and stake taller varieties. Remove faded flowers or cut flowers freely for indoor use; cut flowers when half the buds are open.

Sunflowers (Helianthus annuus)

I leave it to the social historians to determine exactly when and why sunflowers moved from Midwestern roadsides to the pages of fancy New York home magazines. One guess is that it happened in the mid-1980s, after the plant breeders came up with long-stemmed, long-lasting sunflowers small enough to fit through the front door and available at a moment's notice from the florist down the street.

Sunflowers have survived the era nicely — better, say, than *Bonfire of the Vanities,* a detailed and depressing chronicle of 1980s style. Spectacular new varieties seem to come out every year. Old and new, sunflowers are striking, easy to grow, and fun — handsome in the garden as well as begging to be cut and brought indoors.

Sunflowers bloom in a variety of shapes, such as those shown in Figure 4-5. Take a look at the main types of sunflowers:

- ✔ **Giants, monsters, and conversation pieces:** You know the type, fast growing (a foot a week), gangly, clumsy plants that tend to tip over if not staked. Grow them for children to admire, or for seeds for you or the birds. Plants can grow 10 feet tall or more. Flower heads can span 12 inches or more. For the biggest sunflower on your block, choose obviously named varieties such as 'Giganteus' and 'Russian Giant'.

- ✔ **Garden varieties:** These are more compact, less coarse looking, with smaller flowers. Use them at the back of borders or to form a temporary hedge or massed in beds. You can even grow smaller types in containers. 'Teddy Bear' is a 2-footer with 6-inch blooms of densely packed petals with no big dark centers. 'Sunspot' is amazing — what other plant claims a flower (10 inches across) that's half as big as the plant (20 inches tall)?

✔ **Varieties for cutting:** If you want to grow sunflowers to cut and bring indoors, you can try the ones like the commercial growers use: new hybrids with long, single stems that produce several big flowers per plant. You need a lot of space for these; for a long bloom season, stagger plantings every two weeks. Varieties include 'Sunrich Orange' and 'Sunrich Yellow'.

'Teddy Bear'

'Sunrich Orange'

'Prado'

'Sun and Moon Sunbeam'

Figure 4-5:
Choose a short sunflower with a bushy bloom or a tall one with a big, sparsely petaled bloom.

Another group of sunflowers, those with multiple flower stems, also makes excellent cut flowers and looks better in the garden because of a longer bloom season and greater number of blooms. Varieties of this type include: 'Valentine', 5 feet tall, yellow with black centers, 6-inch flowers; 'Velvet Queen', 5 feet tall, reddish, 4- to 8-inch flowers; 'Inca Jewels', up to 8 feet tall, gold, orange, and burgundy shades, 4- to 5-inch flowers.

Sunflowers are easy to grow. Plant in the spring after frost danger and into the summer as long as there's enough growing season ahead. Choose a spot in full sun. The taller types, in particular, produce better in soil that's enriched with organic matter. Nursery transplants are available, but sunflowers are easy to grow from seeds, which take about a week and a half to sprout. Plant seeds an inch deep. Space giants 18 to 24 inches apart and compact types about 12 inches apart.

For cut flowers, pick bouquets when the flowers are just beginning to open. If you want to save the seeds of big flowers, cut off flower heads after the seeds mature (that is, are fully formed and starting to dry) and hang them in a dry, shady place. Just be sure to get to them before the birds do, or your sunflowers will become bird seed.

Sweet Peas *(Lathyrus odoratus)*

They seem to bloom for just minutes, they're picky about the weather, they practically demand that you dig a planting trench deep enough to bury an automobile — so why bother even trying to grow sweet peas? I don't want to dismiss the question by suggesting that it's like asking why go fly-fishing when you can buy trout for a fraction of the cost? So allow me to count the reasons why you should grow sweet peas: (1) Unforgettable fragrance that can fill a room, a garden, or a car; (2) A beautiful range of soft, pastel colors; (3) Sheer old-fashioned charm.

Sweet peas are grouped into two main types:

✓ **Tall climbers:** These familiar sweet peas climb to 5 feet or so and are best for cut flowers. Providing a support for this giant to climb on is a must. Climbing sweet peas bloom in blue, orange, pink, purple, red, and white. 'Royal', whose 12-inch stems sport abundant 1¹/₂-inch flowers in mixed colors, is a long-time favorite and still ranks high among the many varieties sold.

✓ **Bush types:** These sweet peas clamber and sprawl to a height of only 30 inches or so. The stems may be short, but they can still provide cut flowers. They're also great for growing in pots. (Use a big pot, at least 14 inches deep.) The Bijou Strain, which comes in mixed colors, grows just a foot tall and has large flowers.

Sweet peas can't stand heat and do best in cool climates; that's why they're so much at home in British gardens. Before attempting to grow sweet peas, consider whether your environment can support their special needs:

✓ If you live in a typical cold-winter/hot-summer climate, you need to plant early in the spring, as soon as the soil can be dug, so that the plant will bloom while the weather is still cool.

✓ In mild-winter climates, such as California, plant sweet peas in the fall for blooms in winter and early spring. Choose varieties labeled *early-flowering* or *spring-flowering*.

✓ In hot climates, be sure to choose varieties labeled as *heat-resistant*. But be aware that, in the hottest climates, even these varieties don't work.

Sweet peas perform best if you plant the seeds directly where you intend for the plant to grow. Nurseries do sell transplants, and you can start seeds indoors, but seedlings require careful handling and don't save you that much time. Choose a spot in full sun with a climbing surface — a trellis, net, wire fence, or other kind of support. To hasten seed germination, soak the seeds in warm water for at least a few hours up to 24 hours before planting.

Prepare the soil thoroughly. Trenching, shown in Figure 4-6, is the traditional approach. It's a bit extreme, but always worth a try. The idea is to dig a planting trench 12 inches wide and 1 to 2 feet deep. Mix in one part organic matter to two parts soil that you've removed from the trench. While mixing thoroughly, work in dry fertilizer according to label directions. Refill trench with mix and level. Plant seeds 1 inch deep, 6 inches apart (closer, if you later thin to that distance). The seeds take two or three weeks to sprout. When seedlings are 4 to 6 inches tall, pinch the tips carefully to force branching. Never let the soil dry out, and fertilize the plants regularly, as described in Chapter 12.

When flowers start blooming, cut them daily or every other day to prolong the bloom season. Cut the flowers as soon as the buds break open, and remove all seed pods that form.

Figure 4-6:
Give sweet peas the advantage of a full trench of amended soil, and they reward you in spades.

Zinnias (Zinnia elegans)

Easy to grow, sun-loving, and long-blooming, zinnias always rank near the top among summer annuals. The colors seem right for the season — red, yellow, orange, purple, white, salmon, pink, and rose. There's even a green variety called 'Envy'.

Zinnias come in several flower forms, two of which you owe it to yourself to consider:

- *Cactus* refers to large, double blooms with quilled, pointed petals.
- *Dahlia-flowered* types are similar but have flat, rounded petals.

Dwarf types, from 6 to 12 inches, work well as border edgings, in containers, or massed in low plantings. The Peter Pan series grows about a foot tall and has 3-inch flowers in cream, plum, scarlet, white, gold, orange, and pink. 'Small World Cherry' is an All-America winner, with dark red blooms on 14-inch plants — great for beds and cutting.

Taller types do well at the back of a border or massed in beds. 'Ruffles', about 30 inches tall, with 3 to $3\frac{1}{2}$-inch flowers, is excellent for cutting. For a striking midsummer bouquet, try 'Ruffles Cherry'. Also look for bicolor types in candy-cane colors; 'Peppermint Stick' grows about 24 inches tall.

For humid climates or wherever mildew is a problem, your best bet is 'Pinwheel', a compact and bushy zinnia that grows to 12 inches tall and has $3\frac{1}{2}$-inch daisylike flowers. Another zinnia known for its resistance to powdery mildew is Oklahoma Mix, a new mix that grows 2 feet tall and has $1\frac{1}{2}$ inch flowers. (Read more about powdery mildew in Chapter 14.)

A relative of *Zinnia elegans*, *Zinnia angustifolia* is a perennial in mild climates that acts more or less as a 15- or 18-inch ground cover with bright 1-inch flowers. The Star Series is outstanding, with dainty, star-shaped flowers in gold, orange, or white — a great choice for containers or mass plantings.

Plant zinnias in your sunniest spot, preferably in well-drained soil. Wait to plant until late spring, well after frost danger, when the soil and air are definitely warm. Nursery transplants are widely sold but are on the touchy side; be careful not to disturb roots and don't buy overgrown seedlings. Zinnias are so easy to grow from seeds that sowing directly in the ground usually works best. Thin dwarf plants to stand 6 inches apart; thin taller varieties to 12 inches apart.

Pinching the tips of young plants encourages them to develop bushiness; zinnias are highly responsive to pinching. Cut off faded flowers to encourage a long season of blooms.

Zinnias are mildew prone, especially in foggy or humid climates. Reduce the likelihood of mildew by watering them with a ground-level irrigation system rather than overhead sprinklers. Also be on the lookout for snails and slugs. If you spot any, run straight to Chapter 14 for help.

Chapter 5

Annuals from A to Z

· ·

In This Chapter

▶ Old favorites and winning newcomers

▶ When and how to plant each one

▶ Secrets to successful annual gardens

· ·

Maybe the Top Ten is too middle-of-the road for you. If you think about this chapter musically, you can expect to find the gardening equivalent of alternative music (cockscomb, perhaps?), rhythm and blues (dusty miller, you heard him on the South Side), or country (black-eyed Susan). There must be some classical types, but that gets me out of my element.

The annuals listed in this chapter aren't rare or difficult plants. They're grown a bit less often than mainstay annuals such as zinnias and petunias, but they're all very rewarding.

African Daisy to Aster

A is for annuals. Topping the group (alphabetically, at least) are two different plants called African daisy, as well as ageratum and aster.

African daisy (Arctotis)

Plant African daisy seeds randomly, as you would wildflower seeds, for a multicolored spring or summer carpet of cheerful 3-inch-wide daisies in bright orange, red, and yellow, as well as white, pink, and bicolors. *Arctotis* hybrids, the most available types of this plant, grow up to 18 inches tall and produce flowers that make beautiful additions to bouquets, although they last only a few days after cutting.

Sow seeds directly in the ground in full sun. In cold-winter climates, plant in the spring, after the danger of frost has passed; in mild-winter climates, plant in the fall. Thin seedlings so that they stand 10 to 12 inches apart.

African daisies don't withstand high heat and humidity. They bloom best in areas with cool nights, particularly in coastal climates. Remove faded flowers to prolong the bloom season.

African daisy (Dimorphotheca sinuata)

There you have it — an example of the confusion that can be caused by common names! The *Dimorphotheca sinuata* African daisy, compared with the *Arctotis* African daisy, has smaller flowers and lower, more spreading plants — 12 inches tall and 18 inches wide. Bright, dark-centered flowers in shades of orange, pink, red, and white make a cheerful show in late winter in mild climates, and in summer elsewhere. Use the plants for a carpetlike effect, as a border, or to fill in between ground covers.

Sow these seeds directly in the ground in full sun. Plant in early spring in cold-winter climates, or in fall in mild-winter climates. Thin the seedlings to stand 18 inches apart.

African daisies come back from year to year if conditions suit them. For example, in Arizona, they grow like wildflowers among the cacti.

Ageratum, or floss flower (Ageratum houstonianum)

The appeal of ageratum is no secret — it's the blueness. The plants are well-mannered and unprepossessing, mostly 6 to 12 inches tall. In summer, the puffy flowers come in some of the garden's truest shades of blue. (Varieties are available in white and pink, but what's the point?) Dwarf varieties 'Blue Danube' and 'Blue Mink' are reliable favorites. Use ageratum in containers or as an edging for borders.

Set out transplants in spring, when temperatures begin to warm up and the danger of frost has passed. Rich, moist soil is preferred but not essential. Provide full sun unless you live in a hot-summer climate, where part shade is best. Space dwarf varieties 6 inches apart and taller varieties 8 to 10 inches apart.

Nursery plants are often sold in bloom. After you plant them, pinch back the flowers to encourage bushy growth. Make a special effort to cut off faded flowers, especially the white ones, which turn an unsightly brown.

Aster, or China aster (Callistephus chinensis)

Although they're not easy to grow, asters may tempt you to try your luck at raising your own crop of beautiful, richly colored late-summer flowers. In shades of purple, rose, and pink, the flowers are long-stemmed and long-lasting — excellent for cutting. Many varieties are available, offering differ-ent flower forms (including quilled and curved petals) and plants that range from 6- to 12-inch dwarfs to 18- to 30-inch-tall types.

Plant asters in full sun in the spring, after the danger of frost has passed. Nursery transplants are widely sold but not easy to grow; space dwarfs 6 inches apart, tall varieties 12 inches apart. You may do just as well sowing seeds directly in the ground and then thinning seedlings to 6 to 12 inches.

You'll have better luck with asters if you improve the soil with plenty of additional organic matter. (See Chapter 8.) Stake tall varieties to keep flowers from flopping over. Asters are disease-prone; pull out stunted, wilted, or yellowed plants. To keep diseases from spreading, don't plant asters in the same spot two years in a row.

Baby Blue Eyes to Browallia

Annuals can be big, beautiful, bright, and sometimes breathtaking. The plants in this section bloom in shades of blue (baby blue eyes, blue lace flower, and browallia), white (baby's breath), pink (bedding begonia), blazing combinations of red and yellow (blanket flower), and even green (bells of Ireland).

Looking for bachelor's button? It's listed by its other common name, cornflower. Likewise, you can find blue marguerite under F for felicia, black-eyed Susan under G for gloriosa daisy, burning bush under K for kochia, butterfly flower under S for schizanthus, and black-eyed Susan vine under T for thunbergia.

Baby blue eyes (Nemophila menziesii)

Expect this petite California wildflower to brighten a spring garden — especially when it's mixed in with blooming daffodils and other bulbs. Its sky blue flowers with pale centers look like little bells, about 1 inch across. These delicate plants trail low to the ground.

Sow seeds directly in the ground in full sun or part shade. Plant in early spring in cold-winter climates, or in fall in its native state and other mild-winter areas. Thin seedlings to stand 6 inches apart.

Baby blue eyes prefer a soil that's constantly moist. Under favorable conditions, the plants reseed themselves and come back year after year.

Baby's breath (Gypsophila elegans)

Grow baby's breath for graceful, airy bouquets, fresh or dried. It's the annual version of the popular perennial baby's breath that you see at weddings. Tiny flowers in midsummer seem to form white, pink, or red clouds on upright plants up to 18 inches tall. The best-known variety is 'Covent Garden', which has larger white flowers and is widely used for cutting.

Sow seeds directly in the ground in a sunny spot. Plant in spring, after the danger of frost has passed. Thin seedlings to stand 8 to 10 inches apart.

Keep the soil on the dry side. These plants live only six weeks or so; for a longer bloom season, stagger seed sowings over several months. To dry cut flowers, hang them upside down in a cool, dry place. (See Chapter 18 for details.)

Bedding begonia, or wax begonia (Begonia semperflorens)

Crisp, glossy, and succulent, bedding begonias look good enough to eat. Its flowers, which last from late spring through summer, are small but profuse, in shades of pink, red, and white. Begonia leaves can be colorful, too, with dark bronzy tones and bright greens. The plants grow 6 to 12 inches tall. Use them to edge borders, as mass plantings in beds, or in containers.

Set out transplants in full sun in mild-summer climates, or in part shade in hot-summer climates. Plant in spring, after the danger of frost has passed. Space dwarf plants 8 inches apart and taller varieties 12 inches apart.

Bedding begonias are easy to grow and very dependable. You can help them along by improving the soil with plenty of organic matter and keeping the soil moist. In hot climates, bedding begonias need shade from hottest sun.

Bells of Ireland (Moluccella laevis)

The name gives away the surprise of this plant. Spikes of pale green, bell-like blooms make the plant a standout in borders or bouquets. These Irish beauties grow 18 to 36 inches tall, and their cut flowers work well fresh or dried. (To dry cut flowers, hang them upside down in a cool, dry place. Dried flowers turn a tan color.)

Sow seeds directly in the ground in full sun or light shade. Plant in early spring in cold-winter climates, or in fall in mild-winter areas. Thin seedlings to stand 12 inches apart.

Your chances for successful sprouting improve if you chill these seeds in the refrigerator for a week or two before sowing them.

Blanket flower (Gaillardia pulchella)

Blanket flower is another sun-loving, warm-hued daisy that's easy to grow. Its summer flowers of orange, red, yellow, and bicolors are excellent for cutting. Growing up to 24 inches tall, these plants are at home in containers, borders, or mixed wildflower plantings. 'Red Plume' is an All-America Selection with brick red, double-petaled blooms of up to 2 inches across, covering compact 12-inch plants.

Sow seeds directly in the ground in full sun. Plant them in the spring after the danger of frost has passed. Thin seedlings to stand 12 inches apart.

Keep the soil on the dry side after germination and encourage a long bloom season by removing faded flowers.

Blue lace flower (Trachymene coerulea)

Not impressive in the garden, blue lace flower is terrific for cutting. In early summer, its long stems hold distinctive, lacy, 3-inch clusters of lavender blue flowers. Plants grow 24 inches tall.

Sow seeds directly in the ground in full sun. Plant in spring in cold-winter climates, or in fall in mild-winter areas. Thin seedlings to stand 9 to 12 inches apart.

Blue lace flowers are as delicate as their name suggests. They do best in areas with cool summers, the sensitive seedlings don't tolerate transplanting, and the young plants require stakes or other support.

Browallia (Browallia americana)

A hanging basket is the perfect showcase for browallia. The plants sprawl a bit and are covered with intense blue or white flowers in summer. Several species and varieties are available. Compact 'Blue Troll', just 10 inches tall, is well-suited to small pots. 'Blue Bells Improved' is also compact, and thick with lavender blue flowers.

Browallia seedlings can be hard to find at nurseries, so you may want to start seeds yourself. Plant seeds indoors two to three months before the last frost and set out transplants in part shade in the spring, after the danger of frost passes. Containers are your best bets for these plants.

Browallia plants have jungle origins and need warm, moist, shady spots. Provide rich soil well fortified with organic matter. Pinch tip growth frequently and remove faded flowers to prolong the bloom season.

Calendula to Cosmos

This collection of carefree, colorful creations includes calendula, California poppy, calliopsis, canary creeper, candytuft, canterbury bells, carnations, celosia, Chinese forget-me-nots, Chinese lantern, chrysanthemums, cigar plant, cineraria, clarkia, coleus, cornflower, cosmos, and creeping zinnia.

Looking for China aster? Look under A for aster. Find cupflower listed under its other common name, nierembergia.

Calendula, or pot marigold (Calendula officinalis)

The sturdy, robust look of the calendula is your first indication of how reliable and easy to grow this plant is. The big daisylike flowers, 2 to 4 inches across, are typically orange or yellow but are also available in cream and white shades. Use these plants, which grow 12 to 30 inches tall, in containers, in borders, or massed in beds. Pacific Beauty, the best-known taller strain, has double flowers. Bon Bon is a dwarf, 12 to 15 inches tall.

Calendulas are among the stalwarts of winter-spring gardens in mild climates (California and Arizona, for example), where flowers often appear before the New Year and continue blooming through late spring. In cold-winter climates, calendulas bloom best in the spring and early summer.

Plant transplants in full sun, spaced about 12 inches apart. In cold-winter climates, plant in early spring; in mild-winter climates, plant in the fall.

Calendulas thrive in cool weather. Watch for mildew under less than favorable conditions, and bait for snails and slugs. (See Chapter 14.) Remove flowers as soon as they start to fade.

California poppy (Eschscholzia californica)

As a native son, I find the state flower of California to be an appropriate symbol for the Golden State — easygoing, a bit gaudy, sometimes unpredictable, and fun to grow. Pioneer visitors were greeted by bright orange-gold, glossy flowers in vast springtime waves. California poppies still thrive in the foothills and desert plains — and in home gardens all over the world. Grow them in a natural-style border or as fill-in among ground covers; the plants grow 8 to 24 inches tall. Seed companies offer varieties and strains in many colors besides basic orange: yellow, white, pink, and mixes.

Sow seeds directly in the ground in full sun. In cold-winter climates, plant in early spring, as soon as the ground is soft enough for digging. In California and other mild-winter climates, plant in fall. Thin seedlings to stand 6 inches apart. California poppies prefer soil that drains very well and may be on the dry side. Don't try transplanting seedlings; their deep, brittle taproots won't appreciate it.

After they finish blooming, poppies are not a pretty sight; they form dry mounds like hay stacks. Be prepared to get rid of them. In mild climates, plants can reseed themselves and come back year after year. In colder regions, cut off the seedhead, as shown in Figure 5-1, and save the seeds in a cool, dry place until next year.

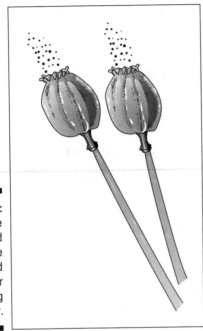

Figure 5-1:
Cut off the
seedhead
of the
poppy and
save it for
planting
next year.

Calliopsis, or annual coreopsis (Coreopsis tinctoria)

The summery appearance of calliopsis is just what you'd expect from this scaled-down member of the sunflower family. Yellow, orange, and red flowers, 2 to 3 inches in diameter, bloom freely through the summer atop plants up to 24 inches tall. Plant calliopsis in masses in beds and borders, or combine them with wildflowers in naturalized settings. The flowers are also great for cutting. Check seed catalogs for dwarf and double-flowered varieties, as well.

Sow seeds directly in the ground in full sun. Plant in early spring, as soon as you can dig the ground. Thin seedlings to stand 6 inches apart and keep the soil on the dry side after seedlings are up. Stake taller varieties.

Canary creeper (Tropaeolum peregrinum)

Canary creeper is a climber — a fast-growing vine that can reach 15 feet in one season. The name comes from the 1-inch, bright yellow flowers that look as though they have wings. Plant this annual near a fence or trellis, or provide stakes for support.

Sow seeds directly in the ground in full sun or part shade after the danger of frost has passed. Thin seedlings to stand 12 inches apart.

Canary creeper does best in cool summer climates. Keep roots cool with an insulating mulch of organic matter.

Candytuft (Iberis umbellata)

Edging borders is candytuft's specialty. Its plants are compact and low to the ground, less than 12 inches tall. In summer, its white flowers resemble familiar sweet alyssum and perennial candytuft *(Iberis sempervirens)*. Look for varieties of annual candytuft in pink and other pastel shades, as well.

Sow the seeds of this plant directly in the ground in full sun or, where summers are hot, part shade. Plant in early spring in cold-winter climates, or in fall or early spring in mild-winter areas. Thin seedlings to stand no more than 6 inches apart.

If your candytuft plants become rangy, shear the top growth like a hedge and wait for new flowers.

Canterbury bells (Campanula medium)

Impressive enough to hold their own at the back of a border, these medium-sized plants (up to 30 inches tall) bear abundant bell-shaped flowers up to 2 inches long. The prized color for these flowers is deep blue, but you can also find mixes in pink, lavender, and white. The flowers are handsome when cut and brought indoors.

Technically, Canterbury bells are biennials. But you can get blooms within a year by setting out nursery transplants in early spring if you live in a cold-winter climate, or in fall if your winters are mild. Plant seedlings in part shade in hot-summer areas, or in full sun where it's cool. Space plants 12 inches apart in soil that you've enriched with plenty of organic matter.

Be sure to stake these tall plants before they begin to flop over.

Carnation (Dianthus)

Unless you have a greenhouse and exceptional dedication, don't expect to grow the carnations you see as long-stemmed cut flowers or as boutonnieres. But border carnations, bushier and compact, are easy to grow and have some of the same fine features as their more exotic cousins — including the spicy, clovelike fragrance. The flowers of border carnations are typically about 2 inches wide and come mainly in red, pink, and white. Look for 'Giant Chabaud' (tall plants, up to 24 inches) and 'Lilliput' (short plants, less than a foot tall). 'Scarlet Luminette' is an All-America Selection winner. Use border carnations to edge a border or in containers; trailing varieties are nice in hanging baskets and window boxes.

Set out transplants in full sun in springtime, after the danger of frost has passed. Space plants 8 to 12 inches apart.

You may need to stake taller varieties of this plant. Remove faded flowers to prolong blooming. Most carnations do better in cooler climates, although some varieties are developed for heat resistance.

Celosia, or cockscomb (Celosia cristata and plumosa)

No one calls celosia charming — unusual, yes; bizarre, yes — but not charming. This plant makes up for its lack of elegance in its intensity of color and ability to thrive in hot weather. As shown in Figure 5-2, celosia (also called cockscomb) comes in two main types: Plumed celosia has feathery flower clusters, and crested celosia has contorted flower heads resembling a rooster's comb. The intensely vivid colors of these blooms include orange, pink, red, and yellow.

Celosia plants grow 12 to 36 inches tall, depending on the variety. Use celosia for masses of bright color in sunny beds; dwarf varieties work well in containers. To dry cut flowers, hang them in a dry, shady spot, as described in Chapter 18.

Set out transplants in full sun in spring, when warm weather has arrived and the danger of frost has passed. Space plants 8 to 12 inches apart. Be sure to keep the soil moist for these plants.

Figure 5-2:
Both feathery plumed celosia *(left)* and gnarled crested celosia *(right)* make unusual and vivid additions to any garden.

Chinese forget-me-not *(Cynoglossum amabile)*

Think of the Chinese forget-me-not as an almost-wildflower. It's easy to grow from seed, spreads and sprawls like a weed, and reseeds to return the next year if conditions suit it. The tiny but abundant skyblue or deep blue flowers are striking in spring borders with bulbs. Plants grow up to 18 inches tall.

In early spring (or fall, in mild-winter climates), sow this plant's seeds directly in the ground. When seedlings appear, thin them so that they stand 9 inches apart. Or you can set out transplants in spring, spacing them at 9 inches. Chinese forget-me-nots prefer to be in full sun.

Chinese forget-me-not resembles the familiar forget-me-not, but its flowers are a bit larger. The seeds of this plant are sticky and can attach themselves to clothing and pets.

Chinese lantern *(Physalis alkekengi)*

The reason to grow this plant is to witness the bright orange, papery 2-inch "lanterns" (actually fruits) that appear in late summer. Use these Chinese lanterns to make striking arrangements all winter. Plants grow up to 2 feet tall.

In spring, after the danger of frost passes, sow these seeds directly in the ground in full sun. When seedlings appear, thin them to stand 18 to 24 inches apart.

To use this plant for dried arrangements, wait until the lanterns turn color and the plants start to dry up. Pull up the entire plant by its roots and hang it upside-down in a cool, dry spot.

Chrysanthemums, annual *(Chrysanthemum)*

The chrysanthemums of football season are actually perennials, but are often bought as annuals in bloom and then discarded after their season. You can also find many attractive chrysanthemums that are true annuals and bloom earlier in the year. The following are all easygoing summer daisies, mostly white and yellow:

- Feverfew *(Chrysanthemum parthenium)* grows compactly from 1 to 3 feet tall.

- Painted daisy or tricolor daisy *(Chrysanthemum carinatum)* grows up to 3 feet tall and spreads about 2 feet.

- Miniature Marguerite *(Chrysanthemum paludosum)* is the most compact, usually less than 12 inches tall. This species is especially suited to container growing.

Sow chrysanthemum seeds directly in the ground in full sun as soon as the ground can be worked. Thin seedlings to stand 12 inches apart. You also can set out transplants in spring, or in fall, if available, in mild-winter climates. These daisies do best in cooler climates. With luck, these plants may reseed themselves and come back year after year.

Cut chrysanthemum flowers are great for bouquets. Flip to Chapter 18 for details.

Cigar plant, or firecracker plant *(Cuphea ignea)*

What came first, this plant's name or the latest cigar-smoking fad? Actually, the plant has gone by many names over the years. The flowers, shown in Figure 5-3, invite descriptive comparisons — they're tubular, about $3/4$ inch long, and bright red with a black ring (the cigar's ashes, I suppose) at one end. The plants themselves grow about a foot tall.

Set out transplants in full sun or part shade in the spring, when the weather and soil have warmed and the danger of frost has passed. Space seedlings 9 inches apart.

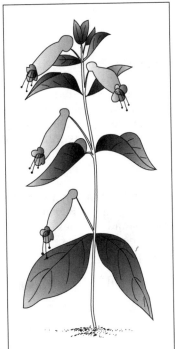

Figure 5-3: Sometimes a cigar isn't just a cigar, as you can see in the oddly shaped flowers of this aptly named plant.

Grow this plant as a curiosity or conversation piece, in a pot or hanging basket, or at the front of a border.

Cineraria (Senecio hybridus)

So beautiful, so temperamental — know anyone like that? Cineraria's daisylike flowers of rich purple, blue, red, and white bloom in clusters that look like bouquets from the florist's shop. But cineraria performs well only in cool-summer climates. It needs rich soil, careful feeding and watering, vigilant pest protection, and every other kind of pampering you can think of. The plants grow about 15 inches tall; dwarf strains grow up to 10 inches tall. Cineraria blooms in spring and early summer — earlier, in mild climates.

In cold-winter climates, set transplants out in spring after the danger of frost passes; in mild-winter climates, set them out in fall or early spring. Plant seedlings 12 inches apart in a shady spot. Enrich the soil by adding plenty of organic matter, as described in Chapter 8.

Cineraria plants are magnets for slugs and snails; set out bait for these pests at the same time you plant. (See Chapter 14 for details.) Also watch for leaf miners and spider mites. This plant is very sensitive to drought, so make sure that the soil never dries out. If you treat cinerarias just right, they reward you by coming back like weeds every year.

Clarkia, or godetia (Clarkia)

Why are these California wildflowers more treasured in Great Britain than in their native state? (Don't think that this is one of those questions with no good answer, like "Why is Jerry Lewis more appreciated in France than in his homeland?") The answer has to do with clarkia's ability to produce cheerful abundant flowers in cool climates early in the season, when they are most welcome. Farewell-to-spring *(Clarkia amoena)* is a favorite type that comes in low- or tall-growing forms and has satiny, 2-inch blooms of mostly red, pink, and white.

Sow clarkia seeds directly in the ground in full sun. Plant in early spring if you live in a cold-winter climate, or in fall if you live in a mild climate such as its native California. Thin seedlings to stand 9 inches apart. Clarkia blooms in spring and early summer and doesn't tolerate hot weather. Plant it in a sunny mixed border or wildflower garden.

Flowers are good for cutting; cut stems when the top bud opens, and the lower ones will follow.

Coleus

Do you think plant breeders may be getting a bit carried away when they name varieties of this foliage plant? 'Molten Lava', 'Dragon Sunset', and 'Volcano' are a just a few variety names inspired by this plant's colorful leaves. (Its flowers are incidental at best.) Grow coleus for a tropical effect in pots and borders — indoors, too. These plants grow quickly, up to 24 inches. 'Scarlet Poncho', with deep scarlet and chartreuse leaves, is a sprawling type bred for hanging baskets.

Set out transplants in spring, after the danger of frost has passed. Plant in light shade. Space 12 to 15 inches apart.

To encourage bushy growth, pinch back tips. Also pinch off flowers if you notice them. At the end of the season, bring plants indoors before frost strikes, and keep them in a sunny window all winter.

Cornflower, or bachelor's button (Centaurea cyanus)

The deep blue of cornflower makes it the traditional flower of boutonnieres. These flowers are also great in bouquets, fresh or dried. The plants, however, are on the homely side. Tall and gawky (up to 36 inches), cornflower is best planted at the back of a border, where it is camouflaged by lower-growing annuals. If height is a concern for you, look for Polka Dot Strain and Jubilee Gem, both of which grow only about a foot tall. The summer blooms, about an inch across, are available in colors other than blue, including pink and white.

Sow seeds in full sun. If you live in a cold-winter climate, plant in early spring. If your winters are mild, plant in fall or early spring. Thin seedlings to stand a foot apart. Stake tall varieties of cornflower. Remove old flowers to prolong bloom, and when flowering slows down and growth looks ragged, pull out the whole plant.

Cosmos (Cosmos bipinnatus)

Why do you see more and more cosmos at the nurseries and in the fancy garden magazines these days? Because plant breeders are busily inventing varieties that bloom earlier and stay more compact, yet still retain cosmos's typically lacy elegance, abundant bloom, and ease of growing. One- to two-inch-wide daisylike flowers appear from late spring through summer in pink, purple, and white, among other colors. These flowers are nice for cutting.

Cosmos grows quickly to 4 feet or more; dwarf types grow half as high. Use cosmos at the back of borders; dwarfs are good for edging or in containers. Look for Sensation Strain, 36 to 48 inches tall, with flowers from white to carmine. Sea Shells Strain has fluted petals. Yellow cosmos (*Cosmos sulphureus*) comes in improved varieties with a wide range of colors; Sunny Strain stays compact, 12 to 18 inches.

Set out transplants in full sun in spring, after the danger of frost has passed, spacing plants 12 inches apart. Or sow seeds directly in the ground in full sun. Stake taller varieties and remove flowers as they fade. Watch for mildew at the end of the season (see Chapter 14); rather than fight the disease, just figure that your cosmos are done for the year — pull them out.

Creeping zinnia (Santvitalia procumbens)

Little bright yellow or orange flowers might fool you into thinking that this low-spreading plant really is a zinnia, which it isn't. Creeping zinnia is a fine plant to use as ground cover or in containers. It only grows 8 inches tall and may spread a foot and a half.

Sow seeds in full sun directly in the ground after the soil and air have warmed up. Thin seedlings to stand 8 inches apart. Creeping zinnia is becoming a popular plant, so you're now more likely to find nurseries selling seedlings.

These plants thrive in hot weather. Just make sure that the soil never dries out.

Dahlberg Daisy to Dusty Miller

The dainty, delightful darlings in this section include the Dahlberg daisy, dahlia, and dusty miller. Looking for more kinds of daisies?

Dahlberg daisy, or golden fleece (Dyssodia tenuiloba)

The bright daisies on this plant are small ($1/2$ inch) but profuse. The flowers cover dark green, sprawling plants no taller than 12 inches. In bloom for most of summer and fall, Dahlberg daisy is a great choice for a pot or hanging basket. Or you can mass-plant it as a ground cover.

In cold-winter climates, set out seedlings in full sun in spring, after the danger of frost has passed. In mild-winter climates, plant in the fall, late winter, or early spring. Space plants 6 inches apart.

Remove dead flowers to encourage a long bloom season. In mild climates, these plants may live through winter like a perennial; don't hesitate to get rid of them, though, if growth becomes scraggly.

Dahlia

Dahlia's flowers can be as large as a dinner plate or as small as a pansy. The annual types grow about 12 to 15 inches tall and produce flowers about 2 to 3 inches wide. Colors include orange, pink, purple, red, white, and yellow. The virtues of dwarf dahlias include a long bloom season (usually from early summer until frost), an abundance of bloom, and handsome, dark green plants. See Chapter 4 for more information about this popular annual.

Dusty miller (Senecio cineraria)

Several plants go by the name dusty miller. This particular one is the annual grown for its handsome silvery gray leaves — its yellow flowers are fairly worthless in comparison. These plants grow about a foot tall and become taller and almost permanent in mild-winter climates. Use them to edge borders or in containers as a contrast with bright flowers, such as geraniums and petunias.

Set out transplants in spring, after the danger of frost has passed. Plant in full sun, 8 inches apart. Cut off flowers as soon as you see them.

If you can't find a dusty miller called *Senecio cineraria,* look for it as *Cineraria maritima.* (Unfortunately, not even botanical names are written in stone, and this one is currently in flux.) Or look for *Centaurea cineraria,* a related annual that's also called dusty miller.

E Is for English Daisy

English daisies are actually perennials, but I include them here because gardeners usually treat them as annuals.

English daisy (Bellis perennis)

The husky little daisies sold in nurseries are versions of the original plants often seen growing in lawns. English daisy forms clumps of dark green leaves and, in spring and early summer, blooms with pink, red, or white double flowers on fairly short stems.

Set out transplants in full sun or part shade in spring. English daisy makes a nice edging for a border and is a traditional companion to spring bulbs.

Felicia to Foxglove

Five friendly fellows — felicia, flax, forget-me-not, four o'clock, and foxglove — follow.

Can't find the annual you're looking for here? It may be listed under another common name. Find floss flower listed under its other common name, ageratum; find flowering tobacco listed as nicotiana; and find firecracker plant under C for cigar plant.

Felicia, or blue marquerite (Felicia amelloides)

This is another small but profuse producer of daisylike flowers. Felicia's blooms are from 1 to 3 inches wide and bright blue with yellow centers. The plants form dense mounds 18 inches tall, up to 5 feet wide. Use these plants in borders or containers (where they can spill over the sides). Felicia is a perennial in mild climates. Kingfisher daisy (Felicia bergeriana) is smaller and more compact, only 6 to 8 inches tall.

Set out transplants in spring in cold-winter climates, or in fall where winters are mild. Plant in full sun, 18 inches apart. Kingfisher daisy is easy to grow from seeds sown directly in the ground.

Keep your pruning shears handy. Cutting back felicia gives you bushier plants and more abundant blooms. Pinch off the tips of young plants to encourage branching, and cut off dead flowers to prolong the bloom season. When many of the flowers have gone to seed (if you haven't cut them off), shear the plant back by as much as a third, and new growth quickly sprouts.

Flax (Linum grandiflorum)

Color as quick and easy as from a wildflower is what you can expect from flax. Spring and summer bring brilliant red flowers (white varieties, too) that are 1 to 2 inches wide. Plants grow up to 30 inches tall, but dwarf varieties are about half that size.

Sow flax seeds directly in the ground in full sun. Plant in early spring in cold-winter climates; plant in fall if your winters are mild. Thin seedlings to stand 6 to 10 inches apart.

Use flax to cover those bare spaces between spring bulbs.

Forget-me-not (Myosotis sylvatica)

How did such poetic names befall certain plants? That's a subject for a more rambling book than this one. Forget-me-nots are prized for producing delicate blue springtime flowers in shady spots. The plants are low and spreading, about 6 to 12 inches tall. Grow them under trees and shrubs, combined with yellow tulips or daffodils, for a classic look.

Set out transplants or sow seeds directly in the ground in spring in cold climates, or in fall where winters are mild. Provide cool, moist conditions and light shade. Space plants 6 to 8 inches apart.

Incorporate plenty of organic matter into the planting bed. (See Chapter 8.) Hot, dry weather makes life tough for forget-me-nots; but under the right conditions, they may reseed and bloom again in fall. In particularly favorable situations, they can reseed themselves permanently. Simply pull out any you don't want.

Four o'clock (Mirabilis jalapa)

These fragrant, 2-inch-long flowers in shades of pink, red, white, and yellow like to sleep in. Although I don't recommend setting your watch by when these flowers open, they are named for their propensity to open in midafternoon each day. The plants themselves are rangy, from 2 to 4 feet tall. Use four o'clocks as big accent plants in beds and border. A bonus of this plant: From summer through fall, its flowers attract hummingbirds.

Sow seeds directly in the soil in full sun. Plant them in spring, after the danger of frost has passed. Thin seedlings so that they stand 12 to 24 inches apart. Four o'clocks are easy to grow in a variety of situations. The plants may reseed and can live through winter, becoming a perennial in mild climates.

All parts of this plant are poisonous. Choose another annual, instead, if you have young children or curious pets.

Foxglove (Digitalis purpurea)

Foxgloves are the towers of flowers you see at the back of old-fashioned borders. The plants grow up to 6 feet tall (although dwarf varieties are also available). Funnel-shaped flowers, like the fingers of a glove, come in many colors, including pink, purple, red, white, and yellow. Foxglove is a biennial, but nursery plants set out in spring bloom in spring and summer. 'Foxy', a 3-foot-tall All-America winner, can bloom the first year after its seeds are planted.

For blooms the first year, set out transplants in a sunny or partly shady spot in spring (or fall, in mild-winter climates). Space the plants 12 inches apart. You can also sow seeds directly in the ground in early spring; most varieties of foxglove will bloom the following spring.

Make sure that the soil is always moist. Watch for insects, such as Japanese beetles, chewing on the big leaves. Put out bait in snail-prone areas. After the first bloom, cut off the main spike to encourage flowers from side shoots.

Foxglove seeds are poisonous if eaten.

Gazania to Gloriosa Daisy

Gaze upon some of the greats: gazania, geranium, gilia, globe amaranth, and gloriosa daisy. Looking for godetia? You can find it under its other common name, clarkia. Searching for the golden fleece? Try its alias, Dahlberg daisy.

Gazania (Gazania hybrida)

The permanent ground cover that brightens up southwestern U.S. gardens also makes a dazzling spring and early summer annual in cold-winter climates. Daisylike flowers, up to 4 inches across, come in gold, orange, red, and other bright shades, as well as white. The plants are low and spreading, usually less than a foot tall. Don't despair if your blooms don't look full on a given day; it may just be the weather! Gazania flowers close at night and don't open fully on cloudy days.

In cold-winter climates, set out transplants in full sun in the spring, when the soil and air have warmed up and the danger of frost has passed. In mild-winter climates, plant in the fall or early spring. Space plants 8 to 12 inches apart.

Gazanias are easy to grow but can suffer root rot from overwatering, especially in slow-draining soil.

Geranium (Pelargonium)

Geraniums are among the most widely recognized annual flowers (not to be confused with the perennial that goes by the same name). This classic has flowers 3 to 4 inches across in a range of colors from white to scarlet. The bushy plants themselves grow from 1 to 3 feet tall. Also available are ivy-leafed types (great when trailing in hanging baskets) and scented types, which emit exotic fragrances when their leaves are crushed. See Chapter 4 for the complete story on this popular annual.

Gilia

These easy-to-grow wildflowers have small, abundant blooms in the summer. Blue thimble flower *(Gilia capitata)*, with blooms resembling pincushions, grows 3 feet and taller. Bird's eyes *(Gilia tricolor)*, with pale purplish flowers, grow only to 2 feet. Use any type of gilia in a border or wildflower garden.

In spring, after the danger of frost has passed, sow gilia seeds directly in the ground in full sun. Thin seedlings to stand 6 inches apart.

Cool-summer climates are best for gilia. Taller plants may need staking. Make sure that the shallow roots don't dry out.

Globe amaranth (Gomphrena)

The little, papery, round blossoms of globe amaranth are great for cutting and drying. The low, mounding varieties make a nice border edging. *Gomphrena globosa,* which produces white, red, or purplish flowers in summer and fall, grows from 6 to 24 inches tall, depending on the variety.

Plant in full sun in spring, after the danger of frost has passed. Set out transplants 6 to 12 inches apart or sow seeds directly in the ground.

To dry the flowers, cut them when they're fully mature and hang them upside down in a shady spot; they retain their shape and color through winter.

Gloriosa daisy, or black-eyed Susan (Rudbeckia hirta)

Descendants of wild black-eyed Susans, these big yellow daisies with black centers have a rugged-looking charm. Gloriosa daisies are easy to grow, reach 2 to 3 feet tall, and bloom through summer with flowers up to 5 inches across — outstanding for cutting. Use these plants in borders or massed plantings.

Gloriosa daisy is actually a perennial, but it is often grown as an annual. The many outstanding varieties (technically, *cultivars*) include 'Goldilocks', which has double blooms on a compact plant, just 10 inches tall, and 'Irish Eyes', whose big yellow petals radiate from an eerily green center. For a very compact version, look for 'Becky'.

Set out transplants in full sun in spring; space 12 inches apart. Or sow seeds directly in the ground in early spring; thin seedlings to stand 12 inches apart.

Watch for snails and slugs and set out bait if necessary. (See Chapter 14.)

Heliotrope, Hollyhock, and Hyacinth Bean

Time for a short but pleasant trip down memory lane. The three annuals covered in this section may send you whirling back to your childhood faster than you can say Marcel Proust.

Heliotrope (Heliotropium arborescens)

The fragrance of heliotrope is as memorable as any you encounter in a garden — sweet, rich, intense . . . you get the idea. This plant's appearance is also distinctive: dark green leaves with prominent veins and regal, deep blue flowers (white varieties, too). Use these plants, which grow from 8 to 24 inches tall, as accents in borders, complementing bright flowers, such as marigolds, or foliage of gray-leafed dusty miller. Or plant them in containers so that you can move the fragrance near a sitting area; 'Marine' and 'Dwarf Marine' are compact types that do well in containers. The flowers are also good for cutting, so you can bring the enchanting perfume indoors.

Set out heliotrope transplants in full sun or part shade in the spring, when warm temperatures have arrived and the danger of frost has passed. Space the plants 12 inches apart and provide well-drained soil enriched with plenty of organic matter.

Hollyhock (Alcea rosea)

Rather gangly and coarse, but oh, the memories this old-fashioned favorite inspires for many of us! Recall the tall spikes of pink, red, and white blooms leaning against grandma's chicken coop, attracting bumblebees and children all summer long. Hollyhocks seem able to grow anywhere, and they reseed themselves year after year. Newer varieties are more compact — 4 or 5 feet, compared to grandma's 9-footers.

Annual strains can bloom the first year from seed. (Original hollyhocks are biennials and don't bloom until their second year.) Two annual hollyhocks are All-America winners: Majorette Mixed, a 30-inch dwarf, and 'Summer Carnival', a 6-footer with full double blooms.

Set out transplants in full sun in spring after warm weather has arrived; space plants 18 to 24 inches apart. Or sow seeds directly in the ground; they may not bloom until the following year.

Make sure that plants get plenty of water. Stake tall plants that start to tip. Watch for Japanese beetles and rust.

Hyacinth bean (Dolichos lablab)

Picture a climbing string-bean vine with purplish-green leaves and little purple or white flowers. This attractive, fast-growing vine is useful for a quick screen or training up a wall or fence. Both the flowers and the bean pods are edible.

Sow the seeds in full sun or part shade in spring, after the danger of frost has passed.

Iceland Poppy and Impatiens

Consider the two annuals in this section as representative of the range of annuals that exist. From the exotic showiness of the Iceland poppy to the simple, accommodating charm of impatiens, you can find exactly the effect you're after somewhere in the world of annuals.

Iceland poppy (Papaver nudicaule)

Iceland poppy is truly an outstanding late-winter and early-spring performer in mild climates. Glistening cup-shaped flowers, up to 3 or 4 inches wide, sit atop elegant, thin stems 1 to 2 feet long; color range is brilliant, including orange, pink, yellow, and white. In cold climates, Iceland poppy has a shorter bloom season but may live on as a perennial. Champagne Bubbles is the most popular strain; it has 12-inch plants and big flowers in a wide range of colors.

In mild-winter climates, set out transplants in full sun in fall or late winter; space 10 to 12 inches apart. In cold-winter climates, set out transplants in early spring as soon as the ground can be worked.

Plants do best in cool weather. Make sure soil stays moist. Diligently remove dead flowers. Rains may batter down long-stemmed flowers, but there's not much you can do about it.

Impatiens (Impatiens walleriana)

Impatiens are probably the most widely known shade flower available. These trouble-free, 8- to 30-inch-tall plants produce flowers that range from classic reds and clean whites to neon shades of lilac and pink. In fact, you can find impatiens in just about every hue except blue and yellow. See Chapter 4 for complete details on this dependable, shade-loving annual.

Kale and Kochia

Okay, so the two annuals in this section are a little, well, weird-looking. Neither kale nor kochia is grown for its flowers, and the foliage on these plants is more likely to inspire a giggle than a gasp.

Kale, or ornamental cabbage (Brassica oleracea)

Grow these plants for their striking multicolored foliage that emerges early in the season, when color is hard to come by. A relative of common kale and cabbage, this ornamental annual is, in fact, edible itself. Plants grow 12 to 18 inches tall and look great massed in a bed or edging a border. They're also striking in containers: Grow a single plant in an 8-inch pot or several in a larger pot.

Set out transplants in early spring in cold-winter climates, or in fall or late winter where winters are mild. Plant in full sun, spacing the plants 12 to 18 inches apart. Ensure that the soil stays constantly moist and watch for caterpillars.

Kochia, or burning bush (Kochia scoparia)

Like kale, kochia is another annual with incidental flowers and big-time foliage. Kochia looks like a little cypress tree (up to 36 inches tall) with bushy, light green leaves that turn bright red in the fall. Use it as a temporary hedge for a border, as an accent, or in containers with low-growing flowers.

Set out transplants in full sun in spring, after the danger of frost has passed. Space plants 18 to 24 inches apart (8 inches for a hedge) or sow seeds directly in the ground at the same intervals.

You can shear these shaggy plants into almost any shape you want.

Larkspur to Love-Lies-Bleeding

Look in this section for lovely larkspur, lavatera, linaria, lisianthus, love-lies-bleeding, love-in-a-mist, and lobelia.

Larkspur (Consolida ambigua)

Think of larkspurs as small, annual versions of the mighty, intense blue delphiniums that tower over British borders. Larkspur plants grow up to 2 feet tall and make wonderful additions to beds and borders. Plant taller types in the back and dwarfs in front. 'Dwarf Blue Butterfly' is a compact size, 12 to 14 inches, that's perfect for containers. Flowers also come in white and shades of purple and pink — all are great for cutting.

Sow seeds directly in the ground in sun or part shade; thin seedlings to stand 12 inches apart. Larkspurs definitely perform best where summers are cool. Make sure that the soil stays moist constantly. Stake taller varieties and remove dead flowers to prolong the bloom season.

Larkspur plants are poisonous if eaten.

Lavatera, or tree mallow (Lavatera trimestris)

Often referred to as "tree mallow," lavatera is not exactly tree size, but it can grow to 6 feet from seeds sown in spring. White, pink, and red flowers that bloom from midsummer into fall resemble hibiscus. Use tall lavatera as a background plant; dwarf varieties are available if you want to bring these lovely flowers to the fore.

Sow seeds directly in the ground in full sun in early spring; sow in fall where winters are mild for blooms in winter and spring. Thin seedlings to stand 24 inches apart.

Moist, cool summers are best for this plant. Remove dead flowers and stake tall varieties.

Linaria, or toadflax (Linaria)

These slight little plants don't amount to much individually, but sown close together, they put on quite a show. Red, pink, blue, purple, yellow, cream, and bicolor flowers look like miniature snapdragons. Bloom time is early summer to fall; in mild-winter climates, flowering can start in winter and continue through spring. Plants typically grow 6 to 12 inches tall — some varieties are twice that size.

Sow seeds directly in the ground in sun or part shade. In cold-winter climates, plant in early spring, as soon as the ground can be worked. In mild climates, sow seeds in fall for winter bloom. Thin seedlings to stand no more than 6 inches apart.

Linaria is very easy to grow. You get your best blooms during cool weather. Try to sow seeds thickly for peak performance.

Lisianthus (Eustoma grandiflorum)

Recent breeding has dramatically upgraded this American prairie native — now a popular flower for cutting. Silky blue, pink, purple, or white flowers can reach 3 inches in diameter. The plants grow 18 to 24 inches tall. 'Tiara White' is a choice white variety growing 12 inches tall. Use lisianthus in borders, pots, or cutting gardens.

Set out transplants in full sun or light shade in spring after the danger of frost has passed. Thin seedlings to stand 12 to 18 inches apart.

Be sure to take some lisianthus indoors as long-lasting cut flowers, and conscientiously cut off faded flowers.

Lobelia (Lobelia)

The first question to ask is, how deep a blue do you want? Lobelia's petite but abundant flowers, blooming through most of the summer, come in a beautiful range of blue shades (as well as more or less incidental white and reddish). The next questions is, do you want a trailing or edging type? The trailers make terrific container plants, especially hanging baskets. The edgers look neat and tidy along a border. 'Crystal Palace' is an edging type that grows 4 to 6 inches tall and has deep blue flowers. 'Cambridge Blue' grows just 4 inches tall and has light blue flowers. 'Sapphire', a trailing type, has rich blue flowers with a white eye.

Set out transplants in full sun or part shade in spring, after the danger of frost has passed. Space plants 6 inches apart. Lobelia prefers cool weather. Provide light shade in hot climates and ensure that the soil stays moist. Plants can reseed in favorable situations or live over winter in mild climates.

Love-in-a-mist (Nigella damascena)

The dainty flowers on this old-timer come fully loaded with fancy accoutrements — pastel colors, feathery foliage, and puffy seed capsules. Love-in-a-mist is striking in borders and bouquets. Plants grow 18 to 24 inches tall. Among the many varieties, 'Miss Jekyll' has deep blue, semi-double flowers, and 'Persian Jewels' comes in a mix of colors.

Sow seeds directly in the ground in full sun or part shade in spring, after the danger of frost has passed, or sow seeds in fall in mild-winter climates. Thin seedlings to stand 6 to 8 inches apart.

Hot summers end the season for love-in-a-mist. To dry the papery, balloon-like seed pods for arrangements, cut off branches with mature pods and hang them upside down in an airy, shady spot. (Chapter 18 contains more information on drying flowers.)

Love-lies-bleeding (Amaranthus caudatus)

Here's another annual from grandma's garden. It's a big plant (4 feet and more) with large, coarse leaves and distinctive flowers — red ropy things drooping as long as 2 feet. Use this unusual annual at the back of a border. 'Joseph's Coat' has multicolored leaves in cream, green, and red.

Sow seeds directly in the ground in full sun or part shade in spring or early summer, after the soil has warmed up. Plant 18 to 36 inches apart, depending on variety size.

Watch for signs of chewing insects, such as Japanese beetles. Bait for snails and slugs if they threaten. Turn to Chapter 14 for help if you spy any of these tiny invaders.

Marigold to Morning Glory

Make way for marigolds, Mexican sunflowers, Mexican tulip poppies, mignonettes, monkey flowers, and morning glories.

Looking for Madagascar periwinkle? You can find it under another common name (which was once its proper botanical name), vinca rosea. You'll also find moss rose hiding under its other common name, portulaca.

Marigold (Tagetes)

Marigolds are the original all-purpose annual. They're dependable flower producers over a long season, summer through frost. Plants can range from 6 inches to 3 feet tall, and flowers can be button-size or whoppers. The plants are fast-growing and easy to grow, and the flowers last a long time when cut. The flower colors range from pure white to bronze and gold. See Chapter 4 for more information about these popular annuals.

Mexican sunflower (Tithonia rotundifolia)

This rangy heat-lover grows up to 6 feet tall and makes a great background plant for sunny spots. Flowers up to 3 inches across are a vivid orange and make great cut flowers in bouquets. 'Goldfinger' is compact, just 3 feet tall.

Sow seeds directly in the ground in full sun in the spring, after the danger of frost has passed. Space plants 2 feet apart. Mexican sunflower is easy to grow and trouble-free.

Mexican tulip poppy (Hunnemannia fumariifolia)

The leaves and shape of these flowers remind you of the related California poppy, but Mexican tulip poppy flowers are a bright, pure yellow and bloom mostly in summer. Plants grow up to 2 feet tall. Use them in mixed plantings and wildflower gardens.

Sow seeds directly in the ground in full sun in spring, after the danger of frost has passed. Thin seedlings to stand 12 inches apart. Make sure that soil is well-drained and keep plants on the dry side.

Mignonette (Reseda odorata)

The intensely sweet fragrance, described as "haunting" by one seed catalog, is why you grow mignonette — unless you're fond of sprawling, medium green, nondescript plants. The flowers are small and greenish yellow, and the plants grow 12 to 18 inches tall. Plant mignonette near walkways, under windows, in containers, or in other spots where you can appreciate the fragrance. Cut flowers from this plant freely to perfume indoor arrangements.

Sow seeds directly in the ground in early spring; or, if you live in a mild-winter climate, sow seeds in the fall. Mignonettes prefer cool weather; plant them in full sun in cool climates, in part shade in hotter areas. Thin seedlings to stand 10 to 12 inches apart.

Monkey flower (Mimulus)

If you have a shady, garden pond, this is the plant to grow at its edge. It's also perfect along shady borders. Plants grow 12 to 18 inches tall. Some people think the 2-inch-long, funnel-shaped flowers look like smiling monkeys. Colors are bright orange, red, and yellow, often with spots and blotches. 'Calypso' has big, early flowers on compact plants less than 8 inches tall. Mystic Strain is compact and spreading, ideal for pots and hanging baskets.

Set out transplants in part to full shade in spring after frost. Space plants 6 inches apart. Monkey flower does best in cool, moist climates and needs lots of water. Remove flowers as they fade.

Morning glory (Ipomoea imperialis)

Also sold as *Ipomoea nil,* morning glory sets the standard for fast-growing, big-leafed, free-flowering summer vines. Varieties can climb as much as 15 feet in one season — some varieties will consume a car left in the way! Trumpet flowers up to 4 or 5 inches wide come in a rich range of blues, pinks, and purples. Newer varieties stay open for longer, not just the morning, as suggested by the name. Plant vines near a trellis, fence, or arbor and let them climb.

The closely related moonflower *(Ipomoea Alba)* is a perennial that's usually treated as an annual. It's very fast-growing, to 20 feet. The beautiful, big white flowers of this plant open in the evening and close the next morning.

Ipomoea seeds don't sprout easily and usually need help; notch the seeds with a knife or file, or soak them for a couple of hours in warm water before planting.

Sow morning glory or moonflower seeds directly in the ground in full sun in spring, after the danger of frost has passed. Space plants 12 inches apart. Don't water or feed this plant too much; doing so encourages leaf growth at the expense of flowers.

Nasturtium to Nierembergia

Now for nasturtium, nemesia, nicotiana, and nierembergia.

Nasturtium (Tropaeolum majus)

Nasturtiums make themselves right at home in a casual garden — or in a casual green salad. Edible flowers in bright orange, yellow, cream, red, or pink blooms are abundant through the summer (or winter and spring, in mild climates). The bright green, round leaves look like waterlilies and can make a thick, low carpet that's attractive in its own right: Water beads artfully on the foliage, and some varieties have multicolored leaves. Use bushy dwarf varieties, up to 15 inches tall, to edge a border; 'Empress of India' is a favorite, with deep crimson flowers on 9-inch plants. Climbing varieties, which trail up to 6 feet, can be trained on a trellis or as a ground cover; Double Green Strain, an All-America Selection, is a semi-trailing type.

Sow seeds directly in the ground in full sun or part shade. In cold-winter climates, plant seeds in the spring; in mild-winter climates, plant seeds in the fall. Thin seedlings to stand 12 inches apart.

Nasturtiums are easy to grow in well-drained soil, and are quick about it. Best in cool-summer climates, they live through winter in mild climates and can reseed themselves — the nicest sort of "weed" if you like a wild look. Both its flowers and young leaves are edible and can add color and peppery flavor to salad greens; wash thoroughly before serving. Cut long-stemmed flowers for use in arrangements. Watch for aphids (especially if you eat the plants).

Nemesia

Nemesia would be a hugely popular annual if it weren't so doggone fussy about the weather. Its red, yellow, pink, and white flowers are as richly and vividly colored as any, and they bloom thickly on compact plants from 8 to 18 inches tall. This is a great plant for pots and hanging baskets, or you can mass plants together to edge a border. Trouble is, nemesia does really well only in cool-summer climates — those coastal areas where spring and summer merge together.

Set out transplants in full sun in spring, after the danger of frost has passed; in mild climates, plant in fall or late winter. Space seedlings 8 to 12 inches apart. Pinch tips of young plants to encourage bushy growth, and remove faded flowers to prolong the bloom.

Nicotiana, or flowering tobacco (Nicotiana)

Nicotiana is an old-fashioned favorite — and, yes, a close relative of smoking tobacco. Newer varieties have some improved habits: flowers that stay open all day instead of closing in the afternoon, and plants with compact growth (12 to 18 inches) rather than tall, weedy growth (4 feet and taller). The blooming season is quite long, lasting through spring and summer, with flowers including pink, purple, red, and white.

Use dwarf types massed like petunias: The Niki Series of semi-dwarf hybrids in various colors, 12 to 24 inches tall, is outstanding. Plant taller varieties at the back of a border. For delightful fragrance at night, choose varieties such as 'Grandiflora' and 'Fragrant Cloud'. Or go with the leggy old-timer, *Nicotiana sylvestris,* which grows up to 5 feet tall and has magnificently scented white flowers.

Set out transplants in full sun or light shade in spring, after the danger of frost has passed. Space plants 12 to 24 inches apart, depending on the size of the variety. Watch for tobacco budworms and aphids.

Nierembergia, or cupflower

Tidy growth and a thick coat of flowers make nierembergia ideal for pots, hanging baskets, or edging. The summertime flowers are tiny (about $1/4$ inch) but abundant and come in purple or white. Plants grow from 6 to 15 inches tall. 'Purple Robe' has royal purple flowers with yellow centers. 'Mont Blanc', with white, yellow-centered flowers, won All-America Selection and its European equivalent, Fleuroselect.

Set out transplants in full sun or part shade in spring, after the danger of frost has passed. Space plants 6 inches apart. Nierembergia prefers cool summers; provide part shade in hot climates. To encourage long and heavy bloom, conscientiously remove dead flowers, even though they're small and time-consuming to pluck.

Pansy to Primrose

Ah, the ever-popular Ps. This section includes some of the most common and beloved annuals of all time, including pansies, petunias, phlox, pincushion flower, pink, portulaca, and primroses. (Look for pot marigold under its other common name, calendula. Find painted tongue under its less-descriptive common name, salpiglossis.)

Pansy (Viola wittrockiana)

Pansies and violas are the "coolest" annuals you can grow. They thrive in cool weather and get ragged-looking in the heat. Pansies are the big ones, with 2- to 4-inch flowers in a range of bright colors: blue, purple, rose, yellow, and white, often striped or dramatically blotched. Plants grow up to 8 inches tall. See Chapter 4 for a complete description of this popular annual.

Petunia (Petunia hybrida)

Petunias are one of the most common annuals in garden centers. The range of flower colors will astound you. They include white, red, pink, blue, yellow, bicolors, and almost every shade in between. The plants are great in beds, hanging baskets, and containers, and some actually double as ground covers. See Chapter 4 for a complete description of this popular annual.

Phlox, annual (Phlox drummondii)

Native to Texas, annual phlox has long been a star of the summer garden in hot climates. Big clusters of 1-inch flowers cover husky plants from 6 to 20 inches tall. Colors include blue, lavender, pink, red, and white. Use for mass plantings in beds and borders. Long-stemmed varieties make great cut flowers. Twinkle Mixed and Beauty Mixed are outstanding dwarfs, in the 6-inch range.

Sow seeds directly in the ground in full sun. In cold-winter climates, plant in the spring, after the danger of frost has passed; in mild-winter climates, plant in the fall. Or you can set out transplants in spring, after frost danger. Space plants 10 inches apart and remove faded flowers to extend the bloom.

Pincushion flower, or sweet scabious (Scabiosa atropurpurea)

Pincushion flower's puffy 2-inch blooms account for its odd name. The plants grow 24 to 36 inches tall and make good additions to mixed beds and cut-flower bouquets.

Sow seeds directly in the ground in full sun in early spring, or in fall if you live in a mild-winter climate. Thin seedlings to stand 8 to 12 inches apart.

This is an easy plant to grow in mild climates with cool summers — it *naturalizes* (naturally self-sows and comes back each year like a perennial without any special care from you) under favorable conditions.

Pink (Dianthus chinensis)

Members of the carnation clan, pinks offer reliability, ease of growing, compact growth, and a wide range of heavy-blooming flowers, mainly in shades of pink, red, and white. The blooms are often bicolored, and some are fragrant. Pinks can grow up to 30 inches tall, but most modern varieties are closer to 12 inches. Taller varieties make outstanding cut flowers. Use compact varieties to edge borders or in containers. Eight-inch varieties with outstanding colors include 'Snowfire', white with red centers, and 'Raspberry Parfait', royal crimson.

Set out transplants in full sun in spring. Space plants 6 to 12 inches apart. The best bloom comes during cool weather. Shear off dead flowers to encourage more blooming.

Portulaca, or moss rose (Portulaca grandiflora)

One look at these fleshy, succulent-like leaves and brilliantly colored flowers, and you can see why portulaca is well equipped for sunny conditions. Its summer flowers look like little roses, in single- or double-flowered strains; colors include intense red, yellow, pink, white, and orange. Plants are ground-huggers, no more than 6 inches tall. Use them as ground cover or spilling from hanging baskets and other containers.

Set out transplants in full sun in spring, after the danger of frost has passed. Space plants 10 to 12 inches apart. This is one of the easiest summer annuals to grow, even in hot, dry places. In fact, these plants prefer their soil to be kept on the dry side.

Primrose (Primula)

Primroses are huge favorites in mild-winter climates, such as California and the Pacific Northwest. They perform famously in regions with cool springs and early summers and are far less successful (as in "total losers") in hot-summer areas. Three kinds of primroses are reliable as annuals:

- ✔ Fairy primrose _(Primula malacoides)_ has delicate pastel flowers (including lavender, pink, rose, and white) on 6-inch stems.

- ✔ _Primula obconica_ has similar, slightly larger flowers on a more robust plant with 12-inch stems.

- ✔ _Primula polyantha_, a familiar indoor flowering plant, has clusters of 2-inch flowers in vivid blues, yellows, oranges, and other shades.

Bloom time for all three types of primrose is spring and summer. Use annual primroses in shady borders, among bulbs, or in containers. Set out transplants in part shade in spring or fall in mild-winter climates. Space plants 6 inches apart.

Primroses need cool, moist soil enriched with plenty of organic matter. Snail and slug damage is just a matter of time; set out bait when you plant. (See Chapter 14.)

Salpiglossis to Sweet William

This selection includes seventeen splendid annuals: salpiglossis, salvia, scaevola, schizanthus, Shirley poppy, snapdragon, snow-on-the-mountain, spider flower, statice, stocks, strawflower, summer forget-me-not, sunflower, Swan River daisy, sweet alyssum, sweet pea, and sweet William. (I haven't overlooked sweet scabious; you can find it listed under its more descriptive common name, pincushion flower.)

Salpiglossis, or painted tongue (Salpiglossis)

Common names that are easier to pronounce — velvet flower and painted tongue — haven't stuck but are highly descriptive. The flowers are stunning, resembling 2-inch petunias with a velvety texture and pronounced veining in the throats. Colors include pink, purple, red, yellow, and white — often with contrasting veins. The plants grow taller than petunias, up to 36 inches high. Use them at the center of borders and beds, in containers, and for cutting.

This is a fabulously beautiful annual, but it's tricky to grow because it demands cool summers. Set out transplants at 12-inch intervals in full sun in the spring, after the danger of frost has passed. Make sure that the soil is well drained and enriched with plenty of organic matter. Pinch tips of young plants to promote bushy growth, and stake taller varieties.

Salvia (Salvia)

If you see brilliant red flowers used in extravagant midsummer beds, chances are they're scarlet sage *(Salvia splendens)* — one of the more colorful and dependable warm-season annuals. This relative of culinary sage is valued for its red spikes of blooms, but its colors also include lilac, purple, and white. The plants grow from 10 to 30 inches tall. 'Red Hot Sally' is only 10 inches tall, with deep red flowers. Use scarlet sage in masses in beds, or as accent plants in mixed borders.

Mealy-cup sage *(Salvia farinacea)* is another choice plant. 'Victoria' grows 24 inches tall and has many spikes of deep blue flowers. It has a long bloom season, lasting well into fall. Figure 5-4 shows some of the common types of salvia.

Set out seedlings in full sun in spring, after the danger of frost has passed and warm weather arrives. Space plants 12 inches apart. Both types of sage thrive in hot weather (though not high humidity) if given plenty of water. In hottest climates, salvia may benefit from partial shade.

Figure 5-4:
Salvia
comes in
many forms
and colors.

Scaevola

More than likely, *scaevola* is the answer to the question, "What's the name of that unusual blue flower in the hanging basket?" This plant, which hasn't been around long enough to pick up a quaint common name, is a real eye-catcher. Blue or purple flowers are tiny but very abundant on long trailing branches. Look for varieties such as 'Blue Wonder' and 'Purple Fanfare'.

Nurseries mostly sell plants already in bloom. Move them into a basket or along a wall where they can trail. Plant in full sun or part shade in spring, after the danger of frost has passed.

Schizanthus, or butterfly flower

Short season, fussy about heat and cold, impossible to spell — why bother with schizanthus? Breathtaking flowers in summer are enough reason to try growing these fussy annuals. They look like little orchids — in pink, purple, orange, white, and yellow — with contrasting yellow throats and many spots. The plants grow 12 to 24 inches tall. Use them for mass displays in beds, at the front of borders, or in containers. 'Bouquet' is an outstanding dwarf variety, less than 12 inches tall.

Set out seedlings in full sun or part shade in spring, after the danger of frost has passed. Space plants 12 inches apart. Cool summers are best for this plant. Enrich the soil with plenty of organic matter and keep it moist.

Shirley poppy (Papaver rhoeas)

Ancestors of today's Shirley poppies are the The American Legion poppies — long-stemmed red flowers fluttering in the fields of France. Colors of modern varieties include pastels and bicolors, as well as brilliant red. Some blooms are as wide as 3 inches across. Plants grow 24 to 36 inches and look lovely planted in clusters in wildflower beds and borders.

Sow seeds directly in the ground in full sun in early spring a few weeks before the date of the last frost. Thin seedlings to stand 12 inches apart.

Remove seed pods to prolong blooming. When cutting flowers for bouquets, seal the stem ends with a flame before immersing in water.

Snapdragon (Antirrhinium majus)

Snapdragons are cool-season annuals that come in sizes ranging from 8 inches to 3 feet tall. The fragrant flowers are arranged in striking spikes of blooms in rich colors: purple, red, lavender, and bronze. They make great cut flowers and can stand a light frost and still look great. See Chapter 4 for more information about this popular annual.

Snow-on-the-mountain (Euphorbia marginata)

A mounding mass of white and bright green leaves, snow-on-the-mountain makes a nice border backdrop for colorful annuals such as low zinnias. The plant grows 18 to 24 inches tall, and its flowers are hardly noticeable. 'Summer Icicle' is a tidy dwarf, about 18 inches tall.

Sow seeds directly in the ground in full sun in spring. Thin seedlings to stand 12 inches apart.

Milky sap in stems can irritate skin and eyes; wash it off immediately if you come into contact with it.

Spider flower (Cleome hasslerana)

When you plant spider flower, expect a shrub in just a few months. Plants grow quickly to 4 to 6 feet. Big clusters of spidery pink or white flowers stand tall. Use spider plant in the back of a border or as a temporary screen.

Sow seeds directly in the ground in full sun. Plant them when warm weather arrives, after the danger of frost has passed. Thin seedlings to stand at least 18 inches apart. Stake these leggy plants if necessary and be prepared for them to reseed themselves like weeds.

Statice *(Limonium sinuatum)*

You may recognize statice as those dainty, papery, purple or yellow flowers in dried arrangements. Statice is also useful in dry, sunny, summer borders. Plants grow up to 30 inches tall.

Set out transplants in full sun in spring, after danger of frost. Or sow seeds directly in the ground. Space plants 12 inches apart.

For dried arrangements, cut flowers after they open and before they start to fade. Hang bunches of flowers upside down in a dry, shady spot. (See Chapter 18 for details.)

Stocks *(Matthiola incana)*

The unforgettable sweet and spicy fragrance of stocks can fill a room. Throughout spring and summer, spikes of flowers bloom in double or single forms. Colors include cream, lavender, pink, purple, red, and white. Plants grow 12 to 30 inches tall. Grow them along walks or in containers where you can enjoy the fragrance. Cut flowers freely for indoor bouquets.

Ten Weeks Strain is a useful dwarf, up to 18 inches tall. If you want flowers for cutting, choose taller types such as Giant Imperial Strain, 24 to 30 inches. Night-scented stocks *(Matthiola longipetala)* are old-fashioned favorites with lilac flowers and a fragrance that's definitely most powerful in the evening.

Set out transplants in full sun in spring in cold-winter climates, or in fall or early spring where winters are mild. Space plants 8 to 12 inches apart. Stocks strongly prefer cool weather — plant early to get blooms before summer heat. Provide plenty of water and well-drained soil.

Strawflower *(Helichrysum and Helipterum)*

Strawflowers are considered *everlastings,* meaning that they hold their shape and color when dried — terrific for permanent bouquets. At least two different types go by the name strawflower:

- ✔ *Helichrysum bracteatum* has 2-inch daisylike flowers in bright colors including orange, pink, red, yellow, and white. Plants grow from 12 to 36 inches tall; Bikini mixes grow only to 15 inches and are more practical in most gardens.

- ✔ *Helipterum roseum* offers softer colors, mostly pastel pink, rose, white, and yellow; plants grow 12 to 24 inches tall.

Both kinds of strawflowers are easy to grow in dry, sunny spots. Sow seeds directly in the ground in full sun in spring, after the danger of frost has passed. Thin seedlings to stand 9 to 12 inches apart.

To dry these flowers, cut long stems when the flowers are fully open, and hang them upside down in a shady place. (See Chapter 18 for more details.)

Summer forget-me-not (Anchusa capensis)

Summer forget-me-nots produce nice blue flowers, just like common forget-me-nots, but this one takes more sun. It's perfect in mixed summer borders. Plants grow 8 to 20 inches tall. 'Blue Angel' is a compact type with ultra-marine flowers.

Set out transplants in full sun in spring, after the danger of frost has passed. Space plants 10 inches apart. Provide plenty of water.

Sunflower (Helianthus annuus)

This North American native has become the chic flower in recent years. The old standard stands about 10 feet tall, with yellow heads 1 foot across. Modern varieties are shorter, more colorful, and multibranched to make cutting the flowers more manageable. (Some novelty types grow only to 20 inches tall.) The flower colors range from white to velvet red. See Chapter 4 for more information about this rustic favorite.

Swan River daisy (Brachycome iridifolia)

Almost everything about Swan River daisy is small — flowers, foliage, plant, and the length of the bloom season. Peak bloom in summer is just a few weeks, but the flowers nearly smother the plant. Flowers are about an inch across and available in blue, pink, or white. Plants grow 9 to 18 inches tall, usually at the lower end of the range. Use them in containers, spilling over the sides of a raised bed, or edging a border.

Sow seeds directly in the ground in full sun in spring, after the danger of frost has passed. Thin seedlings to stand 6 to 8 inches apart. If available, set out transplants after frost danger. Pinch tips of young plants to encourage bushy growth.

Sweet alyssum (Lobularia maritima)

One of the more familiar plants (even though not everyone may know its name), sweet alyssum plays a leading role in the garden. Low-spreading growth makes it ideal for edging a border, filling in between tall annuals or bulbs, and spilling out of containers and between stepping stones. 'Carpet of Snow', with pure white flowers on 4-inch-tall plants, is the most familiar variety. Other colors are available: 'Rosie O'Day', an All-America winner, is a rosy lavender, and Easter Bonnet is a strain with a mix of colors. Bloom season for all varieties is long: from spring to frost, or year-round in mild climates.

Set out transplants in full sun or light shade in spring. Or sow seeds directly in the ground in full sun or light shade in spring. In mild-winter climates, sow seeds in spring or fall. Space plants 8 to 10 inches apart. Sweet alyssum is easy and quick to grow and may reseed itself under favorable conditions. Best blooming comes during cool weather.

Sweet pea (Lathyrus odoratus)

Before attempting to grow sweet peas, keep in mind that sweet peas can't stand heat and do best in cool weather. They come in tall (up to 5 feet) and bushy (2 to 3 feet) varieties. The best reason for growing sweet peas is the fragrant, old-fashioned flowers whose colors range from white to purple to bicolor. See Chapter 4 for more information about this fussy but fulfilling favorite.

Sweet William (Dianthus barbatus)

Although sweet William is related to the carnation, it lacks the family fragrance. But it makes up for this deficiency with its robust growth and big bright flower clusters in pink, purple, red, white, and bicolors. Annual varieties grow 6 to 12 inches tall. Use them to edge borders, in mass plantings, or in containers.

Most sweet Williams are biennials, but they can bloom the first summer if you start seeds early or set out transplants in time. One of several true annual varieties, 'Summer Beauty' flowers in mixed colors and has long stems that are ideal for cutting.

Sow seeds directly in the ground in full sun several weeks before the last frost date. Or set out transplants in early summer. Space plants 6 inches apart.

To be sure of bloom the first season, look for varieties labeled as annuals. Cut back plants after the first bloom in early summer to encourage a second bloom.

Thunbergia and Transvaal Daisy

Two treasures to look into, thunbergia and Transvaal daisies, take the spotlight in this section. (Looking for tree mallow or toadflax? You can find them under the Ls, listed as lavatera and linaria, respectively.)

Thunbergia, or black-eyed Susan vine (Thunbergia alata)

A fast-growing tropical vine, thunbergia looks more difficult to grow than it is. Throughout summer until frost, its 1- to 2-inch-wide tubular flowers bloom in orange, white, or yellow, with a dark eye in the center. Plant near a fence or trellis, and the vine will twine up to 10 feet. 'Susie' is a dwarf variety, climbing 4 or 5 feet; it's great in a container, especially a hanging basket.

If transplants are available, set them out in full sun or part shade in spring, after the danger of frost has passed and when warm weather has arrived. Space plants 12 inches apart. Seeds can be sown directly in the ground at the same time and spacing. Ensure that these plants get plenty of water through their whole season. Blooming is best in cool weather, before and after summer heat.

Transvaal daisy (Gerbera jamesonii)

For sheer good looks, Transvaal daisy is near the top among annuals. (Okay, technically it's one of those perennials typically grown as an annual.) It also ranks close to number one for sheer difficulty to grow. Its flowers are elegant daisies, up to 4 or 5 inches wide, with long, slender petals standing high on slender but sturdy curving stems. These plants bloom off and on from spring through fall in rich, deep colors, including orange, pink, red, yellow, and white. The plants grow up to 18 inches tall; dwarfs are about 8 to 10 inches. Use them at the front of a border or in containers where you can appreciate them up close.

Transvaal daisies are very slow to grow from seeds, taking 6 to 18 months to bloom; some dwarf varieties are speedier and can bloom within 4 or 5 months. Set out transplants in spring, after the danger of frost has passed, in full sun or part shade. Space plants 12 inches apart.

Soil must be perfectly well drained and enriched with plenty of organic matter. Keep the soil moist and provide part shade in hot-summer climates. Set out bait for snails and slugs and watch for mites. The flowers are great for cutting; wait until they're open fully and make a slit at the base of the stem before putting them in water.

Verbena to Viola

Violas, vinca rosea, and most kinds of verbena are tiny treasures of the annual world. Fortunately, good things often come in small packages.

Verbena (Verbena)

Verbena's talent is staying low and spreading wide, covering itself with bright flower clusters 2 or 3 inches wide. Colors include blue, lavender, pink, purple, red, white, and bicolors; bloom season is long, all through the warm months. Plants grow 6 to 12 inches tall and spread as wide as 24 inches. Use them to edge a bed, as a low mass-planting, or in containers.

Wide-spreading strains such as Romance and Showtime work especially well as a ground cover or in hanging baskets. *Verbena bonariensis,* a perennial in mild climates, has a much different look; it's lacy and tall (3 to 6 feet), with purple flowers that look terrific at the back or front of a border.

Set out transplants in full sun in spring, after the danger of frost has passed. Space plants 12 to 15 inches apart. Verbena thrives in hot weather. For bushy growth, pinch back tips of young plants; remove dead flowers.

Vinca rosea, or Madagascar periwinkle (Catharanthus roseus)

This is the champion of hot-climate performers, thriving in desert climates such as the southwestern U.S. and northern Mexico. Even in midsummer, an abundance of $1^{1}/_{2}$-inch white or pink flowers looks crisp and fresh, and the foliage manages to stay shiny and deep green. Plants grow up to 20 inches tall; compact varieties reach half that size or less.

Use vinca rosea to edge a border, as a low-growing mass planting, or spilling from a container. Choose from many new and improved varieties. 'Apricot Delight' is outstanding; it grows 10 or 12 inches tall and has an extra-long bloom season.

Vinca rosea is an easy plant to grow. Set out transplants in full sun in spring, when warm weather has arrived and the danger of frost has passed. Space plants 8 to 12 inches apart. For vigorous and lush growth, make sure that you provide plenty of water — as long as soil drains quickly. Bloom season can extend until the first frost, or later in mild climates.

Viola

Violas are the smaller-flowered cousins of pansies. Violas stay less than 6 or 8 inches tall. Their colors are mostly solid, including blue, apricot, red, purple, white, red, and yellow. See Chapter 4 for more about this petite favorite.

Wallflower and Wishbone Flower

Don't be deceived by the names of the annuals in this section. Wallflowers are far from plain, and wishbone flowers are far prettier than the discarded scraps of a chicken dinner.

Wallflower (Erysimum or Cheiranthus)

It's hard to beat the traditional spring combination of tulips and wallflowers blooming together. Clusters of small flowers come mainly in bright shades of orange and yellow but also mainly cream, purple, and red. Plants grow 12 to 24 inches tall. Use them for mass display in beds and borders. 'Orange Bedder', about 12 inches tall, is an old favorite to combine with spring bulbs or blue forget-me-nots.

For spring bloom, set out transplants in full sun or part shade in early spring; space plants 12 inches apart. For bloom later in summer, sow seeds directly in the ground in full sun in early spring, or fall in mild-winter climates. Wallflowers thrive in cool, moist climates such as Great Britain and the Pacific Northwest, where they enjoy time-honored popularity. Keep their soil moist.

Wishbone flower (Torenia fournieri)

Looking for a low plant to edge a shady border? Wishbone flower is ideal. Small, mainly blue flowers bloom for a long season, through summer and fall. Plants grow 6 to 12 inches tall, with a lushness that looks like they belong around a pond or other water feature. Clown Strain is an All-America winner that grows just 6 or 8 inches tall; flower colors include white and rose pink, as well as shades of blue.

Set out transplants in part shade in spring, after the danger of frost has passed. Space plants 6 to 8 inches apart. Enrich soil with plenty of organic matter and keep it moist. For bushy growth, pinch tips of stems.

Z Is for Zinnia

Here, at the end of the alphabet, you find one of the cheeriest, most diverse annuals around: the zinnia.

Zinnia

Zinnias are easy-to-grow, sun-loving, long-blooming flowers. The colors are red, yellow, orange, purple, white, salmon, pink, rose, and even green. The plants come in several flower forms, including the *cactus* type with large, double blooms and quill-like petals and the *dahlia-flowered* type with flat, rounded petals. See Chapter 4 for more information about this colorful mainstay of the world of annuals.

Part III
Designing Annual Beds and Borders

CARL SAGAN PLANS HIS GARDEN

...and over there, I'm going to plant billions and billions of asters and billions and billions of cosmos...

In this part . . .

Annuals can bring out the artist in everyone. Even if you've never painted on canvas, you can turn your garden into a beautiful work of art by using some of the color and design tips in this part. Discover how to combine flowers of various colors, heights, and shapes and how to create attractive flower beds and borders in places where you can enjoy them the most. If you long to create a symphony of sweet smells, this part also has advice for adding fragrant flowers to your garden.

Chapter 6

Annuals and the Elements of Design

In This Chapter

▶ Playing with color

▶ Deciding on shape and size

▶ Designing for fragrance

▶ Looking at four typical garden styles

*I*f you want to have fun and experiment with flowers, annuals are the perfect plants; they're inexpensive, fast-growing, and long-blooming. You can try out wild color combinations, carpet an entire bed, or fill pots to overflowing with these varied and rewarding plants. Even if you make a hideous mistake (perhaps seeing red and orange together causes a family member to break out in hives), you may have time to replant during the same growing season. If not, just wait until next year and design a whole new planting scheme.

The ways in which you can incorporate annuals in your landscape are endless. You can plant entire beds and borders in swathes of color. You can fill pots and window boxes with flowers that bloom all summer long. Or you can mix annuals into borders of trees, shrubs, and ground covers to add seasonal color, fragrance, and texture.

Playing with Color

Color is the first thing that people notice in a garden, and like music, it goes a long way toward creating a mood. People who talk about the moods that colors create tend to be passionate on the subject. According to common belief, hot colors such as red and orange are energizing, whereas cooler colors have a calming affect. Pastel colors can invoke a mood of serenity and contemplation, whereas an expanse of bright primary colors creates a more playful setting. Consider the tone you'd like for each garden area and choose colors accordingly. Just be sure that you base your choices on your own feelings about the color, not on what so-called experts of design say that the colors should make you feel.

You need to consider more than just the color of the blooms when selecting annuals. The colors of the annual's foliage, the colors of the foliage and flowers of nearby trees and shrubs, the colors and textures of paving materials such as walkways and driveways, and even the color and style of your house are also important factors to consider when choosing an annual. For example, bright pink impatiens contrast nicely with the dark foliage of evergreen trees. Bright red geraniums show up nicely in a window box against a white house.

Gardening has no absolute, cut-and-dried rules about color. Sometimes, your gardening climate can provide guidance about what colors to use. For example, sunlight, which determines how our eyes see the color of flowers, varies dramatically throughout the day and among different climates. The pale color harmonies of pink, cream, and blue that look delightful in a misty Pacific Northwest or British garden appear washed-out in the bright afternoon sun of Texas or southern Italy. And the bright, lively colors that show up so well in desert climates come across as glaring and harsh in the cooler coastal regions of northeastern U.S.

If you're planting a garden that will be viewed mostly in the morning or evening when light is paler, choose flowers with cool colors, such as blue pansies and white petunias. In contrast, if the garden will be viewed in the midday sun, choose flowers with bolder colors, such as red geraniums and orange impatiens. Consider, too, how far away the viewer will be from the planting. When viewed from a distance, flowers with bright, hot colors like red and orange have more impact than those with softer, cooler colors like blue and purple.

The most important way to decide on the colors of your annual garden is to experiment with different combinations of color to find what you enjoy most. Try mixing colors and trust your own eyes. One gardener's favorite combination, such as purple petunias with scarlet geraniums, may be another gardener's worst color-clash nightmare.

Spinning your color wheels

Playing with color in the garden may be the next best thing to finger painting. But now that you're an adult, you may want to put a little more thought into your flower garden than you did with your finger painting. This is where that color wheel that you studied in grade school may come in handy. You may recall that the color wheel is divided into the same colors in the same order as a rainbow:

- ✔ **Primary colors:** These three colors — red, blue, and yellow — are *equidistant* on the wheel. All other colors result from mixing these three. See Photo 114 in the color section of this book for a good example of mixing primary colors. It shows marine blue cherry-pie plant *(Heliotrope)* combined with bright yellow marigolds.

- ✔ **Complementary colors:** These pairs of colors are *opposite* each other on the wheel — orange and blue, yellow and violet, or red and green, for example.

- ✔ **Harmonious colors:** These colors blend gradually *between* two primary colors, such as red to orange to yellow.

- ✔ **Shades of color:** Shades refer to lighter and darker variations of the same color.

Keep these color combinations in mind when designing your annual garden. Use a palette of primary colors to make bold statements. The classic example is the red, white, and blue garden patterned after the American flag; each color stands out distinctly, contrasting with its neighbor.

Complementary colors can be jarring if overused in mass plantings. Rather than alternating yellow marigolds and purple petunias in a large bed, consider intermixing yellow and orange marigolds and using purple sparingly as a bold accent color.

Harmonious colors unify a landscape without creating the monotony of using a single flower or color. A garden that moves like a sunset from yellow to orange to red or various shades of blue like the clear sky creates softer impressions on the viewer.

Finally, you can create a very effective planting by using just one color. Choose one or a few flowers in similar colors and mix them with attractive foliage plants, such as dusty miller. This approach can be especially effective in container plantings. Single-colored beds are also popular for creating a formal look. Plant a single flower of a single color for visual impact when viewed from a distance — like an exclamation point at the end of a sentence, or the cymbals in an orchestra, a bed of yellow marigolds is a statement to behold.

Don't forget the charm and ease of a scheme made up of a single color, accented by varying foliage colors. Gardens planted in all-blue, all-purple, or all-yellow flowers, with a little white mixed in, can be very pleasing and impressive. For a list of annuals by various colors, see Chapter 23.

Separating the hot from the cold

An easy way to select garden colors is to think of all colors as falling within the ranges of *hot* or *cool*. Hot colors are bright and bold, lively, cheerful, and energizing: lemon yellow, hot pink, fire-engine red. Most cool colors — pale pink, sky blue, and lavender — blend well together, creating a feeling of harmony and serenity. No clear, absolute distinction exists between hot and cool; pink can range from a deep, vibrant "hot" pink to a soft, pastel "cool" pink. In general, red, orange, and yellow are considered hot; green, blue, and purple are considered cool.

Don't be afraid to mix and match the two; cool accent colors can really bring out the vibrancy of hot colors. Consider the following ideas for planting flowers in hot and cool colors:

- ✔ For a typical hot-color look, plant a border of cherry-colored zinnias and bright, multicolored nasturtiums backed by a tall row of shaggy golden yellow sunflowers. Such a display of midsummer color is sure to bring a smile to the face of any garden visitor. Choose a variety of nasturtium with variegated leaves ('Alaska' foliage looks as though it's been splashed with white paint), add a splash of cool, cobalt blue bachelor's buttons and lacy love-in-a-mist for accent color and foliage texture, and you've created a colorful border that will bloom for months in full sun.

- ✔ If your taste runs to the cooler, gentler colors, you can re-create the romantic color combinations beloved by master colorists such as British garden writer Gertrude Jekyll and impressionist painter Claude Monet. Pale pink and peach impatiens alongside white or light blue lobelia are perfect for edging beds of taller lilac-colored ageratum and apricot snapdragons. Mix in some tall, dramatic pink and white spider flowers *(Cleome spinosa)*. For a final touch, add a clump or two of purple fountain grass *(Pennisetum setaceum)* to anchor the planting and provide a color contrast that makes the lighter colors appear even more pale and ethereal. Such an annual border can edge a lawn, wrap around a patio, or provide color and texture to an entryway for many months.

Mixing in a little white can spark any color scheme, bringing out the best in the other flower colors. Or you can use white exclusively to create a cool and restful garden that looks its best at dusk and in cloudy, damp weather. The famous white garden at Sissinghurst in England was created by Vita Sackville-West to view in the moonlight. She was inspired by the other-worldly flight of a great horned owl swooping over the garden at twilight. You can choose from many sparkling white annuals to add to such a garden, including daisies, baby's breath, impatiens, sweet alyssum, and the large, fragrant flowers of angel's trumpet *(Datura)*.

Don't forget your leafy greens

Too often, gardeners forget that green is a color, too, and forms the backdrop for all the other colors in the garden. Foliage on annuals varies from a dark forest green to bright emerald to palest chartreuse. Some annuals even have green flowers — nicotiana comes in a pale green, as do bells of Ireland (*Moluccella laevis*).

Many plants now come with variegated (multicolored) foliage, which creates a tapestry of color and pattern even when the plant is not in bloom. Yellow-foliaged plants or those with leaves splotched in cream or white can brighten a dark corner as effectively as white flowers, giving the effect of sunshine lingering on the leaves. Coleus is the classic foliage plant, with its leaves mottled in colors ranging from near-black to lime green, white, and bright fuchsia pink.

Leaves make a rich pattern to accent flower color, and variegation can add its showy speckles and stripes to any color scheme. When planting annuals in front of dark, heavy rhododendrons, for example, add white or brightly colored flowers; in front of yellow-leafed shrubbery, plant blue or purple flowers for a pleasing contrast.

Shape, Height, and Texture

A plant's form is often every bit as important as its color. Like color, the shape, height, and texture of a garden's plants affect the mood it evokes. Neatly-sheared shrubbery combined with orderly mounds of flowers lends an air of formality; rambling vines and sprawling flowers invite you to put your feet up and relax. Tall, lush foliage offers privacy to a small space, whereas low-growing plants can create the illusion of expanse. Fine, feathery foliage creates a delicate, genteel setting; plants with large, broad leaves create a feeling of stability.

All annuals grow from seeds or small plants to mature size in one season, but they vary in form as they develop. Some flowers grow tall; sunflowers, for example, reach heights of 8 to10 feet. Other annuals, such as sweet alyssum and lobelia, prefer to hug the ground, making them perfect for trimming edges of beds and borders. (See Photo 116 in the color section for an example of 'Crystal Palace' lobelia edging a border.) Trailing annuals — such as ivy geraniums, lobelia, and petunias — are ideal for hanging baskets, raised beds, and window boxes.

Contrary to what you may have heard, there's no rule stating that you *must* plant the shortest flowers in front and the tallest flowers in back. For example, some tall, airy annuals, such as *Verbena bonariensis* with its skinny branches topped with tiny purple flowers, can act as scrim plants; the garden is meant to be viewed through scrim plants planted in the foreground, adding a new focus or perspective to the other plantings.

Annuals can quickly add height to a garden, with towering sunflowers or foxgloves creating screening or providing color at the back of the border. (Check out Photos 119 and 123 for examples of these tall annuals in action). As you hike in the woods, notice how nature layers plants: tall trees, understory trees, large shrubs, ferns, and then ground cover plants carpeting the forest floor. Such complexity pleases the eye, and you can mimic that pattern by planting low-growing annuals in front and taller ones in the rear. (See Photo 118 for an example.) You can blend annuals in with other plants to create this same effect in your garden beds. Use flowers of different heights, from statuesque and dramatic hollyhocks to diminutive marigolds.

Texture adds another element to the garden. The droopy, chenillelike softness of love-lies-bleeding *(Amaranthus caudatus)* adds a striking note to a planting scheme. Use the feathery foliage of love-in-a-mist *(Nigella damascena)* to knit together varied plantings in the front of a border. Frilly China asters *(Callistephus chinensis)* or the soft seedheads of annual grasses add fluff and interest. And the spiky spires of foxglove *(Digitalis)* or the candelabra-like heads of woodland tobacco *(Nicotiana sylvestris)* accent the more rounded forms of lower-growing annuals, perennials, and shrubs.

Design for Fragrance

Of all the senses, smell most strongly evokes memory. The fragrance of annual flowers can add another dimension to your garden. The strong perfume of sweet peas or the spicy smell of nasturtiums can bring back an acute longing for a favorite grandmother's garden and for the lazy, hot afternoons of a childhood summer.

Floral fragrances are a matter of personal preference — as personal as your favorite perfume or aftershave — so take the time to choose the flowers that most please your sense of smell. Then mix those flowers in throughout the garden. Plant generously so that you have plenty of flowers to pick for bouquets. Even a few sprays of the unassuming mignonette can scent a room or a front porch. As a rule, choose the old-fashioned varieties of flowers, which usually tend to be the more fragrant. You may need to order seeds by mail to find the older, most strongly scented varieties.

Remember to add a few fragrant blooms to every pot, window box, or hanging basket. Concentrate sweet-smelling flowers near walkways, entries, patios, and decks so that you and your guests can enjoy them often. Some plants don't waste their scent on the daylight hours, as they are pollinated by night-flying moths. Flowering tobacco *(Nicotiana)* and the moonflower vine *(Ipomoea alba)* release their sweet scents in the evening air and so are ideal additions to planting beds or pots near bedroom windows or patios used after dark. Planting the most fragrant flowers may inspire you to slow down, sniff, and enjoy the romance of your garden.

Here are some favorite easy-care annuals that add fragrance to the garden:

- **Heliotrope:** Dark, crinkly leaves show off vanilla-scented purple or dusky white flowers.
- **Mignonette:** An easy little plant to grow from seed, this flower has an amazingly strong, sweet fragrance.
- **Nicotiana or flowering tobacco:** The white flowers have a nearly tropical scent, particularly strong in the evening.
- **Night-scented stock:** This old-fashioned favorite has the scent of cloves.
- **Scented geraniums:** The fuzzy, splotched, and streaked leaves of these annuals come in a wide variety of scents, from chocolate to cinnamon, lemon, and mint.
- **Sweet alyssum:** This favorite edging plant has masses of tiny scented flowers.
- **Sweet peas:** The older varieties of sweet peas, a childhood favorite for many people, retain the sweetest of scents all day long.

Four Styles of Annual Gardens

Annuals fit a wide variety of garden styles. When choosing plants, consider not only your personal taste but also the style of your house and how you use your garden. Do you love backyard barbecues, or do you entertain more formally? Do you have a garden filled with dogs and kids or an outdoor space designed for peace and respite? No matter what your tastes or lifestyle, annuals are available to contribute to the ambiance that you want to create for your garden.

Houses and garden styles vary from region to region across the country and from neighborhood to neighborhood. Try to pick a style that suits your taste, lifestyle, and climate. Then build upon the style to create a garden that carries out the theme instead of haphazardly mixing different trends and ideas. Here are some familiar and effective garden styles:

✔ **Naturalistic:** Easy-care, slightly wild, naturalistic gardens go well with ranch houses or rustic architecture. This style is not just for country gardens; it's an exciting way to bring the feeling of nature to a city lot. Larger, looser, highly textured annuals, such as cosmos and cleome, mix with trees and shrubs to add to the naturalistic feel. Self-seeding annuals, such as nigella, lunaria, and *Verbena bonariensis,* along with any of the annual grasses, such as Japanese blood grass and zebra grass, work well in such gardens. See Figure 6-1 for an example of a naturalistic garden.

✔ **Formal:** Clipped hedges and strong geometric design are characteristic of more formal gardens and are often paired with Georgian- or Tudor-style houses. *Carpet bedding* (thickets of low-growing plants) or masses of single-color plantings are effective in beds edged with brick or in gardens that surround well-groomed lawns. Formal gardens achieve their style not just from specific flowers but also from the overall design of the space. Alyssum, begonias, geraniums, and petunias are classics for filling island beds or surrounding roses grown on *standards* (plants pruned to a small tree form). See Figure 6-2 for an example of a formal garden.

✔ **Cottage:** Cape Cod, timber-style, or other small houses look wonderful surrounded by the profusion of a cottage garden. No lawn, a relaxed design, and paths or stepping stones meandering through cherished flowers characterize cottage gardens. Old-fashioned annuals, such as foxglove, poppies, stocks, sweet peas, and zinnias, are staples of such a planting scheme. See Figure 6-3 for an example of a cottage garden.

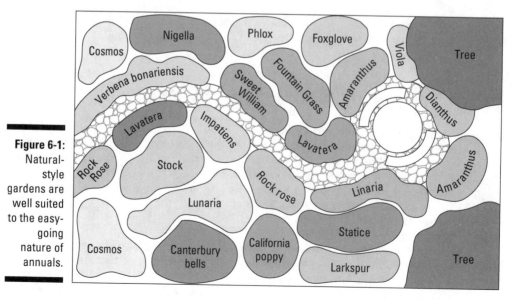

Figure 6-1: Natural-style gardens are well suited to the easy-going nature of annuals.

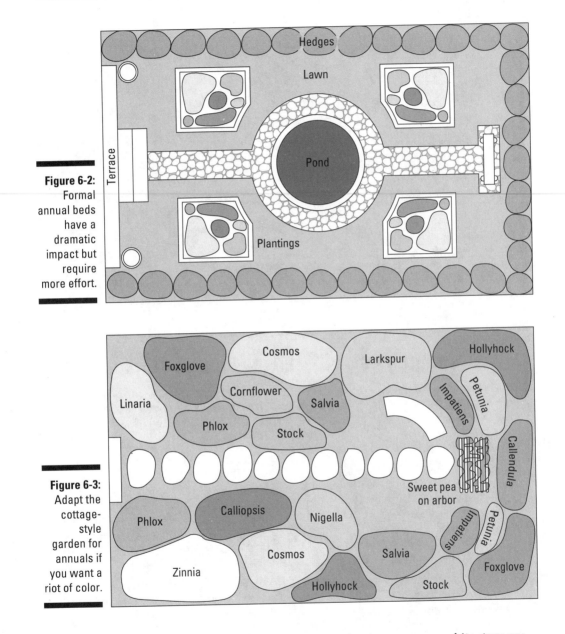

Figure 6-2:
Formal
annual beds
have a
dramatic
impact but
require
more effort.

Figure 6-3:
Adapt the
cottage-
style
garden for
annuals if
you want a
riot of color.

✔ **Modern:** The simplicity and drama of contemporary architecture are
complemented by unusual annuals with interesting foliage and structure. Often such gardens feature large paved areas or decks that can be
softened by annuals in pots or in surrounding beds. Nicotiana, castor
bean *(Ricinus communis),* cupflower *(Nierembergia caudatus),* love-lies-
bleeding *(Amaranthus hippomanica),* and purple fountain grass can all
add a bit of drama to the garden. See Figure 6-4 for an example of a
modern garden.

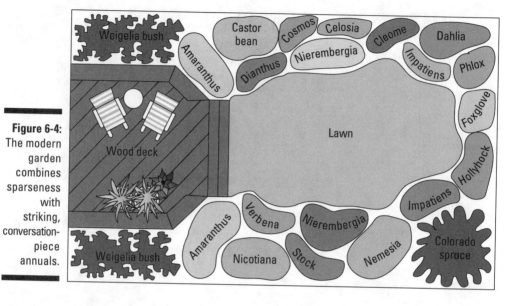

Figure 6-4:
The modern garden combines sparseness with striking, conversation-piece annuals.

Branching out with lesser-known annuals

Nothing's wrong with relying on familiar fixtures such as geraniums and petunias to brighten your garden. But keep in mind that a vast array of lesser-known plants is available. Consider the following ideas for putting unusual annuals to work for you:

✔ Put a large pot in your shady doorway and fill it with fragrant lavender verbena and the felted chartreuse leaves of the licorice plant (*Helichrysum petiolare* 'Limelight'); you and your guests will enjoy a tactile treat all summer long.

✔ Do you have a shed or utility area that you want to hide from view? Turn the area into a thing of beauty by tacking a piece of lattice to it to provide support for a fast-growing annual vine, such as moonflower (*Ipomoea alba*), with its large, heart-shaped leaves and sweetly scented white flowers.

✔ If you're looking for a border or tall backdrop for flowers, consider a hedge that grows 6 to 8 feet tall with feathery foliage and daisylike flowers in elegant shades of pink, lavender, rose, crimson, and white. Plant several packages of cosmos seeds in early spring, and you can enjoy such a hedge from June to October.

Hundreds of different kinds of annuals are available, so search out unusual or particularly fragrant varieties in seed catalogs or specialty nurseries.

Chapter 7
Planning Beds and Borders

. . . .

In This Chapter

▶ Choosing plants of the right height

▶ Deciding where to put your beds and borders

▶ Brightening up your backyard

▶ Encircling a tree with color

▶ Trimming your walkway with annuals

. . . .

Chapter 6 approaches the topic of what annuals to plant where by explaining the principles of design: color, shape, texture, height, and so on. This chapter, on the other hand, takes a pragmatic approach. It gives you suggestions of exactly what to plant where to achieve the effect you want for particular areas in your yard.

Whether you're the type of gardener who loves to plan carefully, or you just returned from the nursery with a load of plants and no idea where to put them, this chapter offers some ideas for one of the best parts of growing annuals: combining them for exciting effects in garden beds and borders.

Getting Bedder All the Time

In just about all cultures and styles of gardening since garden-making began, beds and borders have been the major elements used to organize landscape design. For this reason, understanding the elements of garden beds and borders is a good way to begin to visualize your garden:

> ✔ A garden *bed* (also called an *island bed*) is an area planted with ornamentals (usually flowering plants), surrounded by an open expanse, usually lawn. Beds also can be set amidst paving or used to punctuate any open area that needs color and interest. Because beds are accessible from all sides, gardeners must remember to plant the flowers in

such a way that they can be viewed from any angle. (See Figure 7-1.) Beds enliven a large expanse of grass, add color wherever needed, and are fun to create in different shapes to suit your landscaping.

✔ Garden *borders* are planting strips that follow the edge of fences, driveways, or walkways or that wrap around the perimeter of a lawn. Borders are easier to plan because they are viewed from only one or two sides. A basic guideline when designing borders is to plant larger plants toward the back, with smaller flowers trimming the front edges, as shown in Figure 7-2.

If you study the beds and borders that appeal to you, you will likely find that they demonstrate at least a few of the following qualities:

✔ They combine plants of varying heights and textures, in a pleasing color scheme.

✔ They include fragrant annuals perfuming the air for anyone passing by.

✔ They produce flowers that can be cut for indoor bouquets. Sometimes, smaller flowers, such as pansies, are best viewed close-up, so prudent gardeners plant enough so that they can cut some to fill vases.

✔ They provide color contrasts or accents when planted between or in front of trees, shrubs, and perennials in existing borders.

✔ They include annuals that bloom when bulbs fade away in the spring — filling in holes in beds and borders, while helping to hide dying bulb foliage.

Figure 7-1: Traditionally, gardeners plant the tallest flowers in the center of island beds, and smaller plants at the edge, so that all the plants are visible from every angle.

Figure 7-2:
Planting the tallest plants at the back of a border and the shortest plants at the front ensures that each plant is in clear view.

Rightsizing Your Beds and Borders

When choosing plants for beds and borders, try to use annuals of different heights. Be sure to check plant heights in the flower descriptions of Chapters 4 and 5, as well as on seed packs and in seed catalogs. Many annuals come in different varieties that range in size from dwarfs to giants.

The big guys

Tall-growing annuals, reaching a height of 3 to 4 feet or taller, function in three major ways in beds and borders:

- ✔ Planted along the back edge of borders, they form a backdrop to show off the flowers in the front of the bed.

- ✔ In a planting bed to be viewed from all sides, they provide height down the middle of the bed.

- ✔ They are useful for quick-growing screening — to hide a utility area or cover the wall of a garage, for example.

The following annuals grow to 3 to 4 feet or taller:

- Basket flower *(Centaurea americana)*
- Castor bean *(Ricinus communis)*
- Cosmos *(Cosmos bipinnatus)*
- Flowering tobacco *(Nicotiana sylvestris)*
- Love-lies-bleeding *(Amaranthus caudatus)*
- Spider flower *(Cleome)*
- Sunflower *(Helianthus annus)*
- Verbena *(Verbena bonariensis)*

Middle of the pack

Ranging from 1 to 3 feet, these are the plants that you use the most frequently in all your planting schemes. They are ideal for the middle of beds and borders. They are also the right scale for most containers.

- African daisy *(Arctotis)*
- Ageratum
- Calendula
- Dwarf dahlia
- Geranium, zonal *(Pelargonium hortorum)*
- Gloriosa daisy, or black-eyed Susan *(Rudbeckia hirta)*
- Heliotrope
- Larkspur *(Consolida ambigua)*
- Marigolds *(Tagetes)*
- Phlox, annual *(Phlox drummondii)*
- Snapdragon *(Antirrhinium majus)*
- Zinnia *(Zinnia angustifolia)*

Short stuff

Short annuals (usually less than 8 inches tall) play two of the most important roles in beds and borders: They fill in spaces between larger annuals, and they spill over or trim the edge of a bed, softening the other, more distinct flower shapes.

The following dependable annuals stay under 6 to 8 inches tall. Be sure to choose dwarf varieties when an annual comes in a wide range of sizes. (You don't want 8-foot sunflowers at the front edge of your borders!)

- Bedding or wax begonias *(Begonia semperflorens)*
- Impatiens
- Lobelia *(Lobelia erinus)*
- Mignonette *(Reseda odorata)*
- Nasturtium
- Pansy *(Viola wittrochiana)*
- Petunia
- Sweet alyssum *(Lobularia)*
- Verbena

Choosing the Perfect Spot for Your Beds and Borders

Before you put in your beds and borders, reflect on how the location of your garden can give you viewing pleasure throughout the season. Because annuals grow from seeds or small transplants to maturity over just a few months, you want to plant them where you can most enjoy their color and fragrance during their relatively brief life. For example, you may want your annuals to bloom along the deck or patio where your family gathers to relax or eat, near the kids' play area, and along the sidewalks to your front door and mailbox. Here are a few key considerations for locating beds and borders:

- Do you have a small patio that captures the morning sun, where you like to eat breakfast in late spring? Border the patio with early-blooming annuals, such as sweet alyssum, petunias, or impatiens. You can pop these right out of their plastic nursery containers, water them, and have an instant little garden.

- A west-facing terrace — where you sit to watch sunsets on summer evenings — is an ideal spot to surround with pale flowers, especially those with evening fragrance, such as nicotiana and white evening-scented stock.

- ✔ A shady corner of the lawn, ideal for cooling off on hot afternoons, can be made even more refreshing by planting a perimeter border with white and blue flowers. Cornflower (also called bachelor's button), love-in-a-mist *(Nigella),* and white daisies set against the green lawn create a bright yet cooling display all summer long.

- ✔ If you enjoy cutting flowers to add to salads, plant nasturtiums in a bed right outside the kitchen door.

- ✔ What part of the lawn do the kids most often play on? Plant the surrounding border with plants that catch their attention, such as fragrant sweet William or tall, spindly *Verbena bonariensis.* Odd plants, such as multicolored coleus or the drooping blooms of love-lies-bleeding *(Amaranthus),* also appeal. And children love huge sunflowers or the sweet faces of diminutive pansies. It's best to place the plants in raised beds or containers so kids know not to run through the bed and trample your beautiful garden.

Remember, however, that some plants, such as the castor bean plant, are poisonous. Encourage kids to look and sniff, but never to touch or eat a plant without permission.

Six Designs for Beds and Borders

Almost everyone's yard has some features that are ready-made for planting beds and borders. Find the situation that most closely matches your yard and discover how to re-create a design or adapt it for your own garden.

Sunny patio bed

Many homeowners have a backyard patio that they use for barbecues, outdoor dining, sunbathing, and other summer activities. Creating a flower bed between the patio and the lawn is easy — and a perfect way to show off annuals during the warm months. For example, you can plant a kidney-shaped bed that curves around the sunny sides of the patio, full of colorful flowers that stay low enough so that the patio isn't visually cut off from the lawn area.

Arranging your annuals

If you plant them fairly thickly, water them well, and fertilize them every few weeks, the seven kinds of annuals in the garden plan shown in Figure 7-3 will provide color, fragrance, and pleasure from June until frost.

To re-create the plan shown in Figure 7-3 around your own patio, plant the annuals as follows:

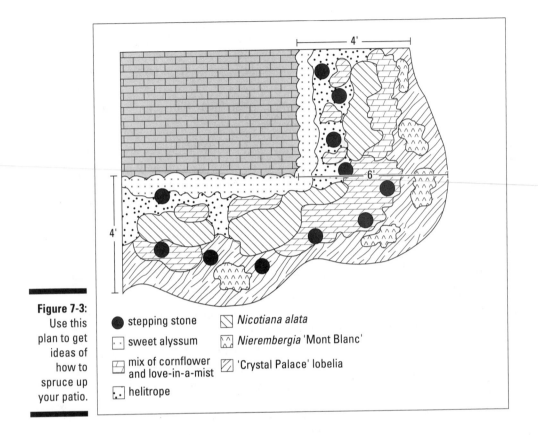

Figure 7-3:
Use this plan to get ideas of how to spruce up your patio.

● stepping stone   ◻ *Nicotiana alata*

⬚ sweet alyssum   ⬚ *Nierembergia* 'Mont Blanc'

⬚ mix of cornflower and love-in-a-mist   ⬚ 'Crystal Palace' lobelia

⬚ helitrope

✔ Because you want your bed to look nice from both the patio and from the lawn, plant the tallest flowers in the interior of the bed. Arrange two dozen white and red flowering tobacco *(Nicotiana alata)* about 4 to 6 inches apart in the center of the bed. Intersperse the two colors or plant them in color blocks, depending on the look you want to achieve.

✔ Surround the flowering tobacco with a wide ribbon of blue cornflower (also called bachelor's buttons), mixed with lacy love-in-a-mist *(Nigella),* to provide a variety of blues. Space seedlings of the cornflower and love-in-a-mist 4 to 6 inches apart.

✔ Along the side of the bed bordering the patio, plant wonderfully fragrant, dark purple heliotrope. The extra-deep purple adds richness to the main color scheme. Heliotrope plants sprawl widely (with handsome thick leaves), so plant them 12 inches apart in a wide swathe, leaving room at the edge of the bed for a trim of white alyssum.

✔ A border of white sweet alyssum *(Lobularia maritima)* edging the patio adds its own enticing fragrance and contrasts nicely with the dark heliotrope leaves. Space the alyssum 8 to 10 inches apart.

✔ On the lawn side of the bed, plant clusters of white cupflower (*Nierembergia* 'Mont Blanc'), an annual that grows about 7 inches tall and has small, deep green leaves and bright white flowers with yellow eyes. Plant several clumps of three cupflower plants, spacing each seedling 8 inches apart.

✔ Surround the cupflowers with an intensely blue edging of 'Crystal Palace' lobelia, spacing each seedling 6 inches apart.

If the bed is so large that you can't reach the middle to weed or water, create a meandering path of a few stepping stones through the bed so that you can reach interior plants when they need care.

Choosing your own annuals

When choosing your own annuals for a border around your sunny backyard patio, use the following criteria to limit your search:

✔ Choose annuals that flourish in the sun.

✔ Look for sturdy, stocky plants — anything too tall or leggy here will probably block the patio from the lawn or may be knocked down by a soccer ball or child chasing a Frisbee.

✔ Plant low, carpeting-type annuals for areas of the bed that get the most traffic. These annuals hold up better throughout a season of use.

✔ Because you likely use your patio from the first warm days of spring until after Labor Day, choose annuals with a long bloom season. Start with healthy transplants in nursery six-packs or 4-inch pots, both of which bloom more quickly than annuals started from seeds.

Because nurseries and garden centers can offer such an overwhelming number of plants to select from, you may want to narrow down the possibilities even more by picking a color scheme. If your house and patio are a neutral color and you have a big lawn, choose a combination of bright and lively colors that you enjoy, because this bed will be the main source of color for the outdoor living area. Or you may decide to plant a flower bed that adds to the festive feeling of a family Fourth of July party that you plan to celebrate on the adjoining patio. If so, choose a red, white, and blue color scheme, softened with plenty of green foliage.

Shady bed around a large tree

Trees are usually the largest and often the most distinctive element in a garden. One way to show them off is to plant a circular flower bed around their trunks. A mix of pastel colors looks great in the shade, particularly with the addition of plenty of white and an accent of green lawn. A nicely pruned specimen tree, encircled by a flower bed, can serve as the main element in creating a stunning front garden.

No matter how good such a garden may look in your mind's eye, make sure you realize that flowers may have difficulty thriving in the shade of the tree because they're competing with the tree roots for water. As you plan such a bed, select less-thirsty annuals that flower well in dappled shade.

The simple planting scheme shown in Figure 7-4 includes annuals that perform under those conditions and, at the same time, add a cool splash of color and a large dose of drama to any garden:

- ✔ In the closest circle surrounding the tree, plant a wide band of spider flowers *(Cleome)* in shades of pink and white. Reaching up to 4 feet high and forming a large clump, spider flower is a striking annual that reseeds easily. Plant eight to a dozen spider flowers, at least 12 to 18 inches apart.

- ✔ As a welcome contrast to the flamboyance of the spider flowers, plant the rest of the bed in variegated coleus hybrids — right out to the surrounding lawn. Choose one or perhaps two hybrids, such as Rainbow or Wizard Mix, that you find particularly pleasing. The large coleus leaves splashed with white and green form an exotic carpet in the shade of the tree. You may like a pale pink coleus to blend with the colors of the spider flower.

- ✔ If you feel the need for more flowers, plant the outer rim of the circle with a foot-wide trim of white or palest pink impatiens.

Figure 7-4:
Most annuals love the sun too much to stand being planted under the shade of a tree. But the flowers in this plan brighten up the shadiest of spots.

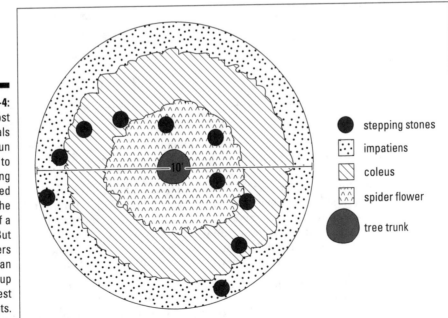

stepping stones

impatiens

coleus

spider flower

tree trunk

TIP

Make the bed large enough to really accent the tree and to allow for a pleasing complexity of plants. A circular bed 10 feet in diameter serves nicely in this situation.

Border for a formal walkway

Annuals can brighten up the skinniest of spaces — such as along a walk or driveway — providing bright color and a sweet scent you can appreciate as you pass by.

A 20-foot-long brick walkway between your entry gate and your front door may only have a 2-foot-wide border along each side. In such restricted spaces, consider a simple color scheme with a minimum of different kinds of plants. For example, you may choose to line a brick walkway leading to a traditional-style home with a classic color scheme of lemon yellow, pale blue, and white, as shown in Figure 7-5.

Figure 7-5:
The blue, white, and yellow flowers in this plan create a stately border for your formal walkway.

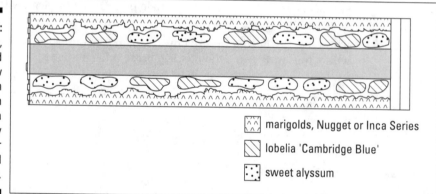

⌃⌃ marigolds, Nugget or Inca Series

▧ lobelia 'Cambridge Blue'

⋰⋱ sweet alyssum

Typically, formal walkways are in full sun. The annuals used in this plan thrive under such conditions:

- ✔ Along the edge farthest from the walkway, plant a row of yellow marigolds. Marigolds in the Nugget Series, with 2-inch fragrant flowers, grow a foot tall. A little taller is the Inca Strain, which grows to 18 inches in height and includes a true yellow variety, 'Inca Yellow'. Space these midsized marigolds about 12 to 15 inches apart and plant them at least two or three deep; they will form a solid ribbon of color by midsummer.

- ✔ In front of the marigolds, interplant lobelia and sweet alyssum to form a thick mat that spills over the brick walkway, softening its edges and blending the taller forms of the marigolds with the more horizontal planes of the walkway. 'Cambridge Blue' lobelia is a good choice because of its sky blue flowers and low-growth habit (to 5 inches). Plant clumps of five to seven lobelia plants (4 to 6 inches apart), interspersed with a slightly larger number of white sweet alyssum. Alyssum is the ideal edging plant, with its tiny white flowers, low-spreading habit, and sweet fragrance. Space alyssum 4 to 6 inches apart.

A month or two into the season, the flowers of the alyssum and lobelia will begin to sprawl and look a bit tired. Cut both back lightly, to help shape the plants and encourage another flush of bloom that will last until the first frost.

Border for an informal walkway

When you're edging a curved walkway made of irregularly shaped paving or stepping stones, you're likely to want different styles and colors of plants than you'd choose to line a straight brick pathway — unless you want the garden design police to come after you.

A curving walkway may lead from a front gate up to the broad front porch of a Dutch colonial or bungalow-style home. The most appropriate planting choices are a loose variety of annuals that duplicate the appearance of a cottage garden border — even within such a confined space as a 3-foot-wide walkway border. The plan in Figure 7-6 assumes that your front walkway is in full sun most of the day.

Figure 7-6: The soothing pastels and irregular plantings of this walkway border create a relaxing welcome for your guests.

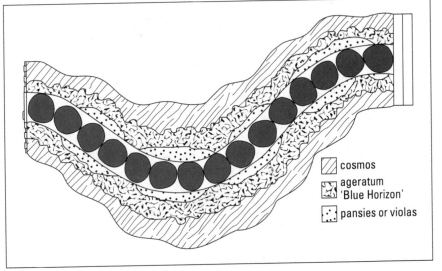

cosmos

ageratum 'Blue Horizon'

pansies or violas

✔ Cosmos are the ideal plants to form the backbone of a curved walkway planting. They are tall, frothy, and easy to grow and come in a variety of soft pastel colors. After the soil begins to warm up in the spring, set transplants 8 to 12 inches apart. Choose plants from the 'Sonata' series: These plants are short enough (about 24 inches tall) that they don't require staking and are available in a mix of white, pink, and lavender. The soft colors look cool even in the blinding sun of midday and form a welcoming, softly ferny walkway border.

Don't plant the cosmos in a line; instead, stagger them three to four plants deep, filling two-thirds of the border's width. Remember to cut off dying blooms frequently throughout the summer to keep your cosmos looking its best. (See Chapter 13 for the specifics of deadheading.)

✔ Loosely fill in the strip of border along the edge of the walkway with transplants of 'Blue Horizon' ageratum, which has fluffy lilac flower clusters, or the more diminutive white 'Summer Snow' or 'Pinkie' ageratum. These colors blend beautifully with the cosmos, and their flat flower heads and rounded leaves offer a pleasing contrast to the airy, fluffy quality of the taller plants. Space ageratum 6 to 8 inches apart.

✔ In the spaces left between the ageratum, and right up along the edge of the stepping stones or paving, plant little pansies or violas, in mixed shades of purple, pink, and white. Their colorful faces nod onto the stepping stones and peek out from beneath the foliage of the larger plants, completing the old-fashioned look of this walkway border planting.

Border for a modern-style walkway

Front pathways leading to ranch-style houses, or more modern-style houses, often stretch from the driveway along the front of the house to the porch and doorway, as shown in Figure 7-7. Such pathways are usually made of poured aggregate or smoothly laid stone.

The border running alongside this pathway is best planted in just one kind of flower. Your goal here is to completely fill the border. This simplicity of single-variety planting suits both the sleekness of the path and the style of house. Even within such a simple scheme, you have plenty of choices.

✔ If you prefer warm colors, plant the border thickly with gloriosa daisy (also called black-eyed Susans). These striking plants are both dramatic and familiar, with their daisylike flowers, sunflower colors, and chocolate brown centers. Choose the variety 'Marmalade' (also known as 'Orange Bedder') for its 4-inch flowers of brilliant gold; plants grow only 18 inches tall and do not need staking. For more variety of color, 'Rustic Dwarfs' (24 inches tall) have smaller flowers in a range of mahogany, brown, orange, and yellow.

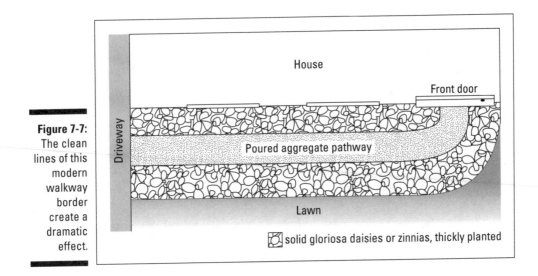

Figure 7-7:
The clean lines of this modern walkway border create a dramatic effect.

House

Front door

Driveway

Poured aggregate pathway

Lawn

solid gloriosa daisies or zinnias, thickly planted

> ✔ If you prefer a paler, softer look, white Mexican zinnias (*Zinnia angustifolia* 'White Star') give a long season of carefree bloom. Thriving in full sun, these white flowers with yellow centers grow to about 18 inches and spread easily to fill a 2- to 3-foot-wide border. The larger-flowered *Zinnia elegans* 'Dreamland Ivory' blooms from early summer to frost with creamy white flowers.

Plant the zinnias or gloriosa daisies to fill the entire border. Space transplants 6 to 8 inches apart, staggering them to avoid the look of soldiers lined up at attention. Keep the plants deadheaded and watered throughout the growing season, and they'll provide a dramatic, colorful walkway border that belies the simplicity and ease of your planting scheme.

Border against a backyard fence

Large borders consisting mainly of trees and shrubs usually form a backdrop in most gardens. You can call on annual flowers to fill in bare spaces between the permanent plants and to brighten the view across the garden.

A border that radiates outward from a fenced-corner and is curved in front (like the one shown in Figure 7-8) is likely to include a variety of shrubs and maybe a small tree or two. These permanent plantings — rhododendrons, daphne, andromeda, and maybe an ornamental cherry or crab apple tree — can put on a spring show and revert to their summer greenery by the time you're ready to plant annual flowers.

Annual plantings between the shady bays formed by the trees and shrubs, and along the front edge of the border, add color and interest to this border during the summer months, when you spend the most time in your backyard.

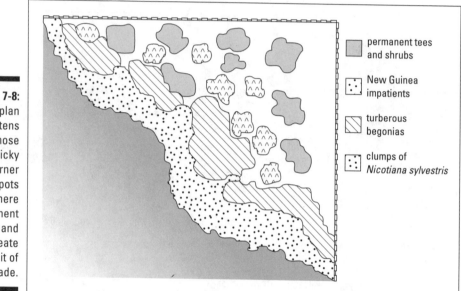

Figure 7-8:
This plan brightens up those tricky corner spots where permanent shrubs and trees create a bit of shade.

permanent tees and shrubs

New Guinea impatients

turberous begonias

clumps of *Nicotiana sylvestris*

✔ In the spaces between trees and shrubs, plant the statuesque, sweetly fragrant flowering tobacco *(Nicotiana sylvestris)*, which will flourish in the light shade cast by the larger plants. This plant is in itself an architectural statement, with its large leaves and 5-foot-tall stems topped with clusters of glowing white trumpet flowers. It brightens up the green of the permanent plantings, and its fragrance wafts to every corner of the garden. Space transplants 18 inches apart.

✔ Tuberous begonias (grown from tubers, and so not actually annuals) grow well in the shaded areas between shrubs and in front of the flowering tobacco *(Nicotiana)*. They add luminous color in beautiful pastel shades, and the flowers are so large that they stand out when viewed across an expanse of lawn. Given adequate water, tuberous begonias grow well between and underneath trees and shrubs — filling in all the empty spaces toward the front of the border with a tapestry of their glowing colors. Bedding begonias (also called wax begonias) work well in the same situation, but they are not as showy as the tuberous type.

✔ Along the very front edge of the border, which receives a bit more sun, continue the slightly-exotic look of the towering flowering tobacco by planting New Guinea impatiens. Choose 'Columbia' for its green and yellow variegated leaves and pale pink flowers, or 'Tonga' for its bronze and green leaves and bicolored lavender-and-deep-purple flowers.

Impatiens and begonias need frequent watering and fertilizing, which they amply repay with months of beautiful bloom.

More annuals to consider for your borders and beds

Tons of annuals perform beautifully in both beds and borders. You can use the following annuals to fill different roles, such as providing long bloom, pleasant fragrance, or bright foliage. Some are especially easy to grow or have the ability to flourish in less-than-ideal situations.

Easy annuals for beginning gardeners
Dwarf pink
Forget-me-not
Impatiens
Lobelia
Pansy
Salvia
Sweet pea

Annuals that reseed themselves
California poppy
Cornflower, or bachelor's button
Forget-me-not
Four o'clock
Nasturtium
Shirley poppy
Spider flower
Statice
Sweet William

Annuals with a long bloom season
Bedding begonia, or wax begonia
Cosmos
Flowering tobacco
Gazania
Globe amaranth
Impatiens
Lobelia
Marigold, African and French
Zinnia

Annuals with colorful foliage
Castor bean
Coleus
Flowering kale and flowering cabbage

Licorice plant
Love-lies-bleeding
Nasturtiums (with variegated leaves)
New Guinea impatiens
Snow-on-the-mountain

Drought-tolerant annuals
Baby's breath
Blanket flower
California poppy
Gloriosa daisy (black-eyed Susan)
Spider flower
Sweet alyssum
Strawflower
Verbena

Fragrant annuals
Flowering tobacco
Heliotrope
Mignonette
Pink
Stock
Sweet alyssum
Sweet pea
Sweet sultan

Annual vines
Black-eyed Susan vine *(Thunbergia)*
Canary creeper
Cup-and-saucer vine *(Cobaea scandens)*
Love-in-a-puff *(Cardiospermum halicacabum)*
Moonflower
Morning glory
Sweet pea

Part IV
Starting at Ground Level

The 5th Wave   By Rich Tennant

©RICHTENNANT

"Yes, they are prehistoric plants. I guess I should have checked the expiration date on the seed package."

In this part . . .

Y ou just brought home several flats of flowers from the nursery or received a shipment of seeds from a mail-order company. What do you do next? You need to give your seeds and seedlings a good start in life if you want them to grow up to be happy, healthy adult flowers. This part shows you how to prepare a good home for your young ones by digging and amending the soil and giving your seeds adequate light, warmth, and moisture. You'll also find suggestions for the best flowers to grow from seed and those that you're better off starting from seedlings.

Chapter 8

Preparing the Soil

● ●

In This Chapter

▶ Improving the earth

▶ Determining the type of soil in your yard

▶ Adding goodies to the soil

▶ Calculating your soil's pH

▶ Dealing with drainage

▶ Digging your flower bed

● ●

"*D*ig a ten-dollar hole for a ten-cent plant." That old gardening expression is a great way to look at soil preparation for annual flowers. You can spend loads of money on fine geraniums or the newest petunias, but they'll grow like ragamuffins if the soil is shabby. The opposite is also true: Plain-Jane annuals can blossom into real knockouts if you grow them in truly superior soil.

For living proof, conduct the following experiment. Pamper a salvia plant by growing it in a hole filled with high-quality potting soil and fertilizer, and plant another salvia in a quickly dug hole without potting soil or fertilizer. The salvia grown in the good soil will be taller and bushier and will produce a double quota of flowers. Annuals this healthy make you feel happy every time you look at them.

Taking Stock of What You've Got

Improving your soil depends on what type of soil you find when you start digging. Based on the size of its particles, soil falls into three basic categories: loam, clay, and sand. See Figure 8-1 for a visual comparison of the three types.

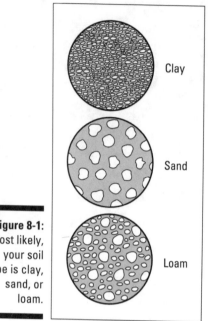

Clay

Sand

Loam

Loam is where the heart is

If your shovel turns up loose, crumbly mounds of earth that fall apart like moist chocolate cake, count yourself lucky. This dreamy type of soil is called *loam,* and it's what everybody else wishes for. Loam is made up of soil particles that are larger than clay particles, but smaller than grains of sand. Loam also may have small rocks and quite a bit of *organic matter* — the material left behind when leaves, plants, and other living things decay. Organic matter gives any soil a slightly spongy character, which helps it hold moisture well and which is wonderfully hospitable to delicate plant roots.

Some people are lucky and have gardens composed of mostly loam soil. If you're one of them, you can skip ahead to the next chapter. But if your soil is coarser or finer than loam, read on. This chapter is for you.

Can you come out and clay?

The best way to visualize clay soil is to think back to your childhood. Remember those little clay figures you made in grade school? Well, plenty of grown-up gardeners are still playing with clay — but not for the fun of it.

Clay soils are over-endowed with extremely fine soil particles. In fact, the particles are so fine that they pack together very tightly, making it hard for roots to penetrate and excluding the air and water that roots need to grow. Technically, any soil composed of more than 35 percent clay particles is a clay soil. But you don't need to take your soil to a laboratory; you know you have clay soil if it feels squishy in your hands when it's wet, or if it sticks to your shovel or to the bottom of your shoes. Try this three-step test to see if your soil is clay.

1. **Dig a spadeful of moist soil and then dump the soil out.**

   Does the mound keep its shape?

2. **Pick up a handful of moist soil and squeeze it together, trying to make it into a hard, little ball.**

   Does the soil retain a ball shape in your palm, or does it crumble apart when you open your hand?

3. **Mix enough soil and water together to make about a tablespoon of mud and rub the mixture between your fingers.**

   Does the mud feel slick and slimy between your fingers?

If your soil can do all these tricks, you can consider it clay.

Gardeners sometimes complain about clay because it dries out slowly, but souped-up, reconditioned clay (that is, clay that's been amended with plenty of organic matter) is great for flowers. Clay soil holds water and nutrients for a long time, because tiny clay particles stick together with very little breathing space between them. Add organic matter to expand the spaces between particles and to help your clay soil hold air, and you have a highly drought-tolerant soil that should serve you very well.

Sand now for something completely different . . .

Sandy soil is pretty obvious. It dries out quickly after it rains, and you can build dirty sand castles with it when it's wet. Rub it between your fingers, and it feels gritty and coarse. If you live in a high-rainfall area, sandy soil is good. Excess rain filters through sand quickly, and that's better than having the water puddling up around plant roots. Of course, as the rainwater flows through your flower bed and down to the groundwater below, so do plant nutrients. The same cure that helps clay soil — adding organic matter — also benefits sandy soil by helping it do a better job of holding onto water and nutrients. Mulches that stop moisture from evaporating from the soil's surface also are a big boon when your soil type is sand.

Building Better Soil

A few places on earth boast soil that is naturally dark, deep, and cushiony and weeds that bend to your will like well-trained dogs. Chances are good that these places are not in your yard — and they're definitely not in mine, either. Instead, you may have one little spot that's not riddled with tree roots or covered with concrete (although it may feel like concrete when you try to stick a shovel in it). Or maybe you moved into a new house whose yard has no topsoil.

The underground status of your chosen site can have any number of problems, but fortunately, you can take steps to make the soil better. And if you really want to, you can always abandon the idea of digging a proper in-ground bed and, instead, grow your annuals in containers or raised beds that you fill with exactly the kind of soil you want.

The soil amendments discussed in this section can greatly improve the texture of your soil, but except for composted manure, they're not great sources of plant nutrients. To provide actual food for your plants, you need to conclude your soil preparation by adding fertilizer to the bed, as described in Chapter 12.

Giving your soil some breathing room

One of the main deficiencies in soil is free: air! You can add air by cultivating the soil, something that's easy to say but hard to do, unless you have a rotary tiller. *Cultivating* is the process of turning over and breaking up the soil — with a shovel, digging fork, or rotary tiller — and then chopping at it with a rake or pronged hoe until the big clods of dirt break into little clods. The next step is gathering up the weeds, rocks, and tree roots that your digging turned up. Finally, you repeat the whole process.

The purpose of all this work is to open up billions and billions of tiny air pockets in the soil. If you don't squeeze the air out again by walking over the bed, these air pockets become little holding tanks for soil moisture and also make cushy surroundings for plant roots.

You can get a lot more air into the soil if you cultivate it when it is reasonably dry. (See the section "Making the Bed" later in this chapter.) Wet soil tends to stick together in globs, and the globs get harder and stickier the more you try to dig. Another drawback of wet soil is that mixing organic matter, fertilizer, and other soil amendments into very wet soil is almost impossible. Try to wait until the soil dries a bit. If your soil tends to be wet and clammy in the spring when you're ready to plant annual flowers, you can avoid the frustration of working with wet soil by preparing your beds in the fall, when dry conditions often prevail. Doing the heavy-lifting of soil preparation in the fall means all the amendments have plenty of time to work their way into the minute recesses of the soil. Come spring, all you need do is a bit of cleanup and you're ready to plant.

Going organic

Transforming plain soil into premium-quality stuff that supports spectacular annuals is usually a simple matter of adding organic matter and fertilizer as you dig and cultivate your bed. For most people, this task involves giving their shock absorbers a good workout as they cart a trunkful of compost or peat moss home from the garden center or discount store. Many types of organic matter are available in 20- to 40-pound bags at very reasonable prices, and bagged soil amendments are the way to go, unless you've got such big plans that you're better off buying by the truckload.

Garden centers sell a wide range of products that qualify as *organic matter* — a substance that is, or was, alive. For example, anything labeled as 100 percent compost is usually a good bet. Many organic amendments are by-products of the forestry industry, such as wood chips and bark. When you buy wood by-products, look for the words "nitrified" and "composted" on the bag. These are your clues that the contents are ready to go to work in your soil by delivering their many benefits.

Compost

When different kinds of dead plant material are piled together, dampened, and stirred or turned every week or so to keep air in the mixture, they become compost after a month (or two or three). Products labeled as compost can be made from all sorts of stuff, but they usually are created by enterprising people who have tapped into nature's wastebasket. Fallen leaves, shredded Christmas trees, and wood chips left from tree trimming crews often find their way to compost manufacturing facilities. Sawdust from lumber mills, peanut hulls from peanut processing plants, and hundreds of other agricultural by-products also are turned into compost.

Unfortunately, you don't know exactly what you are getting in commercial compost unless you open a bag and feel around in there with your hands. You can expect to find little bits of sticks and other recognizable things in a bag of compost, but judge quality mainly by the texture of the material, which should be soft and springy. If you plan to buy big quantities of compost, compare products packaged by different companies to find the best texture. A 3-inch layer of packaged compost, worked into the soil, is a liberal helping that should give instant results. To estimate how much you need, figure that a 40-pound bag (that may actually weigh more or less than that weight, depending on how it's been stored) covers a square yard of bed space.

Of course, the smartest thing to do is make your own compost. Composting your yard trimmings and kitchen scraps is economical because you get for free something you would otherwise have to purchase. It's also environmentally friendly, because it keeps your leftovers out of landfills. Many people, including those working at your local nursery, can get you started making compost. Or check out *Gardening For Dummies,* by Michael MacCaskey and the Editors of the National Gardening Association. It has a whole chapter about composting.

Composted manure

Rotted manure doesn't sound as good as composted manure, does it? But they both mean the same thing — the stuff that you find in bags labeled manure. Composting is almost always necessary to deodorize manure, so you need not worry about stinking up your yard by using packaged manure products. In addition to conditioning soil by improving its texture, composted manure usually contains respectable amounts of nitrogen and other important plant nutrients. The percentage of nutrients varies with the type of manure. Composted chicken manure is very potent, whereas steer manure is comparatively lightweight. Packaged sheep manure is becoming quite popular among some gardeners for its relative ease and pleasantness of use (not to mention increasing availability), and you may even encounter some truly exotic renditions based on the waste from zoo animals, bats, and even crickets.

The amount of manure to use depends on the type of manure and your soil type. Sandy soil can use twice as much manure as clay, but you don't want to overdose either way. With bulky manure from large animals (cows, horses, goats, sheep, and elephants), start with a 1-inch layer, or about 40 pounds per 3 square yards. Follow package application rates when using stronger manure, such as that from rabbits, chickens, and birds.

Humus

Bags labeled *humus* are the wild cards of the soil amendment world. Anything that qualifies as organic matter for soil, or any soil/organic-matter mixture, can be considered humus. Unlike compost, which is supposed to be cultured under controlled conditions, humus comes from more humble beginnings. For example, it may be 2-year-old sawdust and wood chips from a lumber mill mixed with rotten leaves and dark topsoil. Or it may be rotten hay mixed with soil and sand. You just don't know what you'll get until you buy a bag and open it up. If the humus has a loose, spongy texture and dark color, and you like the way it feels and smells, go for it. For a 2- to 3-inch layer, 40 pounds per 2 square yards is a good rough estimate of the quantity to use.

Topsoil

Breaking into bags of topsoil to see what's inside is always interesting. Sometimes, the content is exactly what you may find in bags of humus or compost, and other times it may look more like unbelievably black soil.

Topsoil is almost always cheap. You can use bagged topsoil as a soil amendment, or you can use so much of it that your flower bed is filled with mostly imported topsoil and only a little of the native stuff.

If your soil basically disgusts you, bring home several bags of topsoil, along with humus, manure, and compost. Use the topsoil as the main ingredient for your witch's brew of new soil. Of course, if you want to use primarily topsoil, you must either plant a raised bed or dig out the soil you don't like and dump it somewhere else.

Peat moss

Peat moss is a very spongy brown material taken from peat bogs in Canada, Michigan, and a few other places. The popularity of peat moss, an old standby, has passed its peak now that so many folks have become concerned that gardeners are using up peat moss much faster than Mother Nature can make it.

Peat moss is superb at absorbing and holding huge amounts of water, while frustrating soilborne fungi that can cause plant diseases. Unfortunately, peat bogs take about a thousand years to regenerate after they are harvested. Because of this environmental concern, you may want to limit your use of peat moss to situations where it's most valuable, such as creating special soil mixtures for container-grown plants or for planting shrubs that really love it, such as azaleas and rhododendrons.

Before buying peat moss, check to see if it comes from a source that's managed responsibly and in a sustainable manner. For information about peat moss harvesting and the environment, write to the Canadian Sphagnum Peat Moss Association, 4 Wycliff Place, St. Albert, AB Canada T8N 3Y8.

Checking your soil's pH

When you're out buying fertilizer, you may as well tap into the local expertise to see if you also need some lime. _Lime_ is finely ground limestone, and it's used to raise the pH (acidity or alkalinity) of naturally acidic soil to make it "near neutral." Plants don't like strongly acidic soil because it hampers their ability to take up nutrients and feed themselves. Many soils in areas that were heavily wooded before civilization moved in are naturally acidic. If a nursery professional tells you that everybody in your area has acidic soil that needs added lime, you should do it, too. But if you suspect that people who know more about bubble gum than soil are staffing your garden center, you can buy a simple pH test kit and check your soil yourself. This test takes less than five minutes and is sort of fun.

If you live in the southwestern U.S., you may find out that adding lime is the worst thing you can do for your soil, because you live in an area where the soil pH tends to be alkaline (a high pH rather than a low one). Strongly alkaline soil is difficult for plants, too, and can be corrected by adding small amounts of garden sulfur to the soil or by mixing in acidic soil amendments, such as composted leaves, rotted sawdust, or peat moss. If you go the sulfur route, only buy a little. About 2 pounds is all you should need to lower the pH in 50 square feet of soil.

For growing annuals, your pH need not be exactly on target, but it should not be extreme, either. Soil pH is rated numerically on a scale from 0 to 14. Most annuals grow just fine if the pH is between 5.8 and 7.5. Absolute neutral is 7.0.

Dealing with Delinquent Drainage

If you go to dig your flower bed and find that the soil there is damp and swampy even though the rest of the yard seems dry, you may have a drainage problem. Think back to the last time you witnessed a heavy rain. Did that spot still have a puddle several hours later? If so, the verdict has to be *delinquent drainage,* which means that the soil holds too much water for too long a time.

Sometimes, you can correct a drainage problem by aerating the soil and adding organic matter, but drainage problems usually are caused by factors other than poor-quality soil. For example, an underground spring or other moving water may be beneath the spot, or maybe it's the lowest elevation around, so rainwater is always going to pool up there.

Whatever the cause, you probably should look elsewhere for a place to grow flowers. Bad drainage means that the roots of any plants that do grow there are deprived of air and exposed to excessive amounts of water, instead. Because very few annual flowers are willing to put up with this kind of abuse, they develop root rot in wet soils. One notable exception you might try, if you have wet soil, is the cardinal flower *(Lobelia cardinalis)*. It grows naturally in and around bogs and similar wet spots and requires constant moisture.

The best solution for wet or poorly drained soil is a raised bed. Raised beds can be as simple as mounds of soil that are 6 to 8 inches above the surrounding soil level, or they can be more complex affairs, utilizing boards, stones, or similar materials to make a soil-retaining border. (See the section "Bailing out with raised beds" later in this chapter.)

Making the Bed

Before you dig in to your gardening project, get all your materials together — soil amendments, fertilizer, digging tools (shovel, digging fork, and a dirt rake or hoe), work gloves, a garden hose, and perhaps a wheel-barrow or garden cart, if you plan to do some really serious digging.

1. **Mark off the area you want to dig, for example by using sticks and twine, as shown in Figure 8-2.**

Figure 8-2:
Marking off the area you plan to make into a flower bed keeps you from getting carried away with your digging.

2. **For your first pass, start at the edge of your bed with a flat-tipped spade and skim an inch or two below the surface, stripping off the sod as shown in Figure 8-3.**

Figure 8-3:
Skimming off the sod and setting it aside helps keep grass and weed roots from resprouting and taking over your garden.

3. After removing the sod, use a shovel or digging fork to turn the soil, as shown in Figure 8-4.

Lift up a spadeful of soil and drop it back onto the ground upside-down. Pull out weeds that come loose and toss them into a pile. When you've turned up the entire bed, take a break — you earned it.

Figure 8-4:
Breaking up clods of dirt helps to aerate the soil and make a soft base in which young flower roots can grow.

At this point, if you're unlucky, you may discover that just a few inches below the surface, your soil changes color and becomes very hard. This means that you are working in a site that has only a thin layer of topsoil. That hard stuff is called *hardpan*. See the sidebar, "Double-digging away your hardpan blues," later in this chapter, for advice on handling this situation.

4. Next, using a hoe or rake, hack away at the big clods to break them up, pulling out weeds as you work.

5. Pour on your soil amendments and fertilizer.

6. Dig through the bed again with your shovel, working in the amendments and fertilizer.

The job of digging the bed is much easier the second time!

7. Rake over the bed vigorously with a stiff-tined rake to break up clods.

Your amended, fertilized, cushion-soft flower bed now needs only a bit of polishing before you start planting. Rake the bed so that it has a level top and slightly sloped sides (as shown in Figure 8-5). If you like, you can make a little lip around the top inside edge to help hold water, at least until the lip washes away.

TIP

If you have a dog or cat who has been watching from the sidelines and is poised to continue cultivating your bed as soon as you go inside to rest, sprinkle the surface lightly with cayenne pepper. Martha and Marlon will certainly sniff before they start digging, and one sniff is all it should take to make them change their minds.

Figure 8-5:
Leveling
your flower
bed not only
makes it
look pretty,
but also
helps water
to get
evenly
distributed.

WARNING!

So you think working with a garden spade or digging fork is something you were born knowing how to do? Think again. As with most other types of strenuous work, going about this job the wrong way can result in injury. Keep the following safety tips in mind:

✔ Wear shoes with hard bottoms when digging. Sandals and flip-flops get slippery, which can lead to a nasty gash in the bottom of your foot.

✔ After you fill your shovel with soil and are ready to lift it, choke up on the handle and *bend your knees*. This way, you are lifting with your legs and shoulders more than with your back.

✔ Instead of working ankle-deep in already cultivated soil, stand on a small board or piece of scrap plywood as you finish the job. Besides giving you more balance and control, the board limits compaction of the soil that you're trying to make uncompacted. (It also keeps your shoes a bit cleaner!)

Time for a tiller

Digging a small flower bed is a good exercise program, but preparing a large one by hand can be torture without the help of a tiller. If your bed is larger than 40 square feet (say 10 feet long and 4 feet wide), consider renting, borrowing, or buying a tiller. Rear-tined tillers like the one shown in Figure 8-6 are generally easier to handle than those with digging tines on the front, but any tiller can really wear you down when you need to jockey it around corners and turns. Tillers work best when they're going in a straight line.

Figure 8-6:
Tillers make short work of digging up even the hardest ground.

Another option is to have someone else till your flower bed for you. No matter where you live, someone in your community is sure to sell tilling services in the spring. Look in the classified ads in the newspaper or call local garden centers to find this most valuable resource person. Before the tiller arrives to churn up your soil, have all the soil amendments on hand that you intend to use. After you or the person you hire has tilled the area and raked out the weeds, apply your soil amendments and fertilizer and till the area again.

TIP

Double-digging away your hardpan blues

A hard layer of subsoil is a very bad thing if it is within 10 inches of the surface. Besides being so stiff that plant roots cannot penetrate it, subsoil may block the flow of water through the soil and create a drainage problem.

The best remedy for the problem of hard subsoil is called *double-digging,* but you can call it the French Intensive Method if you want to impress people. (Only the French would develop such murderously intensive work for Americans!) To do it, put your topsoil in a wheelbarrow or garden cart or pile it up just outside the edge of your bed. With all the energy you can muster, dig up the subsoil, too. If

it is tight clay subsoil, you may need a *pick* (the tool that miners use) to break it up. Remove the subsoil to the other side of your bed and keep working until you have a huge hole at least 15 inches deep. Now put your topsoil into the bottom of the bed and layer in huge helpings of soil amendments as you return the subsoil to the topmost layer. By the time you're finished, you will have incorporated so much air and organic matter into the soil that the bed will be raised up several inches higher than the surrounding ground. You also have permanently improved the site and may never need to double-dig it again.

Bailing out with raised beds

If growing flowers sounds like more work than you expected, don't switch to raising tropical fish as a hobby just yet. First, bear in mind that you have to do the really hard digging, or *sodbusting,* only once. In subsequent seasons, as you work your soil and add more organic matter, your garden soil will become so well behaved that digging it will be a pleasure.

Still can't talk you into digging? How about planting your annuals in containers (see Chapter 16) or in enclosed beds on top of the ground? Raised beds are a little harder to set up than containers, but they are a fine solution to hardpan and other situations where working the soil is not a viable option.

If you plan to build a raised bed and fill it with bagged soil, plan to make it about 10 inches high. You can enclose your bed with concrete blocks, landscaping timbers, or nifty new boards made from recycled plastic, which fit together via plastic corner brackets. Plastic raised-bed kits come in several shapes and sizes and can be taken apart and moved in only a few minutes. Figure 8-7 shows some examples of raised-bed options.

Whatever material you use to enclose your raised bed, you need enough topsoil (or mixture of soil, compost, humus, and manure) to reach to the top of the frame. Don't worry if the soil heaps up over the edge, because the first time you water, the soil will begin to settle. After a week or so, the soil level will probably be 2 inches below the rim — just the right margin for adding a little mulch when the time comes.

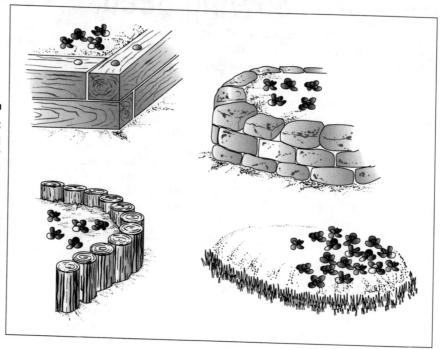

Figure 8-7:
Raising your flower bed enables you to use exactly the soil you want, no matter what kind of ground your yard is blessed with.

Chapter 9

Sowing Seeds

In This Chapter

▶ Discovering what seeds really want

▶ Shopping for seeds

▶ Starting seeds indoors

▶ Sowing seeds directly in the ground

▶ Two dozen easygoing annuals to grow from seeds

*P*lanting a seed and nurturing it into a beautiful flower is an experience that satisfies the primitive, soulful side of gardeners' personalities. You can easily grow many annual flowers by planting their seeds in containers or directly into the ground.

Starting with seeds rather than plants can save you a lot of money. If you grow annuals from seeds, you don't have to buy 12 six-packs in mixed colors in order to get only the red zinnias or purple salvias that you need. But the most compelling reason to grow at least some of your annuals from seeds is the opportunity to have unusual flowers that are impossible to find as bedding plants. Peruse a few seed catalogs, and you quickly see that the variety of choices in terms of color, size, and species is nothing short of mind-boggling when you start with seeds.

Flower seeds come in all shapes and sizes, from begonia seeds the size of salt grains to pea-sized nasturtium and sweet-pea seeds. Larger seeds tend to be easier to handle, and they also grow into comparatively large seedlings. But don't be afraid to try growing small seeds. Just be forewarned that tiny seeds take longer to grow into big plants.

Smart Seed Shopping

In the spring, every garden center and home-supply store puts big seed racks where you can't help but run into them on your way to the checkout line. The seeds you find there are usually good-quality seeds. However, just to be sure, look beyond the beautiful picture on the front of the packet to find the following information (also shown in Figure 9-1):

- Species and/or variety name
- Mature height
- Packing date (don't buy seeds that are more than a year old)
- Special planting instructions

Figure 9-1: Look for the words "packed for . . ." followed by the year of the next gardening season. That way, you'll know you're starting with fresh seeds.

Lobelia $1.39
'Crystal Palace'
Lobelia erinus

Annual
Blooms spring to fall frost
Spreads 12"
2" tall
Sun
Low growing ground cover with intensely rich, deep blue flowers, massed over the top of the plant

net weight
125 mg

To open: Peel this flap back. Peel back side and bottom flaps to find additional information on inside packet!

'Crystal Palace' Lobelia catches your eye with dazzling, vibrant, dark blue flowers.

When to plant outside: Spring after average last day of frost. In mild winter areas, sow late summer for winter color.

When to start inside: 8-10 weeks before last frost. This is the recommended method since Lobelia takes a long time to germinate.

Important! Read inside of packet for more specific information. See top flap for directions.

Packed for 1998

7 36210 00011 9

Some seed packets also include the expected *germination rate,* which is the percentage of seeds in the packet that you can realistically expect to sprout. The rate always should be above 65 percent. If no germination rate is given, you can usually assume that the seeds meet or exceed the germination standards for that species. All the reputable seed companies trash bad seeds rather than sell them. It should ease your mind to know that the seed business is tremendously competitive and that seed quality tends to be very high.

Watch out. Some retailers sell seeds left over from the previous year. Although many flower seeds do remain viable for several years when stored in a cool, dry place, a retailer who sells old seeds is obviously trying to cut corners. For all you know, they kept those seeds in a hot, stuffy warehouse and not one of them is likely to sprout.

TIP

Seeds by mail

Mail-order seed companies are able to maintain huge selections, and they also tend to be meticulous about storage conditions. Any seed company that does not please its customers with high-quality seeds quickly goes out of business. However, because mail-order companies display and guarantee their seeds in their catalogs, the actual packets often give little information beyond variety name and the approximate number of seeds inside.

As soon as your mail-order seeds arrive, read over the packets and write the year on the packet if it is not already stamped there. Noting the date on the packet will remind you not to plant those sweet peas if you forget about them and don't find them until you're cleaning out your desk two years later.

The Needs of Seeds

The process of growing flowers from seeds is pretty straightforward. You plant them in a soft soil, add water, and keep them constantly moist until they sprout. The moisture triggers the germination process and softens the hard outer covering of the seed, called the *seed coat,* so that the sprout can emerge. How quickly this miracle takes place also depends on the temperature. For most seeds, the warm side of 70°F (21°C) is just dandy. From the moment the sprout breaks through the soil, seedlings need light.

Starting seeds indoors

If you plant your annuals too early in the spring, they may be damaged by frost. On the other hand, however, annuals like to do most of their growing before the weather turns too hot. Starting seeds indoors is the perfect solution to the weather challenges facing annuals. Even when the weather is too cold to plant flowers outside, you can start seeds indoors in late winter and early spring. Giving your plants a head start indoors also allows you to control the temperature and moisture so that seeds have no excuses not to sprout. Plus, having little green things growing under lights is a reason to start celebrating spring while winter still rages.

Every seed catalog sells equipment such as various trays, domes, and other paraphernalia for starting seeds. These set-ups help take some of the guesswork out of seed starting, but they aren't required equipment. All you really need are the following:

- **Small containers (with drainage holes in the bottoms) for holding your seed-starting medium:** Many gardeners start seeds in plastic cell-packs saved from the previous year's bedding plants. You can also use bathroom-sized paper cups or 2-inch-deep aluminum pans with little holes punched in the bottom. Forget about using pie pans or egg cartons because they hold so little soil that they dry out within hours and are so shallow that roots hit bottom within a day.

- **A way to keep the containers constantly moist:** To keep your containers consistently moist for the best germination, place them in a larger container, such as a plastic tray, filled with 1 to 2 inches of water. Through the drainage holes, the soil naturally soaks up as much moisture as the plants need. For small seeds that are planted right on the surface of the soil, such as impatiens, mist the top of the container daily with a handheld plant mister.

- **A bag or two of seed-starting soil-less mix:** This mix is usually a finely ground blend of peat moss and vermiculite. It contains no real soil or plant nutrients, but also is totally free of fungi that can cause young seedlings to rot.

- **A source of light:** Although it's possible to grow seedlings in a sunny window, you get better results if you place them under lights. Use fluorescent lights or special *grow lights*. Don't use incandescent light bulbs; they give off too much heat.

To plant seeds in containers, follow these steps (illustrated in Figure 9-2):

1. **Fill containers to the top with seed-starting mix and then level the top by sweeping across it with your hand or a table knife.**

2. **Use your fingertip or a pencil to make small depressions for seeds.**

   The depth of the holes doesn't have to be exact, but try to plant the seeds about three times as deep as the seeds are wide.

3. **Drop one or two seeds into each depression and cover them with pinches of seed-starting mixture.**

   Seed-starting mixture is a lightweight soil mix, usually containing peat moss, vermiculite, and perlite. What makes it special for seeds is the particle size: Compared to potting soils, the particles in a seed-starting mix are smaller. Small particles make controlling sowing depth more precise. Look for seed-starting mixes in garden centers.

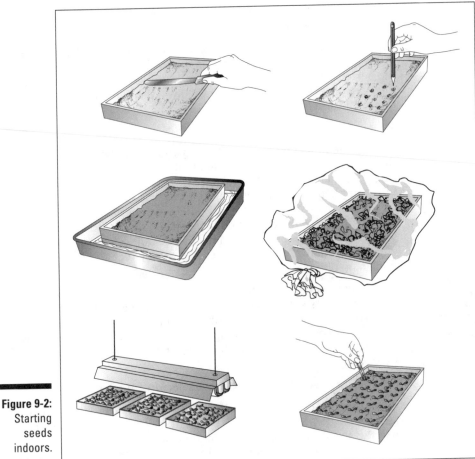

Figure 9-2:
Starting
seeds
indoors.

4. **Dampen the soil thoroughly.**

   To keep from flooding out the planted seeds, use a pump spray bottle to mist the containers repeatedly, or place the containers in small pans or trays and fill the pans with 1 inch of water. After about an hour, the containers will absorb the water from the pans.

5. **To keep the surface of the planted containers from drying out, cover them lightly with plastic wrap or enclose the whole tray in a large plastic bag.**

6. **Keep the containers in a warm place and start checking for germination after three days.**

   Typical warm locations around the home include on top of the refrigerator, near a baseboard heater, or near the furnace in the basement.

7. As soon as the first sprouts emerge, remove the plastic and move the seedlings to good light.

Unless you have a greenhouse, it's best to use some sort of supplemental light to grow stocky seedlings indoors. Tabletop fluorescent fixtures are perfect for this job. Arrange your indoor garden so that the seedlings are always about 2 inches away from the light, and leave the lights on for 12 to 16 hours per day.

8. Thin out the seedlings.

Most of the time, you end up with way too many seedlings. If left alone, the plants will become so crowded that they won't grow well. You must thin your plants so that they are spaced at least 2 inches apart in all directions. Do this by pulling out the weakest sprouts with your fingers or tweezers. It's painful to pull up your precious seedlings, but the remaining ones will grow much better if you do! Try to thin your seedlings when they're just an inch or two tall, before the roots become entangled. That way, you'll be less likely to disturb the roots of the remaining plants.

To thin your seedlings without wasting any plants, dump out the container on its side, tap the mass of roots to make them fall apart, and gingerly transplant the tiny seedlings to individual containers filled with sterile soil-less mix. As long as you handle young seedlings by their leaves, and never, ever touch their tender stems, they transplant very easily.

9. Fertilize the seedlings about two weeks after they emerge.

When the time comes to treat the seedlings to their first meal, use a fertilizer that can be diluted with water (see Chapter 12), and mix it at half the strength recommended on the package. Fertilize seedlings about once a week, or every other time you water them.

10. Prepare your seedlings for outdoor life.

After four to six weeks, your seedlings will be big enough to move outside. To help the seedlings get ready for the big move, spend a little time letting them gradually become accustomed to outdoor sun and wind. In gardening books, this process of gradually acclimating seedlings is called *hardening off*. Whatever you call it, the process is important. Set seedlings outside for a few hours the first day and then gradually increase their time outdoors over a one- to two-week period, until they're staying out all day. Be prepared to bring the seedlings indoors if the temperature drops below 50°F (10°C). Eventually you can leave the seedlings out for several days and nights before you transplant them to flower beds or outdoor containers.

A dozen easy annuals to start indoors

You can start any annual from seed if you really want to, but some annuals are especially satisfying to grow from seed. Here are a dozen easy annuals well worth the trouble of planting early indoors.

- **Sweet alyssum** *(Lobularia maritima):* This dainty little flower can edge beds or serve as a companion plant in containers and window boxes. You want a lot of alyssum if you have any at all, so try planting the seeds in pans or trays. Thin to only 1 inch apart. When transplanting day comes, cut the mass of seedlings into brownie-sized squares and transplant the little clumps without separating the plants.

- **Bells of Ireland** *(Moluccella laevis):* Impress your friends and family with this unusual annual. The large seeds are a cinch to grow, and the plants develop tall spires studded with little green seashell-like structures, which serve as bracts for tiny fragrant flowers.

- **Calendula, or pot marigold** *(Calendula officinalis):* The earlier you get them started, the sooner you can enjoy these pert yellow and orange flowers. Calendulas love cool weather and make great companions for poppies and bachelor's buttons.

- **Celosia:** Celosias need lots of warmth, so wait until you can smell spring in the air before you start the seeds. The plume types are lovely additions to any garden, but some people really like the cockscomb types, with rippled flower heads that look like colorful little brains.

- **Cornflower, or bachelor's button** *(Centaurea cyanus):* Incredibly easy to grow, these guys are hardy enough for you to start moving them out before the last frost. Chances are good that you will have to start the seedlings only one time in your life, because they reseed themselves with

great enthusiasm. The volunteer seedlings are easy to dig and transplant.

- **Globe amaranth** *(Gomphrena):* Gardeners and flower arrangers alike love globe amaranth, with its striking spherical blooms that look great as fresh cut flowers or in dried arrangements. The seedlings need less moisture than some other annuals, but give them plenty of light. Set out these plants late in the spring, after the last frost is long gone.

- **Nicotiana, or flowering tobacco** *(Nicotiana alata):* This old-fashioned strain of flowering tobacco produces fragrant white flowers on tall spikes. Because this flower is in high demand for partially shady spots, the seedlings are often impossible to find; you must grow them yourself or miss all the fun.

- **Salvia:** Every garden center sells salvias as bedding plants, but you can experiment with unique colors by growing the plants from seeds. Offbeat annual species of salvia (and closely related sages) also make enjoyable gardening adventures.

- **Statice** *(Limonium sinuatum):* If you like bringing bouquets indoors to enjoy, statice will become one of your prime picks. The seeds are not difficult to handle, and strains are available in several soft single colors, including purple, rose, and yellow.

- **Strawflower** *(Helichrysum):* The stiff, luminous petals of strawflowers are actually papery bracts. In the garden, the blooms close during rain and open to the sun. Harvested and dried, they last forever. Be sure to thin seedlings to one per 2-inch seedling pot.

(continued)

(continued)

✔ **Tithonia, or torch flower:** An old-time favorite, tall tithonia lights up the background of a sunny garden. Start seeds in late spring and use the plants as replacements for other flowers that melt out in hot weather. This one loves heat.

✔ **Zinnia:** The main reason to start your own zinnias is color choice. Planting from seed is simply the only way to get a large number of plants in the same color. Try going all lemon yellow or all soft pink. Where summers last a long time, start a second crop in July to set out in August.

Sowing seeds directly in the ground

All seedlings grow roots as rapidly as they grow leaves, and some annual flowers put an awesome amount of energy into roots right off the bat. Flowers that spend their infancy developing long, brittle, carrotlike taproots often are difficult or impossible to transplant, so they are best sown right where they will grow. This fact explains why you never see larkspur or Shirley poppies sold as bedding plants, and it's one more reason to find out how to grow annuals from seeds.

When everything goes exactly right, *direct-sowing* (which means sowing seeds right where you want them to grow) is great. Unfortunately, a lot of things can go wrong. Maybe the sun will be so strong the day the seeds are germinating that they dry out and die, and only one out of ten flowers comes up. Or maybe so many weed seeds germinate that you can't tell the flowers from the weeds, and you end up pulling out everything and studding the bed with purchased petunias. Another nightmarish scenario goes like this: You prepare the bed, plant the seeds, and a heavy rain comes along and washes the seeds all over the place.

Direct-sowing doesn't have to be a disaster, however. You can make it a pleasant and rewarding experience if you follow these guidelines:

✔ Give special attention to plants that *must* be grown from direct-seeding, such as poppies and larkspur.

✔ Plant seeds of plants that you will recognize or that have a distinctive appearance. For example, nasturtium leaves look like no other plants (see the sidebar "A dozen easy annuals to direct-sow," later in this chapter), and mistaking a bean or pea seedling for a weed is hard to do.

✔ Soak large seeds in water overnight before planting them. This step really speeds things along when you're sowing hard seeds such as sweet peas and morning glories.

- Sow seeds in the right season. As I explain in the sidebar "A dozen easy annuals to direct-sow," some direct-seeded annuals are best planted in the fall or first thing in the spring; others do best when they're planted in warmer soil in early summer.

- Prepare the planting bed thoroughly, as I describe in Chapter 8. Take extra care to rake smoothly — lumpy soil and clods interfere with germination.

- Sow seeds in a definite pattern. This way, when you see a pattern of little sprouts in your soil, you'll know that those growths are flowers and not weeds. Some seeds are best sown in rows, but others can be scattered.

Sow large seeds by hand directly where you want them to grow. If seeds are too small for your fingers, gently tap them out directly from the packet, as shown in Figure 9-3. Mix seeds with sand to help you broadcast them more evenly, if you like.

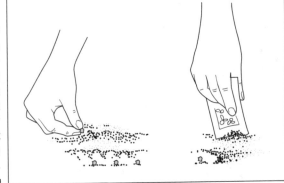

Figure 9-3: Plant larger seeds by hand but shake out smaller seeds right from the packet.

- Pay attention to the seed-packet directions for best planting depth. For many seeds, a light layer of sifted compost is sufficient coverage. At other times, you simply press seeds into the soil with the back of a hoe.

- Water gently and with care. Use a misting nozzle on your garden hose, or a watering can with a perforated spout that creates a gentle sprinkle. Keep the soil damp until seeds sprout. (Chapter 11 discusses the different devices available for watering.)

- Cover seeds with something for a few days after you plant them. An old blanket makes an excellent seed cover, and cardboard boxes are also good. The coverings keep the soil constantly moist while the seeds are germinating. Remove the covering as soon as you see the first sprout.

✔ Weed early and often. If you have trouble weeding around small seedlings, use a table fork to gently pull out awkward little weeds.

✔ After seedlings develop two sets of true leaves, thin out those that stand too close together. Gently pull extra seedlings without disturbing the ones you want to keep, or simply snip them off with scissors just above the soil line, as shown in Figure 9-4.

Figure 9-4:
Thin directly-sown seedlings just as you do indoors: Very carefully pluck them out with your fingers or tweezers, or clip them with small scissors.

A dozen easy annuals to direct-sow

In the age of bedding plants, sowing seeds in carefully prepared beds is a dying art. Grow some of the flowers in the following list to help preserve this ancient gardening skill — and just for fun. It's easier than you think.

✔ **Cosmos:** The feathery foliage of cosmos is easy to identify. Sow plenty of seeds in early spring to be sure of getting a good showing. The yellow or orange flowered species often does best in hot-summer areas.

✔ **Hyacinth bean** *(Dolichos lablab):* This big purple bean looks like an ornamental pole lima. Soak the big seeds before planting them. When the plants are a few inches tall, mulch around them to keep down weeds, and train the vines to climb up the nearest fence or arbor.

- **Larkspur** *(Consolida ambigua):* Impossible to transplant, super-hardy larkspur can be planted in the fall in most areas. The seedlings stand as feathery green mounds through the winter and grow tall first thing in the spring. In very cold areas, sow over melting snow in early spring.

- **Marigold** *(Tagetes):* Marigolds' fernlike foliage is easy to identify, so separating the seedlings from weeds is not really a challenge. You can grow a very nice hedge of little French marigolds from one packet of direct-sown seeds.

- **Melampodium:** Increasingly popular, this low-maintenance flower is best sown in late spring. With little care, the plants grow into big 2-foot-tall mounds covered with small yellow flowers. They also re-seed without taking over your garden.

- **Morning glory** *(Ipomoea imperialis):* Most morning glories have heart-shaped leaves, so they are easy to identify as seedlings. Morning glories produce so many viable seeds that they can become weedy in the garden: Grow this type near mowed areas where they're less likely to get out of control.

- **Nasturtium** *(Tropaeolum majus):* Carefree and easy to grow, nasturtium leaves look like little green, flat umbrellas. Thin them to 8 inches apart to help them grow into big, bushy plants. Both the flowers and leaves are edible.

- **Poppies: Shirley, Iceland, and California** *(Papaver rhoeas, Papaver nudicaule,* and *Eschscholzia californica):* Sow delicate Shirley and Iceland poppies in the fall by scattering the tiny seeds atop cultivated soil. Never try to move them. California poppies can be planted in the fall or the spring. All three types of poppy produce pods filled with seeds that are easy to gather for the next year's sowing.

- **Spider flower** *(Cleome):* Spider flower is best seeded in late spring after the last frost has passed. Cover the soil after planting to keep it moist. In subsequent years, look for volunteer seedlings that appear like magic.

- **Sunflower** *(Helianthus annus):* Some people make a hobby of growing sunflowers, which are now available in a rainbow of hot colors. The large leaves shade out weeds, and the plants often reseed themselves. A few new varieties are truly dwarf, growing to less than 2 feet tall.

- **Sweet pea** *(Lathyrus odoratus):* The seeds of this romantic and elegant flower are so hard that they benefit from soaking for a full day before planting. Sow in late winter, while the soil is still quite cold. Sweet pea seedlings easily survive spring frosts.

- **Thunbergia, or black-eyed Susan vine:** The seeds of this pretty summer vine — a rampant grower — germinate best in warm, moist soil. Soak the seeds overnight before planting and sow them in a group at the base of a fence. This is a fine annual vine for covering chain-link fencing.

Chapter 10

Planting Seedlings

. . . .

In This Chapter

▶ Shopping for bedding plants

▶ Avoiding transplant shock

▶ Planting your seedlings

▶ Caring for your little ones

. . . .

*T*he quickest way to paint your yard with color is to add some ready-grown annuals to your landscape. Generations of nursery professionals and home gardeners have called these flowers *bedding plants* — a name that suggests their most typical use in the garden. You can find these flowers from spring through summer (or all-year in mild climates) at garden centers and nurseries, which pave their sidewalks with bedding plants in three-, four-, and six-packs, or pots of various sizes. And several seed catalogs now sell these flower seedlings by mail.

Some of the flowers commonly offered as bedding plants are simple to start from seed, and it's up to you to decide if you want to take the time and effort to raise your own seedlings or purchase them. Marigolds, sweet alyssum, and calendula, for example, are easy to grow from seed and reach transplant size in just 6 to 8 weeks. Begonias, impatiens, pansies, and petunias, on the other hand, take up to 12 weeks to grow from seeds to transplanting size.

You can't beat the convenience of purchasing your bedding plants already sprouted. In one afternoon, you can transform a patch of soil into a lush and colorful garden. Visiting local gardening centers and stocking up on flower seedlings is a springtime ritual in many cold-winter regions.

Shopping for Seedlings

The bedding plant industry takes some of the guesswork out of shopping for seedlings by shipping plants to nurseries and garden centers at the best time to plant them. Early in the spring and again in the fall, expect to find annuals that grow best in cool conditions. Annuals that require warmer weather generally arrive later in the spring and keep coming as long as customers keep buying. Remember, however, that nurseries can't predict the weather. You need to be prepared to protect tender seedlings from any late frosts.

The following lists show the availability of some of the most popular bedding plants in the spring. The plants that are available in your area and their estimated arrival time depend on your climate. See Chapter 3 for more information about when to plant different annuals in your region.

Popular Bedding Plants Sold in Early Spring	*Popular Bedding Plants Sold in Late Spring*
Calendula	Ageratum
Pink	Begonia
Lobelia	Celosia
Pansy	Dusty miller
Snapdragon	Geranium
Sweet alyssum	Impatiens
Verbena	Marigold
	Petunia
	Salvia
	Vinca rosea

To make sure that you get a healthy plant, check the way the store displays its annuals: Are all the flowers simply lined up in the blazing sun, or have shade-lovers, such as coleus and impatiens, been protected from the sun? Most bedding plants, including those that grow best when they're planted in full sun, do better when kept in partial shade until they're planted.

Be sure to protect your plants as you tote them home in your car. You wouldn't leave the family dog locked up in a hot car with the windows rolled up, so don't treat your plants that way, either.

Nurseries sell annuals in containers of all sizes, as shown in Figure 10-1. If you're looking for immediate impact in a flower bed or container, you may want to purchase annuals grown in 4- to 6-inch (or larger) pots. Plants grown in smaller containers take longer to fill their allotted space; however, they cost significantly less than those in larger pots, so if you can be patient, they may be a better choice.

You're Not in Kansas Anymore

Consider this the moment that you wake up in Oz. Suddenly, you're in a whole new world. I can write volumes about the beauty of annuals, but nothing will inspire you like seeing the plants in living color. The following pages provide a new perspective on the annuals discussed in this book. Let these photos guide you as you choose your own colorful creations and find happiness in your own backyard.

Annuals from A to Z

The annuals pictured on the following pages are listed alphbetically by their most popular common name. Refer to Chapters 4 and 5 for individual descriptions of these plants to determine whether the flower that catches your eye is appropriate for your gardening needs and conditions.

Photo 1: African daisy *(Arctotis)*

Photo 2:
African daisy
(Dimorphotheca sinuata)

Photo 3:
Ageratum, or floss flower
(Ageratum haustonianum)

Photo 4:
Aster, or Chinese aster
(Callistephus chinensis)

Photo 5:
Baby blue eyes
(Nemophila menziesii)

Photo 6:
Baby's breath
*(Gypsophila elegans
'Covent Garden')*

Photo 7: Bedding or wax begonia
(Begonia semperflorens)

Photo 8: Bells of Ireland
(Moluccella laevis)

Photo 9: Blanket flower
(Gaillardia pulchella)

Photo 10: Blue lace flower
(Trachymene coerulea)

Photo 11:
Browallia
(*Browallia americana*
'Blue Bells Improved')

Photo 12:
Calendula, or pot marigold
(*Calendula officinalis*)

Photo 13:
California poppy
(*Eschscholzia californica*)

Photo 14:
Calliopsis, or annual coreopsis
(*Coreopsis tinctoria*)

Photo 15: Canary creeper
(Tropaeolum peregrinum)

Photo 16: Candytuft
(Iberis umbellata)

Photo 17: Canterbury bells
(Campanula medium)

Photo 18: Carnation *(Dianthus)*

Photo 19:
Celosia, or cockscomb
(Celosia cristata)

Photo 20: Celosia *(Celosia plumosa)*

Photo 21: Chinese forget-me-not
(Cynoglossum amabile) blooming
among tulip leaves

Photo 22: Chinese lantern
(Physalis alkekengi)

Photo 23: Chrysanthemum, annual
(Chrysanthemum parthenian)

Photo 24: Chrysanthemum, annual
(Chrysanthemum carinatum
'Eastern Star')

Photo 25: Cigar plant,
or firecracker plant *(Cuphea ignea)*

Photo 26: Cineraria
(Senecio hybridus)

Photo 27: Clarkia, or godetia
(Clarkia amoena)

Photo 28: Coleus *(Coleus)*

Photo 29: Cornflower,
or bachelor's button
(Centaurea cyanus), a pink variety

Photo 30: Cosmos
(Cosmos bipinnatus)

Photo 31: Dahlberg daisy, or golden fleece
(Dyssodia tenuiloba)

Photo 32: Dahlia
(Dahlia 'Cherokee Ideal')

Photo 33: Dusty miller
(Cineraria maritima or
Senecio cinneraria)

Photo 34:
Felicia, or blue marguerite
(Felicia amelloides)

Photo 35: Flax *(Linum grandiflorum)*

Photo 36: Forget-me-not
(Myosotis sylvatica)

Photo 37: Four o'clock
(Mirabilis jalapa)

Photo 38:
Foxglove
(Digitalis purpurea)

Photo 39: Gazania *(Gazania hybrida)*

Photo 40: Geranium, ivy or vining
(Pelargonium peltatum 'Candy Cane')

Photo 41:
Geranium, zonal
(Pelargonium hortorum)

Photo 42:
Gilia, or bird's eye
(Gilia tricolor)

Photo 43: Globe amaranth
(Gomphrena)

Photo 44: Gloriosa daisy, or black-eyed Susan *(Rudbeckia hirta)*

Photo 45: Heliotrope
(Heliotropium arborescens)

Photo 46: Hollyhock *(Alcea rosea)*

Photo 47:
Iceland poppy
(*PaPaver nudicaule*)

Photo 48: Impatiens
(*Impatiens walleriana* Super Elfin Twilight)

Photo 49: Kale, or ornamental cabbage
(*Brassica oleracea*)

Photo 50:
Kochia, or burning bush
(*Kochia scoparia*)

Photo 51: Larkspur
(Consolida ambigua)

Photo 52: Lavatera, or tree mallow
(Lavatera trimestris)

Photo 53:
Linaria, or toadflax
(Linaria)

Photo 54:
Lisianthus
*(Eustoma grandiflorum
'Echo Pink' and 'Prarie Gentian')*

Photo 55:
Lobelia
(Lobelia)

Photo 56: Love-in-a-mist *(Nigella damascena)*

Photo 57: Love-lies-bleeding
(Amaranthus caudatus)

Photo 58: Marigold, African
or American *(Tagetes erecta)*

Photo 59:
Marigold 'French Vanilla'
(Tagetes erecta)

Photo 60: Marigold, Signet
(Tagetes tenuifolia)

Photo 61: Mexican sunflower
(Tithonia rotundifolia)

Photo 62:
Mexican tulip poppy
(Hunnemannia fumariifolia)

Photo 63: Mignonette
(Reseda odorata)

Photo 64: Monkey flower *(Mimulus)*

Photo 65: Morning glory
(Ipomoea imperialis)

Photo 66:
Nasturtium
(Tropaeolum majus)

Photo 67: Nemesia
(*Nemesia strumosa* 'Blue Gem')

Photo 68: Nemesia
(*Nemesia strumosa* 'Carnival')

Photo 69:
Nicotiana, or flowering tobacco
(Nicotiana)

Photo 70:
Nierembergia, or cup flower
(Nierembergia)

Photo 71:
Pansy
(Viola wittrockiana)

Photo 72:
Petunia
(Petunia milliflora)

Photo 73: Phlox, annual *(Phlox)*

Photo 74:
Pincushion flower, or sweet scabious
(Scabiosa atropurpurea)

Photo 75: Pink *(Dianthus chinensis)*

Photo 76: Portulaca, or moss rose *(Portulaca grandiflora)*

Photo 77: Primroses *(Primula malacoides)*

Photo 78: Primroses *(Primula polyantha)*, Silver Laced hybrid

Photo 79:
Salpiglossis, painted tongue, or velvet flower
(Salpiglossis)

Photo 80: Salvia: mealy-cup sage
(Salvia farinacea 'Victoria White')

Photo 81: Salvia: Gentian sage
(Salvia patens)

Photo 82: Salvia: Scarlet sage
(Salvia splendens 'Empire Red')

Photo 83: Schizanthus, or butterfly flower *(Schizanthus)*

Photo 84: Shirley poppy *(PaPaver rhoeas)*

Photo 85: Snapdragon *(Antirrhinum majus)*

Photo 86: Snow-on-the-mountain *(Euphorbia marginata)*

Photo 87: Spider flower
(Cleome hasslerana)

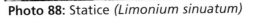

Photo 88: Statice *(Limonium sinuatum)*

Photo 89: Stocks
(Matthiola incana)

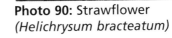

Photo 90: Strawflower
(Helichrysum bracteatum)

Photo 91: Summer forget-me-not
(*Anchusa capensis*)

Photo 92: Sunflower
(*Helianthus annus*)

Photo 93: Sunflower
(*Helianthus annus* 'Teddy Bear')

Photo 94: Swan River daisy
(*Brachycome iridifolia*)

Photo 95: Sweet alyssum
(Lobularia maritima)

Photo 96: Sweet pea
(Lathyrus odoratus)

Photo 97: Sweet William *(Dianthus barbatus)*

Photo 98: Thunbergia, or black-eyed Susan vine *(Thunbergia alata)*

Photo 99: Transvaal daisy *(Gerbera jamesonii)*

Photo 100: Verbena *(Verbena)*

Photo 101: Vinca rosea, or Madagascar periwinkle *(Catharanthus roseus)*

Photo 102: Viola *(Viola cornuta)*

Photo 103: Wallflower *(Erysimum)*

Photo 104: Wishbone flower *(Torenia fournieri)*

Photo 105: Zinnia, mild climate perennial (*Zinnia angustifolia* 'White Star')

Photo 106: Zinnia, Short Stuff perennial mix (*Zinnia elegans* Short Stuff)

Photo 107: Zinnia, annual (*Zinnia elegans*)

Annuals in Action

Annuals are versatile plants. The remaining color pages show just a fraction of the wonderful ways in which annuals can brighten your yard. Use these pages to spark your own ideas for where to plant annuals, how to combine colors, how to vary shape and height, and how to handle challenges such as getting late-summer blooms and perking up shady spots.

Photo 108: Spice-up your herb garden with a dash of annual color.

Photo 109: Annuals give you the power to create a large, lush garden in just one year. This all annual flower bed — now filled with lavatera, zinnias, geraniums, sweet alyssum, and petite marigolds — was bare in early spring.

Photo 110: Looking out or looking in: Planting annuals in window boxes adds color to your home indoors and out. Consider the view from inside when planning near windows. (Chapter 16 discusses container gardening in detail.)

Photo 111: Use annuals to experiment with bold colors, like the purple of this lobelia beside the orange of dwarf African marigold.

Photo 112: Play with pastels. In this garden, heliotrope 'Blue Marine', Domino Strain nicotiana, and 'Peter Pan' zinnia combine to create a soft, romantic effect.

Photo 113: Want punch? Plant marigolds! You have to wear sunglasses to admire the hot colors of marigolds and celosia 'Apricot Brandy'. White-and-blue petunias and red-and-pink dianthus add the spice to this sunny garden.

Photo 114: (above) A classic color combinations of royal blue cherry-pie plant against lemon yellow African marigolds. Photo 115: (below) Sometimes, ignoring the color wheel and following your instincts yields the most striking effects. Here, rusty orange marigolds look great beside lavender and red salvia. See Chapter 6.

Photo 116: 'Crystal Palace' lobelia makes a lovely edge for any border. Turn to Chapter 7 for more ideas on designing annual beds and borders.

Photo 117: Revel in cottage garden charm with spiky foxglove, one of the few annuals (technically a biennial) that can grow and flower in partial shade. Chapter 6 describes four traditional styles of annual gardens, including rustic cottage gardens like the one shown here.

Photo 118: Plant annuals in tiers for levels of color: low in the front, and tall in the back. This garden starts low with petunias and moves up to globe amaranth, salvia, marigolds, and then blue salvia and white cosmos.

Photo 119: Want some privacy? Plant a tall screen using nothing but annuals. In this annual border, sunflowers do the heavy lifting, but tall zinnias and marigolds fill in thick enough to make the strip of soil into a wall of color.

Photo 120: With long and late bloomers like marigolds (edging the path) and zinnias (in the background), this late summer garden gives you color right up to the frost.

Photo 121: Although most annuals love the sun, you can bring color to shady spots by combining impatiens and coleus.

Photo 122: You can find annuals to meet the challenge of nearly any patch of soil. In this narrow, shady strip, for example, coleus and impatiens team up with the yellow flowers of tuberous begonia (another shade-lover) and pink ageratum, an annual that needs partial sun.

Photo 123: Use annuals to accentuate lines and shapes in your yard. Here, foxglove reinforces the vertical line of the fence.

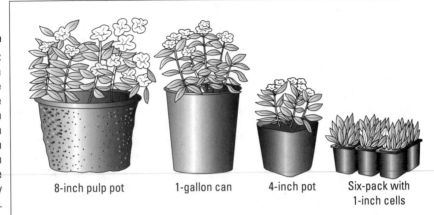

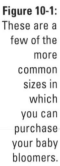

Figure 10-1: These are a few of the more common sizes in which you can purchase your baby bloomers.

8-inch pulp pot   1-gallon can   4-inch pot   Six-pack with 1-inch cells

As you shop, look for bedding annuals that are a good green color, appear to have been watered regularly, and are relatively short and stocky. Although it's tempting to pick out the largest plants with the most flowers, these plants may have grown too large for their containers and will suffer during transplanting. You're better off choosing a healthy, compact plant with few or no flowers. These youngsters transplant better and quickly catch up to larger plants.

Avoid large plants growing in small pots — if a plant's roots entirely fill its container and are poking out of the drainage holes, it may be *rootbound,* meaning that the roots have begun to grow in a tight spiral around the perimeter of the pot and may refuse to spread outward after transplanting, stunting the plant's growth.

At the nursery, don't be shy about tipping the plant out of its pot or pack and inspecting its roots. Avoid plants with thick tangles of root searching for a place to grow — such as out through the container's drainage hole.

Preventing Transplant Shock by Hardening Off

Seedlings that you purchase directly from a greenhouse benefit from a short period of hardening off. (Sounds like the Marine Corps, doesn't it?) *Hardening off* simply means acclimating the seedling to its new surroundings and giving it a chance to adjust to the difference between the comforts of a greenhouse and the cold or heat of an exposed garden bed.

Babes in bloom

Statistics show that consumers are much more likely to buy plants that are already in flower. As a result, plant breeders have tinkered with genes to develop flowers that pop a blossom or two at an early age and then devote a few more weeks to vegetative growth before they start blooming again.

If you buy plants already in flower, pinch off the blossom when you set out the plants — unless you're having guests for dinner, in which case you can wait until the next day. This preemptive pinching encourages the plants to get on with the business of growing buds and branches.

As soon as you get your seedlings home, place them in a bright place that is protected from direct midday sun and strong winds, and water them well. After a few days, move them to full sun. Remember, however, that small pots can dry out very quickly in the midday sun. If you won't be around to check your seedlings every few hours, it's better to leave them in a protected spot until you're ready to transplant. Give them a boost by adding some water-soluble fertilizer next time you give them a drink; choose an all-purpose flower fertilizer and follow label directions. By this time, your seedlings should be nicely accustomed to direct sun and wind and be tough enough to transplant.

If your new seedlings have already spent some time outdoors at the nursery or garden center, they can skip the hardening off and go straight into your garden. Ask the garden center staff whether the seedlings have been hardened off and are ready for transplanting.

Planning to Plant: Give 'em Some Elbow Room

Gardeners tend to have very tight plant spacing in window boxes and containers, but in open beds, the best strategy is to space seedlings so that they will barely touch each other when they reach full maturity. Because different annual flowers grow to different sizes, the amount of space they require varies.

Extras and understudies

Frequently, after planting your garden, you end up with a few extra bedding plants. Don't throw them away. If your garden follows a formal design, where even one additional plant would stand out, transplant the extras to slightly larger individual pots. This way, if a few plants spontaneously expire or get dug up by your neighbor's dog, you can quickly plug in a replacement that's an exact match.

Another way to use annual orphans is to plant them together in large containers. Place the tallest, most upright flowers in the middle and surround them with smaller plants. In a few weeks, you'll have a remarkably pretty container bouquet that looks like you spent hours designing it.

Very small annuals, such as sweet alyssum and lobelia, can be spaced only 4 to 6 inches apart, but big coleus and celosia may do better if they're placed 18 inches apart. Most other annuals grow best planted about 10 to 12 inches apart. The plant tags tucked into the containers of bedding plants often suggest the best spacing. You also can find spacing recommendations in the descriptions of flowers in Chapters 4 and 5.

Instead of setting your annuals in straight lines, try staggering them in a concentrated zigzag pattern so that you have two or more offset rows of plants. This planting design fills a large space more uniformly and looks less rigid than plants lined up in rows. Better yet, plant groups of similar annuals in teardrop-shaped clumps (called *drifts*); this design often looks more natural and helps create focal points in the design. The clump approach also makes many flowers easier to care for. Pinching, pruning, and giving extra water and fertilizer to a closely spaced group of plants is easier than ministering to a long row of flowers.

When planning your planting arrangement, you can estimate the plant spacing and simply make little holes in the prepared bed where you intend to set the plants. Or you can mark the planting spots with craft sticks or lightly dust each spot with plain all-purpose flour. If you already purchased plants in individual containers, simply place the plants where you intend to plant them, and move them around as needed until you're happy with the arrangement.

Planting Seedlings, Step by Step

Whether you buy your seedlings or grow them from seeds, follow these steps to ensure that your plants get off to a good start in your garden.

Transplant during cloudy weather or late in the day. Hot sun during transplanting causes unnecessary stress to the little plants.

1. **The day before transplanting, water the planting bed so that it will be lightly moist when you set out your plants.**

2. **Water your seedlings thoroughly a few hours before transplanting.**

   Watering the seedlings makes them much easier to remove from their containers.

3. **Carefully remove the seedling from the container.**

   If small roots are knotted around the outside of the drainage holes, pinch off the roots and discard them before trying to remove the plants. Then push and squeeze on the bottom of the container to make the entire root ball slip out intact, as shown in Figure 10-2. If it won't come out easily, use a table knife to gently pry it out, the same way you might remove a sticky cake from a pan. Pull on the top of the plant only as a last resort.

Figure 10-2:
Push seedlings out of their container by pressing lightly on the bottom of their pot. Avoid pulling on them from above.

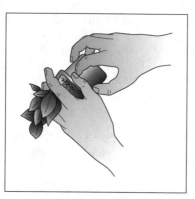

4. **Gently tease apart roots.**

   Use your fingers or a table fork to loosen the tangle of roots at the bottom of the root ball, as shown in Figure 10-3. This step encourages the roots to spread out into the surrounding soil.

Figure 10-3:
Breaking a few roots won't hurt the plant, as long as the mass of roots remains intact.

5. **Make final spacing decisions and dig planting holes slightly larger than the root balls of the plants.**

   Set the plants in the holes at the same depth they grew in their containers, as shown in Figure 10-4.

Figure 10-4:
Scoop a trowelful of soil to one side so that hole is just deep enough to accommodate the seedling.

6. **Lightly firm soil around the roots with your hands, as shown in Figure 10-5, to remove any air pockets that may exist around the plant's roots.**

Figure 10-5: Firm soil around a young plant just enough so that it can remain upright.

7. **If you want, mix a batch of balanced or high-phosphorus, water-soluble fertilizer and give each plant a good slurp.**

   High-phosphorus fertilizers have a large middle number, such as 5-7-4. If you mixed in fertilizer while preparing the planting bed, you shouldn't have to feed your plants again now. (For more about fertilizing annuals, see Chapter 12.)

8. **Gently water the entire bed until it's evenly moist but not muddy, as shown in Figure 10-6.**

   Because you watered the bed before planting (Step 1), the intent is to help the soil settle around the plants' roots. Use a hose with a bubbler nozzle, a sprinkler, or a watering can rosette-type spout. Take care not to wash away surface soil, leaving roots exposed.

9. **After a few days, check to make sure that soil has not washed away from the top of the plants' roots.**

   If it has, use a rake or small trowel to level the soil around the plants.

10. **As soon as new growth shows, mulch around plants with an attractive mulch, such as shredded bark, pine needles, or shredded leaves.**

    A 2- to 3-inch layer of mulch discourages weeds and radically reduces moisture loss from the soil due to evaporation. Chapter 15 discusses the different types of mulch and how to use them.

Figure 10-6:
Use a gentle shower of water, rather than a strong jet-stream, on newly planted annuals.

Special care for beautiful beds

Given warm sun and ample water, most annuals speed right along and come into full bloom in a few short weeks. If you live in a dry area where watering is likely to eat up all your spare time, give some thought to rigging up an irrigation system for your annual flower bed. A series of inexpensive soaker hoses hidden under the mulch can make watering a simple matter of turning on the faucet at very low pressure for a few hours a couple of times each week. For more details on watering, see Chapter 11.

Dwarf varieties of most annual flowers need no pinching right after transplanting, for their natural tendency is to develop numerous branches that emerge from the main stem near the soil line. However, flowers that tend to grow upright, such as snapdragons, tall zinnias, and marigolds, grow bushier if you clip or pinch off the topmost growing tip a week or so after transplanting. If necessary, use scissors or pruning shears so that you don't have to twist and pull to remove the growing tip. If it breaks your heart to pinch off the tip, wait until the first flower opens and promptly cut it and put it in a vase. New branches and buds should quickly pop out from the largest stems of the sheared plant.

Year-round beds

In climates with very long growing seasons, annual beds are often "turned over" two or three times a year. For example, if you live in a warm region where winters don't freeze at all, or where they freeze only slightly (such as southern Texas or Palm Springs, California), you can plant pansies in the fall and enjoy them all the way until May. By then, the pansies are pooped, and it's time to replace them with something new. With a little planning, you can complete such a garden renovation very quickly by following these steps:

1. **Dampen the soil to make the old plants easy to pull out.**

2. **Grab the plants close to the soil and pull to get as many of the roots as you can.**

   Throw out the roots or toss them into a compost heap, if you have one.

3. **Spread a 2-inch layer of compost or composted manure, along with a light dusting of a balanced time-release or organic fertilizer, over the empty section of your bed.**

4. **Dig or till the bed as needed to mix in the compost and fertilizer, and rake the soil smooth.**

   You're now ready to install a new crop of annuals. Simply follow the steps under "Planting Seedlings, Step by Step."

Part V
The Care and Feeding of Annuals

In this part . . .

Annuals are easy to grow, but they still need some routine tender loving care. You can't just plant those little seedlings and then abandon them. The chapters in this part explain how to water, feed, and weed your flowers and what to do for them when they get sick or when insects attack them. You can also find information about staking, pinching, pruning, and deadheading — tasks that may sound like cruel treatment, but are actually compassionate acts that help you get the most from your annuals.

Chapter 11

Quenching Your Flowers' Thirst

· ·

In This Chapter

▶ Looking at the factors that affect an annual's water needs

▶ Comparing different watering methods

▶ Knowing how often to water

▶ Deciding how much to water

▶ Conserving water

· ·

*L*ike many plants, annuals need consistent moisture in the soil in order to grow and bloom beautifully. But the trick is knowing how to get that moisture in the soil and how much of it to apply. In fact, watering may be one of the trickiest aspects of growing annual flowers.

Unlike many plants, annuals are not very forgiving if they don't get the water they want, when they want it. If you let some of these finicky plants dry out, they'll stop growing and quit blooming for good. (Drowning your plants has that same effect.) If they don't die, most under- or overwatered annuals at least shut down for a while. For a more permanent plant, a temporary halt in growth may not be the end of the world. But with annuals, fast, consistent growth is critical. If the plant stalls, you may lose a good part, if not all, of the blooming season.

This chapter shows you how to water wisely and keep your annuals growing strong all season long. No matter what watering method or tools you employ, the most important rule of watering is to observe your plants and soil on a regular basis and respond appropriately to what they're telling you.

Determining a Plant's Water Needs

The amount of water that annuals need to stay healthy and full of blooms depends on a number of factors, including climate, weather, soil type, garden location, and type of annuals used.

Considering climate

The climate of an area encompasses a wide range of factors, such as the amount of average rainfall, the high and low temperatures, the relative humidity, and the amount of wind. If you live in an area where rainfall is regular and reliable (like Seattle, Washington; Vancouver, British Columbia; London, England; or Biloxi, Mississippi) watering isn't a constant chore, except during prolonged dry spells or periods of drought. In drier areas, such as Los Angeles, California, and Phoenix, Arizona, watering is a task you must squeeze into your schedule almost on a daily basis.

You have to water container-grown annuals even more frequently than your plants in the ground. In fact, daily watering of annuals in containers is essential in almost all climates during certain times of the year.

Watching the weather

Climate is determined by the average weather where you live on a season-to-season, year-to-year basis. *Weather* is what's happening outside at any given moment. Out-of-the-ordinary weather can wreak havoc on your plants. Hot, dry winds can fry annuals even when the soil is moist. Prolonged rain can turn zinnias to mush, rot the roots of vinca rosea, and turn cosmos into a mildewy mess.

Table 11-1 shows, in a nutshell, guidelines on how to adjust watering according to weather conditions.

Table 11-1	Watering According to Weather
Water Less	*Water More*
Cooler temperatures	Warmer temperatures
Cloudy or overcast	Bright sunshine
Low wind	High wind
High humidity	Low humidity
Rain	No rain

Studying your soil

Different soil types affect how often a garden needs water. For example, sand holds water about as effectively as a sieve. Water penetrates sandy soil readily and deeply, but tends to filter right on through. Therefore, you need to water plants in sandy soil more frequently than plants in clay soil.

Heavy clay is the exact opposite. Its dense particles crust over and deflect water drops. If you apply water slowly and in stages, it soaks in; if you apply it quickly and all at once, it just runs off. But after clay is saturated, it holds water very well — sometimes so well that the plants rot.

Luckily, when you grow annuals, you can amend the soil with organic matter on a yearly, if not seasonal, basis. Adding organic matter, such as compost, leaf mold, or ground bark, helps sandy soils to retain moisture and helps break up clay soils to improve aeration and drainage. (See Chapter 8 for more information on improving sandy or clay soils.)

Looking at location

In general, shady gardens need less water than those planted in direct sunlight. By blocking the sun's heat, shade cuts down on the amount of water that evaporates from the soil.

However, in places where trees are responsible for casting the shadow, the tree roots may be greedily hogging all the water, leaving little for the flowers. Maples in particular have roots so close to the surface that it's almost impossible to apply enough water to satisfy the tree and the flowers. The farther from the trunk of the tree you place your flowers, the more room they have to spread their roots, and the less they have to compete with the tree for water and nutrients.

If you plan to plant in a shady area, choose annuals that don't need direct sunlight to thrive. Impatiens, forget-me-nots, and browallia are good choices for the dark corners of your yard.

Picking your plants

Although most annual flowers need a consistent supply of moisture to remain healthy and free-blooming, some annuals can get by on less water than others. For example, California poppies, gazanias, portulaca, salvia, and verbena adapt fairly well to hot, dry conditions. Vinca rosea and snapdragons are very sensitive to overly wet soils and can rot if their roots are not allowed to partially dry out between waterings. Skim through Chapter 5 for more ideas of annuals that adapt well to dry conditions.

Knowing when to water

The water needs of your annuals vary with the weather and the seasons. You must learn to be a pretty good observer and make adjustments accordingly.

However, here are some easy ways to tell when your plants need water:

✔ **Look at your plants.** Your annual has ways of telling you when it's thirsty. When an annual starts to dry out, the leaves get droopy and wilt. The plant may also lose its bright green color and start to look a little drab. Your goal is to water before a plant reaches that point, but the plant will tell you when it needs water more often.

✔ **Dig in the ground.** Most annuals need water when the top two to three inches of soil are dry. So take a small trowel or shovel and dig around a bit. If the top of the soil is dry, it's time to water.

Eventually, through observation and digging, you start to develop a watering schedule, and you can eliminate some of the guesswork from this part of your gardening routine.

Still other annuals, such as impatiens, can survive through occasional dry spells, but they look terrible and stop blooming until they receive the water they need.

Read up on the water requirements of the plants you like and then decide whether you can modify your soil or site to accommodate them. Aside from amending your soil, you can group plants according to their water needs. For example, plant a flower that wilts rapidly when it's deprived of water in a location that's partially shaded by other plants during the blazing heat of late afternoon. If you garden in containers (as described in Chapter 16), you have much more control because you can move the pots around if your plants begin to complain about their present location.

Ways to Water

You can choose from a number of ways to apply water to your flowers. Some methods are better than others, but often the best method depends on the size of your flower garden. For example, if you have a small bed of marigolds, a handheld watering can may be all you need. If, however, you have a 200-square-foot flower bed, watering effectively by hand is not just impractical, it's impossible.

In some areas, certain watering techniques become a matter of necessity instead of practicality. In regions where droughts are common or water supplies are unpredictable, conservation is the order of the day. You need to water in ways that hold every drop precious. If foliage diseases such as powdery mildew are common, keep water off the plant leaves and apply it only to the roots. (See Chapter 14 for more information on powdery mildew and other plant diseases.)

Hand watering

If you want to stand around with a hose and water by hand, that's fine. In fact, container gardens require hand watering (that is, unless you install a sophisticated drip-irrigation system). You can buy small hose-end attachments to control the flow of water that gurgles out of your hose. Small _hose-end bubblers_ soften the spray of water; _spray wands_ (Figure 11-1) increase the water pressure for larger areas.

Figure 11-1:
A spray wand on an extension tube lets you reach hanging baskets without washing away the soil.

But hand watering takes time, especially in large gardens, and the time and boredom factors often tempt you to stop watering before your plants have received enough water. Most plants prefer a good soaking every couple of days to a light sprinkling every day. Be sure to water long enough that moisture reaches down to the root zone of the plants.

Sprinklers

Many types of hose-end sprinklers are available, and you've probably used a few of them in your day (even if it was just to play in the arcs of water). The problem with using sprinklers to water your flower beds is that you have to drag the hose all around and frequently move the sprinkler. In addition, most hose-end sprinklers don't apply water very evenly. And if you forget to turn the sprinkler off, you waste a lot of water (though you can solve this problem by installing an automatic timer between the faucet and the hose).

Choose a sprinkler that emits the largest droplets possible because, on a hot day, tiny drops can evaporate before they even reach the ground. Look for a sprinkler that covers a wide area and avoid those that send water straight up into the air (where it can evaporate more quickly).

Sprinklers work best when every flower is the same height. Otherwise, the taller plants get in the way of the spray pattern. In fact, overhead watering can weigh down some taller annuals, such as cosmos, and cause them to flop over on the ground.

The automated system

Automated watering systems can be real time-savers and can give you the freedom to safely take a vacation in the middle of summer. By operating on a timer hooked up to your faucet, these systems turn on and off by themselves at preset intervals. You can find an interesting mixture of timers at your local irrigation supplier or in mail-order catalogs. (See the appendix.)

Some timers are hooked between the end of the faucet and the hose, and others are connected to valves and underground pipes that supply sprinklers. You can even build a moisture sensor into an automated system so that the water comes on only when the soil is dry. (Isn't technology wonderful?) Both drip and sprinkler systems can be fully automated.

Just remember, even an automated system needs to be adjusted to water less in the spring than in the summer.

You may encounter another possible problem from overhead watering and the resulting wet foliage. In humid climates, overhead watering can spread disease and turn your flowers into a moldy mess. On the other hand, in hot, dry climates, wetting the foliage rinses dust off the leaves and helps prevent spider mite infestations.

If you do use sprinklers, don't put them in the same place every time you water. And even during a single watering, move the sprinklers around so that your flowers are evenly watered.

Furrow irrigation

Furrows are shallow trenches that run parallel to your rows of flowers. (See Figure 11-2.) Usually you dig them with a hoe at planting time and then plant a row of flowers on either side of the furrow. Ideally, the flower bed should be sloped just the tiniest bit so that water runs naturally from one end of the furrow to the other. When you want to water, you simply put a slowly running hose at the end of the furrow and wait for the water to reach the other end.

Figure 11-2:
Furrow irrigation makes use of gravity to carry water from one end of the furrow to the other.

Furrow irrigation keeps the foliage dry, and therefore doesn't promote disease the way sprinkler watering does. However, you do have to drag the hose from furrow to furrow. And this type of system doesn't work well on fast-draining, sandy soil. The water soaks in too quickly and never reaches the other end.

Drip irrigation

Drip irrigation is a very effective and efficient way to water annuals. It works well even if your garden is on a slope, which poses a problem for some other systems. Drip irrigation provides water slowly through holes or emitters in a flexible black plastic pipe. You weave this pipe (which is connected to a water supply, a filter, and often a pressure regulator) along the rows of plants so that the water flows directly to the bases of the flowers, as shown in Figure 11-3.

Figure 11-3: Drip irrigation slowly delivers water precisely where you need it, so less is lost to evaporation and runoff.

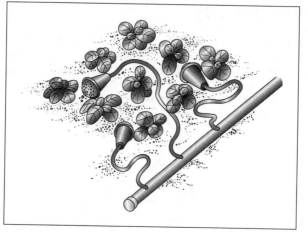

You can wet an entire bed from one end to the other at each watering with drip emitters. (You can snap the emitters in the pipe wherever you want them, or you can buy pipe with the emitters already evenly spaced along the length of the pipe.) The moisture radiates sideways underground and wets the soil between emitters.

You can lay the pipe right on top of the soil and cover it with a mulch, or you can bury the pipe a few inches below the surface of the soil. Most people like to keep the pipe close to the surface so that they can check it for clogs and fix breaks.

You usually have to run drip systems for at least several hours to wet a large area. Watch the system carefully the first few times you water. Dig around to see how far the water has traveled over a given time. Then make adjustments in your watering schedule in the future.

If you live in an area where the soil freezes, don't leave your drip system outside in winter. It may burst. Instead, drain the water out, roll up the tubing, and store it in the garage.

Most nurseries sell drip irrigation systems. You can also purchase them through the mail. (See the appendix.) Emitters are available with different application rates, varying by the number of gallons applied per hour. Pressure-compensating emitters apply water consistently from one end of the line to the other, regardless of pressure changes due to uneven ground.

Soaker-hose irrigation

A soaker-hose system consists of a rubber hose perforated with tiny pores that leak water. You can lay the hose in rows or curve it around plants, similar to the drip irrigation system. Water leaks out of the hose and into the soil, leaving the plant leaves dry and reducing evaporation. A soaker-hose system is simpler than drip irrigation because it involves fewer parts and no nozzles. Its primary limitation is that it works best on flat terrain, often delivering water unevenly in a sloped garden.

Keep your garden looking tidy and improve the efficiency of your soaker hose by laying it on top of the soil and covering it with mulch. You can easily customize a system to fit your garden by threading the hose around your plantings, as shown in Figure 11-4.

Figure 11-4: Soaker hoses are flexible enough to curve around your plants.

Water-saving tips

Water shortages are a reality in almost any climate or region. Here are a few things you can do when water is scarce or limited, when you want to reduce your water bill, or when you just want to conserve the precious resource of fresh water.

✔ **Use a timer.** If you've ever forgotten to turn the water off and ended up flooding half the neighborhood, this tip's for you. Just set an egg timer or an alarm clock to let you know when to shut off the water. Or you can get even more high-tech and use one of the automated timers that I describe in the section "Ways to Water."

✔ **Install drip irrigation.** This method applies water slowly without runoff. Drip is definitely the most frugal watering system you can use.

✔ **Mulch, mulch, and mulch some more.** A mulch is a layer of organic matter that you spread over the root zone beneath a plant. Several inches of compost, shredded fir bark, leaf mold, or other material cool the soil and reduce evaporation, thus saving water. And as the mulch breaks down, it improves the soil. For more on mulches, see Chapter 15.

✔ **Pull weeds.** Weeds steal water meant for your annuals, so keep them pulled. For more on weeds, see Chapter 15.

✔ **Water deeply and infrequently.** Shallow sprinkling does very little good. Water to a depth of 8 to 10 inches and then let the soil dry out partially before you water again. This way, you develop deep roots that can go longer between waterings.

✔ **Use rainwater.** Put a barrel or other collector where the drain pipes from your roof empty. Then use that water on your flowers.

✔ **Measure rainfall.** Keep track of how much rain you get with a rain gauge, available from garden centers and hardware stores. An inch of rain at one time is usually enough to let you skip a watering.

✔ **Plant at the right time.** Plant when your annuals have the best chance of getting fully established before the onset of hot weather. For proper planting times for your area, see Chapter 3.

✔ **Plant drought-tolerant annuals.** I mention a few camels of the annual world earlier in this chapter, in the section "Determining a Plant's Water Needs." You can find more flowers with low water needs in Chapter 5.

How Much Water to Apply

The roots of most annuals grow in the top 8 to 10 inches of soil. That's where the soil is well aerated and conditions suit root growth. When you water, therefore, you must make sure that the moisture reaches a depth of 8 to 10 inches. If you water any shallower, the roots won't be able to grow deeply because they just won't penetrate the dry soil. Shallow-rooted plants are more susceptible to fluctuations in soil moisture because they don't have a large soil reserve to draw from. Bottom line: Don't sprinkle lightly. It does little good.

On the other hand, you don't need to apply so much water that it goes deeper than 8 to 10 inches. Not many roots are growing at that depth, so you'd only be wasting water.

So how do you tell how deep you're watering? Get out your trusty trowel or shovel and dig in an open area of your flower bed. If the water hasn't reached deep enough, water longer. If the soil is still soaking wet at a foot deep, you can cut back some.

Chapter 12

Feeding Those Hungry Annuals

- -

In This Chapter

▶ Supplying nutrients for healthy growth

▶ Reading a fertilizer label

▶ Shopping for fertilizers

▶ Knowing how much and how often to fertilize annuals

▶ Fertilizing annuals in containers

▶ Using organic fertilizers

- -

*I*f annuals are flowering powerhouses (and they are), then fertilizer is the coal that fuels the powerhouse. If you don't create enough steam, the power won't be there and blooming will be sparse. If you create too much steam, the whole thing blows up and you fry the plants.

Proper fertilization, especially when annuals are young, is very important to the quality of bloom. Even though young transplants or seedlings may not be blooming much, their growth during the first six to eight weeks after planting has a huge impact on how well they bloom later. Keeping annuals growing vigorously, never letting them stall, and building healthy foliage early on results in spectacular power when they're ready to bloom. And after annuals have started blooming, proper fertilization keeps them blooming as long as possible.

This chapter covers the what, the how much, and the how often of fertilizing annuals. Get ready to stoke those fires.

In Need of Nutrients

Plants need 16 different elements for healthy growth. Carbon, hydrogen, and oxygen — the foundation blocks for photosynthesis — are required in large quantities, but nature or your watering hose automatically provides these elements.

Plants also need relatively large amounts of nitrogen, phosphorus, and potassium, which are called *macronutrients*. Plants require *secondary nutrients* (calcium, magnesium, and sulfur) in smaller quantities and need the *micronutrients* (iron, manganese, copper, boron, molybdenum, chlorine, and zinc) in even smaller amounts.

Macronutrients, secondary nutrients, and micronutrients are mostly absorbed from the soil by plant roots. If any nutrient is not present in the soil in sufficient quantities, or is present in a form that the plant can't absorb, you must add it as fertilizer or correct the conditions that make it difficult for the nutrient to be absorbed.

Luckily, most soils already contain enough nutrients for healthy growth. In fact, when growing annual flowers, many gardeners may find that nitrogen is the only element that they need to apply via fertilizers. But how do you know for sure? You can look for a yellowing of the lower leaves (a sure sign of nitrogen deficiency), but to be absolutely sure that the problem is lack of nitrogen, you can have your soil tested. A soil test, discussed in detail in Chapter 8, reveals which nutrients are or aren't present in your soil so that you can know the type and quantity of fertilizer to apply.

But a soil test doesn't provide *all* the answers; it only tells you what to work into your soil *before* planting. You still have to apply nitrogen, and maybe other nutrients, later on. To understand why, you need to know a little more about plant nutrients and how they react with the soil.

Nitrogen — once is not enough

Nitrogen is often the only nutrient that you need to apply as a fertilizer. The reason soil tends to be deficient in nitrogen is that plants use more nitrogen than any other nutrient, so the nitrogen supply is quickly depleted from the soil. Nitrogen is also less stationary in the soil. In other words, it can be washed or leached out of the soil when you water. Phosphorus and potassium are less mobile — so once they're there, they stay put for quite a while.

Why do plants need so much nitrogen? Nitrogen promotes healthy growth. As a key part of plant proteins and *chlorophyll,* the plant pigment that plays a vital role in photosynthesis, nitrogen is responsible for the green color of plant leaves. Plants that are deficient in nitrogen show a yellowing of older leaves first, along with a general slowdown in growth.

If your annuals aren't producing their quota of blooms, the reason is probably that the soil doesn't contain enough nitrogen. Luckily, plants usually respond quickly to nitrogen application, so nitrogen deficiency is easy to correct. How? You guessed it — by adding fertilizer.

Keeping the other nutrients in check

In addition to nitrogen, phosphorus and potassium (the other two macronutrients) also play important roles in plant growth. Phosphorus is associated with good root growth and with flower, fruit, and seed production. Potassium is necessary for healthy roots, disease resistance, and fruiting. Deficiencies in either nutrient are not as obvious as nitrogen deficiency and are therefore harder to detect simply from looking at symptoms on a plant. Only a soil test can tell for sure.

Because phosphorus and potassium are less mobile than nitrogen, you can't just water them in to the soil as you can with nitrogen. Instead, you have to work those nutrients into the soil at planting time. That way, they're located right where the roots can absorb them.

Determining the secondary nutrients and the micronutrients that your plants need is also hard, if not impossible, without a soil test. Some of the nutrients may be present, but the *pH,* or the relative acidity or alkalinity, of the soil prevents the plants from being able to absorb them. In such a case, that good old soil test tells you how to adjust your soil pH so that the nutrients can be absorbed. You can find out more about soil pH in Chapter 8.

Shopping for Fertilizers

At first glance, a nursery shelf full of fertilizers is an overwhelming sight. But it really doesn't have to be so confusing. Among all the colorful bags, bottles, and jars, you can find a consistency in labeling to guide you through much of the confusion and lead you to the fertilizer that's best for your annuals.

Checking the guaranteed analysis

When you buy a commercial fertilizer, look on the label for three numbers separated by dashes, as shown in Figure 12-1. These three numbers are a fertilizer's *guaranteed analysis,* telling you how much of each of the macronutrients the fertilizer contains.

- The first number indicates the percentage of nitrogen (N).
- The second number indicates the percentage of phosphate (P_2O_5).
- The third number indicates the percentage of potash (K_2O), which is another name for potassium.

Figure 12-1:
All fertilizer labels show the percentage of nitrogen, phosphorus, and potash (potassium).

For example, a 10-8-6 fertilizer is 10 percent nitrogen, 8 percent phosphorus (a form of phosphate), and 6 percent potash.

Do the math, and you see that a 100-pound bag of 10-5-5 fertilizer contains 10 pounds of nitrogen, 5 pounds of phosphorus, and 5 pounds of potash — a total of 20 pounds of usable nutrients. Although the remaining 80 pounds contains a small amount of other useful nutrients (also listed on the label), most of the extra bulk is just filler left over from manufacturing.

Not all fertilizers contain all three macronutrients:

- ✔ **Complete fertilizers:** These contain all three macronutrients: nitrogen (N), phosphorus (P), and potassium (K). The term *complete* has its basis in laws and regulations that apply to the fertilizer industry: It does not mean that the fertilizer contains *everything* the plant may need.

- ✔ **Incomplete fertilizer:** These are missing one or more of the major nutrients, usually the phosphorus or the potassium. Ammonium sulfate, which has a guaranteed analysis of 21-0-0, is an example of an incomplete fertilizer. Incomplete is not necessarily bad; in fact, it's often good. Incomplete fertilizers are usually less expensive, and besides, if your soil test indicates that your soil has plenty of phosphorus and potassium, why apply more? Too much of those nutrients can harm your plants.

Considering other factors

The guaranteed analysis is your primary shopping guide when buying fertilizer. But you may want to recognize some of the different types of fertilizers and understand more fertilizer-related terminology before you begin filling your cart:

- ✔ **Granular fertilizers:** The most common type of fertilizer, granular fertilizers come in bags or boxes and are either partially or completely soluble. They can be scattered over the soil and watered in, or worked into the soil before planting. You can mix the completely soluble types with water and apply them when you irrigate.

- ✔ **Liquid fertilizers:** You can buy this type of fertilizer in bottles or jugs. On a per-nutrient basis, most liquid fertilizers are more expensive than granular ones. Most liquid fertilizers need to be diluted in water before using, but some are ready to use. You apply liquid fertilizers when you water, and you can inject them into irrigation systems, which is the reason that many professional growers prefer them. They are particularly easy to use on plants grown in containers. Some liquid fertilizers are sold in hose-end applicators (shown in Figure 12-2), which eliminate mixing.

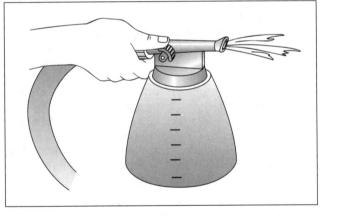

Figure 12-2:
Applying
liquid
fertilizer
with a
hose-end
attachment.

- ✔ **Chelated micronutrients:** This term refers to nutrients in a form that plants can absorb more quickly than the more commonly available sulfated forms. If, no matter how much nitrogen you apply, your plants just won't green up (they stay mottled yellow and green, or just plain yellow), you probably have a micronutrient deficiency of iron, zinc, or manganese. Chelated micronutrients are the quickest fix, although you may also have a soil pH problem that's preventing the nutrients from being absorbed by the plant. (See Chapter 8 for more information.)

- **Foliar fertilizers:** This term refers to fertilizers that you apply to the leaves of plants instead of to the roots. That's right, leaves can absorb nutrients, too. Leaves don't absorb nutrients as effectively as roots do, but they do absorb the nutrients quickly — so foliar feeding is a good fast-food fix for your plants. You can use most liquid fertilizers as foliar fertilizers, but make sure that the label indicates that it's okay to do so. Don't apply foliar fertilizers in hot weather, because they may burn the leaves.

- **Organic fertilizers:** Fertilizers labeled as *organic* derive their nutrients directly from plant, animal, or mineral sources and tend to have a minimum of refining done during their manufacturing process. Some examples include kelp meal, bonemeal, and greensand. Organic fertilizers tend to have lower amounts of all nutrients, and they often have only one main nutrient; greensand, for example, contains mostly potassium.

  To be effective, organic fertilizers need soil containing lots of soil microbes that can break down these products into forms the plant can use. Unlike chemical fertilizers, organic fertilizers make nutrients available to the plant roots slowly over a long period of time — only after the microbes have digested them. Microbes thrive in warm soils with lots of organic matter, such as leaves, grass clippings, and manure. Table 12-1 lists the nutrient contents of the most common organic fertilizers.

- **Slow-release fertilizers:** These chemical fertilizers release nutrients slowly in response to specific environmental conditions, such as temperatures or moisture. Slow-release fertilizers come in the form of pellets that are covered with a thin membrane, which slowly breaks down under the right temperature, moisture, or activity from soil microbes. As the membrane dissolves, the fertilizer inside the pellets is gradually released into the soil, for a period of up to eight months. This type of pellet is especially beneficial for the release of nitrogen, which tends to leach easily from the soil. Slow-release (or *time-release,* as they are sometimes called) fertilizers are best used for annuals grown in pots, but they may also be used as a supplement to other fertilizers if you have vigorous free-growing annuals such as morning glories.

Slow-release fertilizers are good for the environment because they reduce the amount of nutrients that wash out of and away from gardens into rivers and lakes.

Be warned: Slow-release fertilizers are very expensive. And when annuals are growing quickly, they may need more nitrogen than the slow-release fertilizer is providing. Watch your annuals carefully. If they grow slowly or are a bit yellowish in spite of their diet of slow-release fertilizer, give them a boost with an application of regular fertilizer.

✔ **Specialty fertilizers:** This term refers to fertilizers that are supposedly formulated for specific types of plants. For example, you may find a fertilizer labeled Flower Food with an analysis of 0-10-10. The logic behind such a fertilizer is that a blooming plant needs more phosphorus and potassium than it does nitrogen. That's because the phosphorus and potassium are important in the formation of flowers, and the nitrogen promotes the growth of leaves. And you want flowers, right? Well, not so fast. Because phosphorus and potassium don't move into the soil as well as nitrogen does, you can apply all you want of a fertilizer with phosphorus and potassium, and it may not get to the roots. Besides, if your soil test indicated that you have sufficient phosphorus and potassium, adding more does not give you more flowers.

The truth be told, I think specialty fertilizers are more of a marketing strategy than a high-tech solution. They're quite expensive compared to other fertilizers. If your annuals need nitrogen — and they probably do — then nitrogen, and only nitrogen, is what you should apply.

With so many options, how do you know which fertilizer to use on your flower bed? Because annuals aren't particularly fussy, you can use *any* kind of fertilizer that shows a nice balance of the major plant nutrients.

Inexpensive granular fertilizers usually contain only the big guns: nitrogen, phosphorus, and potassium. But why not go high-end with your fertilizer? For a bit more money, you can buy fertilizer that also contains a buffet of micronutrients (such as calcium and magnesium) and is coated to ensure that the nutrients are released very slowly each time you water. If you incorporate one of these slow-release fertilizers into your soil before you plant your flowers, you may never have to think about fertilizer again for the rest of the season.

Fertilizers that are slow-release say so right on the bag. The label also specifies *how* slow the release is. For example, a bag might say "three-month formula," or "six-month formula." Choose the time span that best fits your climate. Where the growing season is only three or four months long, the former is obviously sufficient.

You can use the same approach with balanced organic fertilizers, which are usually bulkier but every bit as good as their chemical counterparts. (In fact, many flower fans who aren't especially concerned about organic practices in their general thinking opt for organic fertilizers for their annual flowers.) Organic fertilizers can be relatively simple concoctions, such as dried, pelleted turkey or chicken manure, or they can be elaborate mixtures of fish meal, bonemeal, feather meal, and even shrimp hulls. You need not worry about possible odors, because you mix the materials into the soil where the smells are hidden from your nose. Because organic fertilizers vary so much in their content and potency, carefully read the label to find out how much you need to use.

Shopping for fertilizer bargains

Fertilizers sell for a range of prices. Some, such as premixed liquid fertilizers, are very expensive considering the amount of nutrients they contain. This is because premixed liquid fertilizers include a lot of water, which makes them heavy and more expensive to ship. When you know how to decipher the information on fertilizer product labels, you can become a better, more price-conscious shopper.

If a 10-pound bag of fertilizer contains 10 percent nitrogen, it includes 1 pound of what's called *actual nitrogen* (determined by multiplying the weight of the package by the percentage of nitrogen). By figuring out the actual nitrogen in different packages of fertilizer, you can compare the price of nutrients. For example, suppose that the 10-pound bag

of fertilizer with 10 percent nitrogen costs $5. The price of the 1 pound of actual nitrogen is $5 (the price divided by the pounds of actual nitrogen). Compare it to a 20-pound bag with 20 percent nitrogen, or 4 pounds of actual nitrogen, costing $10; the cost of the actual nitrogen is $2.50. The larger bag is a better deal, and your plants don't know the difference between more expensive fertilizer and bargain brands.

The amount of actual nitrogen in a package of fertilizer also influences application rates. The more actual nitrogen, the less you use with each application. But don't try to calculate the amount of fertilizer to use yourself; the manufacturer lists recommended application rates on the package.

Fertilizing Your Flower Bed

The best time to start fertilizing your flower bed is before you start planting. Giving your annuals a nutrient-rich home from the get-go ensures healthy development during their most formative period.

For the best results, add your fertilizer no more than a day or so before planting. Organic matter, such as compost, can be added at any time. Here's a fertilizer plan that works well for me:

1. **Before planting, spread a complete, high-nitrogen, granular fertilizer evenly over the planting area at the rates recommended on the package (usually 2 to 3 cups of fertilizer per 100 square feet).**

   You can do the spreading by hand, but be sure to wear gloves. If a test indicated that your soil has enough phosphorus and potassium, then use a product containing only nitrogen.

If you're really ambitious and are planting a large bed of annuals, using a broadcaster to spread the fertilizer will make the job much easier. Broadcasters, like the one shown in Figure 12-3, are commonly used for lawn care but are just as effective in large flower beds. Follow the instructions and rates recommended on the packaging (usually 10 to 20 pounds per 1,000 square feet of garden).

Figure 12-3:
Using a
broadcaster
to spread
granular
fertilizer

2. **Add lime or sulfur if necessary to balance your soil's pH.**

If you discover that your pH needs correcting, apply lime to bring the pH to a more alkaline (higher pH) state, or sulfur to make the pH more acidic (lower). Lime and sulfur are available at garden centers and can be applied either by hand or with a broadcaster like the one shown in Figure 12-3. Read more about when to use lime or sulfur and the proper pH levels for annuals in Chapter 8.

3. **Follow by spreading a 2- or 3-inch layer of organic matter.**

The best type of organic matter to spread just before planting is finished compost or composted manure. These are available in bags from garden centers, or you can create your own compost by allowing your organic matter (leaves, manure, grass clippings, and so on) to decompose. See Chapter 8 of this book for the basics of composting or, for detailed instructions, pick up a copy of *Gardening For Dummies* by Michael MacCaskey and the Editors of the National Gardening Association (published by IDG Books Worldwide, Inc.).

4. **Work everything into the soil, turning it with a shovel or rotary tiller so that all the nutrients end up where the roots can get them.**

   When planting, don't allow the roots of transplants to come in direct contact with the fertilizer. The high nitrogen content may burn the exposed roots.

5. **Now you're ready to plant your flower bed.**

   After planting, be sure to water the bed thoroughly.

6. **Every four to six weeks, fertilize again with a high-nitrogen fertilizer.**

   If you have really sandy soil in which nutrients wash through quickly, you may have to fertilize more often. If plants are slow to respond to these nutrients (say, if you don't see an improvement after a week), apply a foliar fertilizer for an extra boost.

   You can use either a liquid or granular fertilizer, but if you use a granular fertilizer, water well after each application, making sure that you wash off any fertilizer that may have settled on the leaves.

Don't fertilize dry plants, or you may do more harm than good. Plants need water to move fertilizer nutrients to the roots and help them take these fertilizers up into the plant. Without adequate water, the plant roots that do contact the fertilizers may be burned, causing the roots to die and the plant to suffer. Always water your plants well before and after fertilizing to get the most benefit from the fertilizer.

Some gardeners prefer to start cutting back on nitrogen after their annuals reach full bloom, thinking that the nitrogen may force leaf growth at the expense of flowers. I don't believe in this theory. If you're tending annual flowers properly, by removing spent blooms, for example, consistent applications of nitrogen throughout the life of the plant result in more blooms.

Overfertilizing can be much worse than not applying enough fertilizer. Excess nitrogen, for example, can burn the edges of leaves and even kill a plant. Besides that, if you apply too much fertilizer, it can leach into ground water, and then you're a nasty polluter. So always follow instructions on the fertilizer label and apply only nutrients that you're sure are deficient in your soil — too much of any nutrient can cause problems with plants and the environment. If you have doubts about what your soil needs, have your soil professionally tested.

Fertilizing Annuals in Containers

Plants growing in containers need more water than those growing in the ground. The more you water, the more you flush nutrients from the soil, and the more often you have to fertilize.

You can offset some of this constant loss of nutrients by mixing slow-release fertilizers into the soil before planting. But I also like to take a less-fertilizer-more-often approach. The best pots of annuals I've seen are on a constant feeding program. In other words, you give your flowers a little liquid fertilizer every time, or every other time, you water them. Cut the recommended rates on the bottle of fertilizer in half or into quarters, so you're applying only about a teaspoon or so of fertilizer per watering. This may sound like a lot of work, but wait until you see the results. Bloom city!

If fertilizing every time you water is too much hassle for you, use a liquid fertilizer once every week or two. Follow the rates recommended on the label. Your annuals will still do great.

Using Organic Fertilizers

Organic fertilizers come in all shapes and sizes. These days, there are as many definitions of organic as there are cappuccino stands in Seattle. Basically, anything that was once alive (such as seaweed or cows) or was produced by a living thing is considered organic. Some widely accepted organic fertilizers include manure, compost, fish emulsion, bonemeal, and greensand. The appendix lists mail-order suppliers of organic fertilizers.

Manure from horses, cows, and poultry is the most common organic source of nitrogen. The salts in fresh manure can burn plants, so you must make sure that the manure has aged for a while or is completely composted before you apply it. Many gardeners work manure into the soil in the fall and then wait until spring to plant. This approach allows plenty of time for the manure to "mellow."

Bonemeal is a good organic source of phosphorus, but once in the ground, it takes a long time to break down into a form that plants can use. Greensand, a naturally occurring rock mineral found mostly in New Jersey, is an excellent organic source of potassium and also includes many micronutrients.

Many people today prefer to use organic fertilizer because they feel that it's better for their plants. The truth is that your annuals don't know whether the nutrients they're getting have organic or synthetic sources. But organic fertilizers do have an advantage in that, besides providing nutrients, they also add bulk to the soil and improve its structure in ways that synthetic fertilizers cannot.

Organic fertilizers are better for the environment because they support soil-building earthworms and microbes and because they are usually recycled — not manufactured — materials. However, organic fertilizers are often difficult to handle, their nutrient contents are unpredictable, and the nutrients they do contain aren't always immediately available to the plant. They tend to be higher priced, but if you're creative, you can make your own through composting or gathering aged manure from local farms.

You can supply all the nutrients that annuals need by using only organic materials, but you must take some care and effort to ensure that sufficient amounts of nitrogen, phosphorus, and potassium are available to plants throughout the season. You have to observe your plants carefully, noting their vigor and general color, and then add more or less fertilizer with each application until you get the results you want.

Table 12-1 lists some common organic fertilizers, their average nutrient analysis, and moderate rates at which you can apply them. Because nutrient contents of organic fertilizers can vary greatly, use less if you have doubts.

Before applying bonemeal or any other dusty fertilizer, get a good dust mask. Just because a fertilizer is organic doesn't mean that it can't harm you.

Table 12-1	Common Organic Fertilizers	
Organic Fertilizer	*Average Nutrient Analysis*	*Application Rate per 100 Square Feet*
Blood meal	10-0-0	2 pounds
Bonemeal (steamed)	1-11-0	2 pounds
Cow manure	2-2-2	10 to 15 pounds
Fish emulsion	4-1-1	15 to 20 gallons (1 tablespoon per gallon)
Greensand	0-0-7	5 pounds
Horse manure	2-1-2	10 to 15 pounds
Poultry manure	4-4-2	5 pounds

Chapter 13

Staking, Pruning, Deadheading, and Other Joys of Gardening

In This Chapter

▶ Choosing the right tools

▶ Deadheading faded flowers

▶ Staking slumping annuals

▶ Pruning and pinching

▶ Mulching the right way

*Y*ou can view your routine gardening chores in one of two ways: You can think of those tasks as, well, work, or you can view them as opportunities. I recommend the second approach: Deadheading flowers can be an opportunity to visit with your neighbors; pruning the petunias gives you a temporary escape from your teenager's head-banging music; and spreading mulch offers an excuse to enjoy the beauty of nature.

No matter how you view your gardening chores, the payoff is worth your time and effort. By protecting the investment you've made in your annuals, you get a garden that looks good for the long term. Conscientious gardeners are rewarded with prettier, healthier plants that last longer and provide a most impressive display.

This chapter shows you how to efficiently deadhead, stake, pinch, prune, mulch, and do a few wrap-up jobs. It also explains the basic tools and materials that you need to maintain a healthy garden. Use the information in this chapter to keep your annuals in the best shape possible. (Unfortunately, annuals sometimes demand other kinds of care, including pest and weed control, which I cover in Chapters 14 and 15.)

Tackling the Key Gardening Tasks

Garden maintenance involves four simple tasks:

- ✔ **Deadheading:** Removing faded flowers to stimulate new flower production

- ✔ **Staking:** Providing support to stems and blossoms that may otherwise fall over or snap

- ✔ **Pinching and pruning:** Removing parts of the plant to control growth, maximize flower production, and give plants good form

- ✔ **Mulching:** Covering the soil around the plants to keep moisture in and weeds out

Depending on how you approach these chores, you can either slave away for endless hours or get the jobs done quickly and efficiently. Timing is important to help you keep the tasks small and manageable, not large and overwhelming. Here are some key strategies for garden maintenance:

- ✔ **Start the jobs early, before the situation gets out of hand.** This is the most important bit of advice for your garden maintenance. Anyone who has attempted to cut back a jungle of wild and woolly flowers or struggled to upright drooping 4-foot-flower stems can testify that heeding this advice saves you time and toil later. Doing your gardening jobs early makes them significantly smaller and more manageable.

- ✔ **Always do jobs as you notice that they need to be done.** If you head out to the garden to snip a few flowers or pinch back a leggy stem, be on the lookout for faded blossoms to deadhead, debris to clean up, or floppy stems to support. Doing multiple jobs at once is a simple time-saver.

- ✔ **Observe a regular maintenance schedule.** By so doing, you ensure that no chore gets too far out of hand. For example, try to weed and deadhead your flower beds weekly. That doesn't mean spending all day Saturday weeding; it just means that each section of your garden gets attention at least once a week. For example, if you weed and deadhead a small patch of your garden for a half hour every weekday evening, you may be able to cover the entire area over the course of five days. That leaves you Saturday and Sunday to enjoy your handiwork.

- ✔ **Be a bucket gardener.** Hide a plastic bucket near your garden (or take one with you when you go) so that, as you pinch a stem or snap off a flower, you have an easy and convenient place to toss your garden waste until you can take it to the compost pile or recycling bin. For large areas, consider keeping a plastic garbage container (the kind with wheels is great) or a wheelbarrow nearby. Keeping equipment handy means that you are more likely to spend a few minutes doing chores each time you visit the garden rather than waiting until you have a large chunk of time to lug all your equipment from a distant spot.

✔ **Make regular tours of the garden.** Think of these tours as mini-vacations — time away from your kitchen, computer, or laundry room. Don't get your hands dirty on these garden strolls, but do make a mental note of what jobs you need to tackle next. When the time comes to do some work in the garden, you already know what tools you need and what chores are most pressing, so you can work smarter.

✔ **Make sure that you have the materials and tools you need to do the job.** Store tools in a set location where you can always find them, and keep them clean. Keep track of supplies such as stakes, ties, and mulch and restock as amounts get low; don't wait until they're completely gone. I describe the tools you need and how to care for them in the upcoming section "Using the Right Tool for the Right Job."

✔ **Evaluate how much maintenance you're doing.** Is it manageable, or is it taking a toll on you? If it seems that you're spending too much time and effort on your garden, ask yourself whether you could be doing your chores more efficiently to save time. If not, consider scaling down the garden to a size that you can more easily handle.

Using the Right Tool for the Right Job

To do any job right, you need the right tools; gardening is no exception. Fortunately, with a well-planned and properly planted annual bed, you can perform most garden maintenance jobs with a minimum of tools and materials.

Seven essential tools for growing annuals

You need some key tools for maintaining and planting annuals. The good news is that you may already have some of these tools, and because the digging won't have to be very deep, you don't have to get into the "heavy metal."

✔ **Garden spade or shovel:** This is the single most important tool for digging, loosening, turning, amending, and spreading everything from soil to compost to manure. You have lots of choices from a size, price, and quality standpoint. Choose a tool that feels right in both weight and length. Some people prefer a shovel or spade with a long, straight handle; others prefer one with a shorter handle and plastic or metal grip. Mimic the motion you'll use to shovel, and find the size that's most comfortable for you. Remember to pay for quality if you want to invest in a lasting tool.

✓ **Steel bow rake:** This rake is the one with the stiff tines. It's a must-have tool for spreading, leveling, or removing rocks and debris. A steel bow rake helps you break up clods, and when you turn the rake over, the back edge is excellent for leveling and smoothing a seed bed.

✓ **Hand trowel:** This handheld tool is important for digging small holes for planting seedlings or transplants from six-packs or 4-inch containers. It's also handy for popping out weeds and removing small rocks. A thick-bladed farmer's or gardener's knife is an acceptable substitute. These knives have a wide, sturdy blade and are the best for solid digging; they don't bend the way some trowels do. Choose a tool that is the right weight for you and has a comfortable handle.

✓ **Hoe:** Try a scuffle hoe for a more efficient tool than the basic bladed hoe. Compared to an old-fashioned hoe, scuffle hoes work with a push/pull action that cuts off or digs out small weeds right at the soil surface. This tool is good for working between plants and on hard, compacted surfaces such as paths.

✓ **Leaf rake:** Small rakes — about 8 inches wide — are ideal for work in close quarters; large rakes are handy for removing and collecting light debris and, you guessed it, leaves. The tines of a rake may be made of bamboo, plastic, or flexible metal. Consider investing in an expandable rake, which allows you to expand or contract the tines, changing the width so that you can use it over large areas or between plants in a bed.

✓ **Pruners:** No gardener can live without a pair of pruners. Use this hand-held cutting tool for snipping stems up to $^3/_4$-inch diameter or so. Pruners come in handy when you're cutting flowers, pruning plants to improve their shape, or clipping mature plants after they're finished blooming. Pruners are available in a wide price range and several styles. High-quality pruners give you clean cuts with a minimum of effort and will last for years. Look for comfort and sharp blades.

✓ **Garden cart:** Carts are lightweight and stable, allowing you to haul loads of heavy stuff, including soil, compost, or mulch. Let a cart do the work when you need to transport your plants to the garden. It can handle flats of flowers or 1-gallon pots. Look for a cart with four wheels set close together for easy maneuvering through tight spaces. Or if you prefer, you can use a wheelbarrow.

Nonessential but handy garden supplies

If you can afford a few extra gardening goodies, add the following items to your shopping list:

- **Garden gloves:** Choose cloth if don't want to spend a bunch; try sheepskin or pigskin for long-lasting protection.

- **Water wand:** This gadget is an aluminum pipe that attaches to the end of the hose and produces a gentle shower that's perfect for seeds and seedlings.

- **Soft ties:** Garden centers sell various plastic tapes and twist ties for tying stems to stakes and vines to trellises. You can also use regular jute twine, or even strips of soft fabric.

- **Hose guide:** This device keeps hoses outside low beds so that you don't pull the hose over small plants. Use a guide to protect plants along curves or corners.

- **Pronged weeder:** This little tool (about a foot long) is great, especially if you don't have a gardener's knife. One end has a small hoelike blade, and the other end has a dual-pronged point that's perfect for those nasty weeds and general light cultivation.

TIP

Tool tips

Follow these general guidelines for choosing and maintaining your tools and materials, and you're sure to be a happier gardener.

- **You get what you pay for.** Cheap tools may work fine at first, but they may not hold up for more than one season. Over the long haul, you're likely to have trouble with inferior parts and workmanship. Handles may come loose, or metal parts may bend.

  To be sure that the tools you're purchasing are high quality, look for sturdy construction and durable materials. If possible, test the tools before purchasing them. Those pruners may look great, but if they're too large for your grip or give you blisters, you'll dread your pruning chores.

- **Care for your tools.** Store tools indoors in a safe place where small hands can't get to them, and wash and dry tools after each use. Caring for your tools is especially important if you invest in high-quality ones.

- **Keep 'em sharp.** You'll get better results with less effort if your spade, shears, garden scissors, hand trowel, and hoe have sharp edges. Use a file and household oil to sharpen the blades, or bring your tools to a sharpening service.

- **Organize, store, and transport small tools in a bucket or plastic tote.** You can easily lose track of small hand tools, such as trowels, snips, or shears, if you lay them down while you work. Keeping tools in a brightly colored plastic container ensures that they're safe and easy to find.

- **Organize your small supplies.** Keep your garden ties, small stakes, and other items in a handy, lightweight container and store them indoors in a safe and secure spot.

Deadheading: Out with the Old . . .

Avoiding all cheap-shot jokes about touring rock bands, I will simply say that *deadheading* is the act of cutting or pinching off a faded flower. It's an important job: By removing the spent flower, you stimulate the plant to produce a new bud in its exhaustive quest to make seeds to reproduce. Deadheading not only keeps plants looking tidy, but it also prolongs the bloom period and gives you significantly more flowers.

Start deadheading as soon as you see the flowers fade and the petals begin to fall off. Remove part of the stem as well as the faded flower, so that you're sure to get the seed pod, too. With some flowers, such as petunias, you can pull off the petal part and think you've done the job, but the seed pod remains. Use your fingers, as shown in Figure 13-1, to pinch off flowers with fleshy stems. (Marigolds make a particularly satisfying snap.) Use pruners for stiffer or more stubborn flowers.

Watch for flower-producing side shoots a bit down on the stem. When removing spent flowers, cut the stem *above* this point to save the new buds coming on. Cosmos, zinnia, and gloriosa daisy are famous for producing these lower buds. If you don't see any side shoots, cut the stem just above a set of leaves.

Figure 13-1: Removing dead blooms coaxes your annuals into producing new blooms.

Offering Some Support: Basics of Staking

Staking is a simple but important job — especially for plants more than 3 feet tall and for plants with large, heavy flowers or slender stems. Staking keeps plants steady in the wind and ensures that blossoms stay healthy and upright. It gives the garden a neat and tidy look and helps plants produce the maximum number of flowers.

You almost always have to stake tall annuals, such as cosmos, sunflowers, spider flowers, salpiglossis, nicotiana, larkspur, gloriosa daisy, cornflower, and globe amaranthus. You also may need to stake certain tall varieties of zinnia, dahlia, and snapdragon. Keep an eye on all your annuals as they develop to see whether flowers seem to be giving in to gravity, thus requiring you to shake them.

Stake early! You'll have far better results if you put the stake in when you set out transplants or after seedlings reach a few inches tall. By staking early, you can direct the stems to grow upward right from the start and tie them at intervals along the stake as they grow. After a mass of flowers falls over, it's difficult to bring them back to a vertical postion without damaging them. Don't worry about the aethetics of the stake; although the stake may look stark at first, the stems and leaves will quickly surround the stake and hide it from view.

Tie stems to slender bamboo sticks, wooden stakes, or even straight and sturdy woody branches that you saved from your pruning chores. For light plants with sturdy stems, such as cosmos and cornflower, you can use twine or twist ties. For large-flowered plants, such as sunflowers, use plastic garden tape or strips of fabric — under the weight of those heavy flowers, twine can cut into stem tissue. For the largest plants, insert a single stake a few inches from the stem at planting time and loosely tie the seedling to the stake. As the plant grows, continue to tie the stem at intervals along the stake, as shown on the left plant in Figure 13-2.

You can also corral smaller plants by setting stakes in the ground around the circumference and winding ties or twine horizontally to enclose the area. Or you can buy wire stakes with a loop that encircles individual stems (shown on the right-hand plant in Figure 13-2). Also available are mini-fences that hook together in sections to support many plants at once.

Don't forget to stake your container plants. Stake these flowers when they're little by using either one slender stake per plant (pushed several inches down), or three or four stakes around the edge of pot with twine wrapped around the them. Try green wire stakes in containers — they blend in and disappear among the flowers.

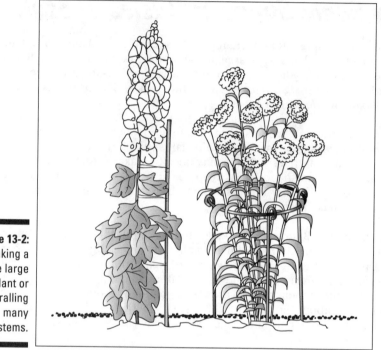

Figure 13-2:
Staking a single large plant or corralling many stems.

If you're growing annual climbers (such as sweet pea, morning glory, scarlet runner bean, and so on), be sure to plant seeds where the flowers will have serious support nearby. Good choices are planting areas near a fence, lattice, post, pillar, or arbor. Many of these climbers twine themselves around the support, but you may need to give some stems guidance by using soft ties. Insert U-shaped staples in posts, pillars, or fence boards to run the ties through.

Pruning and Pinching: It Hurts You More Than It Hurts the Plant

Pinching and pruning annuals are far simpler tasks than similar care for more permanent plants, such as perennials and shrubs. Still, the jobs clearly have their rewards.

Pinching refers to removal of soft tip growth and is usually done with the thumb and forefinger. It encourages plants to become bushy and full rather than rangy and tall. A side effect of pinching is that plants develop uniform growth and plenty of buds — although pinching tends to postpone the flowers a bit if you remove their buds.

Pinch plants when they're young — before they develop long stems. Remove the tip growth by pinching above a set of leaves. To promote good overall shape, pinch both upright and side stems (as shown in Figure 13-3). When you have a mass of plants in the bed, pinch back the tallest ones so that they don't shoot up past their neighbors. Good candidates for pinching include petunias, snapdragons, impatiens, chrysanthemums, marguerites, and geraniums. Avoid pinching plants that send up strong central shoots with flowers at the tip, such as stock and celosia. These flowers don't branch well anyway, so you don't want to pinch off all the flower buds.

Figure 13-3:
Pinching or pruning off side shoots promotes a fuller, more compact plant.

Pruning is the process of cutting back plants to keep them within the boundaries you've set and to promote bushier growth. Annuals rarely need the heavy-duty pruning that perennials and shrubs demand. Trim stems that are rangy, floppy, or sprawling onto neighboring flowers; trim as often as necessary to keep them under control. Make cuts just above a set of leaves or side shoot. This technique promotes both bushiness and new buds. After the first round of blooms, especially if you haven't deadheaded, you can try giving plants an overall trimming to encourage a new round of blooms.

So which annuals require serious pruning? You'll probably need to worry only about globe amaranthus, four o'clocks, felicia, and some types of petunia, especially cascading or trailing varieties that become very leggy.

Mulching Miracles

A *mulch* is simply a soil cover. Mulching an annual garden cuts down on the amount of water needed and helps control weeds. The principle is simple: The soil is cooled and protected by the application of a top layer of some type of material. You can use compost, leaf mold, crushed stone, or bark, or you can use inorganic materials, such as landscape fabric, plastic sheeting, or even newspapers. As long as the material is attractive, you'll have a neat-looking garden, to boot. A layer of mulch also helps hide drip irrigation tubes (discussed in Chapter 11).

Try this trio of quick and easy steps for mulching the annuals in your garden:

1. **Select a mulch material.**

   What do you have on hand that can be used as mulch? Compost or perhaps the by-products of chopped, shredded stuff from a chipper/shredder machine? You also can purchase packaged mulches in bulk or bags; redwood shavings, bark (in small, medium, and coarse chunks or shredded), cocoa or rice hulls, and compost are sold this way. Generally the finer the material, the better it looks with your annuals. Plastic sheeting, landscape fabric, or old newspapers are okay, but they really are ugly and better used in vegetable gardens, where appearance matters less. If you do use an unsightly mulch, you can cover it with a layer of bark, compost, or crushed stone.

2. **Spread your mulch material around annuals but leave a few inches of bare earth around the base of each annual.**

   This technique provides a little reservoir for water and keeps plant stems from rotting or becoming diseased. In general, annuals like a 2- to 3-inch layer of mulch; the thicker the mulch, the fewer weeds. If you use a layer of newspapers or landscape fabric first, you'll need less mulch on top — just enough to cover. Because these are not permanent plants, you don't need anything much thicker.

3. **Make periodic inspections of the garden to see that mulch stays put.**

   Marauding pets, wind, water, and even tiny garden visitors like mice and squirrels can easily displace this soil covering. Keep extra mulch on hand so that you can always add mulch when and where you need it.

For more information about the uses of mulch, see Chapter 15.

Some Final Fun-Filled Activities

Here are a few more quick tasks to help you keep your annual garden looking its best.

- ✔ **Floral management:** For cut flowers, cut stems early in the morning and immediately immerse them in water. Zinnias, cosmos, pinks, snapdragons, marigolds, stock, and poppies are good flowers for cutting. See Chapter 18 for more information.

- ✔ **Replanting:** One way to ensure that your garden earns a place in the hall of fame is to make sure that it's always full and fresh. You may have to replant two to three times during the seasons from spring into fall, especially if you live in a mild climate with a long growing period. If you start early with spring annuals, chances are that the garden will be on its way out by midsummer. At this point, remove tired plants and replant with fresh new annuals that will bloom into late summer and early fall. If you're lucky enough to have a long growing season (and have the energy for it), you may want to replant three times — in early spring, early summer, and fall. And in really warm regions, you can even enjoy a winter annual garden. Local nurseries usually carry plants appropriate for your seasons.

- ✔ **Wrapping up:** Tidying up your garden as the active growing season winds down is your last task. After you collect any seeds, pull up faded plants. Rake and clean up the bed. If anything looks diseased or shows pest damage, bag it and dispose of it properly — don't compost it. Take note: Some plants grown as annuals, such as pansy and primrose, are actually tender perennials. If you leave such plants in place in a protected location, they may grow and flower for several seasons.

Chapter 14

Outsmarting Pests and Diseases

In This Chapter

▶ Preventing problems in your flower bed

▶ Distinguishing between good and evil in the insect world

▶ Choosing the correct insect control measures

▶ Controlling insects that prey on annuals

▶ Identifying a nasty quintet of diseases

Annuals are often called the racehorses of flowers. Few other plants grow so fast and provide so much color so quickly. But that speed can be both a blessing and a curse when dealing with insects and diseases.

First the blessing part: Many annuals grow so fast that they can actually outdistance problems before the problems really get a chance to set in. A beetle may chew on one flower, for example, but what's one flower among a mass of hundreds? You probably won't even notice the damage. (By comparison, gardeners treasure every single bloom on a rose bush.) The vigorous, healthy growth, the modus operandi of annuals, is in itself one of the best ways to fend off many pests. Healthy annuals — flowers planted in well-prepared soil, exposed to the proper amount of sunlight, and watered and fertilized properly — are less susceptible to insects and diseases.

Now the curse: The same fast growth that can outpace some pests is particularly attractive to other pests. Aphids, for example, are very fond of young, tender growth. Also, the fact that annuals are often grown in masses of just one kind creates an ideal breeding ground for pests drawn to that particular food source. And if the pests get out of hand, they don't ruin only one plant here and there — they can nail the whole bed.

But fear not. If you choose adaptable annuals (those that can grow in a variety of conditions and climates), care for them properly, and observe them carefully, few problems will actually send you crying to your neighborhood nursery. I go crying to the nursery no more often than once a week, and it's usually about the bill.

An Ounce of Prevention

Many gardeners, especially beginners, are surprised to find out just how many pest and disease problems that they can actually prevent or avoid. Now I'm not talking about prevention through weekly sprays of scorched-earth pesticides that kill any insect or disease organism before it gets within 10 feet of your annuals. That's not the kind of gardener you want to be.

I recommend a more well-rounded approach to pest control. And the key to this approach is knowledge. The more you know about the plants you grow, the pests that are common to them, the types of pest control measures available, and how to protect the diversity of life that occupies your garden, the less likely it is that you'll have to take drastic measures, such as using strong chemicals.

Becoming a good observer is also important in pest and disease control. The best way to keep pests in check is to walk through your garden at least a few times a week. Don't use this time to plant, weed, or pick, but rather just to observe the plants. Look at the leaves (both sides), stems, flowers, and fruits for any signs of damage or poor plant health. Keep any damage you find in proper perspective; a few chew marks or yellow leaves here and there are not reason to panic. A healthy garden has a balance of organisms, including insects that are harmful to plants, and insects that feed on other bugs.

You can control a few aphids or caterpillars in the garden simply by picking them off and disposing of them, or by waiting for their natural predators, such as ladybugs and lacewings, to have lunch. After frequent visits to the garden, you'll get a sense of the difference between a mild infestation and a serious problem that's out of hand and needs fast, active control measures.

The first step to solving any plant problem is to identify the culprit. Don't always assume that an insect or disease is causing the damage. Sometimes, it may be the result of cold weather, poor nutrition, or physical damage from animals such as deer. To get you started as a gardening super sleuth, this chapter includes some common pests and diseases. If you need more help identifying a problem in your flower bed, local gardening resources such as nursery employees, botanical garden horticulturists, and Master Gardeners at the Cooperative Extension Office can usually recognize a particular insect, disease, or weather condition that's causing the problem. Many times, you can bring them a leaf or fruit sample to examine in person. (Find the telephone number of the extension office under your county government listing for "Cooperative Extension" or "Farm Advisor.") Reference books are also a great way to identify problems. At your nursery, botanical garden, library, or county extension office, ask to see books such as *The Ortho Problem Solver*, a 1,000-page illustrated encyclopedia of garden pests.

The following common-sense pest and disease prevention tips are your first line of defense:

- ✔ **Plant in the right location.** Many pests become more troublesome when annuals are grown in less-than-ideal conditions. For example, when sun-loving annuals are grown in shade, mildew problems often become more severe.

- ✔ **Grow healthy plants.** Healthy plants are less likely to develop problems. Prepare the soil properly before planting and avoid overfertilizing and overwatering. Part V of this book contains information that can help you provide the proper care.

- ✔ **Choose resistant plants.** If you know that a certain disease is common in your area, choose plants that are not susceptible or that resist infection to it. Some varieties of annuals are resistant to specific diseases. For example, some varieties of snapdragon resist rust, and some varieties of delphiniums and zinnias resist mildew. Look for disease-resistance information in seed catalogs and nursery descriptions.

- ✔ **Keep your garden clean.** Cleaning up spent plants, weeds, and other garden debris can eliminate hiding places for many pests.

- ✔ **Rotate your annuals.** Avoid planting the same annuals in the same location year after year. Rotation prevents pests and diseases specific to certain annuals from building up in your soil.

- ✔ **Know the enemy.** The more you know about specific pests and diseases common to your area — when they occur and how they spread — the more easily you can avoid them. For example, some diseases, such as rust and botrytis, run rampant on wet foliage. By simply adjusting your watering so that you don't wet the leaves of the plant, or by watering early in the day so that plants dry out quickly, you can reduce the occurrence of these diseases.

When Bad Bugs Happen to Nice Gardens

Actually, bugs are neither bad nor good. They just do what they're programmed to do: eat, grow, and reproduce. The only problem comes in when bugs and gardeners want to enjoy the same flowers. A little conflict of interest, you might say! A bug becomes a pest only if it meets both these criteria:

- ✔ It wants to eat what you're trying to grow.

- ✔ The damage it causes makes the plant look unsightly and decline in health.

An errant grasshopper may not be cause for concern, but if that same grasshopper brings along his brothers, sisters, and cousins to join in on the zinnia feast at your expense, he becomes a pest. When you start seeing a number of the same type of insects, such as aphids, in your garden, and you notice that their activity is focused on certain plants, such as cosmos, then you need to act quickly and decisively.

Insects that prey on annuals

Here are the most common insect pests that you are likely to find infesting your annuals and the best way to control them:

- **Aphids:** These tiny, pear-shaped pests (shown in Figure 14-1) come in many colors, including black, green, and red. They congregate on new growth and flower buds, sucking plant sap with their needlelike noses. Heavy infestations can cause distorted growth and weaken plants. Vinca and cosmos are two annuals that aphids commonly attack. Aphids leave behind a sticky sap that may turn black with sooty mold.

  Aphids are easy to control. You can knock them off sturdy plants with a strong jet of water from a hose, or you can use insecticidal soap or pyrethrins, described in the section "Botanical insecticides." The soap helps wash off the sooty mold (the harmless black gunk that comes with aphids). But usually if you just wait a week or two, the aphid population boom is followed by a buildup of beneficial insects, especially lady beetles, who usually take matters into their own hands before serious damage occurs.

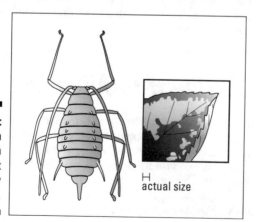

Figure 14-1:
Aphids can weaken plants, but they're easy to control.

actual size

✔ **Geranium budworms:** These frustrating pests (shown in Figure 14-2) love geraniums, nicotiana, ageratum, and petunias. The small caterpillars bore into flower buds and eat the flowers before they open, or they simply feed on open blooms. The result is no flowers, only leaves. Not a pretty sight!

To confirm the presence of these heartless monsters, look for small holes in geranium blossoms or the tiny black droppings that the caterpillars leave behind. You may also see the worms on the flowers. To control, pick off infested geranium buds and spray with Bt. Bt is a naturally occurring bacteria that parasitizes the budworm. It's the most environmentally-friendly pesticide to use, but chemical-based pesticides (such as pyrethrins, carbaryl, and acephate) also work. All are available at local garden centers and are registered for home gardener use.

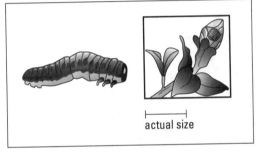

Figure 14-2:
Geranium budworms like to feast on petunias as well as geraniums.

actual size

✔ **Japanese beetles:** Especially troublesome east of the Mississippi River, these pests feed on both flowers and foliage, often skeletonizing leaves. They particularly love zinnias and marigolds. Shown in Figure 14-3, Japanese beetles are about $1/2$ inch long and have coppery bodies and metallic green heads.

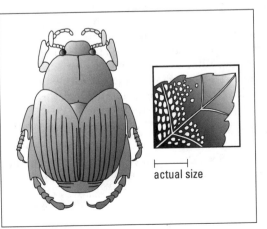

Figure 14-3:
Japanese beetles are especially fond of zinnias and marigolds.

actual size

Controlling this pest can be tough. Treating your lawn and garden soil with parasitic nematodes or milky spore (a form of Bt) may reduce the white C-shaped larvae, but more adults will probably fly in from your neighbor's yard. Turning the soil to expose the grubs to birds also may help. Floral-scented traps that attract adult beetles are available, but the traps may attract more beetles than you had before. If you try the traps, keep them at least 100 feet from your flowers.

Neem, insecticidal soap, and pyrethrins are effective against adult beetles. Traditional chemicals that may help include carbaryl and acephate. You also can simply pick the beetles off your flowers and stomp on them.

✔ **Cutworms:** These 1/2-inch-long, grayish caterpillars (shown in Figure 14-4) emerge during spring and early summer nights to eat the stems of young seedling stems, causing them to fall over like small timbers. They also move on to older plants and feed on leaves and flowers.

Figure 14-4:
Cutworms can do a lot of damage before sprouting wings and flying off.

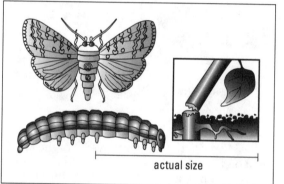

actual size

To protect seedlings, surround their stems with a barrier that prevents the cutworms from crawling close and feeding. These contraptions can be as simple as an empty cardboard toilet-paper roll, a Styrofoam cup with the bottom cut out, or a collar made from aluminum foil — just make sure that the barrier encircles the stem completely and is set 1 inch deep in the soil. You can also trap cutworms by leaving boards around the garden. The worms will hide under the boards during the day, giving you the chance to collect and destroy them. Parasitic nematodes are also effective against cutworms.

✔ **Snails and slugs:** These soft-bodied mollusks feed on tender leaves and flowers during the cool of the night or during rainy weather. Snails have shells; slugs don't. (See Figure 14-5.) Both proliferate in damp areas, hiding under boards, mulch, and other garden debris.

To control these pests, you can roam the garden at night with a flashlight and play pick-and-stomp. Or you can trap them with saucers of beer — these guys can't resist a brewski, even if it means drowning to death. Bury a catfood can, cup, or dish so that the rim is at ground level, and refill regularly. Snails and slugs do not cross copper, so you can also surround raised beds with a thin copper stripping sold in most nurseries. In southern California, you can release *decollate snails,* which prey on pest snails. Ask your cooperative extension office for information. If all else fails, you can use poison snail bait.

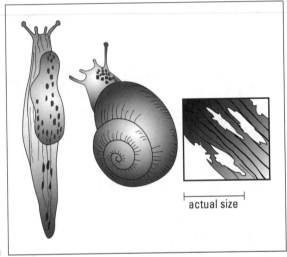

actual size

Figure 14-5:
Slugs and snails like to hide in damp areas.

✔ **Spider mites:** These tiny arachnids can barely be seen without a magnifying glass. If the population gets big enough, you can see their fine webbing beneath the leaves. (See Figure 14-6.) And as they suck plant juices, the leaves become yellowish, with silvery stippling or sheen. If things get really bad, the plant may start dropping leaves. Mites are most common in hot, dry summer climates and on dusty plants. Marigolds and columbines are commonly infested.

A daily bath with a strong jet of water from a hose helps keep infestations down. You can control spider mites with insecticidal soap, which also helps to clean off the plants' leaves. Summer oil is also effective, as is releasing predatory mites.

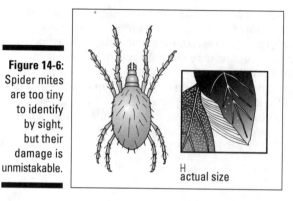

Figure 14-6:
Spider mites
are too tiny
to identify
by sight,
but their
damage is
unmistakable.

✔ **Thrips:** Another nearly invisible troublemaker, thrips feed on flower petals, causing them to be discolored and the buds to be deformed as they open. (See Figure 14-7.) Thrips also feed on leaves, giving the foliage a deformed and stippled look. (You can distinguish thrips from spider mites by the small fecal pellets that thrips leave behind.) Impatiens and many other annuals can become targets of thrips.

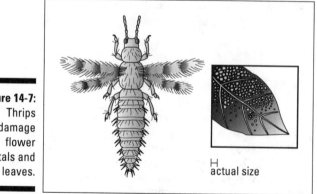

Figure 14-7:
Thrips
damage
flower
petals and
leaves.

Many beneficial insects feed on thrips, especially lacewings. Insecticidal soaps are also effective, as are several stronger insecticides, including acephate.

✔ **Whiteflies:** Looking like small white gnats (see Figure 14-8), whiteflies suck plant juices and can proliferate in warm climates and greenhouses. They tend to congregate on the undersides of leaves. You can trap whiteflies with yellow sticky traps sold in nurseries. In greenhouses, you can release Encarsia wasps, which prey on greenhouse whiteflies. Insecticidal soaps, summer oil, and pyrethrins are effective sprays.

You can buy Encarsia wasps through mail-order pest control suppliers, such as those listed in this book's appendix. Encarsia wasps are very different from the stinging wasps you're probably familiar with; they're small insects that are harmless to people.

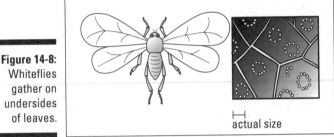

Figure 14-8: Whiteflies gather on undersides of leaves.

actual size

Fighting back

If pests begin to bother your garden in serious ways and you need to take further action, start with the first line of defense: pesticides that are effective against a particular pest, that are relatively safe to use, and that have a mild impact on the rest of your garden's life forms.

In general, these products are short-lived after you use them in the garden — that's what makes them so good. However, in order to get effective control, you often must use them more frequently than stronger chemicals.

Biological controls

Biological controls involve pitting one living thing against another, such as beneficial insects against harmful insects. Beneficial insects are the good soldiers of your garden — the insects that feed on the bugs that bother your annuals. You probably already have many different kinds of beneficial insects in your garden, but you also can purchase them at garden suppliers (see the appendix) and release them into your garden. The more beneficial bugs, the fewer pests.

You can purchase the following beneficial insects to help control the pests that are dining on your annuals:

- **Lady beetles:** These are basic ladybugs. Both the orange-red adult beetles and the lizardlike larvae are especially good at feeding on small insects such as aphids and thrips. Releasing adult beetles is sometimes not very effective because Mother Nature has preprogrammed them to migrate on down the road, so they leave your garden quickly. Try preconditioned lady beetles, which have been deprogrammed (you don't want to know how); they are more likely to stick around. And release them just before sundown. That way, they'll at least spend the night. Release a few thousand of them in spring, as soon as you notice the first aphid.

✔ **Green lacewings:** Their voracious larvae feed on aphids, mites, thrips, and various insect eggs. These insects are among the most effective for garden use. Release them in your garden in late spring, after the danger of frost has passed.

✔ **Parasitic nematodes:** These microscopic worms parasitize many types of soil-dwelling and burrowing insects, including cutworms and grubs of Japanese beetles. Because grubs usually inhabit lawns, you have to apply these worms there, too, as well as around the base of your plants. Apply parasitic nematodes to the soil around the base of your plants once in the spring.

✔ **Predatory mites:** These tiny creatures feed on spider mites and thrips. Add them to your garden in the spring, as soon as frost danger has passed.

✔ **Trichogramma wasps:** Harmless to humans, these insects actually are tiny wasps that attack moth eggs and butterfly larvae (caterpillars, that is). Release the wasps when temperatures are above 72°F (22°C).

To get the good insects to stick around, avoid indiscriminate use of broad-spectrum pesticides, which kill everything, good along with bad. If you do spray, use a type that specifically targets the pest you want to eliminate and that has minimal effect on beneficial insects.

Another way to encourage beneficial insects to make a home of your flower bed is to maintain a diverse garden with many kinds and sizes of plants. Diversity gives the beneficial insects places to hide and reproduce, and it also can provide an alternative food source for beneficial insects that eat pollen and flower nectar as well as other insects. Plants that attract beneficial insects include Queen Anne's lace, parsley (especially if you let the flower develop), sweet alyssum, dill, fennel, and yarrow.

Releasing beneficial insects is one example of biological control, but you can also use different kinds of bacteria that, although harmless to humans, make insect pests very sick and eventually very dead. The most common and useful bacteria are forms of *Bacillus thuringiensis,* or Bt, which kill the larvae of moths and butterflies — that is, caterpillars. One type of Bt (sold as *milky spore*) kills the larvae of Japanese beetles.

ECO-SMART

Empowering garden good guys

Gardens are populated by huge numbers of different insects, most neither good nor bad; they're just hanging out at no expense to the plants. But some insects are definitely beneficial, waging a constant battle with the insects that are bugging your plants. Good bugs are no fools. They hang out in gardens that offer the most diverse and reliable menus. That's why eliminating every last insect pest from your garden makes no sense.

I suggest an approach to pest control that encourages maximum diversity in the garden. That's why having some "bad" bugs around all the time is important. Aphids are like hors d'oeuvres for many helpful insects, so you always hope to have a few aphids in your garden (really). Otherwise, what will the good bugs eat? But accepting the bad bugs also means you have to live with a little damage

once in a while. The idea is to manage the pests, not nuke them off the face of the earth. You want to keep them at acceptable levels, without letting them get out of control.

Observing your garden closely is key to this approach. If an insect or disease gets out of hand, you want to treat it effectively without disrupting all the other life in the garden, from good bugs all the way to birds. The first control measures to try can be as simple as hand picking and squashing snails or knocking off aphids with a strong jet of water from a hose. Or you may decide to protect young seedlings with *floating row covers* — white blankets made from polyester fibers that let air, water, and sunlight through, but block insects from finding your plants. You find other "physical" control measures listed under the individual pests later in this chapter.

Botanical insecticides

Botanical insecticides are those that are made from plants. The following are most useful against the pests of annual flowers:

✔ **Neem:** Derived from the tropical tree *Azadirachta indica,* neem kills young feeding insects and deters adult insects, but is harmless to people and to most beneficial insects. Neem works slowly and is effective against aphids, thrips, whiteflies, and, to a lesser degree, Japanese beetles.

I prefer neem *oil* over neem *extract* (check the product label) because oil is also effective against two common diseases: powdery mildew and rust. Neem oil gets thick when cool, so you must warm it up before mixing it with water.

Use either kind of neem before you have a major pest problem. Neem is most effective when applied early in the morning or late in the evening when humidity is high. Reapply after rain.

Currently, you can buy neem oil only from Green Light Co., Box 17985, San Antonio, TX 78217; phone 210-494-3481. An 8-ounce container costs about $13, and you need to use 2 tablespoons per gallon of water.

✔ **Pyrethrin:** Derived from the painted daisy, *Chrysanthemum cinerariifolium,* pyrethrin is a *broad-spectrum insecticide,* meaning that it kills a wide range of insects, both good and bad. The nondiscriminatory nature of pyrethrin is the downside. The upside is that this insecticide kills pests such as thrips and beetles quickly and has low toxicity to mammals, making it essentially harmless to humans and the environment. (Spray late in the evening to avoid killing bees.)

The terminology can be confusing, here. *Pyrethrum* is the ground-up flower of the daisy. *Pyrethrin* is the insecticidal component of the flower. *Pyrethroids,* such as permethrin and resmethrin, are synthetic compounds that resemble pyrethrins but are more toxic and persistent. Consequently, I prefer to avoid pyrethroids for home garden use.

✔ **Rotenone:** Derived from the roots of tropical legumes, rotenone breaks down quickly but is more toxic than some commonly used traditional insecticides. It is a broad-spectrum insecticide, killing beneficial insects, including bees, and pests alike. Use it as a last resort to control various caterpillars, beetles, and thrips.

Summer oil

When sprayed on a plant, this highly refined oil smothers insect pests and their eggs. The words *highly refined,* in this case, mean that the sulfur and other components of the oil that damage the plant are removed. It is relatively nontoxic and short-lived. Use it to control aphids, mites, thrips, and certain caterpillars.

Don't confuse summer oil with dormant oil. *Dormant oil* is meant to be applied to leafless trees and shrubs during winter; using it on your annuals will fry them. Double-check the product label to make sure that the oil can be used on annual flowers during the growing season. Then follow the mixing instructions carefully. Water the plants before and after applying summer oil, and don't spray if temperatures are likely to rise above 85°F (29°C). When it's that hot, the oil can damage plant leaves.

Insecticidal soaps

Derived from the salts of fatty acids, insecticidal soaps kill mostly soft-bodied pests such as aphids, spider mites, and whiteflies. They also can be effective against Japanese beetles. Insecticidal soaps work fast, break down quickly, and are nontoxic to humans. They are most effective when mixed with soft water. Soaps sometimes burn tender foliage.

WARNING!

Pesticide safety

No matter which pesticides you decide to use, you must use them safely. Even pesticides that have relatively low impact on your garden environment can be dangerous to use and toxic to humans. This potential danger is true of several commonly used botanical insecticides.

Always follow instructions on the product label exactly. Doing otherwise is against the law. Both the pest you are trying to control and the plant you are spraying (sometimes plants are listed as groups, such as flowers) must be listed on the label.

Wear gloves when mixing and spraying pesticides. Spray when the winds are calm. Store chemicals in properly labeled containers well out of reach of children. (A locked cabinet is best.) Dispose of empty containers as described on the label or contact your local waste disposal company for appropriate disposal sites.

Synthetic insecticides

You can successfully control most insect problems by using the techniques and products described in the previous sections. If, however, a pest really gets out of hand on a prized planting, you may want to use something more serious. In the descriptions of insect pests, two synthetic pesticides are listed as possible solutions for a few pests: *carbaryl* (sold as Sevin) and *acephate* (usually sold as Orthene). Try other control measures before you resort to these products — using them will likely disrupt the balance of your garden. When you use any pesticide, make sure that you have the pest identified correctly and follow label instructions precisely.

Disease — When the Flower Bed Becomes a Sick Bed

Only a few diseases are really troublesome for annual flowers, and you can prevent or at least reduce in severity most of them by observing good cultural practices or by planting resistant varieties. If you know that a certain disease is a problem on a particular annual in your area, simply plant something else. You surely have many other choices, and you probably will broaden your gardening enjoyment by looking for other flowers.

Prevention and control

Here are some cultural practices that can help prevent plant diseases:

- **Remove infected plants.** After you notice a plant with a problem, give it the yank.

- **Avoid overhead watering.** Or at least water early in the morning so that plants have a chance to dry off before nightfall. Using drip irrigation or watering in furrows, as described in Chapter 11, also helps keep foliage dry. Overhead watering can cause other problems as well, particularly with petunias and geraniums; it can ruin many flowers, causing them to be washed out or look like they've melted.

- **Space plants properly.** Planting annuals too close together reduces air circulation between plants, creating conditions that favor disease. Follow the spacing recommendations in Part II.

- **Prepare the soil.** Add organic matter to increase drainage and aeration, as described in Chapter 8. Doing so helps you sidestep many soilborne diseases.

- **Keep your garden clean and tidy.** Many diseases spread on plant debris, so rake up fallen leaves and remove dead plants. Simply removing diseased leaves can slow the spread of some organisms.

- **Rotate plants.** Don't put the same annuals in the same beds year after year. Doing so creates a breeding ground for disease. Plant something new.

Chemical fungicides are among the nastiest pesticides. They can contain some very toxic compounds that linger in the environment for a long time. If you can, try not to use them. If, however, a prized planting comes up with a really stubborn disease, you may feel that you have no other choice. Before you spray, make sure to identify the disease properly. Enlist the help of a local nursery or cooperative extension specialist. Then use a product specifically labeled for that disease occurring on the plants that you are growing. Follow the label instructions exactly.

Five feisty diseases

Here are some tips on how to prevent, identify, and — if possible — treat some common diseases of annual flowers:

- **Botrytis blight:** Also called gray mold, this fungal disease *overwinters* (survives in the soil or on plant debris through the winter to reinfect the plant again in spring) on plant debris and is common on petunias and ageratum, among others. It's most notable as gray fuzz forming on old flowers, turning them to moldy mush (see Figure 14-9), but it can also discolor or spot foliage. Botrytis blight is most troublesome on older plant parts and in cool, humid weather. To discourage this disease, make sure that plants are properly spaced and avoid overhead watering. Remove and destroy any infected plant parts and give your garden a good cleaning at the end of each growing season.

Figure 14-9: Botrytis blight can turn flowers to moldy mush.

✔ **Damping off:** This fungus attacks the base of seedling stems, causing them to wilt and fall over. (See Figure 14-10.) The best way to prevent the disease is to plant seeds in sterile potting soil and avoid overwatering. After the disease gets a foothold, it's hard to stop.

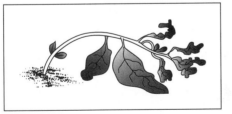

Figure 14-10: Damping off can be hard to control.

✔ **Powdery mildew:** This fungus coats leaves and flowers with a white powder. (See Figure 14-11.) It is most common when days are warm but nights are cool, and it is particularly troublesome on zinnias, dahlias, begonias, and cosmos. Control is difficult, but resistant varieties of those flowers are available. The disease also becomes less of a problem as the weather changes, so if you keep young plants growing vigorously, they may grow out of it. Neem oil also may help. Near the end of the growing season, you may want to pull out the diseased plants early and start with something new next year.

Figure 14-11:
Powdery mildew thrives during warm days and cool nights.

✔ **Rust:** This fungal disease is easy to identify: It forms rusty pustules on the undersides of plant leaves. (See Figure 14-12.) Gradually, the upper sides of the leaves turn yellow, and the whole plant begins to decline. Snapdragons and hollyhocks are common hosts.

To avoid rust, plant resistant varieties. Also, space plants to allow good air circulation, keep the garden clean, and avoid overhead watering. Destroy infected plants.

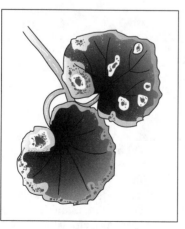

Figure 14-12:
Rust is an easy fungus to identify.

✔ **Root rot:** Several soilborne fungi cause plants to basically all do the same thing — suddenly wilt and die (see Figure 14-13), regardless of whether the soil is moist. Vinca is notorious for checking out like this. The best way to prevent root rot is to prepare the soil properly before planting and make sure that you aren't overwatering — let the soil dry partially in between irrigations. Otherwise, all you can do is remove the dead plants. Few other control measures are effective.

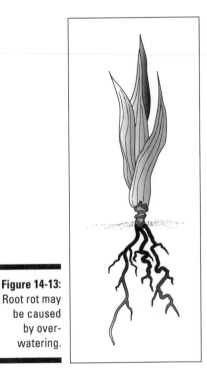

Figure 14-13:
Root rot may
be caused
by over-
watering.

Chapter 15

Weed Wars and Your Ally, Mulch

• •

In This Chapter

▶ Controlling weeds before you plant

▶ Reducing weeds after you plant

▶ Letting mulches do the work

▶ Deciding what type of mulch to use

▶ Knowing when to mulch

• •

*W*eeds and mulches in the same chapter? Well, why not? In the eternal battle against weeds — those aggressive, moisture-stealing plants that always show up where you least want them — mulches can be one of your most valuable weapons.

Outwitting Weeds

A *weed* is any plant growing where you don't want it to. Some weeds are worse than others, but in general, gardeners don't want *any* weeds in their flower beds. Weeds compete with annuals for light, water, and nutrients, resulting in weaker annuals. And weeds make your flower bed look messy.

Luckily, weeds are easier to control in plantings of annual flowers than they are in other garden situations. Pulling out annuals at the end of the season gives you the perfect chance to deal with weeds in an open area and to treat them more aggressively so that they'll never dare to return. In addition, if you grow annuals close together — jowl-to-jowl, so to speak — the flowers can shade the weeds and cause them to die from lack of light.

Before you plant

You can reduce weeds in your annual flower beds in many ways and at many points in the gardening process. Here's what you can do before planting, at the end or beginning of the season, or whenever your beds are empty:

✔ **Presprout weed seeds:** This technique really cuts down on the number of weeds that come up from seeds. Prepare the planting bed several weeks before it's time to plant. Make sure that the soil is nice and level and ready to go, as described in Chapter 8. Then water the soil well and wait for a few days. Presto, young weeds sprout.

You can kill these weeds in one of three ways: Pull them by hand, rake the bed lightly to uproot the seedlings and let them dry out to die, or spray them with an herbicide such as *glyphosate* (sold under a number of brand names). As much as you may oppose the use of herbicides, they do kill the toughest weeds. No matter how you get rid of the young weeds, try to disturb the soil as little as possible — or else you'll simply bring more seeds to the surface, and you'll need to start your eradication process all over again.

✔ **Solarize the soil:** This technique, which uses power from the sun to kill weeds, works best in the middle of summer in climates that get very hot, like the southwestern U.S. Check with your local cooperative extension service to see how effective solarization is in your area. The process does take a while (at least six weeks). Prepare the bed for planting and water it well. Dig a 6- to 12-inch-deep trench around the perimeter. Cover the entire area with thick (4 ml), clear plastic sheeting, place the edges of the plastic in the trenches, and fill the trenches with soil. Then wait. The temperatures underneath can become hot enough to kill insects, disease organisms, and weeds.

✔ **Apply a pre-emergence herbicide:** Pre-emergence herbicides kill seedlings before they can reach the soil surface — after they sprout and before they emerge from the soil. Both liquid and granular forms are available. Apply a pre-emergence herbicide before planting or after annuals are growing; either way, water the ground thoroughly after the application. In addition to weed seeds, the seeds of annual flowers also feel the effects of this herbicide, so don't use pre-emergence herbicides if you plan to sow flower seeds in the bed. After applying a pre-emergence herbicide, you can safely set out transplants; read the product label carefully and follow instructions exactly. How long pre-emergence herbicides remain effective varies by product.

Think carefully before using a pre-emergence herbicide; it may adversely affect what you can grow in the same spot later. For example, after you use such an herbicide on an area, you may not be able to sow seeds there for quite a while. And you probably don't want to grow vegetables there for even longer — food crops and herbicides are not a good mix in home gardens.

After you plant

When annuals are already growing in a bed, here are the approaches you can take to get rid of weeds:

- **Pull weeds out by hand:** Get them while they're young, and they'll come out of the ground easily. Remove the roots, too.

- **Cultivate:** Simply hoeing or lightly turning the soil between annuals exposes the roots of the weeds and kills many of them. The technique is most effective if done often and when the weeds are small. Some cultivating tools, such as three-pronged hand cultivators or special-purpose hoes, are designed especially for this purpose, but a regular hoe or trowel does the trick, too.

- **Spot-spray with herbicide:** You can use weed killers such as glyphosate, which affects weeds after they are growing, to spot-spray tough weeds. But be aware that if you spray any herbicides on your annuals, they'll die, too. Sometimes, you can use a piece of cardboard or a sheet of plastic to protect nearby plants from herbicides that you're spraying on weeds. Or you can put a bottomless box or tin can over a weed before you spray it. Read the entire product label and follow instructions exactly.

- **Mulch:** Mulching is an important weapon in the war against weeds. See the section "Thank You Very Mulch," later in this chapter.

Battling really tough weeds

Some *perennial weeds* (those that live year to year) can really be trouble-some. At the top of that list are Bermuda grass (in mild-winter areas) and bindweed (almost anywhere).

Bermuda grass spreads vigorously by nasty wiry stems. The underground stems are called *rhizomes;* the above-ground stems are called *stolons.* Bermuda grass also produces a ton of seeds, which is another way that it spreads. This monster just spreads and spreads and then spreads some more. That feature makes Bermuda grass desirable for a good lawn, but in flower beds, it's nothing but trouble.

Bindweed, sometimes called wild morning glory, is a rampantly spreading vine that sprawls over and around annuals. You can recognize it by its small, round, white flowers and sword-shaped leaves. If you try pulling it out, it breaks off at ground level and returns the next day. (At least it seems that way.) Bindweed also produces a ton of seeds.

Both of these weeds require persistence to control:

- ✔ Pull seedlings as soon as you see them. Use a trowel or weeding tool to make sure that you remove all the roots.

- ✔ Spot treat with glyphosate as I describe elsewhere in this chapter. Bermuda grass is easiest to kill when its whirlybird-like seedheads appear. But even then, you may have to spray twice. A few herbicides are available that specifically kill grasses but won't hurt your annuals. Ask your nursery expert to recommend one.

- ✔ When you work the soil in the spring or fall, remove the clumps of Bermuda grass roots. You'll never uproot them all, but whatever you can do will help.

Thank You Very Mulch

Any material that you place over the surface of the soil, usually right over the root zone of growing plants, is considered a mulch. Mulches offer many benefits to annuals:

- ✔ They conserve water by reducing soil temperatures and evaporation. The idea is to keep the soil cool by buffering direct sunlight.

- ✔ They prevent wild fluctuations in soil-moisture levels that can really spell disaster in hot weather.

- ✔ They smother weed seeds and prevent them from germinating.

- ✔ Any weeds that come up in a loose mulch are easy to pull.

- ✔ As mulches break down, they add nutrients and improve the texture of the soil.

- ✔ Mulches look good and give the ground a tidy and clean appearance.

Choosing your mulch

The two basic kinds of mulch are organic and inorganic. For flower growers, organic mulches are by far more useful. They look at home with the informal quality of annuals and also help improve planting bed soils.

Organic mulches include grass clippings, compost, wood chips, leaf mold, pine needles, shredded bark, nut shells, cotton gin waste, straw, grain and fruit by-products, composted manure, mushroom compost, peat moss, sawdust, and even newspapers. Some are easier to find in different parts of the country.

As minor as they are, there are some problems with certain organic mulches:

✔ Bark mulches, such as pine needles, are quite acidic. If you use them, keep a close eye on the soil pH and correct it accordingly. (See Chapter 8 for more information about soil pH.)

✔ Grass clippings decay quickly and must be replenished often. But that's okay, because there are usually more grass clippings where the first batch came from. Make sure that the grass hasn't gone to seed before you cut it; otherwise, you may have a lawn coming up in your flower bed. Also, be sure that no herbicides (weed killers) have been used on your lawn, because the residue can damage or kill annuals.

✔ Some organic mulches, such as fresh sawdust, rob your soil of nitrogen as they break down. Counteract this effect by adding supplemental nitrogen to your annuals if they are mysteriously growing slowly or starting to turn yellow. (See Chapter 12 for a discussion of fertilizers.)

✔ Peat moss can become hard and crusty when exposed to weather. Water may not penetrate it, so the water runs off instead of soaking in to the roots. Try to avoid peat moss or mix it with something else — it's so darn expensive anyway.

✔ Some lightweight mulches, such as straw or cocoa hulls, can blow around in the wind. You may want to avoid them if you live in a windy area.

✔ Types of composted manure vary in the amount of nitrogen they contain. If you use them by themselves as a mulch, you run the risk of burning your annuals. If you want to mulch with manure, mix the manure with three times the volume of another organic mulch before applying.

You can purchase organic mulches, such as shredded bark, compost, and leaf mold, in bags, or sometimes in bulk, from nurseries and garden centers. Grass clippings, compost, and wood chips come free from your yard and garden.

Gardeners usually don't use inorganic mulches, such as stone and plastic, in annual flower beds. However, you may want to use products called *landscape fabrics* in your garden. Landscape fabrics, available at many nurseries and garden centers, are made of permeable material that you spread on the ground before planting. You cut little X-shaped holes in the fabric and plant through the holes, as shown in Figure 15-1. The fabrics block weed growth just as an organic mulch does, but you can roll up the fabrics at the end of the season and use them again next year. Some organic landscape fabrics that naturally break down at the end of the year are also now available.

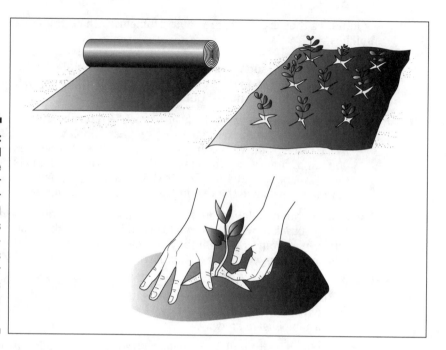

Figure 15-1:
Unroll
landscape
fabric over
your flower
beds and
cut holes
and X-
shaped slits
for your
plants
to poke
through.

Laying it down

Most of the time, a 2- to 3-inch layer of mulch spread evenly beneath the plants is plenty. However, you may have to replenish it during the growing season because many organic mulches break down quickly. Plan on replenishing when the layer thins out or, worse yet, when you see weeds coming through it.

Don't spread mulch all the way to the stem of the plant. Leave several inches of breathing (and drinking!) room for your growing plant. Figure 15-2 shows an example of a well-mulched annual.

Knowing when to mulch

Your mulching schedule really depends on the type of annuals you grow and when you plant them.

Figure 15-2:
Always leave the space immediately surrounding the plant stem free of mulch and debris.

- ✔ **Cool-season annuals planted in early spring:** Pansies and other annuals that do well in cool spring weather will benefit from extra warmth early in the season, when it's a little too cool for cool-season annuals to really thrive. Don't mulch at this point; instead, let the sun hit the soil directly and warm it up. Later on, when the weather starts to get too hot for cool-season annuals, cool things off by mulching. So wait to mulch until after the soil starts to warm and the plants need regular water. As the days heat up, mulch helps the plants thrive and bloom longer into hot weather.

- ✔ **Cool-season annuals planted in late summer or early fall:** For these plants, you want a cooling effect during hot weather, so spread the mulch right after planting. When the weather starts to cool, rake off or remove the mulch so that the soil can warm. Removing the mulch prolongs the bloom longer into the winter. If you really want to go all-out and try to get some of your hardier annuals through the winter so that they bloom very early the following spring, mulch again after the ground starts to freeze. This mulching schedule helps prevent the soil from repeated freezing and thawing, which can literally rip some plants right out of the ground.

- ✔ **Warm-season annuals planted in spring:** You may want to keep the ground clear if you are planting really early — the more heat the better. Otherwise, mulch at planting time.

For more information on the differences between cool-season and warm-season annuals, see Chapter 2.

Part VI
Creating Special Annual Gardens

The 5th Wave   By Rich Tennant

"Now you cut that out!! I should have never planted the canary creeper next to the cattails."

In this part . . .

*I*f you want annuals to do more than fill in the bare spots in your yard, you've come to the right place. The chapters in this part provide a taste of the fun and flexibility of annuals: Grow flowers in pots or hanging baskets, plant wildflower gardens full of annuals that reseed themselves year after year, or bring some of nature's beauty inside by growing cutting gardens for fresh and dried bouquets.

Chapter 16

Growing Annuals in Containers

. . . .

In This Chapter

▶ Discovering great reasons to put annuals in pots

▶ Choosing the right containers for your annuals

▶ Finding out how to plant annuals in containers

▶ Introducing favorite annuals for containers

. . . .

Annuals are terrific choices for containers of all types — ceramic pots, hanging baskets, wood tubs, recycled dinghies, old cowboy boots. (I've never actually seen annuals growing in cowboy boots, but container gardening is the place to let your imagination run wild.) Geraniums, marigolds, petunias, and many other annuals are container fixtures just about everywhere that people grow gardens.

This chapter points out the many reasons to grow annuals in containers, describes how caring for annuals in container is different from growing annuals in the ground, and lists the annuals that are particularly well suited to container life. If, after perusing this chapter, you find that you want to know more about this topic, pick up a copy of *Container Gardening For Dummies,* by yours truly.

Why Grow Annuals in Containers?

Besides the simple fact that annuals are just plain fun to grow, other pragmatic reasons make annuals popular flowers for containers.

> ✔ Maybe your garden doesn't have any other spot for annuals — your soil may be too lousy, or your trees may cast too much shade, for example. Maybe your outdoor space consists of only a patio, deck, or balcony. Containers are your best chance for a garden, and annuals probably top the list of container candidates.

✔ With containers, you can put your favorite annuals where you can best appreciate them. For example, you can move a pot of sweet peas (yes, even sprawling sweet peas) to a site where you can smell their fragrance, or you can position Johnny jump-ups where you can view their tiny splotched faces.

✔ With containers, you can keep annuals out of sight when they're not looking their best — for example, before they bloom or as they dwindle away after blooming.

✔ If you make mistakes, you haven't lost a lot of money. And often you still have time to try growing other types of annuals that same season in the same pot.

✔ You can rotate blooming containers of flowers by the season. Decorate your entryway with pansies in the spring, petunias in the summer, and asters in the fall. In mild-winter climates, you can also grow containers of annuals that bloom from fall through spring — Iceland poppies and stock are great choices.

✔ Nothing dresses up a deck or patio faster for a party than pots of colorful blooming annuals.

Having a Pot to Plant In

Garden centers, nurseries, and even big discount department stores carry a huge variety of containers. When selecting your containers, consider details such as looks, cost, and appropriateness for the plants you want to grow. Whether you buy commercial containers, make your own, or improvise, keep these two main factors in mind:

✔ **Porosity:** Some materials used for containers are more porous than others and allow moisture and air to penetrate more readily. Unglazed terra cotta, wood, and paper pulp dry out faster than some other materials, but they also allow soil to cool by evaporation and to "breathe"(roots need oxygen); porosity has the effect of drawing away excess water, preventing waterlogged soil. Nonporous materials, such as glazed terra cotta, plastic, and metal, hold soil moisture better, which can be both good and bad.

✔ **Drainage:** For healthy root development, soil must drain water properly and have enough space for air. Soil that is too heavy (dense) can slow drainage; so can the lack of a drain hole or a blocked drain hole. If drainage is slow or nonexistent, water may collect at the bottom (it can even stagnate and smell bad); roots can smother, and the plant can die. Look for drain holes when selecting containers. Of course, you can drill, poke, or otherwise create drain holes in containers without them.

Types of container materials

All sorts of things can function as containers for plants. But when you shop at garden centers and other conventional sources, here are the materials you're most likely to encounter.

Unglazed clay or terra cotta

The most familiar material is unglazed clay or terra cotta ("baked earth" in Italian), which is usually reddish orange in color but is available in other colors, as well, including tan, cream, black, and chocolate brown. Pots come in many shapes and sizes. Higher-quality pots, which have thick walls and are fired in high heat, last longer. Pots fired at low heat have a grainier texture and weather away more quickly. Two common styles are the traditional rimmed pot and saucer, and the sleeker Spanish pot, both shown in Figure 16-1.

Figure 16-1: Traditional and Spanish terra cotta pots are attractive and inexpensive.

Unglazed clay pots generally offer good value for the money. Their earthy colors and natural surface look comfortable in almost any garden situation, from rustic to formal. Unglazed clay's porosity allows plant roots to breathe and excess moisture to evaporate — all desirable for many plants. But porosity also means that soil dries out quickly, so you have to remember to water often.

Unglazed clay pots are on the breakable side. In cold climates, pot sides can split when moist soil freezes and expands.

Glazed clay

Usually inexpensive, glazed clay pots come in many more colors than unglazed pots — bright to dark, some with patterns. Many are made in Asia and fit nicely in Japanese-style gardens. They're great in formal situations, or they can liven up a grouping of plain clay pots. Glazed pots are less porous than unglazed and can hold moisture better. They are breakable.

Wood

Wood boxes and tubs are sold in many shapes and styles and usually made of rot-resistant redwood and cedar. They're heavy and durable and stand up well to cold weather. Appearance is usually rustic, at home on decks and other informal situations. Wood containers provide good soil insulation, keeping roots cooler than in terra cotta. Evaporation is also less than in clay pots. Thicker lumber — at least $^7/_8$ inch — is best. Bottoms may rot if they stay too moist; place wood containers on plant stands or little pot "feet" to allow air to circulate underneath them. To make wood last longer, treat the inside with wood preservative.

Half barrels are inexpensive large containers. They used to be made from recycled oak whiskey and wine barrels but now are built specifically for garden purposes. Their look is very rustic. Coat the insides with nontoxic wood preservative.

Plastic

Many plastic pots are designed to imitate standard terra cotta pots. Plastic is less expensive, easier to clean, and lighter than terra cotta. The material is nonporous and doesn't dry out as quickly as terra cotta, so be careful that you don't overwater. Their looks aren't for everyone. You can hide plastic pots inside a more decorative pot. This is a great way to make use of decorative pots that don't have drainage holes; simply place some rocks or pottery shards in the bottom and set an annual planted in a smaller plastic pot on top. *Voilà!* The plastic pot is hidden, and the formerly useless decorative pot is now earning its keep.

Other materials

As you visit secondhand stores and garage sales (or even your own garage) keep an eye out for containers that you can turn into planters.

- ✔ Brass, copper, iron, aluminum, and other metal containers are available at boutiques and antique shops. Create drainage holes if the container doesn't have them. Keep in mind that metal containers heat up more quickly than those made of other materials, so keep them out of direct sun.

- ✔ Cast concrete is durable, heavy, and cold-resistant.

- ✔ Paper pulp pots are made of compressed recycled paper that degrades in several years. You actually can plant the pot and its contents directly in the ground, and the roots grow through the sides as the pot decomposes. They're inexpensive and lightweight but not particularly handsome.

The right size and shape of container

What type of container is good for the plant? What type of container looks nice? You need to consider the answers to both questions before you plant.

A pot that's too small crowds the roots, depriving the flowers of enough moisture, oxygen, and nutrients for healthy growth. If the pot is too big, the superfluous soil may stay too wet and can smother the roots.

As a general rule of scale, if the annuals normally grow 10 or 12 inches tall, provide a pot with a diameter of at least 8 inches. If the plants grow 2 or 3 feet tall, go for a diameter of 24 inches or choose a large container such as a half barrel.

You can crowd seasonal plants, such as annuals and bulbs, together more closely in containers than in the ground. Closer spacing creates much more impact in a much smaller space. Annuals can't grow in crowded conditions for long, but their season is short and the tight quarters within the container make it easier for you to satisfy the crowded plants' demand for extra water and food. If the recommended spacing for ground planting is 10 to 12 inches, you can space the plants 6 to 8 inches apart in a container.

Use this rough guideline for deciding how many annuals to plant per container: In a 10-inch-diameter pot, plant three to four small annuals, such as pansy, lobelia, or sweet alyssum. If you have larger-sized annuals, such as annual geraniums and browallia, a single plant is plenty for a 10-inch container. You can mix and match plants of different sizes, too. Plant two to three cascading annuals, such as lobelia, around the edge of a pot and plant one taller focal point annual, such as salvia, in the center of the pot. The combinations are limited only by your imagination.

Containers come in an assortment of shapes. Some designs are based on practical reasons, and other shapes probably exist because someone likes how they look.

The following list includes some of the traditional shapes:

- ✔ The tapered shape was developed for terra cotta pots to allow plants to slip out more readily for repotting. That design still makes sense.

- ✔ Most pots are taller than they are wide, allowing the roots to grow deep enough. This shape works well for most annuals.

- ✔ Low containers, sometimes called *azalea pots,* are best for shallow-rooted plants that need little soil, such as bulbs. You can also use shallow bowls for small annuals, but make sure that you provide enough soil for growth and that you water and fertilize carefully.

> ✔ To keep the weight to a minimum, hanging baskets come mainly in wood and wire. Wire baskets, lined with sphagnum moss or synthetic material to hold in the soil, offer room on the sides for inserting plants — producing a look of overflowing abundance. The diameter should be at least 9 or 10 inches, but preferably 15 or 16 inches.

Planting Annuals in Containers

An annual growing in a container needs the same things that a plant in the ground does — mainly water, air, and nutrients. Remember that roots in a container are confined and can't forage. Careful watering and feeding are essential. So is starting off with a good soil mix — not dirt dug up from your garden.

Soil mix

With names like Magic Soil, Super Dirt, and Stupendous Stuff for Your Garden, a mind-confusing array of soil mixtures greets shoppers at most nurseries and garden centers. Open up the bags, and the brown stuff inside all looks pretty much the same. The prices range from dirt cheap to expensive, and the labels say almost nothing to help the average gardener. No government agency requires precise labeling; maybe if people started eating soil mix, manufacturers would have to list the ingredients by percentage.

Look for soil mixes labeled "potting soil" — as opposed to "soil amendment." Potting soils are all ready to scoop into your containers. A high-quality potting mix usually contains varying amounts of the following ingredients: organic matter such as peat moss, ground bark, or other wood by-product; vermiculite or perlite to retain moisture as well as provide aeration; sand; nutrients; and ground limestone. A 20-pound bag (about 2 cubic feet) of mix should be enough to fill eight to ten 10- to 12-inch pots.

If you're planting a large quantity of containers, you can buy potting mix in bulk — or ingredients for mixing your own — at local garden supply centers.

Planting steps

You've assembled your containers and soil mix, you've brought home annual seedlings from the nursery, and you're ready to plant.

1. **Before removing plants from their nursery containers, make sure that their root balls are moist.**

Consult the steps for planting annual seedlings described in Chapter 10 for more information about handling root balls of transplants. Pay special attention to the moisture level of the seedling's root ball. If the soil feels dry, soak the plants right inside their nursery pack. Seedlings absorb water much better now than after you plant them. Watch for signs of root-bound seedlings: small white roots woven together so tightly that they repel water. Gently loosen roots at the bottom and sides of the root ball.

2. **Check the size of the drainage holes in the container you plant to use and adjust them, if necessary.**

   Holes should be about $1/2$ inch in diameter, with 4 to 6 drainage holes per 10-inch pot.

   Most commercially made pots have drain holes to allow water to flow through. For some reason, these holes usually are too big, allowing soil and too much water to escape. Partially cover the drain holes by using a small piece of window screen or the time-honored method of placing pot shards (broken pieces of old pots) over the hole. If you don't have any pots that you're willing to smash, use an unevenly shaped rock. (Don't use a flat stone, because it will cover the hole and stop all drainage.)

3. **Fill the container to within 2 or 3 inches of its rim with moistened soil mix and smooth the soil level with your hands.**

   You want the soil mix to be wet enough that it forms a ball when squeezed, but not dripping wet.

4. **With a trowel or your hands, scoop out a planting hole for each seedling.**

   The hole should be deep enough so that, when you place the seedling in it, the top of the seedling's root ball is at the same level as the soil in the container.

5. **Remove seedlings from their containers and place each one in a hole.**

6. **Use your fingers to gently tamp down the soil around each seedling.**

   Ensure that the soil level of the root ball stays even with the soil level in the container. This may require adding more moist soil or taking some soil out.

7. **Water gently with a watering can or hose until the soil is thoroughly moist.**

   A watering can or hose with a bubbler extension works best because it's less likely to wash soil out of the pot. (See Chapter 11 for more about hose attachments and watering tools.)

Watering is much more critical with annuals grown within the confines of a container. Never let the soil dry out. You may want to install a drip system if you have several containers in one area.

Fertilizing container-grown annuals is also more critical than fertilizing the same plants grown in the ground. Establish a regular feeding schedule, as described in Chapter 12. One proven method is to use liquid fertilizer at half the recommended dosage and twice the frequency (every two weeks instead of monthly, for example).

Foolproof Annuals for Container Growing

Some annuals look great when planted alone, and others are *mixers* — best used in combinations with other annuals, perennials, or bulbs. This section offers some suggestions about plant placement and combinations, but annuals are versatile, so feel free to try out your own ideas.

When choosing plants for containers, pay special attention to their eventual sizes and growth habits. In general, compact varieties perform better in containers. (Among sunflower varieties, for example, the 10-foot 'Russian Giant' is out of the question, but the 24-inch 'Teddy Bear' is perfect for containers.) Look for special varieties developed for containers. Names are often a clue to container performance — 'Cascade' petunias, for example, are designed to spill from pots.

The following list contains over a dozen annuals that you can count on to do well in containers in all sorts of conditions:

Cosmos	Phlox
Dahlia	Pinks
Cineraria	Salvia
Dusty miller	Snapdragons (dwarfs)
Iceland poppy	Stocks
Kale	Swan River daisy
Nemesia	Transvaal daisy

Other annuals are more particular. If you have an especially sunny or shady spot, consider an annual better suited to such conditions. For descriptions and advice on care of each of these plants, refer to Chapters 4 and 5.

Old reliables for sunny spots

Most annuals love full sun exposure. By full sun, I mean at least six hours of direct sunshine on the plants each day. The following list includes some of the best annuals to grow in full sun. Keep in mind that the more sun you provide these sun worshipers, the longer and fuller they will flower.

- **Ageratum:** You probably don't want a whole pot full of ageratum, but it's a great plant to edge a container of mixed annuals. Look for dwarf varieties such as 'Blue Mink'.

- **Calendula:** Here's a great choice for containers early in the growing season. Sturdy plants and bright orange or yellow blooms stand up well to cool weather.

- **Geranium:** I can't think of any geranium that won't do well or won't look good in a container. Ivy geraniums are a favorite choice for hanging baskets; Summer Showers was specifically developed for hanging. Scented geraniums are fun in pots that are close enough for you to pinch off their foliage for sniffing.

- **Lobelia:** Call on the compact edging types (such as 'Crystal Palace') to tuck into mixed plantings. Use the trailing types (such as 'Sapphire') to spill from hanging baskets or pots.

- **Marigold:** The tall types are best left in the ground, but the more compact French marigolds and signet marigolds are container classics. Fill a pot with a single variety or combine marigolds with other annuals.

- **Pansy and viola:** Hardy and carefree, these are often the first annuals you see in containers each spring. Combine pansies or violas with bulbs or fill pots with single or mixed colors.

- **Petunia:** Stand-outs for containers are big-flowered grandiflora types, especially Cascade and Supercascade Strains (which are great spillers). Or try much more compact, smaller-flowered millifloras such as Fantasy.

- **Sweet alyssum:** Low and spreading, this annual is a dependable choice for filling in among mixed annuals in a pot or spilling over the edges of a pot.

- **Sweet pea:** Bush types, such as the Bijou Strain, make a fairly restrained container plant. The familiar tall, climbing sweet peas quickly grow out of bounds in a container.

- **Vinca rosea:** Take a lesson from shopping centers and other public spaces where you see vinca rosea in the hottest spots. This is one tough, heat-loving annual for containers that must face hot sun.

- **Zinnia:** Mix colors or use single colors for bright containers in full sun. Compact dwarfs, such as the Peter Pan Series, work best in containers. Avoid tall, lanky types.

Annuals for shady containers

Some annuals provide great color without requiring a full day of sunshine. These annuals perform best with only a few hours of direct sun, and just filtered or dappled light for the rest of the day. Shade-loving annuals like these look great and perform well under trees or on the shady side of a building:

- ✔ **Bedding begonia:** For a neat, well-groomed look, fill pots with solid-colored begonias. Or use them to edge large pots of mixed annuals.

- ✔ **Browallia:** A number of new varieties have been developed specifically for hanging baskets. Look for 'Blue Bells Improved'.

- ✔ **Coleus:** This colorful foliage can brighten up dark parts of your garden. Combine it with shorter shade-lovers, such as impatiens.

- ✔ **Impatiens:** Tall or compact, single or double, just about all impatiens perform brilliantly in containers, including hanging baskets. Plant just one color to a pot for the boldest look. Impatiens combine beautifully with ferns, coleus, begonias, and other annuals in mixed plantings.

Combining Annuals in Mixed Plantings

Pink begonias and blue lobelia. Red geraniums, yellow pansies, and white sweet alyssum. Combining different annuals in the same container is an easy way to create rainbows of color. The key to success is a well-designed mix of different plants that look terrific together. In other words, the plants bloom at the same time, their colors contrast with or complement each other beautifully, and they're in scale with one another.

Secrets of mixed plantings: Color and form

If you want to approach mixed plantings seriously, review the design tips in Chapter 6. And when considering which annuals to combine, keep these pointers in mind:

- ✔ For bold, vibrant looks, choose flowers of contrasting colors (on opposite sides of the color wheel), such as yellow and violet.

- ✔ For pleasing, compatible combinations, choose harmonious blends of related colors, such as blue, violet, and purple.

- ✔ Create a soothing style with variations or shades of the same color — from pale pink to rose, for example.

- Add plenty of pizzazz with energizing warm-color combinations of red, orange, and yellow.

- Cool things down with refreshing blues, greens, and violets.

- Don't forget white. It adds welcome dimension, lightens dark areas, and works with all other colors.

- Consider foliage, too. Green isn't the only color of the leaves on annuals. You can produce stunning results by including flowers that have silver and gray foliage. *Variegated* (two-toned) leaves also add interest.

Classic color schemes are one guideline to container gardening, but personal taste is your ultimate authority. The bottom line: Pick colors that you like — even if that means breaking with tradition and planting orange marigolds with pink petunias. (Somebody, please, tell me what's wrong with that!)

Making sure that plants fit together is usually a matter of balance. A tiny trailing flower in a huge tub, or a wide annual in a narrow box, simply doesn't work. It's okay to dare to be different, but make sure that the jump isn't too great. If you're unsure, test out potential combinations when you're shopping at the nursery. Arrange the plants and pots that you like, and see if the combinations work. You'll know that you've got a winner when the plants fit the pot and the containers fit the location.

Keep in mind a few key points about proportion and scale:

- Make sure the plant fits the pot. Your design looks best if small plants are used for small pots in small spaces, and larger plants are reserved for tubs, barrels, or big pots.

- Catch the eye and add balance with contrasting forms (spiky iris with rounded geraniums, for example), but be careful not to overdo it.

- Create both a soft and pleasing feel with finely textured, lacy plants, such as lobelia, small ferns, or baby's breath. These soften hard container edges and blend well with other textures.

- For a bold focus, try big flowers (zinnias or dahlias) or large, dramatic leaves (coleus). These flowers are particularly effective in large pots alongside smaller plants.

- Group similarly sized plants but feel free to vary height.

- A natural, gradual flow results from tall plants placed toward the back of the container, middle-sized plants in the center, and low or trailing ones along the edges.

- Use balance and scale to determine container placement, too. A huge barrel on a tiny patio looks out of place, and a tiny dish garden is lost on an expansive deck.

A sampling of mixed plantings for containers

Experimenting with different annuals and pots is a great way to get started with container gardening. But if you're the type who likes more direction, plant a few of these tried-and-true mixed plantings:

Terra cotta collection

The versatile styles and sizes of classic terra cotta offer many possibilities for groupings, including the trio of square pots suggested here. Brimming with colorful annuals, the pots are ideal for display anywhere — on a deck, patio, or porch. Their size even allows them to help define and divide seating or dining areas.

- **Containers:** Choose three square terra cotta pots: one large pot that's 18 inches square and two smaller 14-inch pots. Take some time to find the right location for these guys before you plant, because they will be difficult, if not impossible, to lug around after they're planted.

- **Plants:** Plant three annual yellow calliopsis, four blue marguerite daisies, five white sweet alyssum, and seven gold marigolds. Keep these plants deadheaded for a long summer show of flowers.

- **Planting instructions:** Start with the calliopsis, placing one in the center of each pot, slightly toward the back. Next add two daisies in the large pot, one on either side of the calliopsis, and plant one in the front corner of each small pot. Plant sweet alyssums in the side corners of the small pots, and in a front corner of the large pot. Finish by dropping in the marigolds, three per large pot, two per small pot, mixing the colors as you go.

Consider dressing up these pots by adding *pot feet* — small terra cotta pieces that lift the pots off the ground. These feet not only look great, but they also help improve drainage. Place one foot along each side to securely support the containers, making sure that the pot stays balanced. It's best to place the pot on its feet before adding soil, because it will be much heavier after you fill it.

Fragrant window box

An ordinary wooden box comes alive with annuals and trailers that combine good looks with a delicious scent. Upright stock, set along the back of the box, offers a wonderful backdrop of fragrant flowers with a slightly spicy scent in double clusters of purple, pink, rose, and white. Sweet William adds harmony with a touch of fragrance from flowers ranging from ruby red to a dazzling two-toned pink. Old-fashioned sweet peas link all the plants beautifully, climbing and trailing among the other performers. Trailing lobelia, with its delicately shaped leaves and arching stems, spills gracefully from the front of the box.

- ✔ **Container:** Use a window box about 3 feet long by 9 inches wide by 10 inches deep — big enough to hold an impressive array of plants. Use rot-resistant cedar or redwood or treated planter boxes sized to fit right under your windows.

- ✔ **Plants:** Plant five stocks, five sweet Williams, five sweet peas, and two trailing lobelia. If you plant this box in spring, you may find that the annuals are finished blooming by the middle of summer. Replace stock, sweet peas, and sweet William with sweet alyssum, carnations, or scented geraniums.

- ✔ **Planting instructions:** Space the tall stocks along the back of the box, reserving a spot in each corner for a sweet pea. Add one more sweet pea in the center of the box and plant lobelias equidistant from the center along the front rim. Fill in the additional spaces with sweet William, leaving at least a couple of inches between all plants. Water thoroughly and add soil to low spots.

For safety and success, be sure that your box is mounted securely. L-shaped, galvanized steel brackets work best and can be anchored in wood or masonry. They provide the most stability if the box sits inside the "L".

Overflowing hanging basket

Full foliage and flowers can completely hide a moss-lined basket, as illustrated in Figure 16-2.

The following "recipe" for a hanging basic includes a collection of annuals, perennials, and vines that cascade from the sides and top, completely obscuring the container that holds them. Variegated ground ivy, with its two-toned leaves and exceptionally long stems, spills like a living waterfall. Clusters of bright pansies and deep violet lobelias fill the sides and top, a handful of ivy geraniums adds rich pink tones, and ever-reliable sweet alyssum weaves through with a fragrant touch of white.

- ✔ **Container:** You get wonderful results with a galvanized wire basket that you can plant both from the top and *through* the sides. Openings allow you to insert plants just about anywhere to achieve a full, finished look. Use a 20-inch-diameter or larger basket for the best display.

- ✔ **Plants:** Three variegated ground ivies, six purple lobelias, nine light blue pansies, three pink ivy geraniums, and six white sweet alyssums.

Figure 16-2:
Wire
baskets
enable you
to create
the illusion
that you
aren't
using any
container
at all.

✔ **Planting instructions:** Start by thoroughly soaking unmilled *sphagnum moss* (a fluffy, fibrous material available in most garden centers) in a bucket of water. Line the bottom and sides of the basket with large, flat sections of the dripping moss. Gradually add soil to keep the moss in place, filling the basket to the rim with both materials. Plant the ground ivies along the basket rim. Next gently plant through the sides, using a mix of lobelia and pansies, with a few sweet alyssums sprinkled in. Allow space for the ground ivies to cascade. Pull plants through the sides and tuck extra moss around the roots to secure them. Finish by adding ivy geraniums and remaining pansies and sweet alyssum in the top.

Figure 16-3 shows the steps for planting in a wire hanging basket.

Let the wire framework help. When you plant, gently separate the wire sections to create larger openings and then, with the plants in place, push the wires back together to hold everything in place. Water your basket immediately after planting and replace any moss that washes away. Spray the basket often, hitting both the top and sides; otherwise, the soil will dry out quickly. Fertilize regularly with a liquid product.

Figure 16-3:
Line your wire basket with unmilled sphagnum moss and gradually fill it with potting soil as you plant.

Chapter 17

Growing Annual Wildflower Gardens

. . . .

In This Chapter

▶ Getting to know the favorites

▶ Encouraging the best from your wildflowers

▶ Choosing the perfect time to plant

▶ Buying seed mixes or creating your own

▶ Finding the magic spot

▶ Growing wildflowers from seeds or transplants

▶ Keeping the show going

. . . .

*W*hat could be more beautiful and inspiring than strolling through a meadow or backyard border between waist-high, gaily colored wildflowers? The beauty of wildflowers is that they flower all summer long, and the colors of the flower bed change depending on the type of wild-flowers in bloom at the moment.

A *wildflower* is any plant that grows and blooms on its own in natural settings and, in the case of an annual, completes its life cycle in one year. Yes, this plant sounds suspiciously like a weed. Truth be told, the line between wildflower and weed can be pretty fuzzy. On the other hand, when your wildflower garden offers clouds of flowers in a rainbow of colors, when the stars on stage include cheerful two-toned daisies, dazzling poppies, and rich golden hues of black-eyed Susan, you won't have a doubt about whether the plants are wildflowers or weeds.

Any discussion of wildflowers is more about the feelings that wildflowers generate than about botany. These plants can create a natural, carefree mood in your garden and can make a walk to fill your backyard bird feeder feel like a stroll through a mountain meadow.

On the practical side, wildflowers also have a lot to offer. Most are easy to grow under the right conditions. They share an admirable ability to adapt and survive in places that seem less than hospitable. In the friendly confines of your garden (or maybe even in the cracks in your driveway), they become right at home and may even return year after year. You can see why wildflowers are the natural choice for that bare spot along the fence, the border near the lawn, the strip between your yard and your neighbor's driveway, or anywhere you want a full but less formal, less demanding type of landscape. Many wildflowers are even excellent for cutting.

This chapter can help you decide what to plant where. It gives you keys for success, including timetables and steps for selecting and preparing the ground before you sow seeds or set out plants. You find out just how to care for wildflowers and what to do when these annuals wind down.

Who's Who Among Wildflowers

The wildflower family includes some well-known and soul-stirring names, such as bluebonnets, love-in-a mist, and bachelor's buttons, as well as hundreds of other less familiar regional treasures. Be aware, however, that not everyone, everywhere, has equal success with all wildflowers. (For example, in midsummer where I live, the California poppies that have turned to brown straw in the foothills of southern California are being pampered in the borders of gardens in England.) Many wildflowers are easy to grow only where they grow naturally. Others are so adaptable that they can thrive almost anywhere. Some are common annuals (such as sweet alyssum) that do well in the most groomed gardens but have the carefree looks and adaptability to thrive in wildflower settings as well.

The following list contains some of the most widely grown annual wildflowers. All are easy to grow from seed, have an untamed look or feeling, and are able to *naturalize*. Flowers that naturalize reseed themselves to return next year, with little or no effort on your part. For more information about these plants, check Chapter 5.

- African daisy *(Arctotis)* in orange, red, yellow, white, and bicolors
- African daisy *(Dimorphotheca)* in orange, red, yellow, pink, white
- Baby blue eyes in blue or white
- California poppy in orange
- Clarkia in red, pink, and white
- Cornflower in blue, pink, and white

- Cosmos in pink, purple, and white

- Flax in red and white

- Forget-me-not in blue

- Four o'clock in pink, red, white, and yellow

- Bird's eyes *(Gilia tricolor)* in blue

- Gloriosa daisy in yellow

- Linaria in red, pink, blue, purple, yellow, cream, and bicolors

- Love-in-a-mist in blue and pastel colors

- Shirley poppy in red

- Swan River daisy in blue, pink, or white

- Wallflower in orange, yellow, cream, purple, and red

Getting the Most from Your Wildflowers

Growing a wildflower garden may be easier if you start out with some realistic expectations. A successful bed of annual wildflowers can give you many rewards, but you have to do more than throw out the seeds and stand back to watch the show. You can take that approach, of course, (see the section "Alternative planting: Creating a scatter garden," later in this chapter), but your wildflower garden won't reach its full potential. With proper preparation and management, you can double and triple your payoff with bigger, healthier plants that produce more flowers over many weeks.

Don't let the idea of a little work scare you off. Growing wildflowers isn't a matter of a daily grind in the garden. When you select the right plants, choose an appropriate site, and follow simple planting guidelines, you can have lots of color and beauty with minimal effort — especially in comparison to other types of annual gardens. Here, then, is an overview of the steps involved:

- Figure out your timing for spring, summer, or fall flowers so that you can sow seeds or set out plants in the weeks preceding. Yes, this requires planning ahead, especially if you're planting seeds.

- Select a site and prepare the ground. This task involves removing weeds and, in some cases, adding organic material to the soil.

- Choose seeds or a seed mix or buy transplants that can thrive in the conditions in your area.

✔ Sow seeds and/or set out transplants.

✔ Keep young plants moist and remove weeds as they compete with your flowers.

✔ Maintain the garden by watering during dry periods and by staking and supporting tall plants.

✔ Allow the garden to finish naturally. As plants die back and complete the flowering cycle, they just may self-sow, giving you all-new plants when the process repeats down the road.

Picking the Perfect Time to Plant

Your wildflower planting schedule depends on your location and your climate. For the best clues, take a look at nature around you. When do seedlings germinate on hillsides or in fields and vacant lots? If you live in a cold-winter climate, that time will be spring — sometimes late spring — when the ground warms enough and rainfall stimulates the seedlings. If you live in a mild climate with rainy winters and dry summers (such as California and other Mediterranean climates), seeds sprout in winter and begin blooming in early spring.

Seed packs give advice on the best planting times for your area. For basic guidelines, check out the following tips for when to plant:

✔ **Spring:** This is an excellent time to get your garden going, no matter where you live. Wait for the soil to warm if you live in cold regions. Sowing seeds in spring gives you impressive late-spring to summer flowers, depending on the type. You can also start some wildflower seedlings, such as cosmos, indoors and transplant them in early summer to beef up your late-summer blooms. In dry climates, you must water wildflower gardens carefully to keep young plants thriving through summer heat.

✔ **Fall:** If you live where winters are mild, fall is an ideal season to sow seeds for spring blooms. The seeds of annuals such as forget-me-nots and wallflowers absorb moisture from winter rains or your watering, become appropriately chilled by winter temperatures, and then pop into action in early spring. If conditions and plants allow, some seeds may sprout and grow during autumn and winter, perhaps even providing an early spring show.

Shopping for Wildflower Seeds or Seedlings

You'll probably find more wildflowers — both as individual types and in various combinations — in seed form than you will as seedlings for transplanting. (Seeds also offer cost-saving over seedlings.) Look for a wide range of seeds packed as separate varieties (pink clarkia and blue cornflower, for example), as well as numerous specialty mixes. These mixes are usually blended with wildflowers and adapted to grow in certain climatic regions, such as the desert or humid coastal areas. Using a prepared mix is the easiest way to plant a wildflower garden. As you become more familiar with the individual wildflowers — which ones you like, which ones do well in your yard, and so on — you can combine your own mix.

So what's in those mixes? And what exactly do you get in the cute little seed envelopes, 1-pound canisters, or fancy decorated glass jars? The mixes contain seeds for popular and reliable wildflowers, combined to give you a variety of colorful blooms and textures throughout the growing season. These mixes usually also include filler material that adds bulk and enables you to distribute seeds evenly.

You can find regional wildflower mixes designed to suit your geographic area, as well as your fancy. If you have a specific theme in mind, you can probably find a mix to grow it. Look for birds-and-butterflies mixes, hummingbird mixes, meadow mixes, and cut-flower mixes. You can select a mix by color: individual colors or combinations, such as red, white, and blue. Or choose a mix that meets the special needs of your planting locations; in addition to the popular sunny mixes, you can find mixes for dry, moist, and shady areas. Some mixes go by size: knee-high, low-growing, and ground-cover mixes. Some mixes contain only annuals; others include a mixture of annual and perennial wildflowers. Package directions give you the coverage rate, tell you how to plant, and say whether you need to replant each year, which most likely is the case with annual mixes, unless plants reseed for you.

Transplanting seedlings offers you a quicker payoff than sowing seeds, because the plants get a head start and are less threatened by pests, dry conditions, or weeds. Many nurseries offer a number of wildflower varieties in six-packs and 4-inch pots — big enough to give you a sneak preview before you buy of what the plant will eventually look like. Choose dark green plants with good overall shapes and the beginnings of flower buds. Avoid those that are bursting the seams of their pot (probably root-bound) or those that have already begun serious blooming.

Collecting seeds to sow

You can collect some wildflower seeds your-self if you have access to established plants. Always ask permission to collect seeds on private or public land. Check with your local authorities to find out which plants may be protected.

Wait until seed pods dry completely before collecting seeds. Place a small bag over the seed head and shake to free the seeds. Or cut the stem, dry it on a tray, and then gather the seeds. Store seeds in a dark, dry place until you're ready to sow them. Some of the easiest annuals to collect seeds from are California poppies, Shirley poppies, and love-in-a-mist. Refer to Chapter 5 for an illustration of a poppy seedhead.

Choosing and Preparing Your Site

Evaluate your entire landscape as you search for areas that are suited to wildflowers. Consider places where you haven't been able to plant a formal garden, or spots on the edge of the garden where a "wild" area may make a nice transition. The site needs to offer the right conditions — which span quite a range, depending on which wildflowers you're growing. Fortunately, wildflowers are adaptable little fellows, and you can even find types suited specifically to shady, dry, wet, or otherwise poor soil or windy conditions. Consider the following points when evaluating your site:

✔ Choose a sunny, spacious spot for the highest chance of success. Typically six to eight hours of sun a day does the trick. Good drainage is also a must.

✔ Some specialty wildflowers are happy in shady, damp locations. Look for seed mixes that are especially suited to the growing conditions in your garden. Or ask for recommendations at your local nursery.

✔ Remove existing weeds. This task is critical, especially with perennial weeds that can bully little wildflower seedlings. Pull up the weeds or treat them with a weed killer as described in Chapter 15. Remove grassy weeds and seedlings, too.

✔ If you have soil that is considered good, just loosen the planting area with a rake, cultivating to make the soil fine and workable to a depth of about an inch. Remove large rocks and rake the area smooth.

✔ In hard, compacted, rocky, or other poor soils, loosen the soil with a spade or spading fork and spread a generous layer (2 to 4 inches) of organic mulch over the soil. Work this into the soil with a rake, breaking up any large clods. Remove rocks and rake the area smooth.

    ✔ "Water up" the weeds by watering the prepared bed at least a week *before* you sow seeds or set out plants. As weeds sprout, pull them out gently — not because you don't want to hurt the weeds, but because you don't want to churn up more weed seeds.

    ✔ Repeat the previous step, if you have the time before sowing or planting. It really reduces those nasty weeds waiting to rob your seedlings of moisture and nutrients.

Getting Down to Business

Chapters 9 and 10 explain how to plant annuals from seed and from transplants, respectively. Planting wildflowers is essentially the same process, but some steps take on more importance with wildflowers. For example, preparing the bed and removing weeds are more important in a wildflower garden because you do much less mulching, weeding, and other maintenance in wildflower beds than in other types of gardens. Get your wildflowers off to a good start with little competition from weeds, and they can take care of themselves for the rest of the season.

Planting the bed

Although wildflowers naturalize and can compete well with other plants, they do need a head start. Prepare the planting area as you would any annual garden bed (but perhaps a bit more diligently) by tilling and removing weeds, rocks, and other debris. Always use fresh wildflower seeds, and follow these tips for breathtaking results:

    ✔ Measure and follow seed-packet directions for the rate at which to sow seeds. You want enough seeds to fill in your planting area without overcrowding later on. If in doubt, sow more rather than fewer seeds because you can always pull out extra plants after they sprout. For good coverage, sow half the seeds over the entire bed by walking in one direction (say, north to south) and then scatter the other half by moving perpendicular to your first path (east to west, in this case).

    ✔ If you sow bulk seeds, you can get more even distribution by mixing them with a generous amount of fine sand, vermiculite, or rice hulls. Aim for about a 1-to-3 ratio of seeds to broadcast the material.

    ✔ As an option, sow seeds in flats to transplant later into the garden. Use a standard seed-starting soil mix and sprinkle seeds lightly over the surface; cover lightly with soil mix and keep moist. Transplant the seedlings into the ground when they have two sets of leaves.

✔ After sowing seeds in the ground, rake them in very lightly and press them into the soil by walking on the bed or rolling the area with a lawn roller. Water immediately with a fine spray. Keep the seed bed moist by watering if natural rainfall is insufficient. After a month, roots should go deep enough so that you need to water only during dry spells.

✔ Repeat sowing (go lightly this time) a few weeks into the germination process. This allows you to cover any sparse areas and provide plants that will bloom later in the season.

✔ If you plant seedlings, set them out with enough space in between for plants to reach mature size. Add transplants for quick fill-ins if seed beds show bare spots.

✔ If adding wildflowers to established beds, concentrate seeds or transplants so that you have mass plantings of single varieties. This creates a dramatic look.

Alternative planting: Creating a scatter garden

Suppose that you have the space and want wildflowers but simply don't have the time or inclination to go through the process of preparing and planting. Should you give up? Absolutely not. Put the "wild" into wildflower garden by planting a *scatter garden* — duplicating nature by simply throwing the seeds into the breeze and letting fate take over. (Actually, you're better off waiting for a calm day.)

The drawback to the scatter garden idea is that it's somewhat of a calculated risk. But realize that wildflowers have historically done fine on their own anyway. You may not get as many flowers as you would with a more methodical planting, but the plants that do thrive offer extra satisfaction. Time your planting so that the ground is moist and choose areas that are not already overrun with weeds. If you're lucky, some seeds will take root, and the plants that do sprout will reseed to give you more wildflowers year after year.

Keeping Your Garden Just This Side of Wild

Maintaining a wildflower garden involves a bit of work, but it's still less labor than with other annual gardens. Wildflowers don't need as much attention, of course, because the plants have developed some means of living on their own. If you give them a hand, they'll respond with a spectacular display. Follow these tips to hold your garden at its peak:

✔ Keep the seed bed moist as seeds germinate and while plants are young. Deliver a gentle spray, using the tools and tips for watering seedlings discussed in Chapters 10 and 11. During prolonged dry spells, wildflowers act happier with periodic watering in the form of long, thorough soakings. Water this way only if plants start to wilt in the afternoons. As plants mature, they should be able to go longer and longer without water.

✔ Wage war on weeds. And if you start your battles early — even before you plant — you can go a long way toward keeping this job at a minimum. Seeds sown in fall may not sprout until spring if there's too much competition from weeds. Weed as soon as you can tell wildflowers from weeds, and continue weeding regularly during this early stage so that the desirable plants get the upper hand. (Chapter 15 includes detailed weed-whacking strategies.)

✔ Thin crowded beds where seedlings have sprouted too close together. No matter how diligent you are at careful sowing, some areas probably will have too many plants to support mature wildflowers. Let plants reach several inches in growth and then remove any weak seedlings, giving elbow room to the stronger plants.

✔ Support top-heavy plants if they threaten to topple or if stems begin to bend. Keep stems upright with bamboo or plastic-coated metal stakes and soft ties. Insert the stake so that it's hidden behind the flower.

✔ Deadhead spent flowers during the growing season. As Chapter 13 explains, removing faded flowers forces plants to produce new buds and a longer display. If you skip deadheading, the plants go through their natural cycle of producing flowers and making seeds. Near the end of the season, however, you can't do anything to stop nature: Plants wind down, become leggy, produce few flowers, and begin to die back.

When the Show Comes to an End

Eventually, the curtains close on your wildflower display as the plants finish their cycles. At this point, you see no new buds, growth may be rank (bordering on out of control), and leaves start to turn brown. At this point, you have two choices:

✔ You can let plants die back naturally and collect the debris after they are completely dead. This approach allows some seeds to scatter naturally, which may give you new plants in the future.

✔ If time and your climate allow, you can remove faded plants and replant or sow new seeds appropriate for the coming season. Before you start the process all over again, be sure to give abundant praise, ample thanks, and enthusiastic applause to the previous wildflower stars who are exiting the stage.

Chapter 18

Growing Annuals for Cutting

• •

In This Chapter

▶ Discovering annuals that make fabulous cut flowers, fresh and dried

▶ Designing a cutting garden

▶ Harvesting and arranging flowers

▶ Maintaining your cutting garden

• •

A friend says she likes to grow flowers for cutting because it reminds her of her childhood, when she picked favorite fragrant blossoms and "sent the butterflies dancing on air."

I always try to grow a few flowers for cutting in my garden, too. I never know when my wife is going to make a last-minute search-and-rescue mission for something to decorate the dining room table when guests are coming.

People find many good reasons to grow flowers specifically for cutting. Cut flowers can brighten a room, provide cheerful bouquets for friends and families, or surprise a coworker. You can even dry them for winter, when flowers are all the more precious.

This chapter explores why cut flowers are so special, and shows you how to grow flowers for cutting alongside other types of plants or in specialized cutting gardens. I include a list of the dozen best annuals to grow, along with tips for harvesting and using cut flowers in arrangements, both fresh and dried. You also get design plans for three basic gardens: a wide-row garden, a showcase garden in the landscape, and a small-space cutting garden.

If you enjoy the cheer, fragrance, and color that cut flowers offer, or if you have a spot begging for a special garden, read on to find out more about annuals that are great for cutting.

Seven Reasons to Grow Annuals for Cutting

Persuading people to grow annuals for cutting is an easy job. Here's my list of the top seven reasons to grow flowers for cutting:

- ✔ Flowers that are good for cutting (generally) happen to be among the easiest of annuals to grow. In addition to being beautiful, they're reliable, resilient, and refreshing — all this from flowers that also make great bouquets!

- ✔ Growing annuals for cutting can provide you with armloads of beautiful blossoms to use in everyday arrangements in every room in your house. Of course, I'm talking best-case scenario here — like saying a vegetable garden can feed your family every day. But with a little work and the right growing conditions, you can produce an abundance of flowers.

- ✔ You have direct access to the freshest flowers in town.

- ✔ You can create wonderful dried flowers for everlasting bouquets, awesome wreaths, or dozens of holiday crafts.

- ✔ Growing your own flowers reduces your bill at the florist's shop. Instead of ordering expensive arrangements for special occasions, pick bouquets for birthday, get well, and congratulations gifts right from your own backyard — all for free.

- ✔ You can derive satisfaction and pride from your garden by prominently displaying your harvested bouquets and boasting that you grew the flowers right in your own garden.

- ✔ Finally, the same annuals that are suited to cutting also enhance your landscape. They shine alongside other plants and flowers, and on their own, they outdo almost all other annual gardens.

Choosing the Best Annuals for Cutting

Your success at growing annuals for cutting depends, in part, on which plants you choose. Not all annuals can handle the trauma of being cut and transported indoors to the serenity of a few days in a vase. But many do. Here are some basic characteristics that good cutting flowers share:

- ✔ They have sturdy stems that are easy to cut.

- ✔ The cut stems freely take up ample water to allow the flowers to last a long time.

✔ They bloom prolifically, producing an abundance of flowers and buds through the season.

✔ Each flower or cluster of flowers has at least one of these characteristics: excellent form, outstanding color, or interesting texture.

In the following list, I recommend a dozen annuals to grow for cutting. I could easily double or triple the list, but in my experience, these are the most common and the easiest annuals to grow. Let these flowers inspire you to discover more annuals suitable for cutting.

✔ **Aster:** This annual, also called China aster, is an outstanding choice for the late-summer to fall garden, offering abundant flowers in a wide range of colors, from white to burgundy, pink, purple, and blue. Sturdy, straight stems make them easy to work with. Give these plants sun, and stake tall varieties.

✔ **Calendula:** Also called pot marigold, this long-lasting, tough plant is among the easiest to grow. It produces bright yellow or orange flowers in spring, summer, and fall. Cut blooms have a very long life.

✔ **Cosmos:** Good looks and abundant blooms make this flower a standout. Cosmos is a strong background plant that produces large, yellow-centered flowers in pink, white, burgundy, and magenta. Place cut flowers in warm water before putting them in a vase.

✔ **Sweet William:** This annual is an old-fashioned favorite that produces scores of spicy-smelling flowers. The blooms come in shades of pink, red, and purple, as well as bicolors. The plants bloom freely, and cut flowers can last up to two weeks in water.

✔ **Gloriosa daisy:** You may not find a more agreeable and tolerant plant than the gloriosa daisy, also called black-eyed Susan. Traditionally blooming in golden tones of yellow, gloriosa also comes in shades of burgundy, brown, bronze, and orange. Actually a tender perennial, gloriosa daisies are often grown as annuals because they're so easy to grow and they reseed themselves. Immerse cut stems immediately in water.

✔ **Larkspur:** Tall and elegant, this annual can give you both fresh and dried flowers. The spikes in pink, white, blue, and purple shades reach 4 feet — a striking contrast in arrangements. Remove all fernlike foliage when you prepare stems for water.

✔ **Salpiglossis:** Bold colors and velvety textures put this flower, also called a painted tongue, center-stage in arrangements. The blooms come in gold, blue, purple, and maroon, accented by pronounced veins. These plants are easy to grow but prefer a bit of shade during summer. Keep these sticky flowers separate from each other when cutting.

- **Salvia:** A number of plants in the salvia, or garden sage, category produce spikes of reliable flowers while tolerating poor soil and dry conditions. Colors include blue, white, red, purple, rose, and coral. (See photographs 80, 81, and 82 in this book's color section for examples of mealy-cup sage, gentian sage, and scarlet sage.) Upright spikes offer wonderful contrast to round flowers.

- **Snapdragon:** An absolute must for the well-stocked cutting garden, this old favorite offers spikes of brightly colored flowers. Colors include pale pastels, as well as maroon, bronze, white, cream, and orange. Flowers are sturdy and fun to cut. Strip off the lower foliage and use the blooms for upright accents.

- **Sunflower:** One of the most popular flowers these days, the sunflower has expanded its family way beyond the familiar big, bright yellow whoppers. Look for bronze, pale yellow, white, and mahogany varieties. For cut flower use, look for *pollen-free* varieties, which won't shed yellow pollen on furniture and tablecloths. Examples are 'Sunrich Lemon', 'Full Sun', 'Sunbeam', 'Sunbright', and 'Sunrich Orange'. Although dwarf sunflowers such as 'Teddy Bear' are excellent in borders beds, taller kinds produce the most flowers for cutting.

  Cut flowers for indoors just as they begin to open, leaving stems as long as practical. Place in warm water right after cutting, and shorten stems as necessary to fit your vase.

- **Sweet pea:** You'll miss out on fragrance, charm, and nostalgia if you don't grow at least a few sweet peas — nothing else can perfume a room so sweetly in early spring. This flower blooms in white, pink, red, purple, and lavender.

- **Zinnia:** A rainbow of vivid colors and a long blooming season make zinnias ideal for the cutting garden. 'Old Mexico Dwarf' is an exceptional variety for scores of flowers in warm tones. Let cut flowers drink up warm water before arranging.

Mixing Annuals for Cutting into Your Garden

You can intermingle the annuals that you grow for cutting with other plantings, or you can grow a separate cutting garden. If you don't have the space or time to devote to a complete cutting garden, growing individual plants or groups within other beds and borders is a perfect solution. With the right plants, you get lots of flowers to cut and enjoy, and the plants add color and interest wherever you place them.

Follow these guidelines for integrating cutting annuals into your landscape:

✔ Look for open spaces in all your garden areas and evaluate the growing conditions in those areas. Match plant needs (shade or sun, for example) to the site. Have fun as you experiment because, of course, with annuals you're never locked in — you can always plant them somewhere else next year!

✔ Within a shrub border, place cutting annuals where they'll get plenty of sun, in front of larger plants. Plan for enough annuals so that they don't look dwarfed or out of place. Groupings of five, seven, or nine plants of one variety can be attractive and produce plenty of flowers for cutting. Also allow for easy access because you have to be able to reach the plants with your cutting shears.

✔ Cutting annuals are the perfect complement to long-blooming perennials in a perennial bed or border. Be sure that you provide room for these single-season stars to reach full size. Larger and taller annuals (zinnias, gloriosa daisies, sunflowers, and spider flowers, for example) need space toward the back of the bed. Keep low-growers (sweet alyssum and lobelia, for example) in the front.

✔ In a mixed bed or border, choose plants that blend or offer interesting or colorful contrasts. If you have a blooming blush-pink rose, you can try nearby plantings of several mixed shades of cosmos in light pastels. Then add a dash of blue from salvia, larkspur, or cornflower for contrast.

✔ Don't forget containers. Plant a pot full of stunning dwarf zinnias or fragrant sweet William. Or drop pansies into a window box for wonderful blossoms within easy reach.

A Garden Full of Flowers for Cutting

A garden designed specifically to produce cut flowers can be as simple as a single row of cosmos, or as detailed and attractive as a rainbow-colored border with pathways and seating. Or you may have rows and rows of different annuals that produce more flowers than you know what to do with — sort of like those pervasive zucchinis that your neighbors and coworkers try to unload on you every summer. The good news is that you can create a cutting garden to fit your needs, whether you want a small patch of cutting flowers or a more complex garden.

Even if you have room for only a small cutting garden, be prepared for a little bit of work. Planting and caring for a garden of cutting flowers is easy, but it does involve more than simply transplanting some evergreen ground cover and watching from the window as it spreads 4 inches a year. If you want a nice cutting garden, you'll have to plant dozens of flowers and do a bit of watering, and maybe some staking, but that's about it — except for the daily pleasure of harvesting cut blooms.

Designing a cutting garden

Planning your garden of cutting flowers is the easy part, especially if you've worked with annual gardens before. The first step is to decide what you want: Do you prefer rectangles and rows designed for farmlike efficiency so that you can easily gather armloads of plants? Or would you rather have an artistic and attractive garden that you can enjoy as part of the landscape?

Evaluate your site and consider what design might work in the area that you've set aside for your cutting garden. You may need to stand in the yard or pull up a chair and turn your imagination loose for 15 minutes. Perhaps you can sketch some designs of your ideal cutting garden.

Don't forget to check out the resources listed in the appendix of this book for ideas on how to design your cutting garden. A quick way to collect good ideas is to spend a day visiting public gardens and arboreta in your area.

Consider basic design techniques, which I describe in more detail in Chapters 6 and 7. Count on planting in multiples or masses, repeating clusters of certain plants, and dropping in those solitary accent plants for a different look, color, or texture. Consider the size and scale of your flowers. For example, place tall plants in the back and large-flowered plants in larger spaces.

Three designs for cutting gardens

If you don't feel like being creative, this section includes three ready-made garden designs. The first plan is a utilitarian, wide-row, rectangular cutting garden — a workhorse garden that's not fancy but that produces loads of flowers. The second design is a showcase cutting garden that's designed to produce flowers but also serves as a landscape feature. The third plan is a nifty little garden that works well in a small space.

Garden 1: Simple and successful

The cutting garden shown in Figure 18-1 couldn't be more straightforward or, in its simplicity, more effective.

The overall size of this garden is about 850 square feet. Wide 36-inch beds with several plants grown side-by-side allow the maximum number of plants per square foot. Plant the rows in an east-west pattern. Place the tall plants in rows along the northern end so that they don't shade shorter neighbors. Close spacing helps keep plants upright and cuts down on weeds. Mulched paths between the rows allow easy access for harvesting.

The annuals I suggest growing in this plan are proven performers. Each 30-foot row contains a single variety of flower, except the central row, which

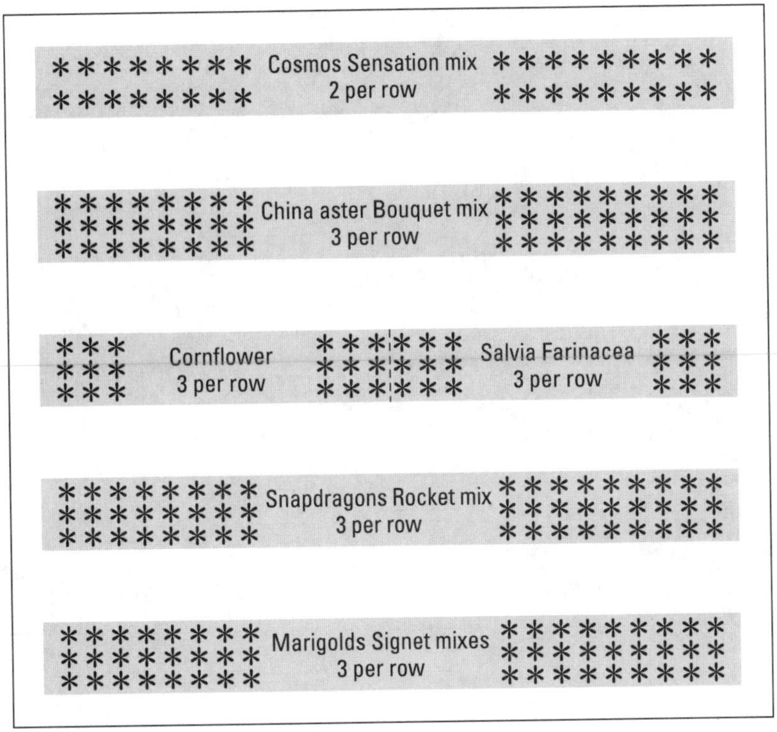

```
* * * * * * *  Cosmos Sensation mix  * * * * * * * *
* * * * * * *        2 per row         * * * * * * * *


* * * * * * * * Cosmos  Bouquet mix * * * * * * * *
* * * * * * * * China aster Bouquet mix * * * * * * * *
* * * * * * * *        3 per row         * * * * * * * *


* * *      Cornflower      * * * * * *  Salvia Farinacea  * * *
* * *      3 per row       * * * * * *    3 per row       * * *
* * *                      * * * * * *                    * *


* * * * * * * *  Snapdragons Rocket mix  * * * * * * * *
* * * * * * * *         3 per row          * * * * * * * *
* * * * * * * *                            * * * * * * * *


* * * * * * * *  Marigolds Signet mixes  * * * * * * * *
* * * * * * * *         3 per row          * * * * * * * *
* * * * * * * *                            * * * * * * * *
```

Figure 18-1: A wide-row cutting garden is easy to plant and allows easy access to the flowers.

cornflower (also known as bachelor's button) shares with mealy-cup sage (*Salvia farinacea*). This garden covers most of the colors in the rainbow, with pastel mixes from cosmos, asters, and snapdragons flanking the central blue row. The warm hues of yellow, orange, and bicolored marigolds round out the collection. Although this garden may not have a complicated design, it overflows with color by midsummer, and produces lots and lots of flowers for cutting.

Garden 2: Showcase display

The garden shown in Figure 18-2 showcases masses of annuals in a design that features two beds divided by a circular path and accentuated with a seating area. Symmetrical and varied, this garden contains nine types of flowers to give you a wide range of colors, sizes, shapes, and textures from late spring through summer.

The outer border of this garden contains lush masses of larkspur, nicotiana, strawflower, gloriosa daisy, sunflower, and cosmos. The island bed, featuring zinnias accented by globe amaranth and verbena, is planted on a raised mound of soil to give the garden depth and add interest. A generous, curving crushed-rock path gives the garden movement and makes harvesting the flowers easy and practical. And for those moments when you simply want to sit and enjoy the space, a bench provides a welcome resting spot.

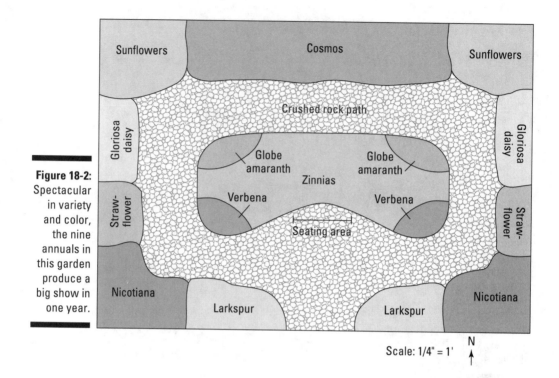

Figure 18-2:
Spectacular in variety and color, the nine annuals in this garden produce a big show in one year.

Scale: 1/4" = 1'

N

Garden 3: Small-space special

The compact and colorful garden shown in Figure 18-3 is adaptable to just about any sunny site. Featuring zinnias and snapdragons, it measures 8 feet by 6 feet and features eight planting areas with a narrow, 1-foot-wide stepping-stone path for access. The flowers are planted in multiples, but because space is tight, some areas, such as the corners, have only six plants per section. Support is critical so that the plants don't lean on neighbors. This collection provides a range of colors in flowers of different sizes and shapes.

Digging in

Before you can turn that first shovelful of dirt to install your cutting garden, you need to choose the right spot. Select a sunny spot that offers easy access to the flowers — perhaps that empty space that's been bothering you since 1987. Next, you can make your plant list, matching selections to conditions. (For the best bets on annuals for cutting, refer to the section "Choosing the Best Annuals for Cutting," earlier in this chapter, for a list of a dozen great options.)

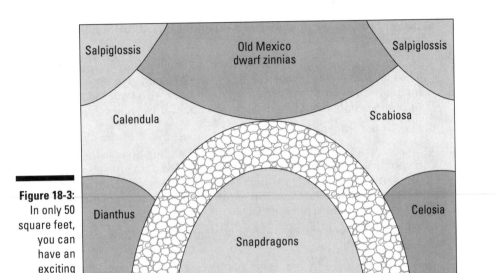

Salpiglossis

Old Mexico
dwarf zinnias

Salpiglossis

Calendula

Scabiosa

Figure 18-3:
In only 50
square feet,
you can
have an
exciting
garden of
annuals.

Dianthus

Snapdragons

Celosia

N

Scale: 1/2" = 1'

Installing a garden is really a pretty simple process, especially if you have a sketch or at least a mental picture of a garden design. If you want to plant flowers in simple rows, you may be able to finish the job in a day. For gardens with a more elaborate design, you may need a weekend or two. (Perhaps you can even enlist the help of a friend or neighbor in return for some lovely larkspur later.) Either way, the following steps should help you get started.

1. **Start by clearing the space and removing weeds.**

2. **If the soil is compacted, heavy clay, or high in sand content, add a 2- to 3-inch layer of compost and dig it in 10 inches or so.**

   Add the compost a minimum of several weeks before planting, if possible. Amending the soil ahead of time gives the materials time to begin to break down and enrich the soil. (Refer to Chapter 8 for advice on amending soil with compost.)

3. **Blend in a complete granular fertilizer according to package directions.**

4. **Rake the area smooth and mark off your beds and paths.**

   Use any material that's handy: string, a disconnected hose, or a light-colored powdery substance, such as flour, lime, or gypsum.

5. **Install border-edging materials — bender-board, bricks, pavers, or stones.**

   Set the border edging so that it sits 1 to 2 inches above the soil level. The elevated edging keeps the dirt in the bed and gives you a couple of inches for a layer of pathway material. Check with your local landscape or home-supply store for more details about these and other options.

6. **Set out the transplants.**

   Space them from 6 to 12 inches apart, depending on mature size. (See recommendations for spacing in Chapters 4 and 5.) Loosen tangled roots or slice vertically through very dense, massed roots in two or three places. Set plants on top of the soil and make any final spacing adjustments before planting them.

   Alternatively, you can sow seeds of plants such as zinnias and calendula directly in the bed where you want them to grow. Wait until late spring, after the soil is thoroughly warm. Mark out rows and press seeds into moist soil. Cover lightly with soil and then cover the area with mulch to help retain moisture. If snails or slugs are a problem in your area, set out traps or bait (see Chapter 14) as soon as seedlings emerge.

7. **Dig holes for the plants.**

   When you have all the plants in the position you want them, begin planting. Using a trowel, scoop out a hole that is slightly larger than the root ball of each plant.

8. **Water the transplants immediately after you finish planting.**

9. **Prepare the pathway by spreading 2 to 4 inches of crushed rock, bark, gravel, or a mulch of straw, shredded leaves, or other organic materials.**

10. **Mulch around the plants with compost, chunkbark, weed-free straw, or similar organic material.**

    Mulching keeps weeds at a minimum and helps the soil hold moisture. (For more on mulching, see Chapter 15.)

Harvesting and Using Cut Flowers

The payoff for all your hard work finally comes when you get to harvest your flowers. What could be more rewarding and enjoyable? To get the most from your flowers, here are some tips on what to harvest, when to cut flowers, and how to treat them so that they last.

✔ Choose flowers that are just reaching maturity. Look for fresh petals and sturdy upright stems.

✔ You can cut flowers almost anytime of the day, but aim for a time when the flowers have high moisture levels — early in the morning or in the cool of the evening, for example.

✔ Use clean, sharp shears or pruners and make your cut above a set of leaves. This may encourage a new bud to grow on the stem you leave behind.

✔ Bring along a plastic pail or bucket and immerse the flowers in a few inches of water if your harvesting will take some time.

✔ After bringing the plant indoors, remove any lower leaves from the stems — especially those that will be under water.

✔ Recut each stem at about a 45-degree angle, keeping in mind the length that will be suitable for your vase.

✔ Use only clean vases or containers.

✔ To get the most from your flowers, change the water daily and help keep it clean by adding two to three drops of household bleach when you refill the vase.

Another helpful idea is to condition flowers before they begin life in a vase. With lower leaves removed, immerse the stem in deep water to just below the flower or top set of leaves. Let the stem stay underwater several hours or overnight before you use it in your arrangement. This step allows the flower to take up as much water as it can in its leaves, stem, and blossom.

Building a Bouquet

You don't need a lot of fancy equipment and a degree in floral design to assemble a beautiful bouquet. Your container can be anything that holds water, and the more water it holds, the better. Bowls, tall vases, mugs, cups, jars, pitchers, and crocks are just fine. Urn-shaped vases with a narrow neck and a deep reservoir make arranging easy.

Applying some basic rules about proportion and balance can help you create an eye-catching arrangement. Heavier flowers look nice when placed near the base (for stability), and lighter ones are suitable for the outside edges. Odd numbers give nice lines. You can add interest and depth by creating layers — placing the flowers at different heights and facing different directions. If you follow these rules, you'll know that a tiny vase of pansies on a large living room table looks strange, and so does a 3-inch-tall bottle holding four snapdragon spikes — even if you *can* stuff them in.

After you finish arranging the flowers, spray them all with a mister bottle of water. As you admire your bouquet, you just may discover an artistic side that you never knew you had.

Creating Everlasting Beauty with Dried Flowers

Simple things like flowers can produce such rewarding results! If you've included flowers that can be dried in your cutting garden — ageratum, baby's breath, celosia, clarkia, cornflower, globe amaranth, larkspur, love-in-a-mist, strawflower, statice, and salvia — you have the ingredients for dried-flower bouquets.

Simply cut several stems when the flowers are fresh and strong and suspend them upside down in a dry, dark place, such as the rafters in your garage or tool shed or an attic or closet. You can hang several bunches from a wire coat hanger to save space, as shown in Figure 18-4. Check the bundles in several weeks to see if they are stiff and crisp — start using them when they reach that stage.

Figure 18-4:
Drying cut flowers is simply a matter of hanging the flowers upside-down from their stems in a cool, dry place.

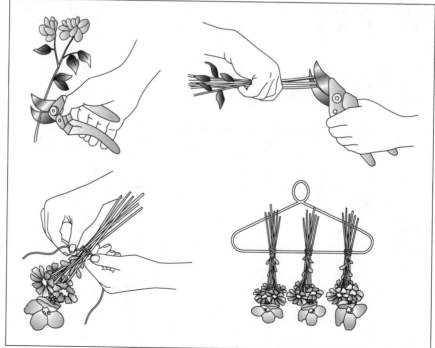

Dried flowers can last a long time, but you can generally expect to enjoy them no longer than through the winter until the following summer. Most dried blooms shatter, get dusty, and otherwise lose their charm, although some can last for years.

Ongoing Care

Because you visit cutting gardens frequently to gather more flowers, you may as well do your gardening chores at the same time. Taking care of cutting annuals is a simple matter because the maintenance chores follow a predictable pattern — water, feed, stake, deadhead, and weed — all of which I explain in Part V. Consistency is the key to giving plants a stress-free environment; in other words, don't wait for your flowers to wilt before you water. Here are a few special tips that apply to a cutting garden.

- ✔ In a garden of wide rows and many plants, tall plants are likely to need staking. At planting time, place single stakes next to plants; be sure that the stakes are tall enough to support the plants when they're fully grown. Or for economy, use several straight and sturdy twigs throughout the bed. Enough of these stakes may provide sufficient support so that you won't have to tie the plants to the stakes.

- ✔ If you grow cutting flowers in landscape settings, use dark green bamboo or wire-coated metal stakes to support tall stems. These stakes disappear discreetly into the foliage, letting the plants, and not the stakes, take center stage.

- ✔ In general, flowers grown for cutting need less fertilization than other annuals. Feeding often stimulates lush vegetative growth, and that's not the goal with cutting flowers. Healthy plants a bit on the "hungry" side actually make the most flowers. However, around midseason, you can give your plants a boost with an application of granular or liquid fertilizer according to package directions.

Winding Down

It'll be a sad day when your cutting annuals — those stalwart friends who've served reliably in the landscape and living room — are struck by frost or otherwise finish their growing season. After you send these zapped annuals to the compost pile, however, you can change your focus to an evaluation of your garden.

Jot down the names, varieties, and descriptions of the plants you grew. Include notes about the planting, care, and harvesting of your flowers. Evaluate the floral performance indoors, too. Some flowers may have an exceptional vase life, so those are the ones that you want to include next year.

A little mental effort as the garden fades will pay off at planning time next season. One big advantage of an annual cutting garden is that each year you start fresh with new options. Scale up, scale down, grow more orange, go with purples and blues, try taller varieties, or add more fragrance. Whatever you do, one thing's for sure: A cutting garden offers you lasting satisfaction.

Part VII
The Part of Tens

In this part . . .

So you have your heart set on filling that sunny spot in your yard with red, white, and blue flowers? And you say you want to include some fragrant flowers and some flowers for cutting, as well? In that case, all you have to do is glance through the lists in this part to find the flowers that meet your needs. Look here for sets of flowers that are easy to grow, short or tall, shade- or sun-loving, fragrant, of a particular color, and much more. You'll also find answers to the most frequently asked questions about annuals.

Chapter 19

Ten Most Frequently Asked Questions about Annuals

. . . .

*I*n the plant kingdom, annuals may be considered fun-loving goof-offs, great to have around for a good time in the summer — and even longer than that in mild climates. But gardeners still have a fair share of questions about these carefree, easy-to-grow flowers.

✔ **What *is* an annual?**

I'm not going to dismiss this question by telling you to read the first chapter of this book (although it does contain lots of handy details on the subject). Here's the short answer: An annual is a plant that goes through its whole life cycle, from seed to bloom to creation of new seeds, in one growing season. Unlike perennials, annuals do not return year after year — although, if you're lucky, the seeds they produce will germinate to take their places.

✔ **Should I plant annuals from seeds or from seedlings?**

The answer depends on the type of annual you want to grow. Some annuals do best when they're sown directly in the ground. Sunflowers and zinnias, for example, don't relish transplanting. Sow seeds of those flowers right where you want them to grow.

Other annuals do well whether you grow them directly from seeds sown in the ground or from seedlings. For example, marigolds grow no matter which way you start them, as seeds or seedlings.

You can start many annuals from seeds indoors and transplant them to the garden at the right time. This method saves money, if you want big quantities of certain plants. It can also be a rewarding aspect of gardening. But you may not want to start difficult, slow-growing types of annuals, such as impatiens or petunias, from seeds. You have better luck if you start slower-growing flowers like these from nursery-grown seedlings.

✔ **Is it better to plant big seedlings or little ones?**

Nurseries usually offer annuals in a small six-pack size or in 4-inch pots or gallon cans. Annuals in larger containers usually are blooming and hard to resist. The blooming plants have one big advantage — they can brighten a garden instantly. But the smaller plants can generally outperform the bigger ones. In fact, if the little seedlings have flowers on them, cut off the blooms when you plant them to encourage bushier growth and more flower production in the long run.

✔ **When can I plant annuals?**

The answer depends on where you live. If you live in a typical cold-winter climate, plant tender annuals (the ones that frost will kill) after all danger of frost has passed. You can plant hardy annuals a few weeks earlier. Some annuals (such as zinnias) need warm soil and air temperatures as well as no threat of frost; plant these flowers when the weather really starts to heat up.

If you live in milder climates, the planting schedule can get a little more complicated (in a good way). For example, you may be able to plant in the fall for winter and spring bloom. See Chapter 3 for a gardening calendar appropriate for your season.

As a general rule, don't plant the instant that nurseries start selling annuals unless you're the kind of person who celebrates the holidays as soon as department stores put up their decorations.

✔ **Why do I see the same plants at every nursery?**

Nurseries sell flowers that are the most popular. (After all, they're in it for the money.) Petunias, impatiens, and marigolds, to name a few of the most popular annuals, are very popular plants because they're reliable, easy to grow, and long-blooming. But hundreds of other wonderful varieties are available, as you can see in Chapter 5. To discover other varieties, check out mail-order catalogs (refer to the appendix) and specialty nurseries.

✔ **What's eating my annuals?**

It's hard to give a simple answer to that question. Most annuals are relatively trouble-free, but they can sometimes run into problems with pests or diseases. (See Chapter 14.) The problem may be that you're growing a plant that's not suited for your climate or garden. With so many terrific annuals, why not choose something else? That's my garden philosophy. Where I live, budworms always eat petunias, and my zinnias always get mildew, so I grow something else. If your nasturtiums are what's getting eaten, the culprit may be your neighbor — nasturtiums make delicious salads!

What's the easiest-to-grow, most colorful annual?

Impatiens. Next question. . . .

SHADY CHARACTER

✔ **What annuals can I get to bloom in the shade?**

Impatiens can do wonders in deep shade, but they can also tolerate a lot of sun in cool climates. Bedding begonias, primroses, coleus, and spider flower also like shady spots. But even these shade-loving plants need some light to bloom well. If your shady spots are too dark, better try ferns.

✔ **Should I always cut off dead flowers?**

This process is called _deadheading,_ and it benefits most annuals by forcing them to concentrate on new flower production rather than seed production. Deadheading is easy with bigger flowers and is essential with zinnias, large-flowered marigolds, and many others. Small-flowered annuals (such as felicias) can sometimes be sheared. Some annuals, such as impatiens, are those miracles of the plant-breeders' art that are considered to be _self-cleaning_ — no deadheading required.

✔ **What annuals can I grow to attract butterflies?**

To get butterflies to linger in your garden, you must provide nectar plants for the adult butterflies and tasty foliage for the caterpillars to chew on. Annuals can't do the whole butterfly-attracting job by themselves, but they can make butterflies happy and add beauty to your garden. Try phlox, verbena, zinnia, and Mexican sunflower _(Tithonia)._

Chapter 20

Ten Annuals That Virtually Care for Themselves

. . . .

*Y*ou've come to the right place if you're looking for information about annuals that grow quickly, need no special watering or fertilizing, run into no particular pest or disease trouble, and still put on a first-rate flower show. Quite a few such annuals do exist, and I list some of my personal favorites in this chapter.

Be forewarned, though, that you can't just stick any of these annuals in the ground and ignore them. You need to prepare the soil, provide the proper sun exposure and moisture, and perform some basic garden maintenance.

Here's my list of the ten easiest annuals that you can grow:

- **Bedding begonia:** (also called wax begonia) Grows in sun or shade; leaves and flowers are always colorful

- **Calendula:** (also called pot marigold) One of the first annuals out of the chute in the spring, looks hardy, and it is

- **California poppy:** A sun-loving flower that's almost too colorful for some people; can become a weed if it likes the conditions

- **Coleus:** Foliage, not flowers, provides the bright colors in shady spots

- **Geranium:** *(Pelargonium)* A classic favorite, but not so easy to grow in hot, dry climates or in places where budworms hang out

- **Impatiens:** As shade-tolerant as any annual; naturally resistant to pests of all kinds

- **Marigold:** A sun-loving favorite that gives the most bloom for your buck

- **Nasturtium:** In favorable conditions, grows like a weed — a beautiful, edible weed with bright green leaves and brilliant flowers

- **Sweet alyssum:** Blooms long and abundantly in cool weather as well as warm weather; may reseed and come back year after year

- **Vinca rosea:** (also called Madagascar periwinkle) Pest-free and glossy-leafed even under the hottest conditions; looks almost plastic

Chapter 21

Annuals for Special Situations: Ten Sets of Ten

● ●

Although annuals are amazingly easy to grow, some do adapt better to certain locations. For example, cosmos and zinnias are sun worshippers, but begonias and impatiens prefer the shade. If you're puzzled about which annuals to take home from the nursery, use the lists in this chapter as a guide. These lists can help you select annuals that grow well in different garden situations. For more specifics, consult the flower descriptions in Chapters 4 and 5.

Annuals for sunny spots

In general, annuals like the sun. These ten *adore* it. If you've got a spot where the sun seems to beat down relentlessly, try some of these sun worshippers:

- ✔ Calendula (also called pot marigold)
- ✔ Celosia (also called cockscomb)
- ✔ Cosmos
- ✔ Dahlia
- ✔ Portulaca (also called moss rose)
- ✔ Salvia (the sage family)
- ✔ Snapdragon
- ✔ Sunflower
- ✔ Sweet pea
- ✔ Zinnia

Annuals for shade

A few annuals thrive in the shade. All the following plants need a bit of sunlight, but not as much as most:

- Bedding begonia (also called wax begonia)
- Browallia
- Coleus
- Forget-me-not
- Impatiens
- Love-in-a-mist (also called nigella)
- Monkey flower
- Nicotiana (also called flowering tobacco)
- Primrose
- Spider flower (also called cleome)

Annuals for hot, dry spots

If water is scarce where you live, don't waste it on thirsty annuals that love to wallow in the mud. Choose one of the following annuals, all of which take more after the camel than the pig.

- African daisy (both *Arctotis* and *Dimorphotheca*)
- Blanket flower (also called gaillardia)
- California poppy
- Calliopsis (also called annual coreopsis)
- Four o'clock
- Globe amaranth
- Portulaca (also called moss rose)
- Salvia (the sage family)
- Verbena
- Vinca rosea (also called Madagascar periwinkle)

Annuals for containers

From window boxes to terra cotta pots, nothing beats a container full of blooming flowers. Turn to Chapter 16 for details about growing annuals in containers. For even more information on this topic, pick up a copy of *Container Gardening For Dummies*.

- ✔ Ageratum (also called floss flower)
- ✔ Calendula (also called pot marigold)
- ✔ Coleus
- ✔ Felicia (also called blue marguerite)
- ✔ Geranium (*Pelargonium,* not the perennial geranium)
- ✔ Impatiens
- ✔ Lobelia
- ✔ Marigold
- ✔ Pansy
- ✔ Zinnia

Annuals for beds and borders

Planning a flower bed or border? Read Chapter 7 for planning ideas, and consider one of the following dependable, yet dramatic annuals:

- ✔ Bedding begonia (also called wax begonia)
- ✔ Geranium
- ✔ Impatiens
- ✔ Marigold
- ✔ Pansy
- ✔ Petunia
- ✔ Snapdragon
- ✔ Salvia
- ✔ Vinca rosea (also called Madagascar periwinkle)
- ✔ Zinnia

Annuals for edging

Want to add some drama to your walkways? The following annuals make perfect borders to your driveway, sidewalk, or pathway:

- Ageratum (also called floss flower)
- Candytuft
- Dusty miller
- Forget-me-not
- Lobelia
- Marigold (dwarf types)
- Pink (also called dianthus)
- Sweet alyssum
- Sweet William
- Viola

Annuals that naturalize (self-seed)

A single annual plant doesn't come back year after year the way perennials do, but some of them do drop seeds that are likely to germinate on their own, taking the place of those that came before them. Here are some of the annuals most prone to self-seeding:

- African daisy (*Dimorphotheca*)
- California poppy
- Cornflower (also called bachelor's button)
- Cosmos
- Forget-me-not
- Foxglove (also called digitalis)
- Nasturtium
- Shirley poppy
- Sweet alyssum
- Wallflower

Annuals for hanging baskets

When you create a hanging basket, like those discussed in Chapter 16, you want some plants that spill over the sides and others that rise dramatically from the center, without getting too tall. All the following annuals work wonders for your hanging baskets:

- ✔ Browallia
- ✔ Creeping zinnia
- ✔ Impatiens
- ✔ Lobelia
- ✔ Nasturtium
- ✔ Nierembergia (also called cupflower)
- ✔ Petunia
- ✔ Scaevola
- ✔ Sweet alyssum
- ✔ Verbena

Annuals that climb or creep

Have a bare wall that you want to cover, or a large patch of yard you want to fill? Consider one of the following annuals, which are prone to climb upwards and creep outwards. Just be prepared to defend your territory in case these spreaders get too carried away.

Climbers:

- ✔ Canary creeper
- ✔ Morning glory
- ✔ Nasturtium (tall varieties)
- ✔ Sweet pea
- ✔ Thunbergia (also called black-eyed Susan vine)

Creepers:

- ✔ Creeping zinnia *(Sanvitalia)*
- ✔ Dahlberg daisy
- ✔ Nasturtium

- Portulaca
- Zinnia (not the annual species, but the tender perennial *Zinnia angustifolia*)

Annuals that are easy to grow from seed outdoors

Seedlings are easy to grow, but they can get expensive. Seeds that you have to start indoors under controlled conditions can take too much of your precious time. The following annuals offer the perfect compromise: They grow easily from seeds planted right in the ground.

- African daisy (both *Arctotis* and *Dimorphotheca*)
- California poppy
- Cosmos
- Linaria (also called toadflax)
- Marigold
- Morning glory
- Shirley poppy
- Sunflower
- Sweet alyssum
- Zinnia

Chapter 22

Ten Annuals for Every Color of the Rainbow

· ·

Color is one of the best things about growing annuals. The lists in this chapter can help you choose plants in the colors you want. Of course, color isn't everything; you still need to look the plants up in Chapter 5 to make sure that they're right for your conditions.

Many annuals have varieties that come in different colors. Sometimes, these varieties are sold as mixtures, so you don't know what you're getting when you plant seeds or buy seedlings before they bloom. If you want a specific color, look for seeds and seedlings sold as separate colors, for example, 'Cherry Pink' grandiflora petunia.

A case of the blues

Nothing beats the true blue of these annuals. If you want a bad case of the blues, or even just a small dose, the following annuals will satisfy your needs:

- ✔ Ageratum (also called floss flower)
- ✔ Aster (also called China aster)
- ✔ Baby blue eyes
- ✔ Browallia
- ✔ Cornflower (also called bachelor's button)
- ✔ Forget-me-not
- ✔ Lobelia
- ✔ Love-in-a-mist (also called nigella)
- ✔ Morning glory
- ✔ Nierembergia (also called cupflower)

Purple passion

Ranging from lavender to grape, these purple flowers add a royal air to your garden:

- Aster (also called China aster)
- Cosmos
- Dahlia
- Heliotrope
- Lisianthus
- Nierembergia (also called cupflower)
- Pansy
- Petunia
- Primrose
- Verbena

Yellow . . . just like this book!

Yellow may mean cowardly, but there's nothing shy about the bold, bright yellows of this lot. Ranging from lemony to the color of egg yolk, these hot colors bring the sunshine to your flower bed:

- Blanket flower (also called gaillardia)
- Calendula (also called pot marigold)
- Dahlberg daisy (also called golden fleece)
- Gloriosa daisy (also called black-eyed Susan or rudbeckia)
- Marigold
- Monkey flower
- Pansy
- Snapdragon
- Thunbergia (black-eyed Susan vine)
- Zinnia

A blaze of orange

The clear, crisp radiance of an orange annual is a sight to behold. The following annuals produce some especially striking shades of orange:

✓ African daisy *(Dimorphotheca)*

✓ Calendula (also called pot marigold)

✓ California poppy

✓ Cosmos

✓ Geranium (*Pelargonium,* not the perennial by the same name)

✓ Marigold

✓ Mexican sunflower (also called tithonia)

✓ Nasturtium

✓ Transvaal daisy

✓ Wallflower

Red hot and spicy

Red is the epitome of a hot color. Think of Monroe's lips, a racy new Mazda, a long-stemmed rose. You can bring a touch of all these elements into your flower bed with the true red of these annuals:

✓ Celosia (also called cockscomb)

✓ Dahlia

✓ Geranium (*Pelargonium,* not the perennial by the same name)

✓ Hollyhock

✓ Impatiens

✓ Love-lies-bleeding

✓ Scarlet sage

✓ Shirley poppy

✓ Snapdragon

✓ Zinnia

Pretty in pink

The color pink is instrumental in giving a romantic appeal to cool, calming pastel gardens. Some of the best pinks that annuals have to offer come from these plants (one of which is even named after the color!):

✓ Bedding begonia (or wax begonia)

✓ Pink (as well as carnation and other members of the *Dianthus* family)

✓ Impatiens

- Nicotiana (also called flowering tobacco)
- Petunia
- Phlox
- Portulaca (also called moss rose)
- Spider flower (also called cleome)
- Sweet pea
- Snapdragon

All dressed in white

White is neither a hot color nor a cold one. Instead, it intensifies the colors of whatever it's next to. Add white to bring out the colors in any flower bed, or create an all-white garden, perfect for evening viewing.

- Baby's breath
- Candytuft
- Cosmos
- Impatiens
- Lobelia
- Marigold (really, white varieties are available)
- Nicotiana (also called flowering tobacco)
- Petunia
- Sweet alyssum
- Vinca rosea (also called Madagascar periwinkle)

Green with envy

Green isn't just for leaves, anymore. The following annuals* actually come in shades of green; just watch out for errant leprechauns:

- Bells of Ireland
- Coleus
- Flowering kale
- Nicotiana (also called flowering tobacco)
- Zinnia

*Yes, there are only five here, but aren't you impressed that I found this many?

Appendix

Sources for More Information about Annuals

• •

Seed catalogs, gardening books, Web sites, master gardeners . . . this appendix is just the beginning of all the resources available to the would-be gardener.

Seeds by mail

W. Atlee Burpee Co., 300 Park Ave., Warminster, PA 18971; phone 800-888-1447, fax 800-487-5530; Web site www.burpee.com. Free catalog. Wide selection of heirloom seeds and the latest hybrid seeds and transplants.

Berlin Seeds, 5371 County Rd. 77, Millersburg, OH 44654; phone 330-893-2030. Free catalog.

Bountiful Gardens, 18001 Shafer Ranch Rd., Willits, CA 95490; phone/fax 707-459-6410; e-mail bountyful@zapcom.net, Web site countrylife.net/ecoaction. Free catalog. All seeds are untreated and open-pollinated. Catalog is free in U.S. and $2 in other countries.

Burrell's, P.O. Box 150, 405 N. Main St., Rocky Ford, CO 81067; phone 719-254-3318, fax 719-254-3319. Free catalog. Wide range of flower seeds.

Comstock, Ferre & Co., 263 Main St., Wethersfield, CT 06109; phone 860-571-6590, fax 860-571-6595. Free catalog. Huge range of lesser-known varieties.

The Cook's Garden, P.O. Box 5010, Hodges, SC 29653-5010; phone 800-457-9703, fax 800-457-9705; Web site www.cooksgarden.com. Extensive range of varieties.

DeGiorgi Seed Company, 6011 N St., Omaha, NE 68117-1634; phone 800-858-2580. Free catalog. Excellent selection of flowering annuals, perennials, grasses, vegetables, herbs, and wildflowers.

Down on the Farm Seed, P.O. Box 184, Hiram, OH 44234. Mail orders only. Sells only untreated seeds, heirlooms, and open-pollinated hybrids. Wide selection.

Fedco Seeds, P.O. Box 520, Waterville, ME 04903; phone 207-873-7333. Catalog $2. Seed cooperative sells annuals of all kinds suited to cold Northeast climate. Will ship seeds to Canada.

Ferry-Morse Seeds, P.O. Box 488, Fulton, KY 42041-0488; phone 800-283-3400, fax 800-283-2700. Free catalog. Standards and new hybrids.

Garden City Seeds, 778 Highway 93 North, Hamilton, MT 59840; phone 406-961-4837, fax 406-961-4877. Organic seeds selected for an early harvest.

Genesee Country Museum, P.O. Box 310, Mumford, NY 14511; phone 716-538-6822, fax 716-538-2887. Only nineteenth-century heirlooms.

Green Mountain Transplants Inc., RR#1, Box 6C, East Montpelier, VT 05651; phone 802-454-1533, fax 802-454-1204, e-mail GMTranspl@aol.com. Greenhouse-propagated transplants.

Gurney's Seed & Nursery Co., 110 Capital St., Yankton, SD 57079; phone 605-665-1930, fax 605-665-9718. Wide range of annuals, dwarf varieties, container fruit trees, houseplants, grasses, and plugs.

Harris Seeds, P.O. Box 22960, Rochester, NY 14692; phone 800-514-4441, fax 716-442-9386. Many annuals, some exclusives, lots on seed starting, and indoor seeds.

Ed Hume Seeds, P.O. Box 1450, Kent, WA 98035; fax 206-859-0694; Web site members.aolcom/Humeseeds. No phone orders. Catalog $1. Untreated seeds for cool climates and short seasons.

Johnny's Selected Seeds, Foss Hill Rd., Albion, ME 04910-9731; phone 207-437-4301, fax 800-437-4290, e-mail homegarden@johnnyseeds.com. Source for seed-starting equipment; flower, herb, and vegetable seeds; container gardening kits; seed collections; and soil mixes.

Jung Quality Seeds, 335 S. High St., Randolph, WI 53957; phone 800-247-5864, fax 800-692-5864. Good selection of annuals and seed-starting equipment and pesticides.

Kilgore's Florida Planting Guide, 1400 W. First St., Sanford, FL 32771; phone 407-323-6630. Free catalog. Annuals suited to Florida. Catalog contains reference table for planting annuals and vegetables in Florida.

Liberty Seed Co., P.O. Box 806, New Philadelphia, OH 44663-0806; phone 800-541-6022, fax 330-364-6415. Excellent selection of pansies, impatiens, and petunias, all available in many colors.

Nichols Garden Nursery, 1190 N. Pacific Highway, Albany, OR 97321-4580; phone 541-928-9280, fax 541-967-8406; e-mail nichols@gardennursery.com, Web site www.pacificharbor.com/nichols. Good selection of pansies and other annuals.

Park Seed Co., Cokesbury Rd., Greenwood, SC 29647-0001; phone 864-223-7333 or 800-948-5487, fax 864-941-4206; e-mail info@park.com, Web site www.parkseed.com.

Pinetree Garden Seeds, Box 300, New Gloucester, ME 04260; phone 207-926-3400, fax 207-926-3886; e-mail seeds@maine.com, Web site www.maine.com/seeds/Welcome.html. Wide assortment of standard, popular varieties in addition to lesser-known varieties.

Reliable Seeds, 3862 Carlsbad Blvd., Carlsbad, CA 92008; phone 760-729-3282. Catalog $2. Seeds for the southern California garden.

Roswell Seed Co., P.O. Box 725, Roswell, NM 88202; phone 505-622-7701, fax 505-623-2885. Limited selection of flowers well adapted to the Southwest and easily grown from seed.

Seeds of Change, P.O. Box 15700, Santa Fe, NM 87506-5700; phone 888-762-7333, fax 888-329-4762; Web site www.seedsofchange.com. Free catalog. Organic, open-pollinated, and old-time varieties as well as new and interesting selections of seeds.

Seeds Trust, P.O. Box 1048, Hailey, ID 83333; phone 208-788-4363, fax 208-788-3452. Catalog $2. Open-pollinated wildflower annuals suited to high-altitude (short-season) gardening. Drought-tolerant and native wildflowers.

Seymour's Selected Seeds, P.O. Box 1346, Sussex, VA 23884-0346; phone 803-663-3084, fax 803-663-9772. From an English lady's cottage garden.

Shepherd's Garden Seeds, 30 Irene St., Torrington, CT 06790; phone 860-482-3638, fax 860-482-0532; Web site www .shepherdseeds.com. Many old-fashioned cottage-garden flowers.

R. H. Shumway's, P.O. Box 1, Graniteville, SC 29829; phone 803-663-9771, fax 803-663-9772. Free catalog. Good selection of flower seeds.

Southern Exposure Seed Exchange, P.O. Box 170, Earlysville, VA 22936; phone 804-973-4703, fax 804-973-8717; Web site www.southernexposure.com. Catalog $2. Specialize in untreated, open-pollinated, heirlooms and seed-saving supplies.

Stokes Seeds, Inc., P.O. Box 548, Buffalo, NY 14240-0548; phone 716-695-6980, fax 716-695-9649. Complete listing of flower seeds, including cultural information.

Territorial Seed Co., P.O. Box 157, Cottage Grove, OR 97424; phone 541-942-9547, fax 888-657-3131. Hardy seeds for year-round gardening, as well as gardening supplies, such as sprinklers, hoes, and wheelbarrows.

Thompson & Morgan Seed Co., P.O. Box 1308, Jackson, NJ 08527; phone 800-274-7333 or 732-363-2225, fax 888-466-4769. Wide selection of English flowers.

Twilley Seed Co., P.O. Box 65, Trevose, PA 19053; phone 800-622-7333, fax 215-245-1949. Broad range of annuals with germination tips.

White Flower Farm, P.O. Box 50, Litchfield, CT 06759; phone 800-503-9624 or 860-496-9600, fax 860-496-1418. Lavishly illustrated catalog includes more than 700 varieties of annuals, perennials, bulbs, and shrubs.

Tools and supplies by mail

Garden Trellises, Inc., P.O. Box 105, LaFayette, NY 13084; phone 315-498-9003. Galvanized steel trellising for vegetables and perennials.

Gardener's Eden, P.O. Box 7307, San Francisco, CA 94120-7307; phone 800-822-9600, fax 415-421-5153. Stylish garden supplies and accessories.

Gardener's Supply Company, 128 Intervale Rd., Burlington, VT 05401; phone 800-863-1700, fax 800-551-6712, e-mail info@gardeners.com, Web site www.gardeners.com. Hundreds of innovative tools and products for gardeners.

Gardens Alive, 5100 Schenley Pl., Lawrenceburg, IN 47025; phone 812-537-8650, fax 812-537-5108. One of the largest organic pest control suppliers.

E. C. Geiger, Inc., Rt. 63, P.O. Box 285, Harleysville, PA 19438; phone 215-256-6511 or 800-443-4437, fax 215-256-6100. Wide selection of horticultural supplies.

Harmony Farm Supply, P.O. Box 460, Graton, CA 95444; phone 707-823-9125, fax 707-823-1734. Drip and sprinkler irrigation equipment, organic fertilizers, beneficial insects, power tools, and composting supplies.

Hoop House Greenhouse Kits, Dept. N, 1358 Route 28, South Yarmouth, MA 02664; phone 800-760-5192. Small, portable greenhouses.

Kinsman Company, River Rd., Pt. Pleasant, PA 18950; phone 800-733-4146, fax 215-297-0450. Gardening supplies and quality tools.

Langenbach, P.O. Box 1420, Lawndale, CA 90260; phone 800-362-1991, fax 800-362-4490. Fine-quality tools and garden gifts.

A. M. Leonard, Inc., 241 Fox Dr., Piqua, OH 45356; phone 800-543-8955, fax 800-433-0633. Free catalog. Professional nursery and gardening supplies.

Mellinger's, Inc., 2310 W. South Range Rd., N. Lima, OH 44452; phone 800-321-7444, fax 216-549-3716. Broad selection of gardening tools, supplies, fertilizers, and pest controls, as well as plants.

Natural Gardening, 217 San Anselmo Ave., San Anselmo, CA 94960; phone 707-766-9303, fax 707-766-9747. Organic gardening supplies and tomato seedlings.

Walt Nicke Co., P.O. Box 433, Topsfield, MA 01983; phone 800-822-4114, fax 508-887-9853. Good selection of gardening tools.

Peaceful Valley Farm Supply, P.O. Box 2209 #NG, Grass Valley, CA 95945; phone 916-272-4769, fax 916-272-4794. Organic gardening supplies, seed-starting equipment, and quality tools.

Planet Nature, P.O. Box 3146, Bozeman, MT 59772; phone 800-289-6656 or 406-587-5891, fax 406-587-0223; e-mail

ecostore@mcn.net. Environmentally friendly products for lawn, garden, and home.

Plow & Hearth, P.O. Box 5000, Madison, VA 22727; phone 800-627-1712. A wide variety of products for home and garden.

Smith & Hawken, 2 Arbor Ln., P.O. Box 6900, Florence, KY 41022; phone 800-776-3336, fax 606-727-1166; Web site www.vgmarketplace.com. Wide selection of high-end tools, furniture, plants, and outdoor clothing.

The Urban Farmer Store, 2833 Vicente St., San Francisco, CA 94116; phone 800-753-3747 or 415-661-2204, fax 415-661-7826. Drip irrigation supplies. Catalog $1.

Master gardeners in the U.S. and Canada

The umbrella organization for all the regional master gardener programs is Master Gardeners International, 424 N. River Dr., Woodstock, VA 22664; phone 540-459-5656. If you write for information, include a self-addressed, stamped envelope. The e-mail address is mgic@capaccess.org. The following is a listing of contact persons and telephone numbers for each state and participating province:

Alabama: Mary Beth Musgrove, 334-844-5481

Alaska: Wayne Vandre, 907-279-6575

Arizona: Lucy Bradley, 602-470-8086, ext. 323

Arkansas: Janet Carson, 501-671-2174

British Columbia: MG Coordinator, Van Dusen Botanical Gardens, 604-257-8672

California: Pam Elam, 209-456-7554, or Nancy Garrison, 408-299-2638

Colorado: Marlo Meakins, 970-491-7887

Connecticut: Norman Gauthier, 860-241-4940

Delaware: Susan Barton, 302-831-2532

District of Columbia: M. Khan, 202-274-6907

Florida: Kathleen C. Ruppert, 352-392-8836

Georgia: Bob Westerfield, 912-875-6269

Hawaii: H. Dale Sato, 808-453-6059

Idaho: Dr. Michael Colt, 208-722-6701

Illinois: Floyd A. Giles, 217-333-2125

Indiana: B. Rosie Lerner, 765-494-1311

Iowa: Linda Naeve, 515-294-2710

Kansas: Charles Marr, 785-532-6173

Kentucky: Sharon Bale, 606-257-8605

Louisiana: Dr. Tom Koske, 504-388-4141

Maine: Lois Berg Stack, 207-581-2949

Maryland: Jon Traunfeld, 800-342-2507 in state; 410-531-5572 out of state (Monday through Friday, 8 a.m. to 1 p.m.)

Massachusetts: Bruce Roberts, 617-536-0916, or Suzanne A. Siegel, 617-536-9280

Michigan: Mary McLellan, 517-353-3774

Minnesota: Dr. Mary H. Meyer, 612-443-2460, ext. 639

Mississippi: Dr. Freddie Rasberry, Mississippi State University, 601-325-2311

Missouri: Denny Shrock, 573-882-9633

Montana: Bob Gough, 406-994-6523

Nebraska: Susan Schoneweis, 402-472-1128

Nevada: Richard Post, 702-784-4848

New Hampshire: Virginia Hast, 603-796-2151

New Jersey: Rutgers Cooperative Extension, 908-526-6293

New Mexico: Dr. Curtis Smith, 505-275-2576

New York: Robert Kozlowski, 607-255-1791

North Carolina: Larry Bass, 919-515-1200

North Dakota: Dr. Ronald Smith, 701-231-8161

Ohio: Mary Riofrio, 614-292-8326

Oklahoma: Dale Hillock, 405-744-5158

Ontario: Ramona Cameletti, 519-826-3115

Oregon: Ann Marie VanDerZanden, 541-737-2503

Pennsylvania: Toni Bilik, 814-863-7716

Rhode Island: Roseanne Sherry, 401-792-2900

Saskatchewan: Sara Williams, 306-966-5593

South Carolina: Robert F. Polomski, 864-656-2604

South Dakota: David F. Graper, 605-688-6253

Tennessee: Dr. David Sams, 901-425-4721

Texas: Dr. Douglas Welsh, 409-845-7341

Utah: Dr. Dan Drost, 801-797-2258

Vermont: Margaret Andrews, 802-773-3349

Virginia: Sheri Dorn, 540-231-6524

Washington: Van Bobbitt, 206-840-4547

West Virginia: John Jett, 304-293-4801

Wisconsin: Helen Harrison, 608-262-1749

Wyoming: Rodney Davis, 307-235-9400

Web sites about annuals

California Garden Calendar: At this site, you can find a detailed monthly calendar of seasonal gardening chores for California gardeners. www.geocities.com/RainForest/1079/calendar.html

Dig the Net — The World of Gardening Online: This site is a gardening database subsection of Time Warner's Virtual Garden. www.digthenet.com

Flowerbase: You can search the site, produced by the Dutch Glasshouse Business Networks, by botanical name or common name in six languages. After you find the flower you're looking for, you can view a picture of it. www.flowerbase.com

Garden Escape: This site is one of the largest online sources for all your gardening needs, from plants to tools to information. www.garden.com

Gardening.com: Turn to this site if you want a searchable plant encyclopedia with over 1,500 plants; access to the Ortho Problem Solver, an illustrated pest and disease guide; a magazine rack, which includes gardening articles from your favorite publications; and information about obtaining gardening software. www.gardening.com

GardenMart: This site offers a searchable database (everything from roses to hoses), an "ask the experts" section, and an electronic bulletin board. The site has links to horticultural resources for areas of interest, such as orchids, water gardening, organic gardening, succulents/cacti, and roses. Other links take you to seed companies and manufacturers of tools and supplies. www.gardenmart.com

GardenNet: This site is the only weekly online gardening publication, The Ardent Gardener, and articles, tips, and a question-and-answer section. The Garden Literature Review offers horticultural samplers and resource leads. `trine.com/GardenNet`

GardenWeb: Forums abound, and features include The Cyber-Plantsman online magazine, gardening tips, a calendar, a bookstore and links to botanical gardens around the world and other sites. The home page can also link you to GardenWeb Europe (practice your French, Italian, or German) and GardenWeb Australia. `www.gardenweb.com`

GardenWeb's The Garden Spider's Web: Created by Karen Fletcher, also the creator of The Garden Gate, this site provides links to numerous other sites. `www.gardenweb.com/spdrsweb`

Horticulture and Crop Science in Virtual Perspective: Winner of numerous awards, this site offers sections on gardening, turfgrass science, and Internet links. The gardening section (WebGarden) features a plant dictionary and an enormous factsheet database. An Ohio State University site. `www.hcs.ohio-state.edu/hcs.html`

Horticulture at Other Sites: This site, maintained by Texas A&M University, provides links to other horticultural sites by region and includes a list of international sites. `aggie-horticulture.tamu.edu/introhtml/univers.html`

Horticulture Solutions Series: Maintained by the University of Illinois College of Agriculture's Cooperative Extension Service, the site contains a vast collection of tips on gardening. Subjects include flowers, house plants, lawns, vegetables, trees, and shrubs as well as a glossary. `ag.uiuc.edu/robsond/solutions/hort.html`

Internet Directory for Botany: This site is presented by the Botanical Museum, Finnish Museum of Natural History, Helsinki University, Finland. Organized by subject category, the site provides links and information on more advanced botanical topics (ethno-botany and paleobotany, for example) as well as the more common topics. It's excellent research tool. `www.helsinki.fi/kmus/botmenu.html`

Internet Gardening: Created and maintained by Harry M. Kriz at Virginia Polytechnic Institute and State University, the site provides descriptions of and links to selected Internet gardening sites, individual Web pages, and discussion groups. `learning.lib.vt.edu/garden.html`

Joe & Mindy's Garden: Created by a husband-and-wife gardening team, the site has a funky, friendly feel. Best of all is the long list of links to *other* Web sites. `www.nhn.ou.edu/%7Ehoward/garden.html`

National Gardening Association: Our personal favorite. Look to this site for everything about the largest national association of home gardeners, including several years of articles from *National Gardening* magazine, applications for Garden Grants, and more. `www.garden.org`

Plant Advisor Desert Southwest Edition: This edition provides regional information on selecting plants, plant locations, and sun requirements for the desert Southwest. Other regional editions were not available at the time this book was written. `www.plantadvisor.com`

Plant World: This site contains a vast collection of information on horticulture, garden festivals, arboreta, gardening societies, and associations. You can also find a library section, news, and links to other gardening and plant-related sites. `www.plantworld.com`

The Royal Botanic Gardens, Kew: Visit the renowned Kew gardens online. `www.rbgkew.org.uk/index.html`

Traditional Gardening: A Journal of Practical Information on Creating and Restoring Classic Gardens: This site is actually an online gardening magazine. `traditionalgardening.com`

USDA Home Gardening Page: This site is comprised of multiple sections, including a horticultural solutions section, lawn and garden care, an eco-regions map, and lots more. www.usda.gov/news/garden.htm

USDA Partners of the Cooperative State Research, Education, and Extension Service. This site is a directory of land-grant universities, which are state partners of the Cooperative State Research Education and Extension Service, with links to all the partners. www.reeusda.gov/new/statepartners/usa.htm

USDA Plants Project: This site includes a database and photo gallery of standardized information about plants found in the U.S. and its territories, with an emphasis on economically important plants. plants.usda.gov

The Virtual Garden: This site features the Electronic Encyclopedia, a database with information on almost 3,000 plants grown in North America. Other resources include excerpts from Time-Life's gardening books, articles from *Sunset* and *Southern Living* magazines, and a tour of the New York Botanical Gardens. www.pathfinder.com/vg

The Virtual Gardener: An Electronic Magazine with Organic Roots: Published in Victoria, British Columbia, this online magazine covers a broad range of gardening topics. www.gardenmag.com

WebGarden Factsheet Database: Compiled by Ohio State University, this site offers online tutorials, a plant dictionary, and a searchable database of over 9,000 factsheets. You can also find weekly Ohio gardening news. www.hcs.ohio-state.edu/hcs/webgarden/FactsheetFind.html

The WWW Virtual Library for Gardening: This is GardenWeb's virtual library for gardening. Among the options are links to general gardening sites, publishers, magazines, regional and international sites, plant databases, and horticultural societies and associations. www.gardenweb.com/vl

Magazines about growing annuals

Country Home Country Gardens. Published quarterly. Meredith Corp., 1716 Locust St., Des Moines, IA 50309-3023. $16. Subscriptions: P.O. Box 37212, Boone, IA 50037-0212; phone 800-677-0484.

Country Living Gardener. Published bi-monthly. The Hearst Corp., 224 W. 57th St., New York, NY 10019; phone 212-649-3824. $19.97. Subscriptions: Customer Service Dept., Country Living Gardener, P.O. Box 7335, Red Oak, IA 51591-0335; phone 800-777-0102.

Fine Gardening. Published bimonthly. The Taunton Press, 63 S. Main St., Newtown, CT 06470-5506; phone 203-426-8171. $32.

Garden Design. Published eight times a year. Meigher Communications, 100 Avenue of the Americas, New York, NY 10013; phone 212-334-1212; e-mail GRDNDDSGN@aol.com.

$27.95. Subscriptions: P.O. Box 5429, Harlan, IA 51593-2929; phone 800-234-5118.

Garden Gate. Published bimonthly. August Home Publishing Co., 2200 Grand Ave., Des Moines, IA 50312. $24.95. Subscriptions: P.O. Box 37115, Boone, IA 50037-2115; phone 800-341-4769.

Horticulture. Published ten times a year. PJS Publications, 98 N. Washington St., Boston, MA 02114-1913; phone 617-742-5600. $26. Subscriptions: P.O. Box 53880, Boulder, CO 80322-3880; phone 800-234-2415.

National Gardening. Published bimonthly. National Gardening Association, 180 Flynn Ave., Burlington, VT 05401; phone 802-863-1308; Web site www.garden.org. $18.95. Subscriptions: P.O. Box 51106, Boulder, CO 80323-1106; phone 800-727-9097.

Index

• A •

AAS (All-America Selections), North American annuals, 15
actual nitrogen, fertilizer bargain shopping, 202
African daisy *(Arctotis),* 77–78, Photo 1
African daisy *(Dimorphotheca sinuata),* 78, Photo 2
African marigold *(Tagetes erecta),* 66, Photo 58
ageratum *(Ageratum haustonianum),* 78, Photo 3
  'Blue Danube', 78
  'Blue Mink', 78
Alcea rosea. See hollyhock
all-year climate zones, planting considerations, 27
alyssum. *See* sweet alyssum
Amaranthus caudatus. See love-lies-bleeding
American marigolds. *See* African marigolds
Anchusa capensis. See summer forget-me-not
annual coreopsis. *See* calliopsis
annuals
  AAS (All-America Selections), 15
  all-year climate zones, 27
  author's Top Ten list, 59–76
  climate zones, 21–24
  container-growing techniques, 247–261
  container mixers, 254–261
  cut flowers, 273–286
  days to bloom/growing season length consideration, 26
  described, 9–11, 289
  easiest-to-grow, 290
  easy care, 293
  Fleuroselect, 15
  growing conditions, 27–29
  growing seasons, 290
  naming conventions, 12–13
  plant form types, 13–15
  reasons for growing, 9–10
  seeds versus seedlings, 289
  shade requirements, 291
  special growing situations, 295–300
  versus biennials, 10
  versus perennials, 10–11
  warm-season versus cool-season, 24–27
Antirrhinium majus. See snapdragon
aphids
  controlling, 222
  seedling indicators, 34
  treatment, 34, 40
April activities
  California, 46
  lowland deserts, 52
  northern region, 34–35
  Pacific Northwest, 54
  southern regions, 40
Arctotis. See African daisy
aster *(Callistephus chinensis),* 78–79, Photo 4
August activities
  California, 48
  lowland deserts, 53
  northern region, 36–37
  Pacific Northwest, 55
  southern regions, 42
automated watering systems, 188
azalea pots, 251

• B •

baby blue eyes *(Nemophila menziesii),* 79, Photo 5
baby's breath *(Gypsophila elegans),* 79–80
  'Covent Garden', 79, Photo 6
bachelor's button. *See* cornflower
Bacillus thuringiensis (Bt), as biological pest control, 44, 223, 228
backyard fence, borders, 139–140
balsam impatiens *(Impatiens balsama),* 63
bedding begonia *(Begonia semperflorens),* 80, Photo 7
bedding plants
  See also seedlings
  described, 171
beds
  annual types, 141
  described, 127–128
  fertilizing techniques, 202–204
  large tree surround, 134–136

beds *(continued)*
  locations, 132–140
  plant sizing, 129–131
  raised, 157–158
  soil preparations, 152–158
  solarizing to control weeds, 238
  special care tips, 179
  wildflower planting techniques, 268–270
  year-round preparations, 180
beds and borders, 297
beer, slug treatment, 225
Begonia semperflorens. See bedding begonia
Bellis perennis. See English daisy
bells of Ireland *(Moluccella laevis)*, 80,
      Photo 8
Bermuda grass, controlling, 239–240
bicolor flowers, described, 14
biennials, versus annuals, 10
bindweed, controlling, 239–240
biological controls
  Bt *(Bacillus thuringiensis)*, 228
  green lacewings, 228
  lady beetles, 227–228
  parasitic nematodes, 228
  plant attractors, 228
  predatory mites, 228
  trichogramma wasps, 228
bird's eyes *(Gilia tricolor)*, 94, Photo 42
black-eyed Susan. *See* gloriosa daisy
black-eyed Susan vine. *See* thunbergia
blanket flower *(Gaillardia pulchella)*, 80–81,
      Photo 9
  'Red Plume', 80
blue flowers, 301
blue lace flower *(Trachymene coerulea)*, 81,
      Photo 10
blue marguerite. *See* felicia
blue thimble flower *(Gilia capitata)*, 94
border edges, Photo 116
borders
  annual types, 141, 297
  backyard fence, 139–140
  described, 128
  formal walkway, 136–137
  informal walkway, 137–138
  locations, 131–132
  modern-style walkway, 138–139
  plant sizing, 129–131
botanical insecticides
  neem oil/extract, 229–230
  pyrethrin, 230
  rotenone, 230

botanical names, components, 12–13
botrytis blight, controlling, 232–233
bottom-heat mat, 43
bouquets, cut flower arrangements, 283–284
Brachycome iridifolia. See Swan River daisy
Brassica oleracea. See kale
browallia *(Browallia americana)*, 81
  'Blue Bells Improved', Photo 11, Photo 81
  'Blue Troll', 81
Bt *(Bacillus thuringiensis)*, caterpillar
      treatment, 44, 223, 228
bucket gardener, described, 208
budworms, treatment, 47–48
bugs, versus pests, 221–222
burning bush. *See* kochia
butterflies, attracting, 291
butterfly flower. *See* schizanthus

• *C* •

calendars
  California region, 44–50
  high-altitude deserts, 50
  lowland deserts, 50–53
  northern region, 32–38
  Pacific Northwest, 53–56
  southern regions, 38–44
  western regions, 44–56
calendula *(Calendula officinalis)*, 82,
      Photo 12
  Bon Bon, 82
  Pacific Beauty Strain, 82
California
  April activities, 46
  August activities, 48
  December activities, 50
  February activities, 45–46
  January activities, 45
  July activities, 48
  June activities, 47
  March activities, 46
  May activities, 47
  November activities, 50
  October activities, 49
  September activities, 48–49
California poppy *(Eschscholzia californica)*,
      82–83, Photo 13
calliopsis *(Coreopsis tinctoria)*, 83, Photo 14
Callistephus chinensis. See aster
Campanula medium. See Canterbury bells

Canadian Sphagnum Peat Moss
  Association, 151
canary creeper *(Tropaeolum peregrinum)*,
  83–84, Photo 15
candytuft, annual *(Iberis umbellata)*, 84,
  Photo 16
candytuft, perennial *(Iberis sempervirens)*, 84
Canterbury bells *(Campanula medium)*, 84,
  Photo 17
cardinal climber *(Ipomea multifida)*, 40, 42
cardinal flower *(Lobelia cardinalis)*, 152
carnation *(Dianthus)*, 84–85, Photo 18
  'Giant Chabuad', 84
  'Lilliput', 84
  'Scarlet Luminette', 84
carpet bedding, described, 124
Cartharanthus roseus. See vinca rosea
cast concrete containers, 250
caterpillars, treatment, 44
cayenne pepper, domestic pet digging
  deterrent, 155
celosia
  Celosia cristata, 85, Photo 19
  Celosia plumosa, 85, Photo 20
Centaurea cineraria. See dusty miller
Centaurea cyannus. See cornflower
Cheiranthus. See wallflower
chelated micronutrients, fertilizers, 199
chemical fungicides, cautions, 232
China aster. *See* aster
Chinese forget-me-not *(Cynoglossum
  amabile)*, 86, Photo 21
Chinese lantern *(Physalis alkekengi)*, 86,
  Photo 22
chlorophyll, described, 196
chrysanthemum, annual *(Chrysanthemum)*,
  86–87
  feverfew *(Chrysanthemum parthenium)*, 86,
    Photo 23
  miniature Marguerite *(Chrysanthemum
    paludosum)*, 86
  painted daisy *(Chrysanthemum
    carinatum)*, 86
  'Easter Star', Photo 24
cigar plant *(Cuphea ignea)*, 87–88, Photo 25
Cineraria maritima. See dusty miller
cineraria *(Senecia hybridus)*, 88, Photo 26
clarkia *(Clarkia)*, 88
  farewell-to-spring *(Clarkia amoena)*, 88,
    Photo 27

clay soils, described, 146–147
Cleome hasslerana. See spider flower
climate
  versus weather, 184
  watering factor, 184
  zones, 21–24, 27
climbing/creeping annuals, 299–300
cloche, described, 35
cockscomb. *See* celosia
cold frame, described, 38
coleus *(Coleus)*, 89, Photo 28
  'Dragon Sunset', 89
  'Molten Lava', 89
  'Scarlet Poncho', 89
  'Volcano', 89
color wheels, 118–119
colors
  blue, 301
  complementary, 119
  experimenting with, Photo 111, Photo 115
  green, 304
  harmonious, 119
  hot versus cool, 117, 120
  in shade, Photo 121
  leafy greens, 121
  orange, 302–303
  pastels, 117–118
  pink, 303–304
  primary, 119
  purple, 302
  red, 303
  selection guidelines, 117–118
  shades, 119
  white, 304
  yellow, 302
common names, variation by location, 12
complementary colors, described, 119
complete fertilizers, described, 198
compost
  as mulch material, 216
  soil amendment, 149–150
compost pile, preparing, 37
composted manure, soil amendment, 150
composting, October activities, 37
Consolida ambigua. See larkspur
container annuals, 297
Container Gardening For Dummies, 17, 247
containers
  advantages, 247–248
  azalea pots, 251
  color/form mixing guidelines, 256–257

(continued)

containers *(continued)*
  construction factors, 248
  drainage, 248
  fertilizing techniques, 205
  full sun annuals, 255
  glazed clay, 249
  material types, 249–250
  mixer plants, 254–261
  planting techniques, 252–254
  plastic, 250
  porosity, 248
  removing seedlings from, 176
  seed starters, 162
  shady annuals, 256
  sizing/shaping, 251–252
  soil mixtures, 252
  terra cotta, 249
  unglazed clay, 249
  wood boxes/tubs, 250
cool colors, versus hot, 117, 120
cool-season annuals
  described, 25
  versus warm-season annuals, 24–27
Cooperative Extension Office, disease/pest
    identification, 220
Coreopsis tinctoria. See calliopsis
cornflower *(Centaurea cyannus)*, 89
  Jubilee Gem, 89
  pink variety, Photo 29
  Polka Dot Strain, 89
cosmos *(Cosmos bipinnatus)*, 89–90, Photo 30
  Sea Shells Strain, 89
  Sensation Strain, 89
  yellow cosmos *(Cosmos sulphureus)*, 89
cottage garden, 124–125, Photo 117
covers, seed, 167
creeping zinnia *(Santvitalia procumbens)*, 90
cultivars
  described, 12–13
  naming conventions, 12–13
cultivating, soil process, 148–149
cupflower. *See* nierembergia
Cuphea ignea. See cigar plant
cut flowers
  bouquet arrangements, 283–284
  dried flowers, 284–285
  end-of-season chores, 285–286
  garden design elements, 277–282
  harvesting techniques, 282–283
  maintenance, 285
  mixed garden techniques, 276–277
  plant types, 274–276
  reasons for growing, 274
  site locations, 280–282
  site preparations, 280–282
cutworms
  controlling, 224
  transplant indicators, 35–36
  treatments, 35–36
Cynoglossum amabile. See Chinese
    forget-me-not

• **D** •

Dahlberg daisy *(Dyssodia tenuiloba)*, 90,
    Photo 31
dahlia *(Dahlia)*, 60–61, 90
  'Cherokee Ideal', Photo 32
  dwarf, 60, 90
  'Figaro', 60
  'Redskin', 60
damping off
  controlling, 233
  preventing, 34
  seedling indicators, 34
days to bloom, described, 26
deadheading, described, 208, 212, 291
December activities
  California, 50
  lowland deserts, 52
  northern region, 38
  southern regions, 44
decollate snails, as pest control, 225
delinquent drainage, described, 152
deserts
  high-altitude, 50
  lowland, 50–53
design elements
  backyard fence border, 139–140
  bed/border locations, 131–132
  bed/border plant sizing, 129–131
  colors, 117–121
  container factors, 248
  cut flower garden, 277–282
  fragrances, 122–123
  heights, 121–122
  large tree beds, 134–136
  lattice, 126
  raised beds, 157–158
  shapes, 121–122
  sunny patio bed, 132–134
  textures, 121–122
  walkways, 136–139

Dianthus. See carnation
Dianthus barbatus. See sweet William
Dianthus chinensis. See pink
diatomaceous earth, described, 40
diatoms, described, 40
digging forks, soil turning tool, 154
Digitalis purpurea. See foxglove
Dimorphotheca sinuata. See African Daisy
direct-sowing, described, 166–168
diseases
  botrytis blight, 232–233
  chemical fungicide concerns, 232
  damping off, 34, 233
  powdery mildew, 233–234
  prevention and control, 220–221, 232, 290
  resistant plant strains, 221
  root rot, 235
  rust, 71, 234
Dolichos lablab. See hyacinth bean
dormant oil, versus summer oil, 230
double flowers, described, 14
double-digging, hardpan remedy, 157
drainage, container design element, 248
drainage, improving, 152
dried flowers, 284–285
drifts, planting technique, 175
drip emitters, watering tool, 190
drip irrigation
  described, 29
  watering tool, 190–191
dusty miller *(Cineraria maritima/Senecia cinneraria),* 91, Photo 33
dwarf dahlias, 60, 90
dwarfs, described, 14
Dyssodia tenuiloba. See Dahlberg daisy

• *E* •

earwigs, treatment, 47
easy-care annuals, 293
edging annuals, 298
English daisy *(Bellis perennis),* 91
Erysimum. See wallflower
Eschscholzia californica. See California poppy
Euphorbia marginata. See snow-on-the-mountain
Eustoma grandiflorum. See lisianthus
expert gardeners, projects, 17–19

• *F* •

F1 hybrid, described, 13
fairy primrose *(Primula malacoides),* 105
farewell-to-spring *(Clarkia amoena),* 88, Photo 27
February activities
  California, 45–46
  lowland deserts, 52
  northern region, 33
  Pacific Northwest, 54
  southern regions, 39
felicia *(Felicia amelloides),* 92, Photo 34
Felicia bergeriana. See kingfisher daisy
fertilizers
  See also nutrients
  bargain shopping techniques, 201
  chelated micronutrients, 199
  complete, 198
  container techniques, 205
  flower bed techniques, 202–204
  foliar, 200
  granular, 199, 202
  guaranteed analysis information, 197–198
  high-phosphorus, 178
  incomplete, 198
  liquid, 199
  nitrogen source, 196
  organic, 200, 202, 205–206
  seedling mix, 178
  shopping for, 197–201
  slow-release, 200, 202
  specialty, 201
feverfew *(Chrysanthemum parthenium),* 86
firecracker plant. *See* cigar plant
flat-tipped spade, sod stripping tool, 153
flax *(Linum grandifloraum),* 92, Photo 35
Fleuroselect, European annual awards, 15
floating row covers, 26, 47, 229
floral management, described, 217
floss flower. *See* ageratum
flower drying, 284–285
flowering tobacco. *See* nicotiana
foliar fertilizers, 200
forget-me-not *(Myosotis stylvatica),* 92, Photo 36
  See also Chinese forget-me-not and summer forget-me-not
formal gardens, described, 124–125
formal walkway, design elements, 136–137
four o'clock *(Mirabilis jalapa),* 93, Photo 37

foxglove *(Digitalis purpurea),* 93, Photo 38
  'Foxy', 93
fragrance, as design element, 122–123
French Intensive Method, hardpan double-
    digging, 157
French marigolds *(Tagetes patula),* 66
frosts
  climate zones, 21–24
  cloche cover, 35
  cool-season annual resistance, 25
  high-altitude desert concerns, 50
  warm-season annual resistance, 25–26
full shade, described, 28
full sun, described, 28
furrow irrigation, described, 189

• *G* •

Gaillardia pulchella. See blanket flower
garden beds, described, 127–128
garden borders, described, 128
garden cart, 210
garden gloves, 210
garden spade, 209
gardeners
  expert projects, 17–19
  master, 308–309
  novice projects, 15–17
gardening chores
  bucket gardener, 208
  deadheading, 212
  floral management, 217
  maintenance schedules, 208
  mulching, 208, 216
  pinching, 208, 214–215
  pruning, 208, 214–215
  replanting, 217
  safety tips, 155–156
  staking, 208, 213–214
  strategies, 208–209
  supplies, 210–211
  tools, 209–210
  wrapping up for the season, 217
gardens
  beds versus borders, 127–128
  borders, described, 128
  clearing at end of growing season, 217
  color mixing, 117–121
  container growing techniques, 247–261
  cottage style, 124–125
  creating in a year, Photo 109
  cut flowers, 277–282
  design, Photo 123
  formal style, 124–125
  late, Photo 120
  lattice as design element, 126
  modern style, 125–126
  naturalistic style, 124
  reflected heat effects, 29
  safety tips, 155–156
  scatter, 270
  screens, Photo 119
  slope challenges, 29
  soil conditions, 28
  soil preparation, 145–158
  soil preparation as disease control, 232
  styles, 123–126
  sun versus shade conditions, 27–28
  weather condition effects, 27–29
  wildflower, 263–271
  wind protection, 28
gazania *(Gazania hybrida),* 94, Photo 39
Gentian sage *(Salvia patens),* Photo 81
genus, botanical name component, 12
geranium budworms, controlling, 223
geraniums *(Pelargonium),* 61–62, 94
  ivy geraniums *(Pelargonium peltatum),*
      11, 62
    'Candy Cane', Photo 40
    Breakaway Hybrid, 62
    Summer Showers, 62
  scented geraniums *(Pelargonium),* 62
  zonal geraniums *(Pelargonium hortorum),*
      62, Photo 41
    Multibloom Strain, 62
    Orbit Strain, 62
Gerbera jamesonii. See transvaal daisy
germination rates, seed packages, 160
gilia *(Gilia),* 94
  blue thimble flower *(Gilia capitata),* 94
  bird's eyes *(Gilia tricolor),* 94, Photo 42
glazed clay containers, 249
globe amaranth *(Gomphrena),* 94–95,
      Photo 43
gloriosa daisy *(Rudbeckia hirta),* 95, Photo 44
  'Becky', 95
  'Goldilocks', 95
  'Irish Eyes', 95
gloves, 210
glyphosate, weed herbicide, 238
godetia. See clarkia
golden fleece. *See* Dahlberg daisy

Gomphrena globosa. See globe amaranth
granular fertilizers, 199, 202
green flowers, 304
green lacewings, as biological pest
    control, 228
Green Light Co, neem oil source, 230
grow lights, seed-starting tool, 162
growing seasons, 290
  all-year climate zone, 27
  calculation methods, 26
  clearing garden, 217
  climate zones, 21–24
  cool-season annuals, 25
  days-to-bloom consideration, 26
  high-altitude deserts, 50
  Pacific Northwest, 53–56
  warm-season annuals, 25–26
  wildflower planting, 266
guaranteed analysis, fertilizer components,
    197–198
Gypsophila elegans. See baby's breath

• *H* •

hand trowel, 210
hanging-basket annuals, 299
hanging basket, mixing plants, 259–261
hardening off, 35, 164, 173–174
hardpan, described, 154, 157
harmonious colors, described, 119
heights
  as design element, 121–122
  bed/border plant sizing, 129–131
Helianthus annuus. See sunflower
Helichrysum bracteatum. See strawflower
heliotrope *(Heliotropium arborescens)*, 95,
    Photo 45
  'Dwarf Marine', 95
  'Marine', 95
Helipterum roseum. See strawflower
herb gardens, annuals to add color,
    Photo 108
herbicides
  glyphosate, 238
  pre-emergence, 238
  spot-spraying, 239
high summer, northern region, 36
high-altitude deserts, 50
high-phosphorous fertilizers, 178
hillside gardens, weather condition
    effects, 29
hoes, soil-breaking tool, 154, 210

hollyhock *(Alcea rosea)*, 96, Photo 46
  Majorette Mixed, 96
  'Summer Carnival', 96
hose guide, 211
hose-end bubblers, watering tool, 187
hose-end sprinklers, 188–189
hot colors, versus cooler colors, 117, 120
hot dry spots annuals, 296
humus, soil amendment, 150
Hunnemannia fumariifolia. See Mexican
    tulip poppy
hyacinth bean *(Dolichos lablab)*, 96
hybrids
  described, 13
  F1, 13
  pollination controls, 13

• *I* •

Iberis umbellata. See candytuft, annual
Iberis sempervirens. See candytuft, perennial
Iceland poppy *(Papaver nudicaule)*, 96–97,
    Photo 47
  Champagne Bubbles Strain, 96
icons, used in book, 4–5
impatiens *(Impatiens walleriana)*, 62–64, 97
  Accent Strain, 63
  balsam *(Impatiens balsama)*, 63
  Fancifrills, 63
  Fiesta, 63
  New Guinea hybrids, 63
  Super Elfin Twilight, Photo 48
  'Victorian Rose', 63
incomplete fertilizers, described, 198
informal walkway, design elements, 137–138
information, sources, 305–311
inorganic mulch, described, 241
insecticidal soaps, 230–231
insecticides
  botanical, 229–230
  handling cautions, 231
  neem, 229–230
  pyrethrin, 230
  rotenone, 230
  synthetic, 231
Ipomoea imperialis. See morning glory
Ipomoea Alba. See moonflower
Ipomoea Nil. See morning glory
irrigation. *See* watering
island beds, described, 127–128
ivy geraniums *(Pelargonium peltatum)*, 11, 62

• J •

January activities
  California, 45
  lowland deserts, 52
  northern region, 33
  Pacific Northwest, 53
  southern regions, 39
Japanese beetles, 36, 223–224
Johnny-jump-up *(Viola tricolor)*, 67
July activities
  California, 48
  lowland deserts, 53
  northern region, 36
  Pacific Northwest, 55
  southern regions, 41–42
June activities
  California, 47
  lowland deserts, 53
  northern region, 36
  Pacific Northwest, 55
  southern regions, 41

• K •

kale *(Brassica oleracea)*, 97, Photo 49
killing frost, climate zones, 21–24
kingfisher daisy *(Felicia bergeriana)*, 92
kochia *(Kochia scoparia)*, 97, Photo 50

• L •

lady beetles, as biological pest control,
  227–228
landscape fabrics, described, 241–242
large tree beds, design elements, 134–136
larkspur *(Consolida ambigua)*, 98, Photo 51
  'Dwarf Blue Butterfly', 98
late bloomers, Photo 120
Lathyrus odoratus. See sweet peas
lattice, vine support, 126
lavatera *(Lavatera trimestris)*, 98, Photo 52
layouts, garden styles, 123–126
leaf rake, 210
leafy green colors, 121
Limonium sinuatum. See statice
linaria *(Linaria)*, 98–99, Photo 53
lime, soil pH ingredient, 151–152
Linum grandiflorum. See flax
liquid fertilizers, 199
lisianthus *(Eustoma grandiflorum)*, 99

'Echo Pink', Photo 54
'Prarie Gentian', Photo 54
'Tiara White', 99
loam soils, described, 146
lobelia *(Lobelia)*, 99, Photo 55
  'Cambridge Blue', 99
  'Crystal Palace', 99, Photo 116
  'Sapphire', 99
Lobularia maritima. See sweet alyssum
locations
  beds/borders, 131–132
  cut flower gardens, 280–282
  disease/pest avoidance, 221
  watering considerations, 185
love-in-a-mist *(Nigella damascena)*, 99,
  Photo 56
  'Miss Jekyll', 99
  'Persian Jewels', 99
love-lies-bleeding *(Amaranthus caudatus)*,
  100, Photo 57
  'Joseph's Coat', 100
lowland deserts
  April activities, 52
  August activities, 53
  December activities, 52
  February activities, 52
  January activities, 52
  July activities, 53
  June activities, 53
  March activities, 52
  May activities, 53
  November activities, 51–52
  October activities, 51
  September activities, 51

• M •

macronutrients, described, 196
Madagascar periwinkle. *See* vinca rosea
magazines, 311
mail-order
  seed companies, 161
  seeds, 305–307
  tools and supplies, 307–308
March activities
  California, 46
  lowland deserts, 52
  northern region, 33–34
  Pacific Northwest, 54
  southern regions, 39–40

marigolds *(Tagetes)*, 65–67, 100
  add punch to a garden, Photo 113
  African marigolds *(Tagetes erecta)*, 66,
    Photo 58
    Climax, 66
    'First Lady', 66
    'French Vanilla', 66, Photo 59
    'Snowdrift', 66
  French *(Tagetes patula)*, 66
    Aurora Series, 66
    'Naughty Marietta', 66
  signet marigolds *(Tagetes tenuifolia)*, 66,
    Photo 60
    'Gem', 66
  tiploid hybrids
    Nugget Supreme Series, 66
Master Gardeners International, 308–309
Matthiola incana. See stocks
Matthiola longipetala. See night-scented
  stocks
May activities
  California, 47
  lowland deserts, 53
  northern region, 35–36
  Pacific Northwest, 54–55
  southern regions, 40–41
mealy-cup sage *(Salvia farinacea)*, 106
  'Victoria', 106
metal containers, 250
Mexican sunflower *(Tithonia rotundifolia)*,
  100, Photo 61
  'Goldfinger', 100
Mexican tulip poppy *(Hunnemania
  fumariifolia)*, 100–101, Photo 62
micronutrients, described, 196
mignonette *(Reseda odorata)*, 101, Photo 63
Mimulus. See monkey flower
miniature Marguerite *(Chrysanthemum
  paludosum)*, 86
Mirabilis jalapa. See four o'clock
misting nozzle, direct-sowing tool, 167
mixers, container plants, 254–261
modern gardens, described, 125–126
modern-style walkway, design elements,
  138–139
Moluccella laveis. See bells of Ireland
monkey flower *(Mimulus)*, 101, Photo 64
  'Calypso', 101
  'Mystic', 101

moonflower *(Ipomoea Alba)*, 101–102
morning glory *(Ipomoea imperialis/Ipomoea
  Nil)*, 101–102, Photo 65
moss rose. *See* portulaca
mulch
  as weed control, 239
  described, 240
  landscape fabrics, 241
  organic versus inorganic, 240–241
  plant benefits, 240
  scheduling, 242–243
  spreading, 242
mulching, described, 208, 216
Myosotis sylvatica. See forget-me-not

• *N* •

nasturtium *(Tropaeolum majus)*, 102,
  Photo 66
  Double Green Strain, 102
  'Empress of India', 102
naturalistic gardens, described, 124
naturalize, described, 264
naturalizing annuals, 298
neem oil/extract, 229–230
nemesia *(Nemesia strumosa)*, 102
  'Blue Gem', Photo 67
  'Carnival', Photo 68
Nemophila menziesii. See baby blue eyes
nicotiana *(Nicotiana)*, 103, Photo 69
  'Fragrant Cloud', 103
  'Grandiflora', 103
  Nicotiana sylvestris, 103
  Niki Series, 103
nierembergia *(Nierembergia)*, 103, Photo 70
  'Mont Blanc', 103
  'Purple Robe', 103
Nigella damascena. See love-in-a-mist
night-scented stocks *(Matthiola
  longipetala)*, 109
nitrogen
  actual, 201
  plant nutrient, 196
northern region
  April activities, 34–35
  August activities, 36–37
  February activities, 33
  high summer, 36
  January activities, 33
  July activities, 36
  June activities, 36

(continued)

northern region *(continued)*
    March activities, 33–34
    May activities, 35–36
    November through December activities, 38
    October activities, 37
    September activities, 37
    warm summers/cold winters, 32–38
November activities
    California, 50
    lowland deserts, 51–52
    northern region, 38
    Pacific Northwest, 56
    southern regions, 43
novice gardeners, projects, 15–17
nurseries, lack of plant variety, 290
nutrients
    See also fertilizers
    growth elements, 195–197
    macronutrients, 196
    micronutrients, 196
    nitrogen, 196
    phosphorus, 197
    potassium, 197
    secondary, 196
    soil tests, 196–197

• *O* •

October activities
    California, 49
    lowland deserts, 51
    northern region, 37
    Pacific Northwest, 55–56
    southern regions, 43
open pollination, described, 13
orange flowers, 302–303
organic amendments, soil transformations,
    149–151
organic fertilizers, 200, 202, 205–206
organic matter, loam element, 146
organic mulch, described, 240–241
ornamental cabbage. *See* kale
Ortho Problem Solver, The, 220
outdoors from seed annuals, 300

• *P* •

Pacific Northwest
    April activities, 54
    August activities, 55
    February activities, 54
    January activities, 53
    July activities, 55
    June activities, 55
    March activities, 54
    May activities, 54–55
    November activities, 56
    October activities, 55–56
    September activities, 55
painted daisy *(Chrysanthemum carinatum),* 86
painted tongue. *See* salpiglossis
pansy *(Viola wittrockiana),* 67, 104, Photo 71
    Johnny-jump-up *(Viola tricolor),* 67
    Majestic Giant Strain, 67
    'Maxim Marina', 67
Papaver nudicaule. See Iceland poppy
Papaver rhoeas. See Shirley poppy
paper pulp pots, 250
parasitic nematodes, as biological pest
    control, 228
part shade, described, 28
pastel colors, 117–118
peat moss, soil amendment, 151
Pelargonium. See geraniums
perennial weeds, controlling, 239–240
perennials
    grown as annuals, 11
    versus annuals, 10–11
Perennials For Dummies, 10
pesticides, handling cautions, 231
pests
    aphids, 34, 40, 222
    biological controls, 227–229
    botanical insecticides, 229–230
    budworm, 47–48
    caterpillars, 44
    controlling, 290
    cutworms, 35–36, 224
    earwigs, 47
    floating row covers, 229
    geranium budworms, 223
    identification sources, 220
    insecticidal soaps, 230–231
    Japanese beetles, 36, 223–224
    prevention methods, 220–221
    slugs, 40, 46, 49, 224–225
    snails, 40, 46, 49, 224–225
    spider mites, 40, 48, 225–226
    summer oil versus dormant oil, 230
    synthetic insecticides, 231
    thrips, 226
    versus bugs, 221–222
    whiteflies, 48, 226–227
pets, cayenne pepper as digging
    deterrent, 155

Petunias *(Petunia hybrida),* 67–69, 104
  'Purple Wave', 68
  Supertunia Strain, 68
  Surfinia Strain, 68
  grandifloras *(Petunia grandiflora)*
    Cascade Strain, 68
    'Fluffy Ruffles', 68
    'Prism Sunshine', 68
    Supercascade Strain, 68
  millifloras *(Petunia milliflora)*
    Fantasy, 68, Photo 72
  multiflora *(Petunia multiflora)*
    Double Delight Series, 68
    'Summer Sun', 68
    Ultra Series, 68
pH balance, soil testing, 151–152
phlox, annual *(Phlox drummondii),* Photo 73
  Beauty Mixed, 104
  Twinkle Mixed, 104
phosphorus, plant nutrient, 197
Physalis alkekengi. See Chinese lantern
picks, double-digging hardpan tool, 157
picotee flowers, described, 14
pinching, described, 208, 214–215
pincushion flower *(Scabiosa atropurpurea),* 104, Photo 74
pink *(Dianthus chinensis),* 104–105, Photo 75
  'Raspberry Parfait', 105
  'Snowfire', 105
pink flowers, 303–304
plants
  See also annuals
  beneficial insect attractors, 228
  container mixers, 254–261
  cut flower annuals, 273–286
  disease resistant strains, 221
  easy care, 293–294
  extras/understudies, 175
  form types, 13–15
  overwatering avoidance, 232
  removing infected, 232
  soil preparation as disease control, 232
  spacing/disease concerns, 232
  watering techniques, 180–193
plastic containers, 250
pollination
  hybrid controls, 13
  open, 13
porosity, container design element, 248

portulaca *(Portulaca grandiflora),* 105, Photo 76
pot marigold. *See* calendula
potassium, plant nutrient, 197
powdery mildew, controlling, 233–234
predatory mites, as biological pest control, 228
pre-emergence herbicide, 238
primary colors, described, 119
primrose *(Primula),* 105
  fairy primrose *(Primula malacoides),* 105, Photo 77
  Primula obconica, 105
  Primula polyantha, 105
    'Silver-Laced hybrid', Photo 78
Primula. See primrose
projects
  expert gardeners, 17–19
  novice gardeners, 15–17
pronged weeder, 211
pruners, 210
pruning, described, 208, 214–215
purple flowers, 302
pyrethrin, 230

• *R* •

rain gauge, 42
rainbows, color, 301–304
raised beds, 157–158
rakes
  leaf, 210
  soil breaking tool, 154–155
  steel bow, 210
red flowers, 303
reflected heat, effects on annuals, 29
replanting, as garden chore, 217
Reseda odorata. See mignonette
resources, 305–311
  magazines, 311
  Web sites, 309–311
root rot, controlling, 235
rootbound, described, 173
rotenone, 230
Rudbeckia hirta. See gloriosa daisy
rust disease, 71, 234

• *S* •

Sackville-West, Vita, 120
safety tips, gardening, 155–156
salpiglossis *(Salpiglossis),* 106, Photo 79

salvia *(Salvia)*, 106
  Gentian sage *(Salvia patens)*, Photo 81
  mealy-cup sage *(Salvia farinacea)*, 106
    'Victoria White', Photo 80
  scarlet sage *(Salvia splendens)*, 106
    'Empire Red', Photo 82
    'Red Hot Sally', 106
sandy soil, described, 147
Santvitalia procumbens. See creeping zinnia
Scabiosa atropurpurea. See pincushion
    flower
scaevola *(Scaevola)*, 107
  'Blue Wonder', 107
  'Purple Fanfare', 107
Scarlet sage. *See* salvia
scatter gardens, wildflowers, 270
schizanthus *(Schizanthus)*, 107, Photo 83
  'Bouquet', 107
screening gardens, Photo 119
seasons
  cool versus warm conditions, 24–27
  growing, 21–24
  wildflower planting guidelines, 266
secondary nutrients, described, 196
seed coat, described, 161
seed packages
  information components, 160
  mail-order companies, 161
seed starters
  container types, 162
  direct-sow annuals, 168–169
  indoor starting annual types, 165–166
  soil-less mix components, 162
seed-area preparation
  California, 45–46
  lowland deserts, 51
  northern region, 33–34
  Pacific Northwest, 53–54
  southern regions, 39
seeding schedules, northern region, 33–34
seedlings
  availability list by season, 172
  container sizing, 172–173
  disease/pest concerns, 34
  drift planting, 175
  early bloomers, 174
  fertilizing, 164
  hardening off, 164, 173–174
  June activities, 36
  planting techniques, 174–179
  rootbound, 173

  shopping for, 171–173
  size considerations, 290
  spacing guidelines, 174–175
  store/nursery display conditions, 172
  thinning, 164, 168
  transporting, 172
  versus seeds, 289
  year-round bed preparations, 180
seeds
  direct-sowing techniques, 166–168
  easy to start outdoors, 300
  germination rates, 160
  indoor planting techniques, 162–164
  mail order, 161, 305–307
  shopping for, 159–161
  starting indoors, 161–166
  versus seedlings, 289
  wildflower gathering/purchasing guide-
    lines, 267–268
seeds by mail, 305–307
seed-starter mixture, components, 162
self-seeding annuals, 298
Senecio cineraria. See dusty miller
Senecio hybridus. See cineraria
September activities
  California, 48–49
  lowland deserts, 51
  northern region, 37
  Pacific Northwest, 55
  southern regions, 42–43
series
  described, 13
  naming conventions, 13
shade
  annual requirements, 27–28, 291
  color in, Photo 121
  flowers, 296
shade cloth, 47
shades of color, described, 119
shady patches, Photo 122
shapes
  as design element, 121–122
  containers, 251–252
Shirley poppy *(Papaver rhoeas)*, 108,
    Photo 84
shovels, soil turning tool, 154
signet marigolds, 66
single flowers, described, 14
sloped gardens
  challenges, 29
  drip irrigation, 29

slow-release fertilizers, 200, 202
slugs, controlling, 40, 46, 49, 224–225
snails, controlling, 40, 46, 49, 224–225
snapdragon *(Antirrhinium majus)*, 69–71, 108, Photo 85
  height ranges, 70
  'Liberty Bell', 70
  'Little Darling', 70
  Madam Butterfly Hybrid, 70
  'Panorama', 70
  'Pixie', 70
  'Rocket', 70
  Royal Carpet, 70
  Sonnet, 70
snow-on-the-mountain *(Euphorbia marginata)*, 108, Photo 86
  'Summer Icicle', 108
soaker hose, 42, 48, 53, 192
soaps, insecticidal, 230–231
sodbusting, described, 157
soft ties, 211
soil tests, pH content, 196–197
soil types
  clay, 146–147
  effects on annuals, 28
  loam, 146
  sand, 157
  watering factor, 185
soils
  bed preparation, 152–158
  container mixtures, 252
  cultivating, 148–149
  delinquent drainage, 152
  nutrient types, 195–196
  organic amendments, 149–151
  pH balance, 151–152
  seed-starter mixture, 162
southern regions
  April activities, 40
  August activities, 42
  December activities, 44
  February activities, 39
  hot summers/mild winters, 38–44
  January activities, 39
  July activities, 41–42
  June activities, 41
  March activities, 39–40
  May activities, 40–41
  November activities, 43
  October activities, 43
  September activities, 42–43

spades, garden, 209
specialty fertilizers, 201
species, botanical name component, 12
spider flower *(Cleome hasslerana)*, 108, Photo 87
spider mites, controlling, 40, 48, 225–226
spray wands, watering tool, 187
sprinklers, watering tool, 188–189
staking, described, 208, 213–214
standards, described, 124
statice *(Limonium sinuatum)*, 109, Photo 88
steel bow rake, 210
stocks *(Matthiola incana)*, 109, Photo 89
  Giant Imperial Strain, 109
  night-scented stocks *(Matthiola longipetala)*, 109
  Ten Weeks Strain, 109
strains
  described, 13
  naming conventions, 13
strawflower *(Helichrysum bracteatum)*, 109–110, Photo 90
  'Bikini', 109
strawflower *(Helipterum roseum)*, 109–110
subspecies
  cultivars, 12–13
  varieties, 12
summer forget-me-not *(Anchusa capensis)*, 110, Photo 91
  'Blue Angel', 110
summer oil, versus dormant oil, 230
sunflowers *(Helianthus annuus)*, 71–73, 110, Photo 92
  'Giganteus', 71
  'Inca Jewels', 72
  'Prado', 72
  'Russian Giant', 71
  'Sun and Moon Sunbeam', 72
  'Sunrich Orange', 72
  'Sunrich Yellow', 72
  'Sunspot', 71
  'Teddy Bear', 71, Photo 93
  'Valentine', 72
  'Velvet Queen', 72
  types, 71–72
sunny patio bed, design elements, 132–134
sunny spots annuals, 295
sunshine, annual requirements, 27–28
supplies
  gardening, 210–211
  mail order, 307–308

Swan River daisy *(Brachycome iridifolia)*, 110, Photo 94
sweet alyssum *(Lobularia maritima)*, 110, Photo 95
 'Carpet of Snow', 110
 Easter Bonnet Strain, 110
 'Rosie O'Day', 110
sweet pea *(Lathyrus odoratus)*, 73–74, 111, Photo 96
 Bijou Strain, 73
 'Royal', 73
sweet scabious. *See* pincushion flower
sweet William *(Dianthus barbatus)*, 111, Photo 97
 'Summer Beauty', 111
synthetic insecticides, 231

• *T* •

Tagetes. See marigold
Tagetes erecta. See marigold, African
Tagetes patula. See marigold, French
Tagetes tenuifolia. See marigold, Signet
terra cotta
 containers, 249
 mixing plants, 258
textures, as design element, 121–122
thermostats, bottom-heat mat, 43
thrips, controlling, 226
thunbergia *(Thunbergia alata)*, 111–112, Photo 98
 'Susie', 111
tiers, planting, Photo 118
tillers, soil breaking/turning tool, 156
timers
 automated watering systems, 188
 soaker hose, 53
Tithonia rotundifolia. See Mexican sunflower
toadflax. *See* lineria
tools
 automated watering systems, 188
 bottom-heat mat, 43
 digging forks, 154
 direct-sowing technique, 167
 drip emitters, 190
 drip irrigation, 190–191
 flat-tipped spade, 153
 floating row covers, 26, 47, 229
 garden cart, 210
 garden gloves, 210
 garden spade, 209

grow lights, 162
 hand trowel, 210
 hand watering, 187–188
 hoes, 154, 210
 hose guide, 211
 hose-end bubblers, 187
 leaf rake, 210
 mail order, 307–308
 misting nozzle, 167
 picks, 157
 pronged weeder, 211
 pruners, 210
 purchasing/caring guidelines, 211
 rain gauge, 42
 rakes, 154–155
 seed covers, 167
 seed starters, 162
 shade cloth, 47
 shovels, 154
 soaker hose, 42, 48, 53, 192
 soaker hose timer, 53
 soft ties, 211
 spray wands, 187
 sprinklers, 188–189
 steel bow rake, 210
 tillers, 156
 trowels, 193
 water wand, 211
 watering can, 167
topsoil, soil amendment, 150–151
Torenia fournieri. See wishbone flower
Trachymene coerulea. See blue lace flower
trailers, described, 14
transplanting
 California, 45–46
 lowland deserts, 51
 northern region, 35–36
 southern regions, 39–40
transplants
 cold frame, 38
 diatomaceous earth, 40
 harden off (acclimate) procedure, 35
transvaal daisy *(Gerbera jamesonii)*, 112, Photo 99
tree mallow. *See* lavatera
trees, bedding around, 134–136
trichogramma wasps, as biological pest control, 228
tricolor daisy. *See* painted daisy
Tropaeolum majus. See nasturtium

Tropaeolum peregrinum. See canary creeper
tropical climates, all-year growing season, 32
trowel, hand, 210
trowels, water depth-level measuring, 193

● *U* ●

unglazed clay containers, 249

● *V* ●

varieties
  described, 12–13
  naming conventions, 12–13
velvet flower. *See* salpiglossis
verbena *(Verbena),* 112–113, Photo 100
  Romance, 112
  Showtime, 112
  Verbena bonariensis, 112
vinca rosea *(Cartharanthus roseus),* 113,
    Photo 101
  'Apricot Delight', 113
viola *(Viola),* 113
  Viola cornuta, Photo 102
Viola wittrochiana. See pansy

● *W* ●

walkways, borders, 136–139
wallflower *(Erysimum/Cheiranthus),* 113–114,
    Photo 103
  'Orange Bedder', 113
warm-season annuals
  described, 25
  floating row covers, 26
  versus cool-season annuals, 24–27
water wand, 211
watering
  automated systems, 188
  climate factors, 184
  conservation tips, 191
  depth-level measurement techniques, 193
  drip irrigation, 190–191
  furrow irrigation, 189
  hand methods, 187–188
  knowing when to water, 186
  location considerations, 185
  methods, 186–192
  plant type needs, 185–186
  soaker-hose irrigation, 192
  soil type considerations, 185
  sprinkler types, 188–180
  weather factors, 184

watering can, direct-sowing tool, 167
wax begonia. *See* bedding begonia
weather conditions, effects on gardens,
    27–29
weather
  versus climate, 184
  watering factor, 184
Web sites
  annuals, 309–311
  Master Gardeners International, 308
weeds
  Bermuda grass, 239–240
  bindweed, 239–240
  cultivating, 239
  described, 237
  glyphosate herbicide, 238
  mulching to control, 239
  perennial, 239–240
  post-planting techniques, 239
  pre-emergence herbicide, 238
  pre-planting preparations, 237–238
  pulling by hand, 239
  solarizing, 238
  spot-spraying with herbicides, 239
western regions
  California activity calendar, 44–50
  dry, mild summers/wet, mild winters,
    44–56
  high-altitude deserts, 50
  lowland deserts, 50–53
  Pacific Northwest, 53–56
white flowers, 304
whiteflies, controlling, 48, 226–227
wildflowers
  advantages, 264
  collecting seeds from established
    plants, 268
  described, 263
  end of season chores, 271
  growing strategies, 265–266
  maintenance, 270–271
  naturalizing, 264
  planting techniques, 269–270
  prepared mixes, 267
  scatter garden, 270
  seasonal planting, 266
  seedling advantages, 267
  shopping guidelines, 267
  site preparations, 268–269
  types, 264–265
wind, effects on annuals, 28

window box, mixing plants, 258–259,
    Photo 110
wishbone flower *(Torenia fournieri)*, 114,
    Photo 104
  Clown Strain, 114
wood boxes/tub containers, 250

• 𝒴 •

year-round beds, preparations, 180
yellow cosmos *(Cosmos sulphureus)*, 89
  Sunny Strain, 89
yellow flowers, 302

• 𝒵 •

zinnias, annual *(Zinnia elegans)*, 75–76, 114,
    Photo 107
  cactus type, 75
  dahlia-flowered type, 75
  'Envy', 75
  flower forms, 75
  Oklahoma Mix, 75
  'Peppermint Stick', 75
  Peter Pan Series, 75
  'Pinwheel', 75
  'Ruffles Cherry', 75
  'Short Stuff', Photo 106
  'Small World Cherry', 75
zinnias, tender perennial *(Zinnia angustifolia)*
  Star Series, 75
  'White Star', Photo 105
zonal geraniums *(Pelargonium hortorum)*,
    61–62
zones, climate, 21–24

IDG BOOKS WORLDWIDE BOOK REGISTRATION